Shari'ah and Common Law

De Gruyter Studies in Global Asia

Series Editors
Pervaiz K. Ahmed and Mahendhiran S. Nair

Volume 4

Shari'ah and Common Law

The Challenge of Harmonisation

Edited by
Adnan Trakic

DE GRUYTER

ISBN 978-3-11-076668-4
e-ISBN (PDF) 978-3-11-076670-7
e-ISBN (EPUB) 978-3-11-076671-4
ISSN 2698-4776

Library of Congress Control Number: 2022943167

Bibliographic information published by the Deutsche Nationalbibliothek
The Deutsche Nationalbibliothek lists this publication in the Deutsche Nationalbibliografie; detailed bibliographic data are available on the internet at http://dnb.dnb.de.

Cover image: titoOnz/iStock/Getty Images Plus
Typesetting: Integra Software Services Pvt. Ltd.
Printing and binding: CPI books GmbH, Leck

www.degruyter.com

Foreword

The Federal Constitution of Malaysia provides for a dual system of law. The first, which is mainly based on the English common law and federal statutes, is governed by the federal court system, while the second, based on Shari'ah, comes under the purview of the Shari'ah courts, which derive their jurisdiction from state enactments, with the exception of the federal territories. The distinct and separate jurisdiction of the two courts system is recognised in article 121(1A) of the Federal Constitution.

Since the independence of Malaya in 1957 and the formation of Malaysia in 1963, the parallel systems of law where the secular legal system exists alongside the Shari'ah legal system have served the nation well. This has, to some extent, allowed Malaysia to be regarded as a role model of a thriving multi-cultural and multi-religious nation, where people of various faiths and ethnicities have built a peaceful and vibrant society based on shared experiences of moderation and pluralism. The Shari'ah courts have limited jurisdiction over Muslims, primarily in areas of personal law relating to matrimonial and inheritance issues and some aspects of criminal law relating to offences against the precepts of Islam. While the federal court system has jurisdiction over all persons and on all matters that were not reserved to the Shari'ah courts. This includes the powers of juridical review.

However, as in any dual systems of law, there are bound to be challenges as the parallel tracks do sometimes cross paths and cut into the jurisdiction of the other. There have been contentious issues and conflicts of laws, such as those relating to freedom of religion, leading to questions of which court system had jurisdiction to determine such issues. These experiences have led to calls for harmonisation of the two court systems so that the dual systems work seamlessly without impinging on each other's jurisdiction.

Against this background, Dr Adnan Trakic has undertaken this timely task of looking into the challenges of harmonising the Shari'ah and common law. This has led to the compilation of 15 academic essays written by subject experts in various areas of law, including contract, banking and finance, insurance, employment, corporate governance, defamation, protection of privacy, family, criminal justice system, human rights, alternative dispute resolution, and state involvement in religion. These are now contained as chapters of this book.

I have always held the belief that commonalities between the two systems of law were far larger than their dissimilarities. Conflicts there may be, but they are far fewer when compared to similarities. Hence, it is not surprising when Dr Adnan Trakic concluded that the need for harmonisation has been exaggerated for the large body of similarities in many areas of the law are complimentary to each other, and they do not need harmonisation. There just needs to be a specific focus on the few areas of differences that must be attended to and resolved by reasoned discourse.

https://doi.org/10.1515/9783110766707-202

That is the theme of this book, which has been well addressed by the authors. This is a commendable effort, and I am confident that the views expressed by these subject expert authors would encourage meaningful debate on the need for harmonisation of the Shari'ah and common law in Malaysia and far beyond. And that is most welcome.

Datuk Vazeer Alam Mydin Meera
Judge
Court of Appeal, Malaysia
Putrajaya

Preface

When I was a student many years ago at Ahmad Ibrahim Faculty of Law, International Islamic University Malaysia, I was privileged to have had a chance to study both common law and Shari'ah. The emphasis perhaps was more on common law, but equivalent Islamic law units were taught where possible. So, for instance, the Contract Law unit was based on common law, while the Shari'ah comparable was the Islamic Law of Transactions. The same goes for Banking and Finance Law, Family Law, Inheritance Law, Criminal Law, Evidence Law units and their counterparts, Islamic Banking and Finance Law, Islamic Family Law, Islamic Inheritance Law, Islamic Criminal Law, and Islamic Evidence Law. Throughout my time as a student of both legal traditions, it never struck me that Shari'ah and common law have irreconcilable differences or, worse, that they have hostile tendencies towards one another. That differences between the two exist is not disputed. They certainly do like they do between any other different legal systems. But, I was always under the impression that Shari'ah and common law share many more commonalities than differences, let alone differences that are irreconcilable.

I have lately come across opinion pieces and commentaries where the term "harmonisation of Shari'ah and common law" is coloured in a negative context, as if one system of law is trying to forcefully convert the other. These views began to create confusion and, I would dare say, even resentment among the ordinary public, some of whom started to believe that Shari'ah and common law are so different and that any attempt to harmonise their differences should not be welcome. They just need to keep to their own boundaries, and when their paths cross, well, that is when the problems start. Hostility created by the impression that they are so different and that they aim to convert one another prevents the meaningful conversation from taking place so that their differences can be harmonised and an optimal comprise reached.

What struck me as someone observing this phenomenon was that these apparent irreconcilable differences and antagonism between Shari'ah and common law are not how I learned them to be. As such, this prompted me to assemble a group of experts on both common law and Shari'ah to explore similarities and differences as well as the possibility of reconciling the differences that exist between Shari'ah and common law. I selected the topics in the areas of law that appear to me as the most contentious. Each chapter in the monograph provides a detailed account of the developments in that area of law with reference to both Shari'ah and common law. They also do not shy away from differences. But, their approach to them is constructive in that they provide to the regulators and our readers practical solutions that are reflective of the harmonisation of law. Harmonisation is an effort to bring two different things/concepts into harmony with one another and not an effort to subdue one by the other. It is my sincere hope that this monograph will help the

https://doi.org/10.1515/9783110766707-203

readers understand both Shari'ah and common law better and aid harmonisation efforts when needed.

I want to use this opportunity to express my heartfelt appreciation to all contributors for their painstaking efforts and participation in this project. I am immensely grateful to you all. The monograph attests to your great collegiality and lucid scholarship, from which I have benefited greatly.

I should also like to record a debt of gratitude to the De Gruyter team, particularly Ms Lucy Jarman, for her timely assistance and helpful guidance throughout the publication process.

I want to thank my family for graciously allowing me to dedicate my time and effort to this book so that it may *see* the light of day.

Finally, thank you to you, dear reader! I hope you will find the book interesting and helpful. Happy reading!

Adnan Trakic
June 2022

Contents

Adnan Trakic

1 Harmonisation of Shari'ah and Common Law: An Overview

1.1 Introduction

Shari'ah, in a narrow sense, refers to Islamic law. But, its actual meaning is broader. It also includes religious and ethical norms. For Muslims, it represents a complete system of life.[1] Common law, on the other hand, refers to a strictly normative body of law that has been developing through customs and, more importantly, judicial decisions of precedential value.[2] In a broader context, it depicts a secular legal system of countries that have adopted it as a predominant source of law.[3] While statutes introduced through the legislative process would typically not be considered as part of Shari'ah or common law, in instances where they influenced their enactments, they could also be regarded as part of Shari'ah or common law. Furthermore, the state apparatus entrusted with the administration and enforcement of Shari'ah or common law legal systems should also be included in the discussion of laws and their harmonisation.

Occasional non-alignment between Shari'ah and common law is unavoidable in countries that practice both legal systems. But, the problem of inconsistency between the two tends to be exaggerated, leaving one with an impression that the two systems of law are so different to the extent that their differences cannot be reconciled. Is this really the case? Are the differences between the two significantly more than the similarities? Given that some differences are likely to exist, as they would between any other different legal systems, can they be reconciled? Is the harmonisation of law a reconciliation solution? These and similar questions have prompted the author (who is the editor of this monograph) to assemble a group of scholars to conduct research and produce scholarly chapters on the topics within their respective expertise. This monograph is the outcome of that initiative.

The monograph seeks to explore and discuss the basic legal concepts in Shari'ah and common law and identify their most prominent similarities and differences. Practical examples are provided with reference to the respective jurisdiction/s where the two legal systems are practiced. For clarity and ease of reference, all

1 *See* Yusuf Talal DeLorenzo and Michael JT McMillen, "Law and Islamic Finance: An Interactive Analysis," in *Islamic Finance: The Regulatory Challenge*, ed. Simon Archer and Rifaat Ahmed Abdel Karim (Singapore: John Wiley and Sons, 2007) 132–198.

2 *See* Ashgar Ali Ali Mohamed, "Major Legal Systems in the World," in *Malaysian Legal System*, ed. Ashgar Ali Ali Mohamed (Kuala Lumpur: Current Law Journal, 2014) 57–78.

3 Countries in which common law is regarded as a predominant source of law are: United Kingdom, United States, Ireland, Malaysia, Singapore, Hong Kong, Pakistan, India, Bangladesh, and South Africa, to name but a few.

https://doi.org/10.1515/9783110766707-001

contributors have been requested to structure their discussions around the following objectives:

- Identify similarities and differences between Shari'ah and common law in the selected area of law,
- Ascertain if the differences, if any, are reconcilable,
- Suggest ways in which the two systems of law could be harmonised where necessary, and
- Other questions that authors of the respective chapters deem appropriate may also be addressed.

While concerted efforts have been made to provide compelling answers to the many pertinent questions, including the ones mentioned above, the author is aware that there could be other questions and areas that might not have been dealt with. Given the time and space constraints, the author selected areas and topics that, in his view, are not only reflective of the ongoing challenges and debates, but also forward-looking and conciliatory in their approach to legal issues.

The selected chapters are suitably placed within the proper jurisdictional context. The idea behind that was to provide a practical element to the discussion so that the similarities and differences between Shari'ah and common law and their harmonisation where necessary, can be observed in context. As many of the contributors are either based in Malaysia or are linked to this jurisdiction in one way or another, naturally, their tendency was to illustrate their points with reference to Malaysian laws. Besides, the author believes that Malaysia might just be the best jurisdiction for this type of research as it provides good access to legislation, written court judgments, and plenty of scholarly writings on both legal systems. Malaysia is also seen as a leading Muslim jurisdiction in Islamic banking and finance, and its Muslim personal laws are regarded as one of the most advanced in the world. While Malaysia appears throughout the book as a predominant jurisdiction of choice, occasional references to laws of other jurisdictions and international laws and instruments have also been made where appropriate. The jurisdictional context of harmonisation of law discussion has been detailed below for clarity and ease of reference.

1.2 Harmonisation of Laws: Jurisdictional Context

Harmonisation of Shari'ah and common law can be considered in two different jurisdictional contexts. First is jurisdictions where both legal systems operate in parallel with each other, or at least in the presence of each other in situations where one tends to be more prevalent than the other. Malaysia is a good example where both legal systems coexist within their legislative and judicial boundaries. For the most part, they operate independently of each other without major interference.

However, occasional conflicts do arise, and when they do, they further become compounded by the considerable distrust instigated by the belief that one wishes to dominate the other. This can be seen from several recent cases where civil (common law) and Shari'ah courts and legislatures (Federal and State) have claimed exclusive jurisdiction over the subject matter in dispute or parties involved.

In *Indira Gandhi a/p Mutho v Pengarah Jabatan Agama Islam Perak,*[4] both civil and Shari'ah courts claimed jurisdiction over a dispute involving the conversion of children to Islam by a Muslim father. Malaysia's apex court (the Federal Court) concluded that the civil court has jurisdiction over the matter as one of the parties (children's mother who objected to conversion) could not appear before the Shari'ah court as she was a non-Muslim. The court also added that it is within the civil court's exclusive jurisdiction to interpret state or federal legislation, including the Federal Constitution. On 25 February 2021, the Federal Court delivered another ground-breaking decision in *Iki Putra Mubarrak v Kerajaan Negeri Selangor.*[5] In this case, the court held that section 28 of the Shari'ah Criminal Offences (Selangor) Enactment 1995, which criminalised unnatural sex, was null and void as it was not within the State's power to enact. Such offences were within the Federal Parliament's power to pass laws. The court clarified that federal and state legislatures must observe their constitutional boundaries when legislating offences. Soon after, on 17 March 2021, in *Lill Ireland Lawrance Bill v Menteri Bagi Kementerian Dalam Negeri Malaysia,*[6] the High Court held that the Home Affairs Ministry Directive prohibiting the use of certain words such as "Allah" by non-Muslims was unconstitutional.

The decisions like these have made some segments of society, particularly Muslims, uncomfortable. As a result, some political leaders and government ministers voiced their concerns. Ahmad Zahid Hamidi, the leader of UMNO, a major political party in the country, is reported to have said: "In my opinion, these two decisions (*Iki Putra Mubarrak* and *Lill Ireland Lawrance*) have touched on the rights of Muslims as enshrined in the Federal Constitution. Thus, we may need to amend the constitution to ensure shariah laws are strengthened in our legal system."[7] Others have been more measured in their commentary, adding that while the court decisions must be respected, greater efforts must be made, particularly, by the Islamic Development Department (JAKIM), to "strengthen and streamline syariah laws in Malaysia."[8]

---

4 [2018] 1 MLJ 545.

5 [2021] 3 CLJ 465.

6 [2021] 4 CLJ 231.

7 FMT Reporters, "We must Amend Constitution to Protect Shariah Laws, says Zahid," *FMT*, March 28, 2021, https://www.freemalaysiatoday.com/category/nation/2021/03/28/we-must-amend-constitution-to-protect-syariah-laws-says-zahid/ (emphasis added).

8 Bernama, "Jakim Committee to Review, Strengthen Shariah Criminal Laws After Landmark Ruling on 'unnatural sex'," *Malay Mail*, February 27, 2021, https://www.malaymail.com/news/malay

Situations like these are sensitive not only to the parties involved but also to their wider religious and cultural community and necessitate a delicate solution that would promote inclusiveness and understanding among the multireligious and multicultural society and not hostility and division. Harmonisation of law could be that solution. Harmonisation is, by its very nature, a process by which two different legal traditions are recognised and allowed to operate uninterruptedly, and when their paths intertwine, it produces an amicable solution that is reflective of the values of both legal systems. A good example of successful harmonisation of Shari'ah and common law is the case of *Latifah Mat Zin v Rosmawati Sharibun*.[9] In this case, the issue pertained to the status of the monies in an account of a widow. She claimed that the monies were a gift from the deceased husband. Thus, she filed a case before the civil court as probate and letter of administration is within the civil court's jurisdiction.[10] One of the deceased beneficiaries, on the other hand, claimed that the monies were part of the estate and, as such, subject to *faraid* (Islamic inheritance law) and lodged a case before the Shari'ah court, which has exclusive jurisdiction over Islamic inheritance law.[11] As the dispute evolved into a conflict of jurisdiction and constitutional interpretation, the Federal Court was asked to offer the solution. Abdul Hamid Mohamad FCJ (as he then was), delivering the court's decision, came up with an interesting solution. Both courts were asked to work together in harmony to achieve the best outcome. Shari'ah court was requested to decide the Islamic inheritance law issue (i.e., whether monies in the account were part of the deceased estate or a gift). The civil court then made the distribution order in accordance with the order of the Shari'ah court.

The other context in which the harmonisation of Shari'ah and common law could be considered is jurisdictions where the common law-based legal system is the only legal system recognised. Shari'ah here is not viewed as part of the legal system, but due to a substantial presence of the Muslim minority community, certain aspects of Shari'ah could be practiced in the form of what Rowan Williams, former Archbishop of Canterbury, calls a "supplementary jurisdiction."[12] The United Kingdom (UK) is a good example. Muslims in the UK are a minority, but that did not prevent them from having certain aspects of their personal matters governed by Shari'ah,

---

sia/2021/02/27/jakim-committee-to-review-strengthen-shariah-criminal-laws-after-landmark-r/1953418. *See* also FMT Reporters, "Don't Challenge More State Laws, Says PAS After Court Ruling," FMT, February 28, 2021, https://www.freemalaysiatoday.com/category/nation/2021/02/28/dont-challenge-more-state-laws-says-pas-after-court-ruling/.

9 [2007] 5 CLJ 253.

10 Art. 74 (1) of the Federal Constitution. *See* also Ninth Schedule (List I – Federal List) of the Constitution.

11 Art. 74 (2) of the Federal Constitution. *See* also Ninth Schedule (List II – State List) of the Constitution.

12 Rowan Williams, "Civil and Religious Law in England: A Religious Perspective," *Ecclesiastical Law Journal* 10, (2008): 262–282.

such as marriage, divorce, inheritance, and commercial dealings. Under English law, particularly the Arbitration Act 1996, the parties are allowed to decide in their personal contractual dealings on the law that would govern their contractual obligations and the forum to settle the possible disputes as long as the chosen law and forum are consistent with English law. At first, Muslims in the UK were able to refer their disputes to Shari'ah Councils and their local Imams. But, the councils' decisions were not legally enforceable, and it was up to the parties involved if they wanted to observe them. In order to have an alternative dispute resolution mechanism recognised under the UK law, in 2007, Muslim Arbitration Tribunal was established.[13] The decision of the tribunal is binding in accordance with the Arbitration Act 1996.

Some notable individuals like Rowan Williams and former Lord Chief Justice Lord Phillips have been somewhat sympathetic to the needs of the minorities to be governed by religious laws in certain specified matters.[14] They opined that there is a scope for the application of Shari'ah not as part of English law but rather through what Ayelet Shachar calls "transformative accommodation" in which individuals are allowed to freely decide on whether they would like their dispute to be decided by the communal religious entity (like Shari'ah Council and Muslim Arbitration Tribunal) or state-administered courts.[15] In a way, this approach has elements of free market in which the two legal traditions are supposed to compete for the loyalty of their constituents. It needs to be emphasised, however, that transformative accommodation is predicated on the conviction that all citizens (Muslims and non-Muslims) must have uninterrupted access to the state-administered courts at all times. In fact, this already happened in the case of *Uddin v Choudhury*,[16] in which the English Court of Appeal heard the dispute between two Muslim families as a result of a failed arranged marriage. The court considered the Shari'ah expert's testimony in deciding the dispute. While the court ultimately decided the dispute by considering the marriage agreement as a legally enforceable contract under English law, the court's reference to the Shari'ah expert's opinion in interpreting the agreement was of major significance. Again, the cooperation between both legal traditions resulted in a harmonious and amicable solution.

It needs to be noted, however, that not everyone is supportive of the harmonisation of the law approach. Some have called for the abolishment of communal and religious courts such as Shari'ah Councils and Muslim Arbitration Tribunals on the

---

13 Muslim Arbitration Tribunal, accessed June 13, 2021, http://www.matribunal.com/index.php.

14 Rowan Williams, "Civil and Religious Law in England: A Religious Perspective," *Ecclesiastical Law Journal* 10, (2008): 262–282. *See* also Steve Doughty, "Sharia Law SHOULD Be Used in Britain, Says UK's Top Judge," *Daily Mail*, July 4, 2008, https://www.dailymail.co.uk/news/article-1031611/Sharia-law-SHOULD-used-Britain-says-UKs-judge.html.

15 Ayelet Shachar, *Multicultural Jurisdictions: Cultural Differences and Women's Rights* (Cambridge: Cambridge University Press, 2004), 122.

16 [2009] EWCA (Civ) 1205.

basis that they allegedly enable gender-based discrimination against women and transform the historically acceptable role of arbitration.[17] There have also been concerns around the so-called “creeping Islamization” in Malaysia.[18] These perceptions, just like the narrow views of some Muslim clerics and politicians, may become a significant obstacle towards harmonisation efforts if not addressed promptly and transparently. Therefore, this book addresses these and similar concerns to correct some of the misconceptions and suggests ways in which harmonisation could be achieved where necessary.

1.3 Structure and Framework

The monograph consists of fifteen chapters. The first and the last chapters are written by the editor. By authoring Chapters 1 and 15, the editor hopes to accomplish two things. First, he wants to help readers understand the context in which the harmonisation of Shari’ah and common law is discussed in this monograph and provide a summary in the end with his own commentary where necessary. Second, he wishes to reassure the readers that the selection of the chapter titles was carefully made, and the expectations for each chapter were set with a harmonisation theme in mind. The chapters are not a mere compilation of random topics. Quite the contrary, they can be classified into those dealing with contract/commercial law (Chapters 2, 3, and 4), employment law (Chapter 5), corporate governance (Chapter 6), tort law (Chapters 7 and 8), environmental law (Chapter 9), family law (Chapter 10), criminal law (Chapter 11), human rights law (Chapter 12), dispute resolution (Chapter 13), and miscellaneous (Chapter 15). All these areas of law have been selected by the editor based on relevance, importance, and availability of corresponding expertise. The selected areas of law and issues dealt with are briefly introduced below.

Contract law is arguably the most significant area of commercial law. While there are many types of specialised contracts, such as hire and purchase, leasing, loan, sale, partnership, and employment contracts, they are all “contracts” in a general sense of the word. Thus, the contract law principles on formation, terms, vitiating factors, and discharge are applicable to all of them. In countries that

17 Madeleine Davies, “Baroness Cox to Draft Anti-Sharia Bill,” *Church Times*, April 10, 2015, https://www.churchtimes.co.uk/articles/2015/10-april/news/uk/baroness-cox-to-draft-anti-sharia-bill. *See* also Rebecca E. Maret, “Mind the Gap: The Equality Bill and Sharia Arbitration in the United Kingdom,” *Boston College International and Comparative Law Review* 36, (2013): 255–283.

18 Joseph Chinyong Liow, “Malaysia’s Creeping Islamization – and Dimming Prospects for Covenantal Pluralism,” *The Review of Faith & International Affairs* 19, no. 2 (2021): 1–13. *See* also Ahmad Fauzi Abdul Hamid, “The Politicisation of Syariah Law in Muhyiddin’s Malaysia,” *East Asia Forum*, May 13, 2021, https://www.eastasiaforum.org/2021/05/13/the-politicisation-of-syariah-law-in-muhyiddins-malaysia/.

practice Islamic banking and finance, the contracts must also comply with Shari'ah. Therefore, in Chapter 2, Aishath Muneeza examines the compatibility of contract law principles of common law with Shari'ah. But before that, she explains the basic contract law principles in both legal systems and points to their similarities as well as differences.

The harmonisation efforts in Islamic finance are discussed in Chapter 3 by Noor Suhaida Kasri. The author examines the following themes: the divergence between the Islamic law theory and the Islamic finance practices, the decline in the usage of equity-based as compared to sale or fee-based modes of financing and investment, the extent to which the form and the substance are embraced in Islamic finance practices, and the jurisdictional battle between the Malaysian judiciary and the Bank Negara's Shariah Advisory Council (SAC) pertaining to the resolution of Shari'ah issues in Islamic finance disputes. One aspect of harmonisation is of particular interest here. Since Islamic finance contracts commonly used by Islamic financial institutions must comply with both conventional contract law as well as Shari'ah, what would be the effect of non-compliance with either law? While non-compliance with the conventional contract law could render the contract illegal and as such null and void, the same cannot be said for non-compliance with Shari'ah. Is this seemingly discriminatory arrangement acceptable? Is harmonisation of law a solution, and what would that harmonisation practically look like? Noor Suhaida provides the answers to these and many other questions with reference to recent court decisions and relevant statutory provisions.

Chapter 4 also deals with Islamic finance as it relates to the financing of energy projects. In this chapter, Ridoan Karim explores to what extent the lack of standardised Islamic finance contracts hinders the much-needed financing in the renewable energy sector. He considers ways in which Islamic finance contracts could be harmonised. One aspect of harmonisation of particular interest is the use of the Accounting and Auditing Organisation for Islamic Financial Institutions (AAOIFI) standards as a model that could be adopted by Islamic financial institutions and regulators into Islamic finance contracts. The lack of standardisation, he argues, causes uncertainty in the enforcement of the Islamic finance contracts, which is not good for either the parties involved or the wider industry.

Chapter 5 looks into an important area in employment law. Ashgar Ali Ali Mohamed and Mohamad Hassan Ahmad examine and compare the treatment of insubordination under common law and Shari'ah. While it is clear that both legal systems agree that employees have the duty to obey the employer's lawful and reasonable orders, there seems to be uncertainty on how so-called "dubious" orders are to be approached. These are the orders which, when given by the employer, the employee is not sure whether they are lawful and reasonable. Should employees risk and disobey these orders on the basis that they are dangerous? What if they turn out to be lawful (after court litigation, for example); would the employer be able to dismiss the employee for disobeying lawful orders? The authors address these and similar questions in a way that provides not only the answers but also the jurisprudential basis behind the adopted positions.

In Chapter 6, we turn to corporations and examine the need for a robust corporate governance framework, especially in the intuitions that carry "Islamic" label. Elsa Satkunasingam points out that an intuition carrying this label must demonstrate strict compliance with corporate governance principles like accountability and transparency as they form the bedrock of Islamic belief and value system. The author decided to examine the extent to which the Islamic corporate governance principles align with the common law through a case study approach. She explores the topic in the context of Tabung Haji (TH), the Malaysian pilgrimage fund board. While the analysis of the TH provides useful lessons, the conclusions deduced should be considered in a wider context of corporate governance.

We now move on to the abuse of freedom of speech and expression. While free speech and expression is a fundamental human right under both Shari'ah and common law, both legal systems impose certain limitations on them. In Chapter 7, Farheen Baig Sardar Baig and Ashgar Ali Ali Mohamed examine the limitations of this right with specific reference to the legal cause of action under defamation. As the name suggests, defamation is destroying someone's reputation by uttering or publishing lies about them. As such, it is the abuse of freedom of speech and expression. Defamation is both criminal and civil wrong. The authors detail the treatment of defamation under both Shari'ah and common law and point to some areas where they are the same as well as where they seem to differ.

Another notable human right protected under both Shari'ah and common law is the right to privacy. In Chapter 8, Ridoan Karim and Normann Witzleb discuss privacy and data protection with reference to several Muslim jurisdictions and note that their current laws are mostly based on Western concepts. While Islam equally values privacy and data protection, they opine that countries' desire to comply with Western-originated privacy laws is for economic reasons. That said, the authors argue that there are many Islamic law concepts like *muhasbah* (self-accountability) and *amanah* (preservation of trust) that are worth exploring further and perhaps adopting into the contemporary privacy and data protection jurisprudence. The authors also note that there could be some differences, like those stemming from Shari'ah's reservations about recognising personal data (information) as property. Does this mean that the theft of private date cannot be considered an offence of theft? The authors provide useful context and explanation to this and other similar questions.

Islamic law principle of *amanah* (preservation of trust) as well as other principles like *khalifah* (God's vicegerent on Earth), *mizan* (balance), and *maqasid* Shari'ah (preservation of Shari'ah objectives), Maizatun Mustafa, in Chapter 9 explains, are equally useful in the preservation of the environment. Humanity needs to achieve a healthy balance between the need for economic development and the preservation of the environment. The two are not necessarily exclusive of each other, Maizatun argues. While Muslims believe that God has entrusted human beings with the management of the Earth and its resources, they have to manage it sustainably. What does the principle of sustainability exactly mean? Does it have the same meaning under both Shari'ah and common law? How do we deal with environmental denigration and abuse of trust to manage the Earth sustainably? The author addresses all of the above questions with reference to practical examples and authoritative legal provisions.

In Chapter 10, Sridevi Thambapillay examines various challenges pertaining to the harmonisation of family law in jurisdictions where Shari'ah and common law principles are applicable. The issues that have arisen before the courts in countries like Malaysia are reflective of the complexities involved in achieving harmonisation. This is a challenge that could be amicably resolved if given sufficient attention. Sridevi acknowledges that a lot of progress has been made but at the same time highlights areas that remain unresolved. She offers practical solutions to many of these problems.

When the criminal justice system is mentioned in the context of harmonisation of law, one might be under the impression that there is little scope for harmonisation as the two systems of law have some irreconcilable differences in this regard. For example, there are types of offences like *zina* (illicit sexual intercourse) and *shurb al khamr* (drinking alcohol) that are punishable under Shari'ah. The same are not crimes under common law. For this and other reasons, the harmonisation of Shari'ah and common law in the area of criminal law perhaps seems least likely to happen. However, there have been multiple examples where the two systems of law may have the same objectives. One such example is the progressive concept of restorative justice, which finds strong support in both legal systems. In Chapter 11, Hanifah Haydar Ali Tajuddin and Nasimah Hussin discuss harmonisation efforts in the criminal justice system and offer their views on the best way forward for countries like Malaysia that practice both legal systems. Although, it is worth mentioning that the Federal Constitution limits the extent to which Islamic criminal law is practiced in Malaysia. The restrictions are detailed in the chapter.

In Chapter 12, Muhamad Hassan Ahmad, Muhammad Naqib Ishan Jan, and Ashgar Ali Ali Mohamed explore the similarities and differences between the concept of human rights and the rule of law in both common law and Shari'ah. It has been often claimed that Shari'ah concept of human rights is incompatible with generally accepted norms in western societies. There is this notion that the concept and scope of human rights in Shari'ah remain unchanged, while in the West, human rights have constantly been evolving in line with societal changes and popular views. Is this a fair characterisation of Islamic and Western traditions' approach to human rights? The authors seek to ascertain if this notion still holds and propose ways in which this area of law should be considered.

Chapter 13 presents alternatives to litigation and court adjudication. Ashgar Ali Ali Mohamed and Muhamad Hassan Ahmad discuss not only the most prevailing

Alternative Dispute Resolution (ADR) mechanisms like conciliation, mediation, and arbitration but also indicate their equivalents in Islamic law like *sulh* (mediation) and *tahkim* (arbitration). The use of ADR, however, has not been without criticism. It has been suggested that arbitration, for example, can be quite expensive. In some industries like Islamic finance, litigation seems to be the preferred choice among the disputing parties. In view of these criticisms, Is ADR genuinely a better option than litigation? What is Islamic law's position on this? The authors will address these questions and offer their views.

Chapter 14 is slightly different than others in that it examines the position of Islam and Islamic law in the United States (US). Julio C Colon reviews the relevant jurisprudence of US first amendment law as it pertains to religious practice and applies it to recent cases that encountered a legal issue involving Islamic jurisprudence, whether personal or transactional. In doing so, other issues that may not have been addressed in US courts will be analysed by comparison to other common law jurisdictions, such as probate matters, corporate finance, and various types of damages.

1.4 Conclusion

The foregoing discussion shows that the harmonisation of Shari'ah and common law needs to be understood in the proper context. The selected areas of law in the two systems of law require detailed expert analysis before we can begin to talk about the need for harmonisation. If the analysis indicates the existence of many more similarities/commonalities than differences, then the need for harmonisation may not be as dire as one may think. The commonalities do not need to be harmonised. They just need to be acknowledged and appreciated. Harmonisation is required when there are differences. There are surely many examples where Shari'ah and common law do not share common values and principles. But, that does not mean that they are not malleable enough to adapt to reach a compromise even in those circumstances. The chapters in this monograph are written with this objective in mind. Their main aim is to show how the differences between the two law systems can be reconciled. But, they also highlight the many commonalities that exist between Shari'ah and common law to demonstrate that the need for harmonisation is not as dire as the need for the appreciation for the commonalities.

Aishath Muneeza

2 Harmonisation of Contract Law: How Far Have We Gone – and Where Are We Going?

2.1 Introduction

The law of contract is a significant area of commercial law, which is a substantive law. Common law principles of contract law are used in many countries in the world especially by those countries that were British colonies. This is the case in Muslim countries as well. Since the sixteenth century, Muslim countries were ruled by the British, and since then, the Islamic legal system in these countries slowed its progress, and the application of English law became a common practice up until today.[1] Islamic law's application was reduced to personal matters of Muslims. However, due to the institutionalisation of Islamic finance, the adoption and application of Islamic law in commercial transactions have been revived, and research in this regard has gained momentum. For the sake of sustainable development of Islamic finance globally, law harmonisation between Islamic law and common law has been viewed as an important aspect that requires attention.[2]

Islamic finance requires dual compliance of laws in its transactions. This means that the primary law that ought to be applied to validate all of its transactions is Shari'ah, and to ensure that the legal system of the country recognises such transactions, the law of the land needs to be applied as well. Therefore, if there is any conflict between the law of the land and Shari'ah, the law of the land will prevail. This point can be illustrated using the case of *Shamil Bank of Bahrain EC v Beximco Pharmaceuticals Ltd and others*,[3] where even though the parties intended to apply Shari'ah to determine the matters arising from the contract entered between the parties, the court held that Shari'ah is a non-national law and as such, under Rome Convention on the Law Applicable to Contractual Obligations 1980 (Rome Convention) which was the applicable law at that time, a non-national law cannot be applied to resolve the dispute between the parties. However, today the position in *Beximco* case is no longer applicable as the Rome Convention was replaced by the Regulation (EC) No. 593/2008 of the European Parliament and the Council on the Law Applicable to

1 Md Abdul Jalil and Muhammad Khalilur Rahman, "Islamic Law of Contract is Getting Momentum," *International Journal of Business and Social Science* 1, no. 2 (November, 2010): 179–180.
2 Aishath Muneeza, *Legislative Conflicts Facing Islamic Banking in Malaysia* (Kuala Lumpur: Dar Al Wahi, 2015).
3 [2004] 4 All ER 1072.

https://doi.org/10.1515/9783110766707-002

Contractual Obligations, known as the Rome I Regulation (Rome I Regulation) which came into force in the UK on 17 December 2009.[4] The Rome I Regulation allows the Shari'ah to be the governing law of a contract.

That being said, the objective of this chapter is to examine the compatibility of contract law principles of common law with Shari'ah. The key principles of contract law in both legal systems will be analysed to *see* where they converge and diverge. This chapter looks at the contract law principles from common law and Shari'ah perspective, in a nutshell, followed by their comparison.

2.2 Contract Law Principles from Common Law and Shari'ah Perspective

2.2.1 Contract Law under Common Law

Under common law, there are four main parts of contract law principles:
1. Formation of a contract (an offer, acceptance, consideration, contractual intention, and the form);
2. Contents of a contract (express terms and implied terms);
3. The end of a contract (expiration, termination, vitiation, and frustration); and
4. Remedies (e.g. damages).[5]

In common law, to make a contract, three essential elements must be present: agreement, contractual intention, and consideration. To make a contract under the common law, an agreement must be reached by accepting the offer made, and to decide whether there is an agreement made between the parties, the court may use an objective test.[6] In the case of *Stover v Manchester City Council*,[7] the courts observed that an offer is an expression of willingness to contract on specified terms, made with the intention that it is to be binding once accepted by the person to whom it is addressed. An offer can be addressed to a particular person or group of persons or to the world at large.[8] It is not compulsory to make an offer by using

4 Abdullah Abdul Rahman, "Shari'ah as the Governing Law of Islamic Finance Contracts in the UK: The Impact of Rome I Regulation and the Position in Arbitration," April, 2019, https://www.ccalaw.com/index.php/home/knowledge/article/item/shariah-as-the-governing-law-of-islamic-finance-contracts-in-the-uk-the-impact-of-rome-i-regulation-and-the-position-in-arbitration.

5 Allen & Overy, "At a Glance Guide to Basic Principles of English Contract Law," accessed March 25, 2022, http://www.a4id.org/wp-content/uploads/2016/10/A4ID-english-contract-law-at-a-glance.pdf.

6 Allen & Overy, "At a Glance Guide to Basic Principles of English Contract Law," accessed March 25, 2022, http://www.a4id.org/wp-content/uploads/2016/10/A4ID-english-contract-law-at-a-glance.pdf.

7 [1974] 1 WLR 1403.

8 *Carlill v Carbolic Smoke Ball Company* [1892] EWCA Civ 1.

words only; it could be made by way of conduct as well.[9] An offer needs to be differentiated from an invitation to treat[10] and a counter-offer.[11] An offer can be terminated due to the death of the offeror or the offeree or due to a lapse of reasonable time.

Generally, an offer can be revoked at any time before its acceptance.[12] An acceptance is a final and unqualified expression of assent to the terms of an offer. It is imperative to note that the communication of the acceptance shall be communicated to the offeror for it to have legal effect.[13] As such, silence will not amount to a valid acceptance,[14] though acceptance could be made through conduct.[15] An exception to this is the postal rule, where a postal acceptance will become effective when the letter of acceptance is posted even if the posted letter of acceptance is delayed, lost, or destroyed[16] unless the express terms of the offer exclude the postal rule.[17]

There will be no binding contract unless a promise is made with consideration. Consideration made in this case must be sufficient but need not be adequate;[18] it must be not from the past[19] unless it was proceeded by request;[20] and it must move from the promise.[21] Mere performance of an existing public duty will not amount to valid consideration[22] unless the promisor goes beyond their duty.[23] Likewise, an existing contractual duty will not amount to valid consideration[24] unless the party goes beyond their existing duty[25] or if they confer a practical advantage.[26] If the existing contractual duty is owed to a third party, this may be used as valid consider-

9 *Thornton v Shoe Lane Parking* [1971] 2 WLR 585.

10 Instances like goods on display in shops – *Fisher v Bell* [1961] 1 QB 394; *Pharmaceutical Society of Great Britain v Boots* [1953] 1 QB 40; and advertisements – *Partridge v Crittenden* (1968) 2 All ER 425.

11 *Hyde v Wrench* (1840) 49 ER 132.

12 *Dickinson v Dodds* (1876) 2 Ch D 463.

13 *Entores v Miles Far East Corp* [1955] 2 QB 327.

14 *Felthouse v Bindley* [1862] EWHC CP J35.

15 *Brogden v Metropolitan Railway Co.* (1877) 2 App. Cas. 666; *Butler Machine Tool v Ex-cell-o Corporation* [1979] 1 WLR 401.

16 *Adams v Lindsell* (1818) 106 ER 250.

17 *Holwell Securities v Hughes* [1974] 1 WLR 155.

18 *Chappell v Nestle* [1960] AC 87.

19 *Re McArdle* (1951) Ch 669.

20 *Lampleigh v Braithwaite* [1615] EWHC KB J17.

21 *Tweddle v Atkinson* [1861] EWHC QB J57.

22 *Collins v Godefrey* (1831) 1 B & AD 950.

23 *Glasbrook Bros v Glamorgan County Council* [1925] AC 270.

24 *Stilk v Myrrick* [1809] EWHC KB J58.

25 *Hartley v Ponsonby* [1857] 7 EB 872.

26 *Williams v Roffey Bros* [1990] 2 WLR 1153.

ation for a new promise.[27] It is also essential to note that part-payment of debt is not a valid consideration for a promise to release the debt in full.[28]

For a contract to be binding, the parties making the contract shall have the intention to create a legally binding relationship. If it is a commercial transaction, the court will presume that there is the intention to create a legal relationship among the parties unless otherwise proven.[29] For social and domestic arrangements, it will be presumed that there is no such intention[30] unless otherwise proven.[31]

Contracts can be made formally by putting everything agreed between the parties in writing. They could also be made orally or by conduct unless legislation requires otherwise.[32] Contents of a contract can include express terms (ones that the parties have set out in their agreement) and implied terms (terms that are not expressly stated but implied, either because the parties intended this, or implied by operation of law, or by custom and usage).

A contract can be brought to an end in several ways: upon reaching of expiry date or in accordance with the terms agreed; termination due to breach[33] or antici-

27 *New Zealand Shipping v Satterthwaite* [1975] AC 154.

28 In *Pinnel's* case 1602 5 Rep, 117 it was held that part payment of a debt is not valid consideration for a promise to forebear the balance unless at the promisor's request part payment is made: (a) before the due date; (b) with a chattel; and (c) to a different destination. This was affirmed in the case of *Foakes v Beer* (1883–84) LR 9 App Cas 605. Further exceptions to the rule in *Pinnel's* case are: where part payment is made by a third party; and promissory estoppel.

29 *Edwards v Skyways Ltd* [1964] 1 WLR 349.

30 *Jones v Padavatton* [1969] 1 WLR 328; *Balfour v Balfour* [1919] 2 KB 571.

31 For example, by producing a written agreement like in the case of *Errington v Errington Woods* [1952] 1 KB 290; where the parties have been separated like in the case of *Merritt v Merritt* [1970] 1 WLR 1211; where there is a third party to the agreement like in the case of *Simpkins v Pays* [1955] 1 WLR 975.

32 For example: (i) a lease for more than 3 years must be made by deed: Law of Property Act 1925, ss 52, 54(2); (ii) most contracts for the sale or disposition of an interest in land must be "made in writing": Law of Property (Miscellaneous Provisions) Act 1989, s 2; (iii) contracts of guarantee are required to be evidenced in writing: Statute of Frauds, s 4.

33 A breach may occur due to: (a) Failure or refusal to perform – a failure or refusal to perform a contractual promise when performance has fallen due is prima facie a breach. (b) Defective performance – where a person promises to do one thing but does another, which differs, for example, in time, quantity or quality, this amounts to a breach. The effect of such a breach often differs from those of a complete failure or refusal to perform (*see* below). Note that where the "defect" in performance is particularly serious, the breach may amount to non-performance rather than defective performance (for example, if a seller promises beans but delivers peas). (c) Incapacitating oneself – for example, a seller commits a breach of contract for the sale of a specific thing if he sells it to a third party.

patory breach[34] or termination for breach.[35] There are certain factors that can vitiate the contract, such as the presence of misrepresentation and mistake. A contract can also be discharged by frustration if, after its formation, an unforeseen event occurs which makes the performance of the contract impossible, illegal, or fundamentally different from what was contemplated. It is essential to note that the position at common law is that frustration discharges the parties only from duties of future performance, and rights accrued before the frustrating event will remain enforceable.

There are remedies (most commonly damages – monetary compensation) available for breach of contract.[36] In case of breach of contract, the injured party must show that: there was actual loss arising from the breach, the kind of loss is recognised as giving a right to get compensation, and the loss is not too remote. Even if there is no actual loss suffered by the party, a breach of contract can be established, and in this case, there will be an entitlement to only nominal damages. If damages are inadequate, equitable remedies such as specific performance[37] and injunction[38] are available.

2.2.2 Contract Law under Shari'ah

The contract law principles from Shari'ah perspective are derived from Islamic law. The Arabic word used to indicate contract is *'aqd* (singular) or *'uqud* (plural), which means "to tie" or "to bind" or "to combine." A contract can be defined as an agreement between two or more parties with the intention to create a legally enforceable

34 An anticipatory breach occurs when, before performance is due, a party either repudiates the contract or disables himself from performing it. (a) Repudiation – clear and absolute refusal to perform, which includes conduct showing the party is unwilling, even though he may be able, to perform. (b) Disablement – for example, where a party disposes elsewhere of the specific thing which forms the subject matter of the contract. Where one party commits an anticipatory breach, the other can elect to: (i) keep the contract alive by continuing to press for performance (in which case the anticipatory breach will have the same effect as an actual breach); or (ii) "accept" the breach (in which case he has a right to damages and termination.

35 At law, the right to terminate for breach arises in three situations: (a) repudiation – where a party evinces a clear and absolute refusal to perform; (b) impossibility – where a party disables himself from performing; (c) substantial failure to perform. Any defect in performance must attain a certain minimum degree of seriousness to entitle the injured party to terminate. A failure in performance is "substantial" when it deprives the party of what he bargained for or when it "goes to the root" of the contract. For less serious breaches, a right to damages may arise, but not a right to terminate.

36 It is essential to note that damages are designed to compensate for an established loss and not to provide a gratuitous benefit to the aggrieved party.

37 Where damages are deemed inadequate, the court may make an order for specific performance which will compel the party in breach to fulfil the terms of a contract.

38 A court may restrain a party from committing a breach of contract by way of injunction.

relationship. From a technical sense, it could be stated that a contract creates an obligation that results from offer and acceptance. A codified rule in this regard is the *Al-Majalla Al Ahkam Al Adaliyyah* (The Ottoman Courts Manual (Hanafi)), which consists of 16 books.[39] In Book 1 on sale, a contract is defined as what the parties bind themselves and undertake to do with reference to a particular matter, and it is stated that a contract is composed of the combination of offer and acceptance.[40] An offer is described as a statement made in the first place with a view to making a disposition of property, and such disposition is proved thereby[41] while acceptance is defined as the statement made in the second place with a view to making a disposition of property and the contract becomes completed thereby.[42] The conclusion of a contract consists of connecting offer and acceptance together legally in such a manner that the result may be perfectly clear.[43] As such, it can be observed that an offer is the first stage of entering into a contract. An offer can be made in a number of ways, such as verbally, in writing, through a message,[44] and through signs and gestures, especially if the person is deaf or dumb or when the receiver does not understand the language of the offeror.[45] An offer can also be made by conduct,[46] but silence does not constitute an offer.[47]

It is also stated that sale consists of exchanging property for property. It may be concluded (valid, voidable, executory, and conditional) and a non-concluded contract.[48] In this context, a valid sale, or a sale which is permitted, is a sale that is lawful both in itself and as regards matters incidental thereto, while the voidable

---

39 Book 1 is on sale; book 2 is on hire; book 3 is on guarantee; book 4 is on transfer of debt; book 5 on pledges; book 6 on trust and trusteeship; book 7 on gift; book 8 on wrongful appropriation and destruction; book 9 on interdiction, constraint and pre-emption; book 10 on joint ownership; book 11 on agency; book 12 on settlement and release; book 13 on admission; book 14 on actions; book 15 on evidence and administration of an oath; and book 16 on administration of justice by the courts. *See Al-Majalla Al Ahkam Al Adaliyyah* (Beirut: al-Matba'at al-Adabiyyah, 1302 H), accessed March 25, 2022, http://legal.pipa.ps/files/server/ENG%20Ottoman%20Majalle%20(Civil%20Law).pdf.

40 *Al-Majalla Al Ahkam Al Adaliyyah*, art 103.

41 *Al-Majalla Al Ahkam Al Adaliyyah*, art 101.

42 *Al-Majalla Al Ahkam Al Adaliyyah*, art 102.

43 *Al-Majalla Al Ahkam Al Adaliyyah*, art 104.

44 The Maliki, Shafi, Hanbali jurists are of the view that the offer must be made by the owner of the property in return for a consideration; but Hanafi jurists are of the opinion that it can come from either of the parties.

45 The Maliki school consider this way as valid even if it is made by a perfect person as the main criteria that needs to be fulfilled is communication the offer to the recipient, but most of the jurists are of the view that known signs of dumb persons made to constitute an offer are valid while some jurists consider signs and gestures invalid as modes to make an offer.

46 An offer made through delivery of goods are considered as a good offer according to Maliki school.

47 Hasbullah Hj Abd Rahman, "Offer and Acceptance in Islamic law of Contract," *Jurnal Syariah* 8, no. 2 (2000):15–32.

48 *Al-Majalla Al Ahkam Al Adaliyyah*, artt 105–107.

sale is a sale which, while valid in itself, is invalid as regards matters incidental thereto. A void sale is a sale that is invalid in itself, and a conditional sale is a sale dependent upon the rights of some third party, such as a sale by an unauthorised person. An unauthorised person is a person who, without any legal permission, deals with some other person's property. An executory sale is a sale not dependent upon the right of any third person. Such sales are divided into irrevocable and revocable sales. It is essential to note that under Islamic law, there are specific types of contracts such as sale (*bai'*), pledge (*rahn*), guarantee (*kafalah*), agency (*wakalah*), hire (*ijarah*), partnership (*musharakah*), (*limited*) partnership (*mudaraba/qirad*), and gift (*hibah*) that have their own rules to follow apart from the general rules of contract that apply to all types of contracts.[49]

In Shari'ah, the parties entering into the contract must be free to decide the objectives, terms, and conditions they want to apply to their private transaction.[50] The upholding of the sanctity of the contract can be derived from Qur'an, (*Surah* 2): verse 282, and there is also a need to uphold the principles of equity and equality as found in Qur'an, (5): 58.[51] Further, the prohibition of *gharar* (uncertainty), *riba* (usury), *maysir* (gambling), or any other element prohibited by Shari'ah needs to be considered when entering into a contract. There is no specific form required under Shari'ah to conclude an agreement. What is required is consent from all parties derived through making a proposal or an offer by one party and accepting it by the other party. The offer and acceptance must be made at the same meeting (*majlis*).[52]

There are three essential elements of Islamic law of contract derived from the divine sources of Shari'ah, namely *sigha*, which refers to an offer and acceptance (*ijab* and *qabul*); contracting parties (*al-aqidayn*); and subject matter (*mahal al-aqd*). For a contract to be valid, mutual consent between the contracting parties must be obtained. However, there is no specific way that needs to be followed to establish consent, and Muslim scholars are of the opinion that consent can be derived from offer and acceptance. Parties to the contract must possess a legal capacity (*ahliyyah*) before entering into a contract. If not, the contract will be void and will have no legal effect. *Ahliyyah,* in this context, refers to "the competency of an individual to accept or to perform the responsibilities or rights imposed on him or against him."[53] The contracting parties must be of sound mind, puberty and prudence, and

49 Nicholas HD Foster, *Islamic Commercial Law (II): An Overview* (Barcelona: InDret, 2007), 3–4, https://indret.com/wp-content/themes/indret/pdf/405_en.pdf.

50 SE Rayner, *The Theory of Contracts in Islamic Law: A Comparative Analysis With Particular Reference to the Modern Legislation in Kuwait, Bahrain, and the United Arab Emirates* (London, Boston: Graham & Trotman, 1991).

51 Nicholas HD Foster, *Islamic Commercial Law (II): An Overview* (Barcelona: InDret, 2007), 5, https://indret.com/wp-content/themes/indret/pdf/405_en.pdf.

52 Hasbullah Hj Abd Rahman, "Offer and Acceptance in Islamic Law of Contract," *Jurnal Syariah* 8, no. 2 (2000):15–32.

53 Abdul Karim Zaidan, *Al-Wajiz Fi Usul al-Fiqh* (Beirut: Muassah al-Risalah Beirut, 1985), 95.

competent; and have no legal impediments (*al-hajr*)[54] such as bankruptcy to conclude a valid contract.

The subject matter of a contract may include a commodity or the object of a contract or the performance of an act. When it comes to the subject matter of the contract, there are certain conditions that ought to be fulfilled. Firstly, the subject matter must be legal from Shari'ah perspective. This means that subject matter should not be something prohibited by Shari'ah like liquor or a service or an act prohibited such as gambling, and the commodity must be capable of being traded in (*mal mutaqawwim*). Secondly, the subject matter shall be in existence at the time of entering into the contract except when entering into *salam* (forward sale) and *istisna'* (manufacturing contract). If the subject matter does not exist at the time of the conclusion of the contract, the contract will be void. There are differences of opinion among scholars on the existence of the subject matter. Hanafis and Shafis are of the opinion that a subject matter which is not in existence or only exist in the future is void based on the following two Hadith or Prophet (SAW): "It is prohibited to sell the foetus of camel in the womb"[55] and "Do not sell what you do not have."[56] According to Malikis, in a commutative contract, it is a requirement to have the subject matter in existence, but not in a gratuitous contract. This means that, in the latter, there is no requirement to have the subject matter in existence at the time of concluding the contract.

The third condition that must be fulfilled when it comes to the subject matter is that it shall be known to the parties entering into a contract. This means that the parties shall know the particulars of the subject matter, such as its nature, value, quality, and quantity. If the contracting parties lack knowledge about these details, the contract will be void. Therefore, the parties will have to physically examine the subject matter and indicate its attributes in the contract. These requirements are stipulated by Shafi scholars both on commutative and gratuitous contracts. Article 200 of *Al-Majalla Al Ahkam Al Adaliyyah* states that a thing sold must be known by the buyer. Article 201 further clarifies that the thing sold becomes known by a description of its qualities and state, which will distinguish it from other things. Article 202 states if the thing sold is present at the meeting at which the sale is made, a pointing out, which can be perceived, is sufficient. The Malikis are of the view that the knowledge of the contracting parties on the nature of the subject matter is required in commutative contracts and not in gratuitous contracts.

Fourthly, there must be certainty in the delivery of the subject matter. Article 198 of *Al-Majalla Al Ahkam Al Adaliyyah* states that the delivery of the thing must

54 Contracts entered by minors (*sabiyy*), lunatic or of unsound mind (*al-majnun*), idiot or imbecilic (*al-ma'tuh*), the prodigal person (*al-safih*), death or the sick (*marad al-mawt*) and bankrupts (*iflas*) will be void and will have no legal effect.

55 Sahih Muslim, Hadith No. 3615–3616.

56 Sunan Abu Dawud, Vol. 3, No. 3503.

be possible, and article 209 of *Al-Majalla Al Ahkam Al Adaliyyah* reiterates that the sale of a thing, the delivery of which is not possible, is invalid. It is imperative to note here that the contract will be void if the subject matter is incapable of being delivered. The majority of the scholars are of the opinion that except for *salam* and *istisna'* contract, a sale contract must result with instant transfer of ownership and delivery of the subject matter from the seller to the buyer. Imam Ahmad ibn Hanbal opines that it is allowed to delay the delivery of the subject matter of sale based on the customary practice of the society.[57] An example of this could be when a large quantity of goods is sold, and the delivery of them is not possible instantly.[58]

The final condition is related to the determination of consideration: the monetary price or the commodity exchanged for another commodity where the consideration is paid in kind. Under Shari'ah, the price must be decided at the time of the contract. If not, the contract would be void. Further, in determining the price, *riba* should be eliminated.

It is also important to determine the effect of void and voidable contracts under Shari'ah. If a contract fulfils all the elements and conditions of it, then it would be considered as a valid contract, and if there is any defect found in the essential conditions of a contract, then that contract could be either void or voidable. Majority of the scholars have divided the types of contracts in this regard into valid (*sahih*) and void (*batil*) contracts, while Hanafis have divided them into three categories: *sahih*[59] (valid), *fasid*[60] (voidable/irregular), and *batil*[61] (void) contracts.[62] It is essential to note that a void in Shari'ah is automatically terminated, while voidable contracts can be saved provided that the contract is rectified by removing the irregular element from it.

57 There is also a hadith (Sahih Muslim, Book 22, Hadith 142) relied in this regard. Jabir (Allah be pleased with him) reported: My camel had grown tired as Allah's Messenger (SAW) came to me. He goaded it and it began to jump. After that I tried to restrain its rein so that I could listen to his (Prophet's) words, but I could not do that. Allah's Apostle (SAW) met me and said: Sell it to me, and I sold it for five 'uqiyas. I said: On the condition that I may use it as a ride (for going back) to Medina. He (the Holy Prophet) said: Well, you may use it as a ride up till Medina. When I came to Medina I handed over that to him and he made an addition of an uqiya (to that amount which had been agreed upon) and then presented that (camel) to me.

58 Hashim Kamali, *Islamic Commercial Law, An Analysis of Futures and Options* (Kuala Lumpur: Ilmiah Publisher, 2002), 107.

59 A contract which has fulfilled all the essential requirements of a valid contract.

60 A contract where the essential elements and conditions of a contract are complete, but it is associated with a quality which is prohibited by the Lawgiver.

61 A contract in which one of the essential elements is missing, or any condition is not fulfilled.

62 Ahmad Hasan, *The Principles of Islamic Jurisprudence: The Command of the* Shari'ah *and Juridical Norm*, vol. 1 (Islamabad: Islamic Research Institute Islamabad, 1993), 206.

2.3 Comparisons Between Two Legal Systems

2.3.1 Nature of Contracts

In Shari'ah, contracts can be classified into unilateral and bilateral contracts. However, in common law, even in unilateral contracts, consent from the person accepting the offer is required to enforce it as a contract. Therefore, it would not be wrong to state that the concept of unilateral contract as it is in Shari'ah does not exist in the common law. Under common law, the concept of unilateral contract exists as an offeror like in the landmark case of *Carlill v Carbolic Smoke Ball Company*[63] openly makes an offer, it is considered as a valid offer. It is true that common law acknowledges its own concept of unilateral contract, where an offer can be made open to all who are willing to pay for a specified act. But, without acceptance from a person, the contract cannot be enforceable. The point that needs to be differentiated here is, in Shari'ah no consent from the person accepting the offer is required, while under the common law, even if it is a unilateral contract, acceptance is required. As such, only bilateral contracts have been acknowledged as contracts.[64] A unilateral contract can be defined as a contract or a promise made by one party only. It can also be described as a one-sided contract where its nature is gratuitous, and there is no need to obtain consent from the party at the receiving end. Some of the examples of unilateral contracts are *hibah* (gift), *ibra* (set-off debt), *waqf* (endowment), *wasiyyah* (will), and *qard* (loan). A bilateral contract is a two-sided contract that is recognised in the common law.

2.3.2 Invitation to Treat

The importance of determining whether a statement is an invitation to treat or an offer is that if a statement is an invitation to treat, then the acceptance of it will not make a legally binding contract between the parties. In other words, an invitation to treat is not an offer capable of acceptance. Table 2.1 summarises some examples of these instances.

---

63 [1892] EWCA Civ 1.

64 Nicholas HD Foster, *Islamic Commercial Law (II): An Overview* (Barcelona: InDret, 2007), 3–4, https://indret.com/wp-content/themes/indret/pdf/405_en.pdf p.4.

Table 2.1: Examples of the Instances that the Court Considered Invitations to Treat.

Instance	General Rule	Exception
Displaying of goods	Displaying goods with a price tag in a shop is an invitation treat.	If the display of goods with a statement in the shop clearly signifies the intention of the shopkeeper to be legally bound, then if a customer accepts the terms of the display, there is a binding contract and the shopkeeper will be legally bound to sell the goods to the buyer.
Advertisement	Advertisement is an invitation to treat.	In certain circumstances, an advertisement might be considered as an offer. This may happen when the advertisement includes a promise to all potential customers for using the item.
Reply to inquiry	Reply to an inquiry is an invitation to treat.	–
Auction sale	A call for bid by an auctioneer is an invitation to treat.	In circumstances where the auction sale explicitly states that particular goods will be auctioned "without reserve" price, then such auction will be an offer, and anyone can, in this case, accept the offer by placing the bid.
Tenders	When tenders are invited from the public to supply the required item/ service or for a particular project, it is considered as a mere invitation treat.	Under certain circumstances, an invitation to submit tenders is considered as an offer like where it is expressly stated that in the invitation for tenders, the tender will be given to whoever offers the highest price for the tendered items or services or whoever offers the lowest price to supply the required items, etc.

Source: Extracted from Jalil.[65]

65 Md Abdul Jalil, "Adoption of the Principle of 'Invitation to Treat' in Islamic Law of Contracts," *International Journal of Computer Science, Information Technology and Management* 1, no. 1 (2016): 51–68.

Md Abdul Jalil explains that how the Shari'ah scholars view the concept of invitation to treat in Shari'ah is different from that of common law.[66] In Shari'ah, if there is a price stated in the goods offered, then it is not considered an invitation to treat but rather, it is considered an offer.[67] However, if there is no price stated in the goods offered, it would not be considered an offer as there is excessive uncertainty in it warranting it to be treated as an invitation to treat. Further, whether a statement is considered an offer or an invitation to treat from Shari'ah perspective, the sign of intention to create legal relation (*qarina*) shall be examined. This means that from the statement made, if it is evident that the intention of the maker of the statement is to create legal relation, then it will be considered as an offer, while if it is otherwise, it would be merely an invitation to treat. There are also some scholars who view invitation to treat as a promise by the maker to do an act making it from Shari'ah perspective as an offer; rather than an invitation to treat. Common law views some proposals made as invitations to treat to protect the seller from being sued multiple times for breach of contract due to shortage of stocks, and this view is made considering business convenience. Jalil views that this is an important aspect that should be considered in Shari'ah. It is important to have a balance in this regard where the rights of both sellers and buyers shall be protected, and any unfairness arising from the transaction shall be avoided. As such, Jalil concluded that the common law principles of invitation to treat does not violate any express Shari'ah principles like *riba* (usury), *gharar* (uncertainty), and *maysir* (gambling) and as such is acceptable under Shari'ah.

2.3.3 The Concept of Promise

Promise (*wa'd*[68]), according to Islamic jurists, can be defined as a statement made by the maker to another expressing his intention to do an act of kindness in the future. Under Islamic law, the promise to do bad things is not binding.[69] From a Shari'ah perspective making a promise to enter into a contract and actually entering into a contract are different things. The scholars, by referring to Qur'an, (5):1, unanimously agree that fulfilling the promise made by a person is mandatory; but they

66 Md Abdul Jalil, "Adoption of the Principle of 'Invitation to Treat' in Islamic Law of Contracts," *International Journal of Computer Science, Information Technology and Management* 1, no. 1 (2016): 51–68.

67 Md Abdul Jalil, "Adoption of the Principle of 'Invitation to Treat' in Islamic Law of Contracts," *International Journal of Computer Science, Information Technology and Management* 1, no. 1 (2016): 51–68.

68 There are two words used as substitutes for the word *wa'd*, which are *'iddah* and *maw'idah*.

69 Nasrul Hisyam Nor Muhamad, Mohd Fauzi Abu @ Hussin, Buerah Tunggak and Abdul Hafiz Abdullah, "The Promise in the Contract of Islamic Law: A Special Focus on Promise Contract," *Mediterranean Journal of Social Sciences* 7, no. 4 (July 2016): 136.

differ on the legal action that could be taken against breaching of a promise. There is no doubt that it is a religious obligation in Islam to fulfil the promise made, and one will be held accountable in the hereafter. As for whether the court has the authority to decide that the one who makes a promise has responsibility to carry out his promise or not, the opinions of scholars differ and are shown in Table 2.2.

Table 2.2: Views of Scholars on a Promise.[70]

#	View	Scholars
1	Promises must be fulfilled in all circumstances.	Umar bin Abdul Aziz Ibn Shubrumah, Ibn al-Ashwin, al-Hasan al-Basri, Ishaq bin Rahawayh, view of Hanbali School given by Ibn Taymiyyah and also a view of Malik.
2	The general rule is that a promise must be executed except in circumstances where there is a valid and reasonable excuse.	The view of Maliki
3	The scholars in this group are of the opinion that adhering to a promise is not mandatory, and the court cannot compel a person to fulfil his promise. For these scholars, breaching the promise is an abominable act, and it is not a sin. This view is based on the notion that promise is a *tabarru'* (voluntary) that is similar to *hibah*.	The view of the majority of scholars composed of Imam Abu Hanifa, al-Shafi'i, Ahmad bin Hanbal, Zahiri's school and also some Malikis' fuqaha.
4	A promise is binding and can be enforced by the court if that particular promise is bound to a reason even if such a commitment is not made from the other side.	The famous views within the Maliki School
5	A promise which is subject to certain stipulations or conditions can be enforceable, and a promise which is not enforceable is a promise without any such stipulations or conditions.	Hanafi School

Various Shari'ah advisory bodies have decided that promise is binding and can be enforceable in the context of Islamic finance transactions. For instance, in this regard OIC Fiqh Academy in its 5th Conference held on 10th and 15th December 1988 in Kuwait, has held that promise made by a party is binding from a religious perspective

70 Nasrul Hisyam Nor Muhamad, Mohd Fauzi Abu @ Hussin, Buerah Tunggak and Abdul Hafiz Abdullah, "The Promise in the Contract of Islamic Law: A Special Focus on Promise Contract," *Mediterranean Journal of Social Sciences* 7, no. 4 (July 2016): 136–137.

unless there is a valid and reasonable excuse not to abide by it. Ismail Wisham et al. reviewed the status of promise under Shari'ah and in the common law. They concluded that the opinion of Maliki scholars on it is similar to the bindingness of a promise in the common law.[71] To understand the position of promise under common law, the concept of promise and promissory estoppel has been reviewed. It is viewed that the promise forms the basis of legal contracts and is self-imposed.[72] It is imperative to note that in terms of the bindingness of a promise, the position in common law and civil law differs. In common law promise is binding, whereas in civil law it is not.[73]

Marjan Muhammad et al. studied *wa'd* in the context of the Contracts Act 1950 (Malaysia), which derives its principles mainly from common law. They concluded that the Contracts Act 1950 does not recognise *wa'd,* and it only recognises binding *muwā'adah* (mutual promise), which is not permissible in the Shari'ah.[74] About the implication of a binding *wa'd*, paragraph 12 of the policy document issued on *wa'd* by Bank Negara Malaysia states that: "the promisor shall not unilaterally revoke his wa`d and the promisor shall fulfil his *wa'd* in accordance with the specified condition."[75] Further, it is stated that "the promisee has a right to claim compensation for any actual loss suffered due to the failure of the promisor to fulfil his *wa'd*."[76] In this case, "the promisee's actual loss shall be determined either by: (a) an authoritative body; or (b) a methodology accepted as customary market practice (*`urf tijari*)."[77] It is worth noting that offer and acceptance in Shari'ah are not promises.

71 Ismail Wisham, Aishath Muneeza and Rusni Hassan, "Special Legal Features of the Islamic Wa'd or Pledge: Comparison with the Conventional Law on Promise Within the Sphere of Islamic Finance," *International Journal of Law and Management* 53, no. 3 (2011): 221–234.

72 Charles Fried, *Contract as Promise: A Theory of Contractual Obligation* (Cambridge: Harvard University Press, 1981).

73 James Gordley, *The Enforceability of Promises in European Contract Law* (Cambridge: Cambridge University Press, 2004).

74 Marjan Muhammad, Hakimah Yaacob & Shabana Hasan, *The Bindingness and Enforceability of a Unilateral Promise (wa'd): An Analysis from Islamic Law and Legal Perspectives* (Kuala Lumpur: International Shari'ah Research Academy for Islamic Finance (ISRA), Research paper no. 30, 2011), 2.

75 Bank Negara Malaysia, "Wa'd," accessed March 26, 2022, https://www.bnm.gov.my/documents/20124/761688/20170202+-+PD+on+Wa%60d.pdf/6db13262-5299-4c9b-a4ac-96895ca02537?t=1580887370995.

76 Bank Negara Malaysia, "Wa'd," accessed March 26, 2022, https://www.bnm.gov.my/documents/20124/761688/20170202+-+PD+on+Wa%60d.pdf/6db13262-5299-4c9b-a4ac-96895ca02537?t=1580887370995.

77 Bank Negara Malaysia, "Wa'd," accessed March 26, 2022, https://www.bnm.gov.my/documents/20124/761688/20170202+-+PD+on+Wa%60d.pdf/6db13262-5299-4c9b-a4ac-96895ca02537?t=1580887370995.

2.3.4 Offer and Acceptance

In offer and acceptance (*sigha*), it can be stated that general rules applicable in common law and Shari'ah overlap. However, certain points might have some differences. For instance, the postal rule applied for acceptance of an offer under common law is not compatible with Shari'ah. This is because, under Shari'ah, the knowledge of the acceptance is essential to form a valid contract. Further, if the opinion of Shafi school of law is applied, acceptance should be made instantly after the offer is made. If not, the offer will lapse.[78] The unity of the meeting place and the option to acceptance rules applied (*Khiyar al-qabul*)[79] ensures this. For Hanafis, unlike Shafis it is not a must for the party accepting the offer to immediately accept it as time is required for the person accepting it to contemplate and decide on the offer made. As such, the option of acceptance as per Hanafis can be made prior to the breaking up of the meeting. Therefore, it would be not wrong to state that even though common law has various ways in which offer and acceptance could be made, the Shari'ah parameters ought to be followed when concluding contracts that opt to follow Shari'ah rules. It is also argued that the role played by offer and acceptance in Shari'ah is more vital than in common law of contract. Islamic law of contract is more similar to the medieval action of debt than the modern contract law.[80] Offer and acceptance under Islamic law are not promises made, and even when it is made, future tense cannot be used, and past tense should be used to indicate finality.[81]

2.3.5 Consideration

In determining consideration, unlike in common law, Shari'ah requires to abide by *riba*-related rules. As such, this again is a point of difference between common law and Shari'ah rules applied to contracts. The rules related to consideration found in common law are not part of Shari'ah. However, if those principles do not conflict with Shari'ah, there is no issue in applying them in Shari'ah applied contracts. One thing that is important is to determine consideration at the time of the contract, not after the contract is concluded. This is an essential principle to be followed in this regard.

78 Hasbullah Hj Abd Rahman, "Offer and Acceptance in Islamic Law of Contract," *Jurnal Syariah* 8, no. 2 (2000):15–32.
79 The option to accept or reject a proposal, in a contract of sale, before the proposal is accepted, the option is surrendered by giving acceptance to the proposal.
80 Aron Zysow, "The Problem of Offer and Acceptance: A Study of Implied-in-Fact Contracts in Islamic Law and Common Law," *Cleveland State Law Review* 34, no. 1 (1985–1986): 69–77.
81 Aron Zysow, "The Problem of Offer and Acceptance: A Study of Implied-in-Fact Contracts in Islamic Law and Common Law," *Cleveland State Law Review* 34, no. 1 (1985–1986): 69–77.

2.3.6 Intention to Create Legal Relations

Unlike in common law, Shari'ah does not differentiate between commercial and social/domestic agreements to determine whether the parties intended to create a binding contract or not. As long as the essential elements of a valid contract are fulfilled, it is deemed that the parties intended to create legal relations.

2.3.7 Form

There is no particular form required to create a contract under common law and Shari'ah. In common law, the only exception would be when legislation requires the parties to enter a contract in a specific way prescribed in the law. However, under Shari'ah, Quran, (2):282 encourage parties to write contracts or/and have witnesses in cases where contracts are entered where some future obligations are involved. But it is not mandatory to write contracts. Therefore, there is no significant difference between common law and Shari'ah in this regard.

2.3.8 Contents of a Contract

There are no specific contents that are required under the Shari'ah except for the essential conditions that must be agreed upon between the parties. As such, no such essential condition could be put as an implied term. This means that those essential conditions should be put as express terms. The autonomy to decide this is not given to the parties entering into the contract like in common law. Other than that, the parties are free to put their stipulations as long as the stipulation is within the parameters of Islamic law. This is in line with the hadith of the Prophet (SAW) where it is stated: "Muslims are bound by their stipulations except for a stipulation which makes the unlawful lawful or makes the lawful unlawful."[82]

2.3.9 The End of a Contract

The Arabic term used for the termination of a contract is *faskh al 'aqd*. There is no difference between common law and Shari'ah when it comes to ending a contract due to expiry date or discharging of duty under the contract or in the manner provided in the contract as that is what has been agreed between the parties. Under Shari'ah, a contract can also be terminated via *iqalah* (mutual consent). As for the

82 Sunan Abu-Dawud Hadith No 1419.

doctrine of frustration, it is reflected in the Shari'ah concept of *'Istihalah al-tanfidh'* that arises due to the impossibility of the performance of contract because of change in circumstance (*udhr*).[83] Further, the principle of *Quwa Qahira* (or *Quwat al-Qanun*) or act of God is considered to be wider than the common law doctrine of frustration.[84] As such, it can be said that there is no issue in accepting the doctrine of frustration under Shari'ah as this principle is in line with Qur'an.[85] Article 443 of *Al-Majalla Al Ahkam Al Adaliyyah* provides that if any event happens whereby the reason for the conclusion of the contract disappears so that the contract cannot be performed, such a contract is terminated.

Like the common law, Shari'ah also acknowledges that the existence of vitiating factors will negate the consent of the parties affecting the validity of the contract under the principle of *Uyuub Alaqd* (defects of a contract).[86] Mistake and misrepresentation are also considered in this regard as vitiating factors in Shari'ah. In the case of mistake (*ghalad*), the effect of mistake in a contract is divided into two categories: mistakes that invalidate the contract (void)[87] and mistakes that do not invalidate the contract (voidable).[88] As for the breach of contract, it is said that under traditional Islamic law, the only remedies available were monetary compensation or damages and specific performance of the contract for failure of performance of a valid contract. The concept of breach of contract was not used as a general rule.[89] It is essential to note that Islam promotes the fulfilment of contracts. This is evident from the following three verses of the Qur'an:

83 Al-Barak Hada Ahmad, Zuhairah Ariff Abd Ghadas, Farhanin Abdullah Asuhaimi, Nurzihan Mohammad Udin, "The Principle of Force Majeure in Shari'ah: A Special Reference to Saudi Contract," *The Turkish Online Journal of Design Art and Communication* 8 (2018):1097–1106.

84 Al-Barak Hada Ahmad, Zuhairah Ariff Abd Ghadas, Farhanin Abdullah Asuhaimi, Nurzihan Mohammad Udin, "The Principle of Force Majeure in Shari'ah: A Special Reference to Saudi Contract," *The Turkish Online Journal of Design Art and Communication* 8 (2018):1097–1106.

85 *See* Qur'an: "Allah intends ever facility for you; He does not want to put to difficulties" (2):185; "On no soul does Allah place a burden greater than it can bear" (2):286; "Allah has imposed no difficulties on you" (22):78; "Allah does not burden a person beyond his capacity" (7):42.

86 Ibrahim Yaro Gambo, "Mistake as Vitiating Element of a Contract: A Comparative Analysis Between Sharia and Contemporary Laws," *International Journal of Business & Law Research* 8, no. 3 (July–Sept, 2020):109–113.

87 Example provided by Ibrahim Yaro Gambo is: non-conformity between the subject matter mentioned and the subject matter pointed during the contract.

88 Example provided by Ibrahim Yaro Gambo is: here somebody contracts to buy an animal (he) by mentioning and what was pointed at him an animal of the same class and description only that it eventually turned out to be (she). In this situation the contract is valid but voidable at the discretion of the party who made the mistake.

89 Adnan Amkhan, "Termination for Breach in Arab Contract Law," *Arab Law Quarterly* 10, no. 1 (Jan 1995): 17–30.

> O you who believe! Fully discharge (the obligations arising through) contracts[90]
>
> . . . and those who truly care for their trusts (left by others in their care) and their covenants[91]
>
> Fully discharge the volume (to be provided to the client) when you measure in volume, and weigh (the commodities sold by weight) by an accurate scale. That is goodness and better (as a material and practical) interpretation (of the contract of sale you have concluded).[92]

By referring to al-Zarqa, it was observed that termination for breach of contract was not an option traditionally available under the traditional Shari'ah. But this does not mean that it should remain the same even today, as it could be validated from Shari'ah perspective on justice and fairness grounds.[93] It shall be observed here that Shari'ah law allows compensation for actual damages, but due to *gharar* (uncertainty or speculation), foreseeable or future damages are disallowed. Therefore, damages for loss of anticipated future profits, loss of business reputation, and loss of goodwill are not generally recoverable as claims of this nature are considered speculative. On the other hand, liquidated damages create certainty in a contract by defining the rights and obligations of contracting parties, and hence, liquidated damages agreements are valid and enforceable under Islamic law.

This is in line with the view of Shari'ah Advisory Council of Bank Negara on the late payment charge imposed by an Islamic financial institution encompassing both concepts of *gharamah* (fine or penalty) and *ta'wid* (compensation). It is ruled that the late payment charge imposed by an Islamic financial institution encircling both concepts of *gharamah* and *ta'wid* is permissible, provided that:
- *ta'wid* may be charged on late payment of financial obligations resulting from exchange contracts (such as sale and lease) and *qard* (loan);
- *ta'wid* may only be imposed after the settlement date of the financing became due as agreed between both contracting parties;
- Islamic financial institutions may recognise *ta'wid* as income on the basis that it is charged as compensation for actual loss suffered by the institution; and
- *gharamah* shall not be recognised as income, and therefore, it has to be channelled to certain charitable bodies.[94]

90 Qur'an (5): 1.

91 Qur'an (23): 8.

92 Qur'an (17): 34.

93 Adnan Amkhan, "Termination for breach in Arab Contract law," *Arab Law Quarterly* 10, no. 1 (Jan 1995): 17–30.

94 Bank Negara Malaysia, Shari'ah *Resolutions in Islamic Finance* (Kuala Lumpur: Bank Negara Malaysia, 2010), 129–130.

2.4 Conclusion

From the foregoing discussion, it is evident that the principles of contract law in common law and Shari'ah overlap though there are some differences. Not every difference identified in this regard will require harmonisation between the two, as harmonisation will be required in instances where there is a conflict between the two. If not, there will be room to acknowledge and adopt the difference without any issue. Table 2.3 summarises the discussion made in this chapter, answering the question of whether there is a need to harmonise principles of contract law in common law with Shari'ah.

Table 2.3: Is There a Need to Harmonize Principles of Contract Law in Common Law with Shari'ah?

Key Areas	Conflict	Need for Harmonisation
Nature of contracts	Shari'ah divides contracts into unilateral and bilateral contracts.	The unilateral contract needs to be recognised by common law.
Invitation to treat	From a Shari'ah perspective, an invitation to treat is determined based on the intention of the maker of the statement and could be considered a promise.	Not required as there is room to decide what is considered an invitation to treat in the common law based on the circumstance.
The concept of promise	From a Shari'ah perspective, a breach of promise generally does not allow the parties to bring an action in court, though one is committing a sin. Common law acknowledges binding *muwa'adah*, which is not permissible in the Shari'ah. However, due to the growth of Islamic finance, the view adopted is breach of promise can be enforced in courts, and damage for the actual amount of loss can be awarded.	Required as Shari'ah parameters need to be considered in dealing with breach of promise cases. The parameters stated in paragraph 12 of the policy document issued on *wa'd* by Bank Negara Malaysia can be considered.
Offer and acceptance	In Shari'ah, offer and acceptance need to be made in the same Majlis,[95] and the offer and acceptance must be clearly communicated to be effective. For an offer to be accepted, the knowledge of the person who made the offer about the acceptance of his offer is required and essential. Therefore, the postal rule of acceptance is not recognised in Islamic law.	Required as offer and acceptance in the same Majlis concept needs to be acknowledged, and the application of the postal rule in acceptance needs to be abolished.

95 Unity of the meeting place and the option to acceptance rules applied need to be adhered to.

Table 2.3 (continued)

Key Areas	**Conflict**	**Need for Harmonisation**
Consideration	In determining the consideration, Shari'ah requires the consideration to be determined at the time of the conclusion of the contract, and rules of *riba*[96] need to be observed in determining the consideration.	Required to ensure that consideration is determined at the time of the conclusion of the contract without ambiguity as required by Shari'ah and rules of *riba* are followed.
Intention to create legal relations	From a Shari'h perspective, to determine whether the parties have the intention to create legal relations, there are no presumptions made by looking at the type of agreement entered. Rather, what is considered is the existence of the essential elements in a contract that reflects the parties' intention.	Required, as from the Shari'ah perspective, the moment the essential elements of a contract are fulfilled, irrespective of whether it is a commercial or domestic/social contract, the parties will be bound to follow what they have agreed.
Form	From Shari'ah and common law perspectives, the general rule is that contracts could be entered orally, by writing, or by conduct. However, under common law, if legislation requires contracts to be in a specific form, then that form must be followed. Based on *maslahah* (public interest) and *siyasah shariyyah* (public policy), such stipulations made by legislation can be accepted in Shari'ah.	Not required
Contents of a contract	From a Shari'ah perspective, there is no issue in having express and implied terms in a contract. However, all essential elements of a contract shall be expressed terms of a contract, and if not, due to the existence of *gharar* (uncertainty), the contract may be invalid from Shari'ah perspective. Having said this, even in common law, if the essential	Required as parties will have to agree to the essential elements of the contract explicitly, and there should be no contents agreed upon which will be contrary to Shari'ah.

96 For instance, when gold and fiat money are exchanged, deferred sale cannot be possible as *riba al fadl* rules need to be observed.

Table 2.3 (continued)

Key Areas	Conflict	Need for Harmonisation
	requirements of a contract are missing, then the contract will have no legal effect as well. Further, any condition contrary to Shari'ah will have no legal effect even if the parties do agree to abide by them.	
The end of a contract	There is no difference between common law and Shari'ah in how the contracts are brought to an end. Even the effect of vitiating factors invalidating the consent given is similar in both common law and Shari'ah. However, there is a difference in how compensation is given for breach of contract. Shari'ah allows only actual damage to be claimed.	Required as in cases where monetary compensation is awarded for breach of contract, there is a need to limit it to actual losses suffered.

Source: Author's own elaboration.

As seen in Table 2.3, there is a need to harmonise some areas of principles of contract applied in common law with Shari'ah. This is inevitable as the sources of these two types of legal systems differ, and due to this, there would be some differences in their application in governing contracts as well. It is anticipated that the findings of this chapter will assist in understanding the differences and similarities between contract law principles applied in common law and Shari'ah and the aspects that require harmonisation in this regard.

Noor Suhaida Kasri

3 Islamic Banking, Islamic Capital Market, and *Takaful*: The Shari'ah and Common Law Harmonisation Analysis

3.1 Introduction

Islamic finance is one of the prominent sectors driving the Malaysian economy. As at 2020, the market share of Islamic finance in Malaysia stood at 18.4 percent out of the total global Islamic financial assets worth USD 2.7 trillion.[1] Among the key drivers facilitating industrial growth is its enabling legal and regulatory framework, which creates a conducive and comprehensive ecosystem. This chapter examines how the conventional legal and regulatory framework is harmonised with the Shari'ah requirements in three Islamic finance focal areas – Islamic banking, Islamic insurance (*takaful*), and Islamic Capital Market (ICM). Malaysia's harmonisation journey is not free from any legal tussles, though, in hindsight, the issues and challenges faced in the adaptation process have pushed the Islamic finance industry to be more innovative and proactive in finding solutions to remain relevant and competitive.

This chapter begins with an introduction, and then it proceeds with the legal discussion on the issue of jurisdiction for Islamic banking, ICM, and Islamic insurance. The crux of this chapter is the discussion on five important subjects that depict the intriguing harmonisation development as well as the relevant issues and challenges faced in positioning the Shari'ah requirement within the conventional setting. These subjects relate to the Shariah Advisory Council (SAC), the Islamic Financial Services Act 2013 (IFSA), the decline of equity-based financing, conditional *hibah* in takaful products, and compensation for breach of *wa'd* in Islamic profit rate swap.

3.2 Jurisdiction of Islamic Banking, Islamic Capital Market and *Takaful*

Despite Islamic banking and finance, ICM, and Islamic insurance carrying the title "Islamic," their jurisdiction may not be subjected to Islamic or Shari'ah courts. In Malaysia, the jurisdiction of civil and Shari'ah courts is provided for in the Federal Constitution. The Federal List (the Ninth Schedule) of the Federal Constitution lists out

1 BNM, *Financial Sector Blueprint (2022–2026)* (Kuala Lumpur: Bank Negara Malaysia, 2022), 103 and 105, https://www.bnm.gov.my/publications/fsb3.

https://doi.org/10.1515/9783110766707-003

matters that fall under the civil court's jurisdiction. Included in the said list are matters pertaining to contract, property, and mercantile law (under item 4(e)); finance (item 7), banking (item 7(e)), capital issues (item 7(m)), insurance (item 8(d)) as well as ascertainment of Islamic law and other personal laws for the purposes of federal law (item 4(k)).

Though the Federal List is silent on matters pertaining to Islamic finance, Islamic banking, ICM, and Islamic insurance, the inclusion of these subjects under the purview of the civil judiciary has been duly explicated in several case laws. Among them is the celebrated case of *Latifah Mat Zin v Rosmawati Sharibun & Anor.*[2] In this case, the Federal Court expounded item 4(k) of the Federal Constitution and said:

> Item 4(k) provides: "Ascertainment of Islamic Law and other personal laws for purposes of federal law" is a federal matter. A good example is in the area of Islamic banking, Islamic finance and takaful. Banking, finance and insurance are matters enumerated in the federal list, items 7 and 8 respectively. The ascertainment whether a particular product of banking, finance and insurance (or takaful) is Shariah-compliant or not falls within item 4(k) and is a federal matter. For this purpose, the Parliament has established the Syariah Advisory Council – *see* s. 16B of the Central Bank of Malaysia Act 1958 (Act 519).[3]

Notwithstanding the clarity given on the civil jurisdiction of matters pertaining to Islamic finance – Islamic banking, ICM, and Islamic insurance, the reality is civil court judges are trained and qualified in common law and not Shari'ah. Thus, they may not be equipped to deal with the related Shari'ah issues. In this regard, Raus Sharif CJA, in *Bank Islamic Malaysia Berhad v Lim Kok Hoe & Anor and other appeals,*[4] said:

> In this respect, it is our view that judges in civil court should not take upon themselves to declare whether a matter is in accordance to the religion of Islam or otherwise . . . that in the civil court not every presiding judge is a Muslim, and even if so, may not be sufficiently equipped to deal with matters, which ulama' take years to comprehend. Thus, whether the bank business is in accordance with the religion of Islam, it needs consideration by eminent jurists who are properly qualified in the field of Islamic jurisprudence . . . Thus it is a requirement for any Islamic bank to establish a Syariah advisory body to advice the bank and to ensure the operation of its banking business do not involve any element which is not approved by the religion of Islam . . . In fact, in 2003, a single Syariah (Shariah) Advisory Council was established through an amendment of the Central Bank of Malaysia Act 1958 . . . The court, will have to assume that the Syariah advisory body of the individual bank and now the Syariah Advisory Council under the aegis of Bank Negara Malaysia, would have discharged their statutory duty to ensure that the operation of Islamic banks are within the ambit of the religion of Islam.[5]

Such position is further reinforced in a later case, *Bank Kerjasama Rakyat Malaysia Bhd v Brampton Holdings Sdn Bhd,*[6] where Wong Kian Kheong JC said:

2 [2007] 5 CLJ 253.
3 [2007] 5 CLJ 272.
4 [2009] 6 MLJ 839.
5 [2009] 6 MLJ 853.
6 [2015] 4 CLJ 636.

> Based on *Lim Kok Hoe*, as well as the above provisions in CBMA (Central Bank Malaysia Act), a court cannot simply decide that an Islamic financing facility is not Shariah compliant. The court shall be guided by the advice and ruling of the SAC. Accordingly, the defendant cannot merely allege that the Islamic Financing Facility is illegal and unenforceable in this case. The defendant shall have obtained advice or ruling from the SAC as to whether the Islamic Financing Facility in this case has complied with Shariah or otherwise.[7]

While the role of the SAC is undeniably important in ensuring that products and services offered by the Islamic finance industry comply with Shari'ah, its presence within the realm of civil judiciary and arbitration has brewed legal debates surrounding its constitutionality.

3.3 Shari'ah Advisory Council – A Harmonising Tool in Shari'ah Ascertainment vis-a-vis Court and Arbitration Adjudication

In May 1997, the Bank Negara Malaysia (BNM) established the National Shari'ah Advisory Council (later known as the SAC) (BNM-SC) as the highest Shari'ah authority to ascertain relevant Shari'ah rulings on matters related to Islamic financial business operations, activities, or transactions in Malaysia. Its function is spelled out in section 52 of the Central Bank of Malaysia Act 2009 (CBMA) as follows:

(1) The Shariah Advisory Council shall have the following functions:
   (a) to ascertain the Islamic law on any financial matter and issue a ruling upon reference made to it in accordance with this Part;
   (b) to advise the Bank on any Shariah issue relating to Islamic financial business, the activities or transactions of the Bank;
   (c) to provide advice to any Islamic financial institution or any other person as may be provided under any written law; and
   (d) such other functions as may be determined by the Bank.

(2) For the purposes of this Part, "ruling" means any ruling made by the Shariah Advisory Council for the ascertainment of Islamic law for the purposes of Islamic financial business.

A separate SAC was also established by the Securities Commission of Malaysia (SC) for the ICM though its SAC was established a year earlier, in May 1996 (SC-SAC). The SC-SAC sits as the highest Shari'ah authority in ascertaining the application of Shari'ah principles for the purposes of the ICM sector. Its function is provided for in section 31ZJ of the Securities Commission Act 1993 (SCA), which carries the same

7 [2015] 4 CLJ 637.

functions as the BNM-SAC, only that the mandate of the SC-SAC is on ICM businesses and transactions.

The relevance and duties of the BNM-SAC and the SC-SAC apply and extend not only to the respective market regulators and the Islamic financial industry but also to the judiciary and arbitrators. Section 56 of the Central Bank of Malaysia Act (CBMA)[8] provides that:

(1) Where in any proceedings relating to Islamic financial business before any court or arbitrator any question arises concerning a Shariah matter, the court or the arbitrator, as the case may be, shall:
   (a) take into consideration any published rulings of the Shariah Advisory Council; or
   (b) refer such question to the Shariah Advisory Council for its ruling.

Upon such reference and issuance of Shari'ah ruling by the SAC, section 57 of the CBMA[9] states that: "Any ruling made by the Shariah Advisory Council pursuant to a reference made under this Part shall be binding on the Islamic financial institutions under section 55 and court or arbitrator making a reference under section 56."

To shed light on the referral requirement stipulated in sections 56 and 57 of the CBMA, the BNM-SAC issued a Manual for Reference by the Court and Arbitrator to the SAC[10] (the BNM-SAC Manual) in 2012. The BNM-SAC Manual defines what and how questions concerning Shari'ah matters arising from the court and arbitration proceeding can be referred to the BNM-SAC. The term "question concerning Shariah matters" is defined in paragraph 6 of the BNM-SAC Manual as: "A Shariah question on a matter relating to Islamic finance involving matters that have not been determined by the SAC. Such questions include, but are not limited to, aspects of the Islamic finance business such as the structure of the business, products or services, implementation or operation, terms and conditions or documentation."

The BNM-SAC Manual also noted that the BNM-SAC is only to ascertain Shari'ah rulings regarding the Shari'ah issue forwarded. It has no jurisdiction to make findings on facts or apply a particular ruling on the facts of the case and make a decision as those are within the jurisdiction of the court and arbitrator.[11]

Notwithstanding the BNM-SAC Manual attempted to clarify the context of the referral as envisaged in the legislation, the binding nature of the BNM-SAC ruling,

---

8 Similar provision can be found in the SCA, s 31ZN.

9 Similar provision can be found in the SCA, s 31ZO.

10 BNM, Manual for Reference by the Court and Arbitrator to the SAC, translated by Abdul Hamid Mohamad Mohamad and Adnan Trakic, (Kuala Lumpur: International Shariah Research Academy for Islamic Finance, 2012), 8.

11 Abdul Hamid Mohamad Mohamad and Adnan Trakic, *The Shariah Advisory Council's Role in Resolving Islamic Banking Disputes in Malaysia: A Model to Follow?* (Research paper no. 47) (Kuala Lumpur: International Shariah Research Academy for Islamic Finance, 2012), 11.

the constitutionality of the BNM-SAC and its rulings, including sections 56 and 57 of CBMA continue to be challenged in numerous courtrooms. Despite these challenges, the constitutionality of the BNM-SAC and its rulings, including sections 56 and 57 of CBMA, was made clear in the recent landmark Federal Court judgment in the case of *JRI Resources Sdn Bhd v Kuwait Finance House (Malaysia) Berhad.*[12]

The Federal Court in *JRI Resources* raised and addressed four issues. The first issue relates to the context of "ascertainment of Islamic law" as prescribed by item 4(k) of the Federal List of the Federal Constitution, as this forms the basis for the issuance of the BNM-SAC rulings for matters on Islamic financial business. On this issue, the Federal Court accepted the argument of the BNM (one of the interveners in this case) where the word "ruling" mentioned in section 57 of the CBMA, i.e., "Any ruling made by the Shariah Advisory Council" is not for "determination" of the dispute between the parties. Rather, the BNM-SAC's "ruling" only "ascertains" the applicable Islamic law for Islamic financial business. It does not conclude or settle the dispute between the parties, nor does it determine the liability of the parties. The determination of the customer's liability under any banking facility lies with the presiding judge and not the BNM-SAC.

The second issue relates to the judicial function of the BNM-SAC. The court held that the BNM-SAC does not have any judiciary characteristics, nor sections 56 and 57 of the CBMA confer judicial power onto the BNM-SAC. Therefore, the BNM-SAC cannot be said to be usurping the judicial power of the court. Instead, the ruling made by the BNM-SAC is solely confined to the Shari'ah issues. This is because the presiding judge, who referred the matter to the BNM-SAC, would still have to exercise his/her judicial power and decide the case based on the evidence submitted before the court.

The third issue relates to the binding effect of the BNM-SAC ruling. The court held that the BNM-SAC's ruling was not an outcome of the exercise of judicial power. Instead, the BNM-SAC merely ascertained the Islamic law for Islamic banking, and it is for the court to apply the ascertained Islamic law to the facts of the case. The ascertained Islamic law does not settle the dispute between the parties before the court. The BNM-SAC did not determine or pronounce an authoritative decision as to the parties' rights and/or liabilities before the court. It did not convert the court into a mere rubber stamp.

Finally, the fourth issue is regarding the use of expert opinion. The court found that the civil courts are not in a position to appreciate and determine the divergence of opinions among Islamic law experts and to decide based on Shari'ah principles. It further envisaged that if the parties were to be allowed to lead expert evidence, it would fall upon the civil courts to ascertain what would be the applicable Islamic law for Islamic banking and to apply the ascertained Islamic laws to the facts of the

12 [2019] 3 MLJ 561 (*JRI Resources*).

case. This can be further complicated with each expert giving his/her opinion based on different schools of jurisprudence.[13]

In short, the presence of the SAC in assuring the products offering and services are Shari'ah compliant cannot be understated. This assurance bodes well with the continuous growth of Islamic finance in Malaysia and elevates its position as the leading Islamic finance market globally. Despite the legal battle against its constitutionality, the SAC has performed a key harmonisation role by assisting civil courts and arbitrators through the ascertainment of the applicable Shari'ah principles on the disputed Islamic financial businesses.

3.4 Harmonising Shari'ah via Conducive Legislative Framework – Islamic Financial Services Act 2013

Besides establishing the SAC as a harmonisation and development tool for the Islamic finance industry, the harmonisation of Shari'ah in the realm of conventional finance has also taken place. The initiation of this harmonisation journey started with the promulgation of the Islamic Bank Act 1983 (IBA), which introduced the first Islamic bank in Malaysia, Bank Islam Malaysia Berhad. This was followed by the introduction of the Takaful Act 1984 (TA), which led to the setting up of the first *takaful* (Islamic insurance) operating company, Syarikat Takaful Malaysia Berhad, in 1984. Later in 1990, the world's first ringgit *sukuk* (Islamic financial certificate) was issued by Shell MDS (M) Sdn. Bhd. This was followed by the introduction of the first Islamic unit trust fund, Tabung Ittikal, established by Arab-Malaysian Securities in 1993, and the Shariah-compliant securities list endorsed in 1997 by the SC-SAC.

While Islamic banking and *takaful* are governed by their respective independent legislations, separate from conventional banking and insurance legislation, the ICM however is governed by a single framework regulating both conventional and ICM activities. The choice for having a single legislative regime for Islamic and conventional capital markets, i.e., the Capital Market Services Act 2007, is influenced by the finding of the IOSCO Task Force on Islamic Capital Market in 2004, which found that conventional securities regulation framework and principles

13 An interesting read on the constitutionality of sectons 56 and 57 CBM and solutions to address the constitutionality conundrum can be found in Adnan Trakic, "Shari'ah Compliance in Islamic finance Contracts: The Malaysian Constitutional Dilemma," *Oxford University Commonwealth Law Journal* 20, no. 2, (2020): 289–309, DOI: 10.1080/14729342.2020.1812025, accessible via https://doi.org/10.1080/14729342.2020.1812025.

apply equally to ICM with an additional requirement for Shari'ah approval or certification processes.[14]

3.4.1 Ensuring Shariah-Compliance via Islamic Financial Services Act 2013

Today, the Islamic banking and takaful industry are governed by one single omnibus legislation, Islamic Financial Services Act 2013 (IFSA), which repealed IBA and TA on the same date that IFSA came into force. IFSA promotes not only financial stability and compliance with Shari'ah principles but also strengthens the regulation of financial institutions. It introduces and ensures end-to-end Shari'ah compliance through Shari'ah governance and Shari'ah-contract-based regulatory framework for the Islamic finance industry in Malaysia.[15] Figure 3.1 gives an overview of the end-to-end Shari'ah compliance from the aspect of Shari'ah contracts for Islamic finance products and services, Shari'ah governance, Shari'ah and operational standards.

Since Shari'ah compliance is the *raison de etre* for the existence of Islamic financial institutions, the regular issuance of standards and guiding policies by the BNM assisted and guided the industry with the relevant Shari'ah prerequisites and general best practices. As of to date, the BNM has issued 14 Shari'ah Standards and Operational Requirements, which give effect to rulings by the BNM-SAC and serve to promote the effective management of risks in Islamic financial business.[16]

These standards and guiding policies must be complied with by Islamic financial institutions as well as their Shari'ah committees. The institutions must ensure that their internal policies and procedures are in line with the standards and guiding policies specified by the BNM. Even if the standards and guiding policies are silent on certain matters, the institutions are duty-bound to ensure that they continue to manage their businesses, affairs, and activities in a manner not contrary to Shari'ah – breach of which will entail supervisory intervention as well as punitive penalty and imprisonment.

---

14 IOSCO, "*Islamic Capital Market Fact Finding Report*, Report of the Islamic Capital Market Task Force of the International Organization of Securities Commissions," July, 2004, 52, https://www.iosco.org/library/pubdocs/pdf/IOSCOPD170.pdf.

15 Umar A Oseni and Noor Suhaida Kasri. *The Application of Hibah In The Islamic Financial Services Industry In Malaysia: Towards A Sharī'ah-Oriented Legal Framework.* (Kuala Lumpur: International Shariah Research Academy for Islamic Finance, 2016), 3.

16 BNM, *Financial Stability and Payment Systems Report 2018* (Kuala Lumpur: Bank Negara Malaysia, 2019), 88, https://www.bnm.gov.my/-/fspr2018.

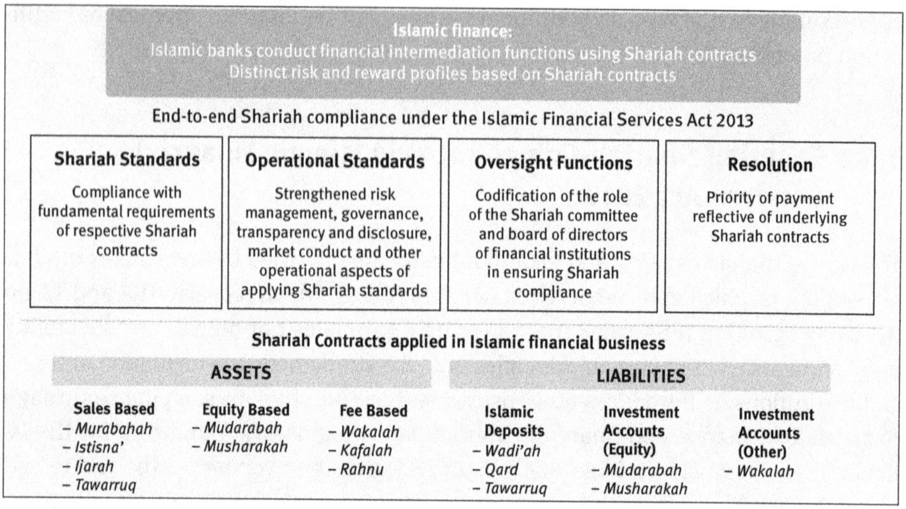

Figure 3.1: End-to-End Shariah Compliance Under the IFSA.
Source: BNM, 2013.[17]

3.4.2 Validity of Islamic Financing Contract in the Event of Non-Shari'ah Compliance

The strict compliance with Shari'ah requirement in IFSA is pursued with a hefty requirement governing the event of breach or non-compliance. Section 28(1), (2), (3), and (5) provide that,

(1) An institution shall at all times ensure that its aims and operations, business, affairs and activities are in compliance with Shariah.
(2) For the purposes of this Act, a compliance with any ruling of the Shariah Advisory Council in respect of any particular aim and operation, business, affair or activity shall be deemed to be a compliance with Shariah in respect of that aims and operations, business, affair or activity.
(3) Where an institution becomes aware that it is carrying on any of its business, affair or activity in a manner which is not in compliance with Shariah or the advice of its Shariah committee or the advice or ruling of the Shariah Advisory Council, the institution shall –
    (a) immediately notify the Bank and its Shariah committee of the fact;
    (b) immediately cease from carrying on such business, affair or activity and from taking on any other similar business, affair or activity;

17 BNM, *Financial Stability and Payment System Report 2012* (Kuala Lumpur: Bank Negara Malaysia, 2013), 80, https://www.bnm.gov.my/files/publication/fsps/en/2012/fs2012_book.pdf.

(c) within thirty days of becoming aware of such non-compliance or such further period as may be specified by the Bank, submit to the Bank a plan on the rectification of the non-compliance.

(4) Any person who contravenes subsection (1) or (3) commits an offence and shall, on conviction, be liable to imprisonment for a term not exceeding eight years or to a fine not exceeding twenty-five million ringgit or to both.

While the above section provides for the required measures to be undertaken by the affected Islamic financial institutions in the case of Shari'ah-non-compliance, IFSA is said to be silent on the validity of the impugned Islamic financing contract governing the underlying Islamic transactions or arrangements. This stance is seen to be adopted in several court judgments, as elaborated below.

In *Bank Kerjasama Rakyat (M) Berhad V Koperasi Serbaguna Iman Malaysia Berhad,*[18] the defendant alleged, among others, that the Asset Sale Agreements (ASA) and Asset Purchase Agreements (APA) for the Islamic financing facilities are invalid as they contravened the general Shari'ah concept and the *Bal-Ai Inah* (sale and repurchase) principle. The defendants claimed that the parties entered into the ASA and the APA on the same date. This, therefore, triggered an element of *gharar* (uncertainty) as to whether the ASA was entered into before the APA as required by the principle of *Bal-Ai Inah.*

To address this issue, the High Court asked: "Whether as a matter of law, irrespective of the defence raised by the Defendant of the purported Syariah non-compliance, the Asset Sale Agreements and Asset Purchase Agreements between the Plaintiff and the Defendant in relation to the Financing Facilities are enforceable? ('First Question')."[19]

In other words, whether the Islamic financing agreements that are in breach of provisions of the IFSA are valid and enforceable?

The Court then observed that,

> The First Question does not require any fact for the Court to make deliberations as the question is whether the Asset Sale Agreements and Asset Purchase Agreements are enforceable irrespective of the sequence in signing of the Asset Sale Agreements and Asset Purchase Agreements. In this instance I am not required to examine whether the Plaintiff and Defendant have executed the Asset Sale Agreements before the execution of Asset Purchase Agreements in respect of each of the Financing Facilities.
>
> Proceeding further on this basis, non-compliance with Shariah principles of Bai Al-lnah will not be the determinant factor for the Asset Sale Agreements and Asset Purchase Agreements to be deemed unenforceable. In the final analysis, the Court has to determine whether this situation falls under any of the circumstances provided under Section 24 of the Contracts

18 [2020] MLJU 438.
19 [2020] MLJU 446.

> Act 1950[20] ("Contracts Act") which will render the Asset Sale Agreements and Asset Purchase Agreements void.[21]

Though the court opined that the timing of the execution of the ASA and APA is a non-issue, the court remarked that: "In my further analysis I treated the Asset Sale Agreements and Asset Purchase Agreements as already being non- compliant with Shariah principles of Bai Al-lnah due to the timing of the executions of the agreement, adopting the hypothetical position that the Asset Purchase Agreements were executed before the Asset Sale Agreements."[22]

Relying on the obiter of the Court of Appeal's *Bank Islam Malaysia Berhad v Lim Kok Hoe & Anor and other appeals,*[23] *Bank Muamalat Malaysia & Ors v Redha Resources Sdn Bhd & Ors,*[24] *and Maybank Islamic Bhd v M-IO Builders Sdn vs Bhd & Anor,*[25] the court held:

> The validity of the said Asset Sale Agreements and Asset Purchase Agreements is therefore governed by the Contracts Act . . . Given that Islamic financing facilities fall within the scope of the Contracts Act, if the Asset Purchase Agreements were executed before the Asset Sale Agreements and therefore were not in compliance with Shariah principles of Bai Al-lnah would the agreements be rendered void and unenforceable? The answer is in the negative as an agreement may only be rendered void and unenforceable if the consideration or object of the agreement is vitiated by the vitiating factors as stipulated in Section 24 of the Contracts Act. A financing facility which is not compliant with Shariah principles of Bai Al-lnah does not satisfy any of the circumstances provided under Section 24 of the Contracts Act . . . In arriving at my decision, I applied the principle that non-compliance with Shariah principles does not render a financing facility contract illegal and unenforceable unless it is vitiated by the vitiating factors as stipulated in Section 24 of the Contracts Act. . . .[26]

The court further considered the application of section 281 of IFSA in determining whether Islamic financing agreements that are in breach of provisions of the IFSA are valid and enforceable. Section 281 provides that:

---

20 Contracts Act 1950, s 24 states: "The consideration or object of an agreement is lawful, unless –
(a) it is forbidden by a law;
(b) it is of such a nature that, if permitted, it would defeat any law;
(c) it is fraudulent;
(d) it involves or implies injury to the person or property of another; or
(e) the court regards it as immoral, or opposed to public policy.

In each of the above cases, the consideration or object of an agreement is said to be unlawful. Every agreement of which the object or consideration is unlawful is void."

21 [2020] MLJU 438, 449.

22 [2020] MLJU 438, 449.

23 [2009] 6 MLJ 839, [37].

24 [2017] 2 MLJ 686.

25 [2017] 2 MLJ 69.

26 [2020] MLJU 438, 451.

> Except as otherwise provided in this Act, or in pursuance of any provision of this Act, no contract, agreement or arrangement, entered into in breach or contravention of any provision of this Act shall be void solely by reason of such breach or contravention:
>
> Provided that nothing contained in this section shall affect any liability of any person for any administrative, civil or criminal actions under this Act in respect of such breach or contravention.

Concurring with the submission of the Plaintiffs, the court viewed that by virtue of section 281, any non-compliance with Shari'ah principles of *Bai Al-lnah* will not render the ASA and the APA between the plaintiff and defendant void, invalid and unenforceable. This position is supported by the silence in the relevant sections 29, 28(1),(2),(3), and (5) of IFSA in providing that a contract is void or invalid when these provisions are breached.

This judicial stance on the application of section 281 of IFSA is further upheld in a recent Court of Appeal decision held on 6 January 2021 in *Maybank Islamic Berhad v Golden Base Construction Sdn Bhd & 2 Ors.*[27] In this case, the appellant granted an Islamic *Murabahah* financing facility of RM50 million to the Respondent for the construction of a highway. The facility was secured by two individual guarantors. The financing was structured on the Shari'ah principle of *Murabahah* whereby the respondent made a request to the appellant to purchase underlying Shari'ah compliant commodities (*Murabahah* Asset) at a purchase price equivalent to the financing amount, and an undertaking by the respondent to purchase the same *Murabahah* Asset from the appellant payable on deferred payment terms. The respondent and their guarantors defaulted on the payments.[28]

The appellant commenced a suit at the High Court. In their defence and counterclaim, the appellant and their guarantors alleged, *inter alia*, that the financing is void and unenforceable for being non-*Shariah* compliant and counterclaimed for a sum of RM 95,835,335.57 for loss of profit and loss of investment. The court found there were two triable issues. The triable issues were whether the *Murabahah* transaction complies with BNM's Policy Document on Murabahah and whether the *Murabahah* Asset has been identified in the financing documents. The court, *inter alia*, held that the mere use of the words "Shariah compliant commodities determined by the Appellant as per the e-certificate" in the financing documents was insufficient to identify the underlying asset. Thus, the legality of the *Murabahah* transaction was in question due to the uncertainty of the underlying *Murabahah* asset, and this called for evidence of

27 At the point of writing this chapter, the full decision of the Court of Appeal has yet to be published. Hence the inability to provide the full citation for the case.

28 Leong Wai Hong, Claudia Cheah and Aufa Radzi, "Court of Appeal Allowed Maybank Islamic Berhad's Appeals for Summary Judgment of RM 45 mil and Struck out Counterclaim of RM 95 mil in Relation to a Murabahah Financing Transaction," *Skrine*, January 7, 2021, https://www.skrine.com/insights/alerts/january-2021/court-of-appeal-allowed-maybank-islamic-berhad%E2%80%99s-a.

a Shari'ah expert to be given at a full trial. The appellant's applications for summary judgment and striking out of counterclaim were therefore dismissed.[29]

The appellant then appealed to the Court of Appeal and argued that the High Court erred because non-compliance with Shari'ah principles does not render a financing facility contract illegal and unenforceable based on existing case law and section 281 of the IFSA 2013. Agreeing with the appellant's contention, the Court of Appeal unanimously allowed the appellant's appeal – entered summary judgment against the respondent and their guarantors, and struck out the respondent's counterclaim.[30]

Based on these cases and by virtue of section 281, contracting parties cannot avoid a contract solely on the ground that it has contravened the provisions of IFSA and that non-compliance with Shari'ah principles does not render the Islamic financing facility contract illegal and unenforceable. Nonetheless, Islamic banks are not held free from their Shari'ah compliance statutory obligation. In this regard, the High Courts in *Golden Base* and *Sigur Ros Sdn. Bhd. & Anor v Maybank Islamic Berhad & Anor*,[31] opined that in line with the requirement in section 28 of IFSA, the Islamic banking institutions that granted the non-Shariah compliant financing product will be subjected to penalty/punishment by the BNM for offering such product to their customers.

The importance of valid Shariah contracts in Islamic banking products seems to be outrightly displaced as shown in these recent judgments. While Shariah compliance is the backbone of Islamic banking products, the use of section 24 of Contract Act (CA) and section 281 of IFSA to disregard non-compliant Shariah contract in favour of debt contractual obligation inadvertently distorted the spirit of Shariah compliance statutory prerequisite. The fundamental requirement for Shariah compliance is cleary underlined in IFSA's principal regulatory objectives – which is to promote financial stability and compliance with Shariah. While section 28 of IFSA further requires for every Islamic banking institution to ensure at all times its aims and operations, business, affairs, and activities are in compliance with Shariah which includes compliance with BNM Policy Documents.

It is further argued that since section 24 of the CA is used as the baseline in invalidating contracts, section 24(b) could potentially be applied in cases involving Shariah non-compliance contracts in Islamic banking products. Section 24(b) states that:

> The consideration or object of an agreement is lawful, unless –
> *(b)* it is of such a nature that, if permitted, it would defeat any law;

29 Leong, Claudia and Radzi, "Court of Appeal."
30 Leong, Claudia and Radzi, "Court of Appeal."
31 [2018] MLJU 642.

In this regards, it follows that by allowing debt agreement that is tainted with Shariah non-compliance element to prevail would defeat the very essence of IFSA (including BNM Policy Documents which is part and parcel of IFSA hence deemed as subsidiary law of IFSA). The existence of Shariah non-compliance element has effectively caused the object of the debt agreement to be unlawful hence render the debt agreement to be void.

The repercussion of Shariah non-compliance over contract validity and on Islamic banks' reputation and their balance sheet is succinctly described by the learned Mohd Zawawi Saleh FCJ in *JRI Resources*: "Contracts containing Shariah repugnant elements which had already been executed are liable to be deemed null and void, which would in turn render the profits derived thereof non-halal. As a result the tainted income arising from such transactions must be channelled to charity and cannot be kept by the bank."[32]

Having said the above, it is worth noting that the way Islamic banking is practised in the industry could perhaps influence the mindset and approach adopted by the judiciary. In reality, the expansion of Islamic banking in Malaysia in the last decades has been dominated by debt-based portfolios rather than equity-based products. The economic effect of debt-based Islamic banking products thus mimics conventional banking products. In this regard, it should not come as a surprise for others to assess Islamic banking arrangement from the lens of conventional banking. The question then is, why are the debt-based instead of equity-based financing solutions dominating the Islamic banking industry?

3.5 Equity-based Financing

The provision for equity-based financing is provided for in section 2 of IFSA, which states: "'provision of finance' means entering into, or making an arrangement for another person to enter into, the businesses or activities which are in accordance with Shariah including – (*a*) equity or partnership financing, including *musyarakah*, *musyarakah mutanaqisah* and *mudarabah*."

To assist in offering such financing, BNM has issued Shari'ah and operational standards, particularly the Policy Documents on Musyarakah and Mudharabah, both on 20 April 2015. Through these Policy Documents, Islamic banks are guided particularly on the governance and risk management measures that are appropriate for the risks inherent in the structures of these Shari'ah contracts.

Musyarakah (profit and loss sharing) and *Mudharabah* (profit sharing contract) contracts entail a unique underlying character that offers an important distinctive feature – mutual risk-sharing – differentiating Islamic banking and conventional

32 [2019] 3 MLJ 561, 588.

banking products. In Shari'ah, the relationship between risk and return is captured in the Islamic legal maxim of '*Al ghunm bil ghurm*', which in essence refers to the concept of "no risk, no return." This legal maxim requires a contracting party to undertake risk and bear responsibilities as a precondition for entitlement to profits. In this regard, both Islamic banks and customers are to assume certain responsibilities, which include mutual risk-taking. The responsibilities and the level of risk borne by each party must correspond and be reflected in the profits earned by Islamic banks and the pricing of the banking services.[33]

3.5.1 The Common Plight of Equity-based Financing

Notwithstanding the distinctive characteristic, *Musyarakah* and *Mudharabah* banking products are not widely used, instead Islamic banking market share in terms of product offerings is dominated by debt-based banking products, namely *Tawarruq*[34] and *Murabahah*. Figure 3.2 illustrates the breakdown of Shari'ah contracts used in the Islamic banking industry in Malaysia in 2019. It showcases *Musyarakah* financing product and *Mudarabah* investment account are represented by only 8 percent of the total financing products and total deposit and investment account products, respectively.

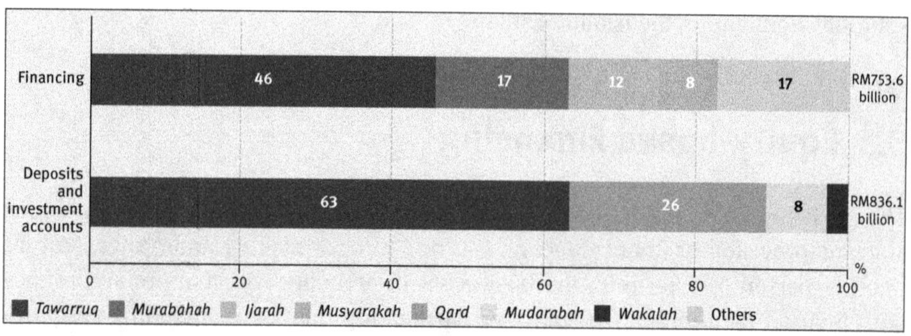

Figure 3.2: The Breakdown of Shari'ah Contracts Used by the End of 2019.
Source: BNM, 2019[35]

33 BNM. *Financial Stability Report 2012*, 87.

34 Tawarruq refers to the purchase of an asset with deferred price, either on the basis of musawamah or murabahah, then selling it to a third party to obtain cash.

35 BNM, *Financial Stability Review – Second Half 2019* (Kuala Lumpur: Bank Negara Malaysia, 2019), 49, https://www.bnm.gov.my/files/publication/fsps/en/2012/fs2012_book.pdf.

Several factors contributed to this sluggish performance. In general, the issue lies in the deep capability challenges and associated costs in moving towards the risk-sharing model, given that extending credit is far easier compared to extending risk-sharing instruments that can be traded in the capital market.[36] The Islamic banking business model is profit-driven; hence, to survive, Islamic banks must meet their yearly profit target. The competition between Islamic and conventional banks exacerbates this survival need further. Another dilemma is information asymmetry that results in adverse selection of granting financing to clients with poor credit standing and moral hazard when financing is utilised inappropriately.[37]

Given the above factors, it is easier for Islamic banks to promote and implement a debt-based financing model than an equity-based financing model due to its resemblance to conventional products and the low risk associated with it. This aptly fits the role of Islamic banks as intermediaries that receive deposits and give out credit to their customers. In such a structure, shifting the risk or taking it at its lowest level is deemed the best option.[38]

3.5.2 The Future of Equity-based Financing in Malaysia

The Covid-19 pandemic may perhaps be the game-changer for equity-based solutions as the pandemic exposed the reality of debt-based banking. The increased reliance and concentration of debt-based financing in the banking system led to unsustainable corporate leverage and even excessive risk-taking by banks, which tantamount to systemic implications. In cognizance of this reality, the BNM, in its Financial Sector Blueprint (2022–2026), spotlighted alternative finance as an important solution that includes debt and equity-based instruments. Alternative finance solutions will play a critical role in complementing bank-led debt financing to fund the economy, promoting more sustainable long-term growth.[39]

Alternative finance solutions are also listed as one of the strategic thrusts in transforming Malaysia into a high-income nation. To do so, the BNM undertakes that it will (i) sustain and grow the alternative finance ecosystem and its supporting infrastructure; (ii) strengthen the regulatory framework and collaboration to promote the development of non-debt finance; and (iii) reinforce the finance ecosystem

36 Said Bouheraoua, et. al., *Implementing the IFSA Investment Account: A Risk-Sharing Banking Model* (Kuala Lumpur: International Shariah Research Academy for Islamic Finance, 2016), 83.
37 Amiruddin and Ismail, "Profit and Loss Sharing (PLS) and Non-PLS Financing in Malaysia."
38 Amiruddin Mohd Nor and Shafinar Ismail, "Profit and Loss Sharing (PLS) and Non-PLS Financing in Malaysia: Which One Should Be the One?" Knowledge E, accessed April 1, 2022, https://knepublishing.com/index.php/KnE-Social/article/view/6585/12118#figures
39 BNM, *Financial Sector Blueprint (2022–2026)* (Kuala Lumpur: Bank Negara Malaysia, 2022), 42, https://www.bnm.gov.my/publications/fsb3.

for micro-enterprises for sustainable and inclusive growth. This includes reviewing the taxation framework for alternative finance instruments towards a more equitable tax regime for debt and equity finance that will encourage the growth of alternative finance.[40]

3.5.3 *Hibah* in *Takaful* Nomination

Like insurance, *takaful* is a form of protection that avail to *takaful* participants as well as their nominees and beneficiaries at the occurrence of misfortune events like death or permanent disability befallen on the *takaful* participants. When this occurs, the *takaful* benefit received under the coverage will help the takaful participant's nominee and beneficiaries in managing the financial consequences of the loss.[41]

Being in an industry that was (and still is) largely dominated by insurance products and services, *takaful* industry players needed to remain viable, relevant, and competitive. Against this backdrop and with the support of the BNM-SAC resolution issued in its 34th meeting dated 21 April 2003 (2003 BNM-SAC Resolution),[42] *takaful* operators in Malaysia introduced the concept of *hibah* (gift) as part of their product structure. *Hibah* is a form of benevolent (*tabarru`*) contract, and it denotes a transfer of ownership of an asset from a donor (*wahib*) to a recipient (*mawhub lahu*) without any consideration. The inherent nature of a *hibah* is that it allows for a unilateral transfer of ownership of a *hibah* asset from the donor to the recipient without any consideration.[43]

The introduction of *hibah* in the structuring of Shari'ah-compliant products is likened to "the icing on the cake" that has helped Islamic banking and *takaful* players to favourably compete with conventional banking and insurance players.[44] A similar sentiment is echoed by a senior *takaful* practitioner, Wan Deraman (2016 as cited in Soualhi, 2017),[45] who urged for the issuance of more *hibah*-based products to make *takaful* products more competitive with conventional insurance products. According to Wan Deraman, the nature of *hibah* would help the relatives of the

40 BNM, *Financial Sector Blueprint*, 45–46.

41 Umar and Noor, *The Application of Hibah*, 15.

42 The SAC, in its 34th meeting dated 21 April 2003, resolved among others: "The takaful benefit may be made as hibah because the objective of takaful is to provide coverage for takaful participant. Since the takaful benefit is the right of takaful participant, the participant is at liberty to exercise his right in accordance with Shariah."

43 BNM, *Hibah* (Kuala Lumpur: Bank Negara Malaysia, 2016), 4, https://www.bnm.gov.my/banking-islamic-banking.

44 Umar and Noor, *The Application of Hibah*, 3.

45 Younes Soualhi, et., *Nomination in the Context of IFSA 2013: A Critical* Shari'ah *Appraisal* (Kuala Lumpur: International Shariah Research Academy for Islamic Finance, 2017), 9.

takaful participants, regardless of whether these relatives would be entitled to any shares of inheritance.

3.5.4 Harmonising Nomination in the Takaful Practice

Nomination plays a key role in the *takaful* practice of conditional *hibah* as it facilitates the process of naming a person (nominee) in the *takaful* certificate by the certificate holder/*takaful* participant. It is a right given to the *takaful* participant to choose someone to receive or manage the money disbursed by the *takaful* operator upon the death of the *takaful* participant. The purpose of nomination is to ensure that the benefits can be disbursed much faster without the need to obtain the Grant of Probate or Letters of Administration or Distribution Order.[46]

According to Younes et al., the nomination is a concept that originated and developed in conventional insurance.[47] It is part and parcel of wealth management that allows funds to be attended to before and after the death of the funds' owner. Thus, the nomination is extant in insurance laws across jurisdictions, including Malaysia, and the same is provided for in the Insurance Act 1996 and later, Financial Services Act 2013 (FSA). Nomination is practised in *takaful* as part of its product offerings and provided for in the TA and later IFSA. Nonetheless, compared to TA, IFSA is more comprehensive in provisioning for nomination and resembles the nomination provisions for insurance in the FSA.

The practice of nomination in *takaful* products went through two phases of development – pre and post 2003 BNM-SAC resolution issuance. Prior to the 2003 BNM-SAC Resolution, nomination in the practice of the *takaful* industry in Malaysia then was to only accept the said nomination based on *wasiyyah* (will, testament, bequest). During this period, the nominee would merely act as an executor entrusted to distribute the *takaful* benefits according to the law of *faraid* (Islamic law of inheritance). The nominee was described as a proper claimant who would hold the capacity of an executor or estate administrator. However, with the approval of conditional *hibah* by the 2003 SAC Resolution, a nominee(s) could now be named the sole beneficiary of the *takaful* benefit.[48]

---

46 Malaysian Takaful Association, "Frequently Ask Question (FAQ) on Making a Nomination," accessed April 3, 2022, https://www.malaysiantakaful.com.my/media/media-release-press-statement/frequently-ask-question-faq-making-nomination-soalan-soalan.

47 Younes, et., *Nomination in IFSA*, 5.

48 Younes, et., *Nomination in IFSA*, 59.

3.5.5 Harmonising Conditional Hibah in the Takaful Nomination Practice

The 2003 BNM-SAC Resolution resolves that *hibah* and conditional *hibah*, also known as *hibah ruqba*, are permissible contracts and allowed to be used as part and parcel of *takaful* products. According to BNM-SAC:[49]

> Takaful benefit[50] may be given as hibah ruqba which refers to a conditional gift contingent upon death of one of the parties (either the giver or the recipient of hibah) as a condition of ownership for the surviving party. In this situation, the hibah property will be owned by the recipient upon death of the giver. However, upon death of the recipient, the hibah property will be returned to the giver.[51]

Due to the 2003 BNM-SAC Shariah Resolution, conditional *hibah* is widely practiced in the *takaful* industry, particularly in the family *takaful*[52] plan.

To ensure that the conditional *hibah* is practiced in accordance with the conditions laid out by the 2003 BNM-SAC Resolution (as well as a later BNM-SAC resolution made in its 165th meeting dated 26 January 2016), these conditions have been incorporated in Schedule 10 of IFSA, which states:

> 2. (1) A takaful participant who has attained the age of sixteen years may nominate an individual to receive takaful benefits payable upon his death under the takaful certificate, either as an executor, or as a beneficiary under a conditional *hibah* by notifying the licensed takaful operator in writing the name, date of birth, national registration identity card number or birth certificate number and address of the nominee.
>
> (4) The licensed takaful operator –
>
> (a) shall prominently display in the nomination form that the takaful participant may –
>
> (i) assign the takaful benefits to a nominee or designate the nominee to receive the takaful benefits as a beneficiary under conditional *hibah*; or
>
> (ii) designate the nominee to receive the takaful benefits as an executor;
>
> (b) shall record the nomination and the particulars of the nominee in its register of takaful certificates.

---

49 BNM, *Shariah Resolutions in Islamic Finance* (Kuala Lumpur: BNM, Second Edition, 2010), 85, https://www.islamicfinance.com/wp-content/uploads/2015/01/Shariah-Resolutions-2nd-Edition-En.pdf.

50 IFSA, s 2 states that takaful benefits include "any benefit, whether pecuniary or not, which is payable under a takaful certificate."

51 BNM, *Shariah Resolutions in Islamic Finance* (Kuala Lumpur: BNM, Second Edition, 2010), 86.

52 IFSA, s 2 defines "family takaful certificate" as "a takaful certificate by which takaful benefits are payable on death or survival, including those takaful benefits payable in respect of personal accidents, disease or sickness, and includes an annuity but excludes a personal accident takaful certificate."

Despite the availability of the 2003 and 2016 BNM-SAC Resolutions approving the conditional *hibah* and provisions providing for the implementation of conditional *hibah* is incorporated in IFSA, several works of literature have raised legal issues pertaining to the legal status of *hibah* under the extant conventional legal system. Shari'ah issues have also been deliberated in the literature relating to the practice of nominating nominees under conditional *hibah* in family *takaful* products. However, because the current chapter is legal in nature, the ensuing discussion focuses only on related legal issues.

3.5.6 Jurisdiction of Hibah

The issue pertaining to *hibah* jurisdiction has been discussed in several cases, though at this juncture, it is sufficient to discuss the judgment of the celebrated case of *Latifah Mat Zin v Rosmawati Sharibun & Anor.*[53] This case involved a petition for a Letter of Administration in the civil High Court. The issue was whether the joint accounts form part of the deceased's estate or not, which depends on whether there was a gift *inter vivos*. In this case, the parties agreed for the term gift *inter vivos* to also refer to *hibah*. The High Court then ruled that Islamic law is to be applied in determining the issue of *hibah*. Hence applying what he found to be the Islamic law of *hibah* and based on the facts before him, the judge ruled that there had been no *hibah* or gift of the monies in the joint accounts to the appellant.

Discontended with the High Court decision, the appellant appealed to the Court of Appeal. In the Court of Appeal, the appellant argued that the applicable law was the federal law of banking and contract and not the Islamic law of *hibah*. This argument was rejected by the court. The court held that the applicable law was the law of gifts, not the law of banking or contract. The question would then be whether the applicable law, in this case, is the civil law of gifts *inter vivos* or the Islamic law of gifts.

The appellant then appealed to the Federal Court. Delivering the court judgment, the learned Abdul Hamid Mohamad FCJ stated the following:

> In the circumstances, I agree with the Court of Appeal that it is the Islamic law of "hibah" that applies. We have seen that para. (ii) of item 4(e) of the Federal List excludes "Islamic personal law relating to . . . gifts or succession." This is further reinforced by item 1 of the State List which specifically provides that "Islamic law . . . of persons professing the religion of Islam, including . . . gifts . . . " Section 61(3) of the Administration of the Religion of Islam (State of Selangor) Enactment 2003 (the relevant law, in this case) also provides:

53 [2007] 5 CLJ 253.

> (3) The Syariah High Court shall:
> (a) . . .
> (b) in its civil jurisdiction, hear and determine all actions and proceedings if all the parties to the actions or proceedings are Muslims and the actions and proceedings relate to:
> (vi) gifts inter vivos, or settlements made without adequate consideration in money or money's worth by a Muslim; (emphasis added).
>
> So, it is very clear that the determination whether the assets in question had been given as a valid "hibah" by the deceased to the appellant is a matter that falls within the jurisdiction of the syariah court. The Court of Appeal was right on this point.[54]

The court also made further reference to *hibah* instrument that is bundled together with *takaful* products – whether they also fall under the jurisdiction of the Shari'ah court as described above. Abdul Hamid Mohamad FCJ remarked that:

> Item 4(k) provides: "Ascertainment of Islamic Law and other personal laws for purposes of federal law" is a federal matter. A good example is in the area of Islamic banking, Islamic finance and takaful. Banking, finance and insurance are matters enumerated in the federal list, items 7 and 8 respectively. The ascertainment whether a particular product of banking, finance and insurance (or takaful) is Shariah-compliant or not falls within item 4(k) and is a federal matter.[55]

Based on the above *obiter*, *hibah* bundled together with takaful, Islamic banking and finance product offerings falls under the ambit of List I of the Federal List as they are considered financial tools. In this respect, the proper jurisdiction to resolve any disputes that arise from such *hibah* would be the civil court and not the Shari'ah court.[56]

3.5.7 Harmonising Hibah under the Contract Act 1950

Based on the legal premise above, the next important issue to be considered is the application of the CA to *hibah,* including conditional *hibah* embedded in a *takaful* instrument. The reason for considering the CA's application is that based on the cases deliberated in the earlier sub-section, the validity and enforceability of the contract evidencing the Shari'ah transaction and arrangement will be governed by it. In particular, section 26 of the CA stipulates that: "An agreement made without consideration is void, unless – (a) it is in writing and registered . . . (b) or is a

54 [2007] 5 CLJ 280.
55 [2007] 5 CLJ 272.
56 Umar and Noor, *The Application of Hibah,* 4.

promise to compensate for something done . . . (c) or is a promise to pay a debt barred by limitation law . . . In any of these cases, such an agreement is a contract." Further, explanation 1 of section 26 provides: "Nothing in this section shall affect the validity, as between the donor and donee, of any gift actually made."

Relying on explanation 1 above, it is argued that *hibah,* which is equivalent to a gift, as determined by *Latifah Mat Zain* earlier, is valid, binding, and enforceable despite being an agreement entered into without consideration. Further, it is argued that from the perspective of statutory interpretation, the phrase "of any gift actually made" would include both conditional and absolute gifts, based on the maxim that provides *generalia specialibus non derogant* (the general does not detract from the specific).[57]

This position is further strengthened by the interpretation given in *Kwan Teck Meng & Ors v Liew Sam Lee,*[58] where the High Court gave a purposive interpretation to section 26(a) of the Contracts (Malay States) Ordinance, 1950: "[A] transfer by way of gift is void until it is registered but . . . the validity of the gift by way of such transfer, as between the donor and donee, is not affected."[59] This implies that the gift is valid, but the transfer of the gift will be void pending the fulfilment of the requirement of registration.[60]

Though there is no case law that challenges the validity of Shari'ah-compliance of *hibah* in *takaful* products, the discussion above indicates that harmonisation augurs well in *hibah* in *takaful* products. This could be explained by the similar nature shared by the Shari'ah and the common law in products like *hibah* and gifts, hence the seemingly smooth process of harmonisation.

3.6 Damages for Breach of Promise in the Case of Islamic Profit Rate Swap

Islamic Profit Rate Swap (IPRS) is referred to by the BNM-SAC as:

> . . . an agreement entered between two parties to mutually exchange profit rates (between fixed rate and floating rate) through the execution of a series of Shariah compliant sales contracts to trade certain assets. The objective of IPRS is to enable the bank to manage the mismatch between cash inflow generated from the asset and cash outflow arising from payment of expenditure or cost of funding associated with the liability side of the balance sheet.[61]

57 Umar and Noor, *The Application of Hibah,* 26.
58 [1963] 1 MLJ 333.
59 [1963] 1 MLJ 337.
60 Umar and Noor, *The Application of Hibah,* 26.
61 BNM, *Shariah Resolutions in Islamic Finance,* 139.

While the main objective of IPRS is similar to a conventional interest rate swap (i.e., to exchange a fixed interest rate for a floating rate, or vice versa, so parties can either reduce or increase exposure to fluctuations in interest rates), IPRS is obliged to undertake additional trading arrangement as to make the exchange of profit rate Shari'ah compliant. Figure 3.3 depicts the arrangement of IPRS as practiced in the Islamic financial market in Malaysia.

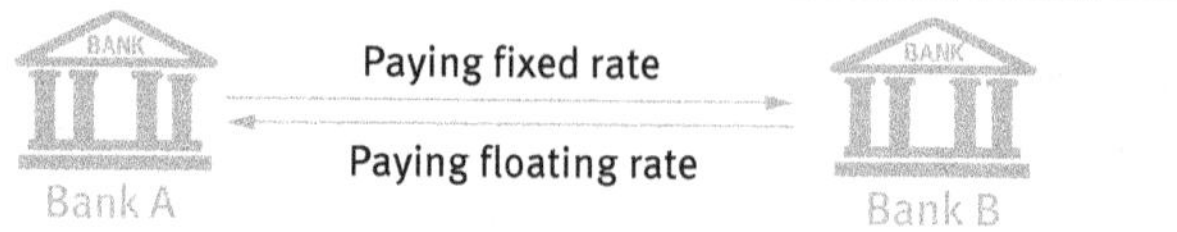

Source: Authors own

Explanation:

1. Both parties, Bank A and Bank B, want to hedge against their fixed and floating rate exposures. To do so, both enter into a three-year fixed and floating profit rate swap whereby Bank A agrees to pay to Bank B a fixed rate amount and Bank B agrees to pay to Bank A a floating-rate amount.
2. Fixed profit rate: On day one, Bank A gives Bank B a *wa'd* under which it promises to enter into a commodity *murābahah* purchase agreement with Bank B if Bank B exercises the *wa'd* at an agreed time in the future. The exercise of Bank A's *wa'd* results in Bank A paying to Bank B the amount of the fixed rate leg for the first calculation period.
3. Floating profit rate: On day one, Bank B gives Bank A a *wa'd* under which Bank B promises to enter into a commodity *murābahah* purchase agreement with Bank A if Bank A exercises the *wa'd* at an agreed time in the future. The execution of Bank B's *wa'd* results in Bank B paying to Bank A the amount of the floating rate leg.
4. Similar exercises will take place throughout the three years of the profit rate swap between Bank A and Bank B.

Figure 3.3: Islamic Profit Rate Swap Arrangement.
Source: Kasri and Zainalabiddin, 2016[62]

IPRS is duly approved by the BNM-SAC as a Shariah-compliant hedging product. In its 44th meeting dated 24 June 2004[63] (BNM-SAC 2004 Resolution), the BNM-SAC

62 Noor Suhaida Kasri and Siti Syafira Zainalabiddin, *Breach Of Wa'd And Its Compensation Payment: A Critical Analysis of Islamic Profit Rate Swap* (Kuala Lumpur: International Shariah Research Academy for Islamic Finance, 2015), 8.
63 BNM, *Shariah Resolutions*, 139.

approved the arrangement of IPRS through the use of *bay al-inah* contract[64] conducted amongst financial institutions or between an Islamic financial institution and another counterparty. Though the SAC resolution on the permissibility of IPRS is based on *bai al-inah* contract, in the current practice of IPRS, as shown in Figure 3.3, the Shari'ah contract of *murabahah* or *tawarruq* arrangement (popularly known as commodity *murabahah*), as well as *wa'd* (promise/undertaking) are used. The approval of these contracts can be seen in several BNM-SAC resolutions, for example, its 79th meeting dated 29 October 2008,[65] which resolved that foreign currency option product based on *waʿd* and two independent *tawarruq* transactions is permissible.

3.6.1 Early Termination of Islamic Profit Rate Swap

While the above SAC resolutions have clearly established the permissibility of IPRS, the issue pertaining to the compensation/damages arising from early termination of IPRS still lingers. It is common for one of the contracting parties under the IPRS to decide to withdraw his/its position before the maturity of the IPRS. Among the well-known reasons is the unfavourable movement of the rate/price against his/its position, thus the early withdrawal to avoid further losses. In this regard, the said party is said to terminate the IPRS, earlier than agreed. In early termination, one of the parties holding a debt obligation to the other party shall be responsible for settling the amount due, known as the "close-out amount." In the conventional interest rate swap, the close-out amount is determined based on the market quote methodology, which refers to the standard formula adopted by market participants to determine the payable compensation amount.[66]

With regard to the permissibility of early termination of IPRS, the BNM-SAC 2004 resolved that "that the proposed offset practice in the IPRS structure is permissible and does not tantamount to the sale of debt with debt, which is prohibited by the Shariah."[67] While on the issue of using interest rate swap conventional methodology in determining the close-out amount for IPRS, the BNM-SAC, in its 54th meeting dated 27 October 2005, resolved that "the methodology to determine the close-out amount under the conventional interest rate swap is also applicable to the IPRS."[68]

In supporting its decision, BNM-SAC argued that "(t)The principle of muqasah (offset) is a common practice and acceptable in the event where two parties are indebted to each other, and the debts are settled based on the payment of the difference

64 Bai inah refers to sale contract followed by repurchase by the seller at a different price.

65 BNM, *Shariah Resolutions*, 145.

66 BNM, *Shariah Resolutions*, 141–142.

67 BNM, *Shariah Resolutions*, 141.

68 BNM, *Shariah Resolutions*, 142.

between the two debts amount."[69] Nevertheless the SAC further cautioned that in the case of IPRS's early termination:

> the methodology to determine the close-out amount in IPRS, the SAC is of the view that the market quote methodology may be applied to IPRS if the contracting parties are convinced that the outcome of the application represents the actual loss suffered by a party to the contract as a result of a default by the other party. This view has considered the fact that the methodology for determination of ta`widh by a third party in the context of profit rate swap is not practical.[70]

3.6.2 Breach of Waad under Islamic Profit Rate Swap

As shown in Figure 3.3, if one of the parties wishes to terminate his/its position/obligation under IPRS, he/it would not proceed to execute his/its *wa'd* to enter into commodity *murabahah* contract. In this regard, the defaulting party is said to breach his/its promise to purchase the agreed commodity from the non-defaulting party, which he had promised at the inception of the IPRS. For the party who has breached his/its *wa'd*, the BNM in 2017 has issued a Policy Document on *Wa'd,*[71] which provides that if the promisor fails to fulfil his *wa`d*, the promisee has the right to claim for actual loss. The Policy Document further states that in the case of breach of *wa`d* arising from a default in derivative obligations, the "actual loss to the promisee may consist of costs/loss in relation to promisee's risk mitigation arrangements whether conducted on actual basis (i.e. specific back-to-back arrangement with a third party) or on estimated basis (i.e. risk mitigation on portfolio basis)."[72]

The above scenario can be discerned from the back-to-back hedging arrangement shown in Figure 3.4.

Based on the arrangement flow shown in the said Figure, Kasri and Abidin[73] argue that there could be two general scenarios involved in the early termination of IPRS:

(a) At the time of the breach, Bank A has purchased the Shari'ah-compliant commodity from Broker A but has yet to deliver it to Client A;
(b) At the time of the breach, Bank A has yet to purchase the Shari'ah-compliant commodity from Broker A.

69 BNM, *Shariah Resolutions*, 143.
70 BNM, *Shariah Resolutions*, 142.
71 BNM, *Wa'd* (Kuala Lumpur: Bank Negara Malaysia, 2017), 12, https://www.bnm.gov.my/banking-islamic-banking.
72 BNM, *Wa'd, 12.*
73 Noor and Siti, *Breach Of Wa'd*, 13.

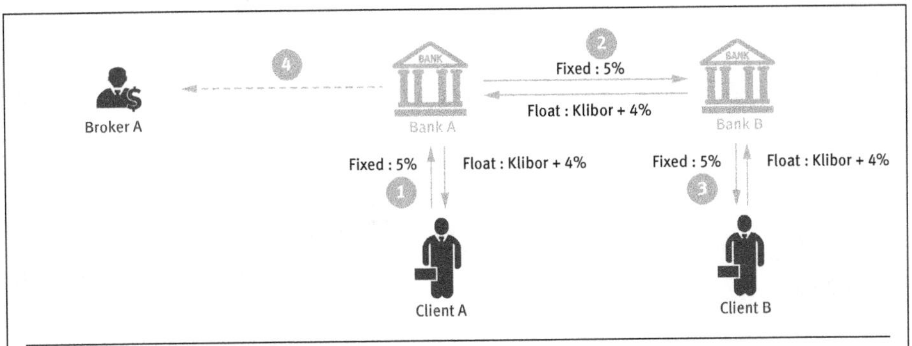

Explanation:

1. Upon the request and the need of Client A to hedge its floating profit rate exposure and convert it into a fixed profit rate exposure, Bank A agrees to pay to Client A a floating profit rate amount at KLIBOR+4.0%. In return, Client A agrees to pay to Bank A a fixed profit rate amount at 5%.

2. As Bank A does not "house the risk", Bank A enters into a back-to-back hedging arrangement with another party, Bank B. Under this hedging arrangement with Bank B, Bank A agrees to pay to Bank B a fixed profit rate amount at 5% (equivalent to the amount that Bank A will receive from Client A). In return, Bank B agrees to pay to Bank A a floating profit rate amount at KLIBOR+4.0% (equivalent to the amount that Bank B will receive from its client, Client B).

3. At the same time, Bank B has entered into a hedging arrangement with its client, Client B, whereby Bank B agrees to pay to Client B a fixed profit rate at 5% (equivalent to the amount that Bank B will receive from Bank A). In return, Client B agrees to pay to Bank B a floating profit rate amount at KLIBOR+4.0%.

4. At the time agreed to execute the payment and in order to materialise such payment either from Bank A to Client A or from Client A to Bank A, depending on who is exercising the *wa'd*, a broker will be appointed, Broker A. (The parties agreed to the terms and conditions of the broker's appointment in the DFTA.) Broker A will purchase a Sharī'ah-compliant commodity and thereafter sell the commodity to the exercising party (seller). The seller then sells the commodity to the undertaking party (buyer). The buyer will then pay the selling price to the seller based on the cost plus profit.

Figure 3.4: Back-to-Back Hedging Arrangement.
Source: Kasri and Zainalabiddin, 2016[74]

'These two scenarios are further captured in Figures 3.5 and 3.6 respectively where they depict two typical circumstances surrounding the case of breach of wa'd in IPRS.'

Based on these two scenarios and the discussion with the relevant Islamic banking industry practitioners in Malaysia, Kasri and Abidin[75] contend that the claim for the loss incurred due to the breach of *wa'd* could be identified as follows:

74 Noor and Siti, *Breach Of Wa'd*, 10.
75 Noor and Siti, *Breach Of Wa'd*, 17.

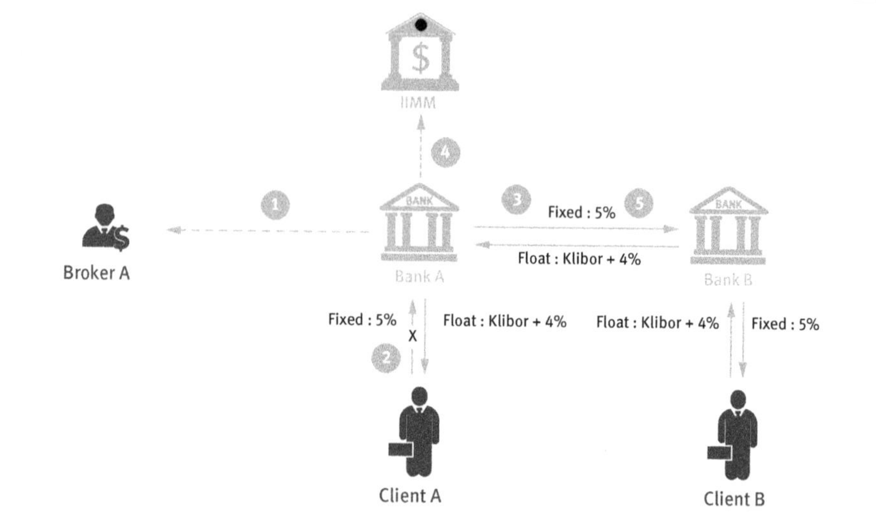

Explanation:

1. Bank A purchases the Sharīʿah-compliant commodity from Broker A . Thereafter Bank A delivers an exercise notice and *murābahah* sale confirmation to Client A.
2. Client A refuses to execute the *murābahah* sale confirmation, hence breaches its *waʿd* to purchase the commodity from Bank A.
3. Despite Bank A not receiving the payment from Client A, Bank A is still bound to pay Bank B the agreed fixed profit rate amount at 5%. At the same time, Bank A is still holding the commodity purchased from Broker A.
4. In order for Bank A to pay Bank B, Bank A will have to borrow money from the Islamic Interbank Money Market (IIMM). Bank A may incur some cost in getting such funds from the IIMM.
5. Using the money borrowed from the IIMM, Bank A pays Bank B the agreed fixed profit rate amount at 5%.

Figure 3.5: Breach of *Waʿd* by Client A in the Event that Bank A Has Purchased the Shari'ah-Compliant Commodity from Broker A.
Source: Kasri and Zainalabiddin, 2016.[76]

(a) in case the breach of *waʿd* occurs at the time when the promisee (say, Bank A) has acquired the commodity Bank A would typically incur loss pertaining to:
   (i) the commodity price paid to Broker A;
   (ii) the payment of the agreed fixed profit rate amount at 5 percent made to Bank B;
   (iii) the cost of borrowing money from IIMM (cost of funds); and
   (iv) the penalty for the breach of promise by Client A.

76 Noor and Siti, *Breach Of Wa'd*, 14.

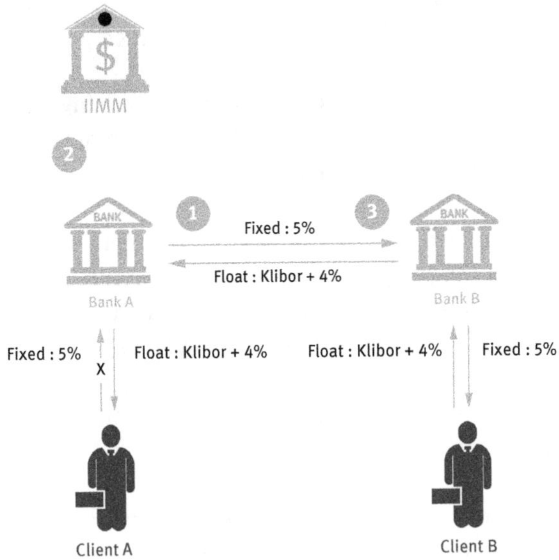

Explanation:

1. Despite Bank A not having purchased the Sharīʿah-compliant commodity from Broker A, Bank A is still bound to pay Bank B the agreed fixed profit rate amount at 5%.
2. As mentioned earlier, to pay Bank B, Bank A will have to borrow money from the Islamic Interbank Money Market (IIMM). Bank A may incur some cost in getting such funds from the IIMM.
3. Using the money borrowed from the IIMM, Bank A pays Bank B the agreed fixed profit rate amount at 5%.

Figure 3.6: Breach of *Waʿd* by Client A in the Event that Bank A Has Yet to Purchase the Shari'ah-Compliant Commodity.
Source: Kasri and Zainalabiddin[77]

(b) in case the breach of waʿd occurs at the time when the promisee has yet to acquire the commodity, the promisee would typically incur loss pertaining to:
   (i) the payment of the agreed fixed profit rate amount at 5 percent to Bank B;
   (ii) the cost of borrowing money from IIMM (cost of funds); and
   (iii) the penalty for the breach of promise by Client A.

As the above scenarios is argued to reflect the practice of claim for damages in the case of breach of *wa'd* under IPRS in the Islamic banking industry in Malaysia, the question then is whether these damages claimed as compensation amount is in harmony with the common law requirement.

77 Noor and Siti, *Breach Of Wa'd*, 15.

3.6.3 Harmonising Requirement for Damages for Loss or Damages Caused by Breach of Promise

The Shari'ah requirement for the compensation amount arising from the breach of *wa'd* to be on an actual basis resonates well with the legal requirement provided for in section 74 of the CA. The said section provides for compensation for loss or damage caused by a breach of contract, and it reads as follows:

(1) When a contract has been broken, the party who suffers by the breach is entitled to receive, from the party who has broken the contract, compensation for any loss or damage caused to him thereby, which naturally arose in the usual course of things from the breach, or which the parties knew, when they made the contract, to be likely to result from the breach of it.

(2) Such compensation is not to be given for any remote and indirect loss or damage sustained by reason of the breach.

Though the above section provides for breach of contract and not promise/undertaking, it is submitted that section 74 may still apply to breach of promise in view that promise is legally viewed as equivalent to a contract. This is argued based on section 2 of the CA which states that, "every promise and every set of promises, forming the consideration for each other, is an agreement" as well as section 26(b) of the CA which provides that: "An agreement made without consideration is void, unless – (b) it is a promise to compensate, wholly or in part, a person who has already voluntarily done something for the promisor, or something which the promisor was legally compellable to do."

The judicial interpretation of section 74(1) CA can be found in the Federal Court decision of *Toeh Kee Keong v Tambun Mining Company Ltd*,[78] where Azmi CJ held as follows:

> Section 74(1) of the Contracts Ordinance, 1950, is a statutory enunciation of the rule in Hadlex v. Baxendale [1854], 9 Exch 341. This section reads:
>
> When a contract has been broken, the party who suffers by such breach is entitled to receive, from the party who has broken the contract, compensation for any loss or damage caused to him thereby, which naturally arose in the usual course of things from such breach, or which the parties knew when they made the contract, to be likely result from the breach of it.The rule lays down the main principles as follows:-
>
> Where two parties have made a contract which one of them has broken, the damages which the other party ought to receive in respect of such breach of contract should be such as may fairly and reasonably considered either arising naturally, i.e. according to the usual course of things, from such breach of contract itself, or such as may reasonably be supposed to have been in contemplation of both parties, at the time they made the contract, as the probable result of the breach of it . . .

78 [1968] 1 MLJ 39.

> In cases of breach of contract the aggrieved party is only entitled to recover such part of the loss actually resulting as was at the time of the contract reasonably foreseeable as liable to result from the breach. What was at that time reasonably so foreseeable depends on the knowledge then possessed by the parties or, at all events, by the party who later commits the breach.[79]

The use of the term "compensation" instead of "damages" in section 74 is further analysed in *Akitek Tenggara Sdn Bhd v Mid Valley City Sdn Bhd*,[80] where the Federal Court referred to section 73 of the Indian Contract Act (equivalent to section 74 of the CA) and said:

> The general principle for the assessment of damages is compensatory, ie the innocent party is to be placed, so far as money can do, in the same position as if the contract had been performed. In explaining the distinction between "compensation" and "damages" Mookerjee J said in Mahamed Mozaharal Ahmad v Mahamed Azimaddin Bhuinya AIR 1923 Cal 507 at pp 511 – 512:
>
> As Lord Esher observed in Dixon v Calcraft (64) the expression compensation is not ordinarily used as an equivalent to damages, although as remarked by Fry, LJ in Skinner's Co v Knight (65) compensation may often have to be measured by the same rule as damages in an action for the breach. The term compensation as pointed out in the Oxford Dictionary, signifies that which is given in recompense, an equivalent rendered. Damages, on the other hand; constitute the sum of money claimed or adjudged to be paid in compensation for loss or injury sustained; the value estimated in money, of something lost or withheld. The term compensation etymologically suggest the image of balancing one thing against another; its primary signification is equivalence, and the secondary and more common meaning is something given or obtained as an equivalent. The word "compensation" therefore refers to an award made which is equivalent to what has been lost.[81]

While the position for the compensation for any loss or damage out of breach of promise must be actual loss or actually suffered as a result of the said breach, the next question is whether penalty, as listed as one of the compensated items, as argued earlier, can be claimed as actual loss hence deemed as part of the compensation amount.

Penalty for breach of contract is provided for in section 75 of CA, which reads as follows:

> When a contract has been broken, if a sum is named in the contract as the amount to be paid in case of such breach, or if the contract contains any other stipulation by way of penalty, the party complaining of the breach is entitled, whether or not actual damage or loss is proved to have been caused thereby, to receive from the party who has broken the contract reasonable compensation not exceeding the amount so named or, as the case may be, the penalty stipulated for.

79 [1968] 1 MLJ 40.
80 [2007] MLJU 404.
81 [2007] MLJU 425.

The application of section 75 above is deliberated in *Cubic Electronics Sdn Bhd (in liquidation) v Mars Telecommunications Sdn Bhd.*[82] In this case, the Federal Court held that there is no necessity for proof of actual loss and damage when an innocent party seeks to enforce a damage clause under section 75 of the CA. The court further held that proof of actual loss is not the sole conclusive determinant of reasonable compensation although evidence of that may be a useful starting point.

Based on the analysis of sections 74 and 75, it can be argued that the element of compensation, including the penalty charged on the promisor who defaulted or breached his/its *wa'd* as identified earlier, is in harmony with the legal requirement under the statute and the common law. For a claim for compensation or damages out of breach of contract/promise, it must be on an actual loss basis, while for a penalty, it is to be reasonable compensation without the need for further proof of actual loss.

3.7 Conclusion

This chapter depicts the development of the Shari'ah and legal harmonisation in the selected subjects under Islamic banking, ICM, and *Takaful* namely the SAC, the IFSA, the equity-based financing, *hibah* in *takaful* products, and compensation for breach of *wa'd* in IPRS. While compliance with the Shari'ah prerequisites is mandatory, the discussion of these subjects showed that the theory might not be easily adaptable on the ground. For a meaningful growth of the Islamic finance industry in line with the spirit of *Maqasid* Shari'ah, there is a need for the industry stakeholders to further engage and collaborate with one another. This will forge a better understanding and implementation of Islamic finance solutions. In the long run, the nation will benefit as the Islamic finance industry becomes more impactful, inclusive, and sustainable-driven, thus meeting the very notion of Islamic finance.

82 [2019] 1 AMR 737; [2018] MLJU 1935.

Ridoan Karim

4 Shari'ah-Compliant Financing for Energy Projects: A Call for Standardisation of Islamic Finance Contracts

4.1 Introduction

Covid-19 has a significant influence on the world's energy systems by reducing investments and slowing the growth of renewable energy technologies.[1] According to the International Energy Agency's (IEA) most recent Worldwide Energy Review, global energy consumption decreased by 3.8 percent in the first three months of 2020.[2] Interestingly, demand for fossil fuels like coal, oil, and natural gas has declined while demand for renewable energy has grown.[3] The price of energy stocks has been fluctuating unprecedently due to the influence of the pandemic on financial markets.[4] Hence, a new paradigm is unavoidable in response to recurring crises and global economic slowdown caused by the pandemic, especially in the energy sector. Institutionalised risk-sharing can assist the global economy in resisting shocks and reviving the economy.[5] As a strong proponent of the investment risk-sharing concepts, Islamic finance should be revisited to *see* if it can produce the desired outcomes in this space.

---

1 Daoxia Wan et al., "The Impact of Investor Attention during COVID-19 on Investment in Clean Energy versus Fossil Fuel Firms," *Finance Research Letters* 43 (2021):1–6, https://doi.org/10.1016/j.frl.2021.101955.

2 "Global Energy Review 2020," 2020, https://www.iea.org/reports/global-energy-review-2020.

3 For example, Iberdrola, a leading clean energy company, has demonstrated a robust financial performance in the first quarter of this year. As the director of the IEA highlights, "only renewables are holding up during the previously unheard-of slump in electricity use." *See* also Andrew Fawthrop, "Is Clean Energy Better Placed than Fossil Fuels to Navigate the Coronavirus Crisis?" NS Energy, 2020, https://www.nsenergybusiness.com/features/coronavirus-clean-energy-fossil-fuels/.

4 However, with "green recovery" stimulus measures being introduced in some countries, renewable energy firms have experienced the pandemic somewhat differently. More voices are calling for the need to rapidly transition to a clean energy future, which suggests investors will pay more attention to the potential to invest in clean energy stocks. *See* Elena Sanchez Nicolas, "Germany Ready to Lead Green Recovery Post Coronavirus," euobserver, 2020, https://euobserver.com/green-deal/148206. *See* also Dayong Zhang, Min Hu, and Qiang Ji, "Financial Markets under the Global Pandemic of COVID-19," *Finance Research Letters* 36 (2020): 2, https://doi.org/10.1016/j.frl.2020.101528.

5 Yu Chung Tsao et al., "A Risk-Sharing-Based Resilient Renewable Energy Supply Network Model under the COVID-19 Pandemic," *Sustainable Production and Consumption* 25 (2021): 484–498, https://doi.org/10.1016/j.spc.2020.12.003.

https://doi.org/10.1515/9783110766707-004

Islamic finance is portrayed as "ethical capitalism."[6] Islamic principles relating to financing are linked to sustainability as it is founded on equality, fairness, and justice. The overreaching influence of these principles also covers the issues relating to environmental protection and preservation.[7] Hence, it is interesting to *see* how *istisna-ijara* (procurement and lease contract), *wakala-ijara* (agency and lease contract), *murabaha* (credit sale agreement), *sukuk* (Islamic equivalent of a bond), and *tawarooq* (commodity sales contract), Islamic financing concepts used in energy projects, stand in comparison with conventional financing. Nevertheless, to put this into reality, many well-functioning principles and institutions must be harmonised with Islamic finance to convert the ideas into reality. Additionally, certain legal issues must be resolved before widespread adoption may occur, especially issues relating to the standardisation of Islamic finance contracts.

Hence, this chapter attempts to present a legal analysis to understand the nature of standardisation efforts and clarify the objectives and legal trajectory of Islamic finance in the energy sector. Most of the countries implementing Shari'ah-compliant financing for energy projects follow civil law systems; some follow common law; many are hybrid legal systems. These systems differ from country to country and, indeed, from continent to continent. Hence, a detailed analysis of the legal mechanisms of the standardisation challenges is required to understand how the Interest-Free Loan (IFL) can be facilitated in the energy industries.

4.2 Islamic Finance Developments in the Energy Sector

The push for a greener energy transition has reached the Middle East and North Africa (MENA) region, which has sparked a renewed interest in developing greener energy technologies. This significantly expanded the share of solar-generated electricity, led by Morocco and Jordan, who have accomplished several successful projects.[8] Saudi Arabia has also adopted "Vision 2030," which aims to install 9.5 gigawatts (GW) of

6 Mehmet Asutay, "Islamic Moral Economy as the Foundation of Islamic Finance," in *Islamic Finance in Europe: Towards a Plural Financial System*, ed. Valentino Cattelan (Cheltenham: Edward Elgar Publishing, 2013), 55–68.

7 *See* generally U.F Moghul & S. Safar-Aly, "Green Sukuk : The Introduction of Islam's Environmental Ethics to Contemporary Islamic Finance," *Georgetown International Environmental Law Review* 27, no. 1 (2014): 4.

8 Steven Griffiths, "Strategic Considerations for Deployment of Solar Photovoltaics in the Middle East and North Africa," *Energy Strategy Reviews* 2, no. 1 (2013): 125–131, https://doi.org/10.1016/j.esr.2012.11.001.

renewable energy.[9] Dubai is no different, and with the expansion of the Sheikh Maktoum Solar Park, it will produce 1,000 MW of electricity through renewable means.[10] The Egyptian Government also hopes to secure 2,000 megawatts of solar energy through a "feed-in-tariff" scheme and expects to confirm further developments in other renewable energy projects, such as wind and hydro.[11] The energy crisis and worsening environmental circumstances have propelled the development of renewable energy sources not only in the Arab world but also in Europe.[12] Despite elevated goals, the wind and solar energy market shrank dramatically over the last decade as government incentives were reduced all over the world.[13] Even though incentives played a role, other factors like the conventional financing model also significantly contributed to such reduction of renewable energy production.[14]

Generally, in conventional energy projects, the private sponsor (or sponsors) would create a special purpose vehicle (SPV)[15] or company to construct, own, operate, and maintain the project.[16] Electricity buyers (typically a government entity if the project is connected to a grid system) enter into Power Purchase Agreements (PPA) for project operation and maintenance.[17] This model is known as Independent Power Project (IPP).[18] This model allows lenders (such as commercial banks, multilateral agencies, and organisations that provide initial capital) to reimburse from the project's income stream through conventional arrangements. The project's funding is typically provided through a combination of debt and equity. If the project

9 Y. H.Ahssein Amran et al., "Renewable and Sustainable Energy Production in Saudi Arabia According to Saudi Vision 2030; Current Status and Future Prospects," *Journal of Cleaner Production* 247 (2020): 2–6, https://doi.org/10.1016/j.jclepro.2019.119602.

10 Farkhod Aminjonov, "Policy Innovations and Rationale for Sustainable Energy Transition in the UAE," *Social Science Quarterly* 101, no. 7 (2020): 2398–2412, https://doi.org/10.1111/ssqu.12909.

11 Doaa Salman and Nadine Amr Hosny, "The Nexus between Egyptian Renewable Energy Resources and Economic Growth for Achieving Sustainable Development Goals," *Future Business Journal* 7, no. 1 (2021): 1–12, https://doi.org/10.1186/s43093-021-00091-8.

12 European Commission, "Second Report on the State of the Energy Union" (Brussels, Belgium, 2017).

13 Brett Christophers, "Fossilised Capital: Price and Profit in the Energy Transition," *New Political Economy* 27, no. 1 (2022): 146–159, https://doi.org/10.1080/13563467.2021.1926957.

14 Christophers, "Fossilised Capital, 146–159.

15 A Special Purpose Vehicle (SPV) is a separate legal entity created by an organisation. The SPV is a distinct company with its own assets and liabilities, as well as its own legal status. Usually, they are created for a specific objective, often to isolate financial risk. As it is a separate legal entity, if the parent company goes bankrupt, the special purpose vehicle can carry on.

16 Patrick T.I. Lam and Angel O.K. Law, "Financing for Renewable Energy Projects: A Decision Guide by Developmental Stages with Case Studies," *Renewable and Sustainable Energy Reviews* 90 (2018): 937–944, https://doi.org/10.1016/j.rser.2018.03.083.

17 Patrick and Angel, "Financing for Renewable Energy Projects", 937–944.

18 Independent power producers (IPPs) are typically not owned by the national electricity company or public utility. IPPs may utilise the national grid or a commercial distributive system to supply electricity for consumers.

is riskier, the debt and costs ratio will be lower. Factors such as project location, reliability of the technology used, and creditworthiness of the PPA counterparty all have an effect on this model.[19] The SPV has the responsibility of repaying the loan(s). As a result, lenders will be given a security package to ensure that their debt will be repaid. This will include: a security interest over the SPV's assets (pledged by the sponsors) and sharing bank accounts of the SPV (the SPV will be restricted from maintaining any bank account not expressly permitted by the lenders).[20] This particular conventional financing model has a growing opposition, not only in the MENA region but also elsewhere, as it involves high interest (*riba*).[21]

When it comes to renewable energy projects, Islamic financing takes a different approach than traditional financing. All Islamic financial institutions prohibit the charging of interest (*riba*). Instead, the financier charges a premium or gets a portion of the company's earnings. The investor can also engage in contracts with third parties relating to lease arrangements or equity investment. Returns to invest depend on several risk factors that the investor has accepted. Islamic law principles urge financiers to become partners in the company rather than be only a conventional creditor.[22] Nevertheless, such a process does not guarantee an inevitable return on investment. Hence, Islamic finance imposes certain principles to safeguard the investor. For example, the contract must be free from ambiguity (*gharar*), speculation or gambling (*maisir*), and disjuncture from Shari'ah-compliance.[23]

Now, the question is how Islamic financial instruments might be useful for financing the renewable energy industry. Among various Islamic financial structures, "*istisna-ijara*" is the most popular for funding renewable energy projects.[24] This is a hybrid arrangement that combines *istisna* (procurement) and *ijara* (forward leasing). *Istisna* is a sales contract in which one party agrees to create a specific asset in accordance with the agreed specifications and then deliver it in a predetermined time

19 Patrick T.I.Lam and Angel O.K.Law, "Financing for Renewable Energy Projects: A Decision Guide by Developmental Stages with Case Studies," *Renewable and Sustainable Energy Reviews* 90 (2018): 937–944, https://doi.org/10.1016/j.rser.2018.03.083.

20 Patrick and Angel, "Financing for Renewable Energy Projects", 937–944.

21 Luluk Widyawati, "A Systematic Literature Review of Socially Responsible Investment and Environmental Social Governance Metrics," *Business Strategy and the Environment* 29, no. 2 (2020): 619–637, https://doi.org/10.1002/bse.2393.

22 Rasem N. Kayed, "The Entrepreneurial Role of Profit-and-Loss Sharing Modes of Finance: Theory and Practice," *International Journal of Islamic and Middle Eastern Finance and Management* 5, no. 3 (2012): 203–228, https://doi.org/10.1108/17538391211255205.

23 Rasem, "The Entrepreneurial Role of Profit-and-Loss Sharing Modes of Finance", 203–228.

24 Paolo Pietro Biancone and Maha Radwan, "Sharia-Compliant Financing for Public Utility Infrastructure," *Utilities Policy* 52 (2018): 88–94, https://doi.org/10.1016/j.jup.2018.03.006.

frame for a predetermined fee.[25] During the construction phase, the Project Company or the SPV undertakes an *istisna* contract to procure the construction, development and delivery of the assets.[26] The Project Company simultaneously enters into a construction contract with the engineering, procurement, and construction (EPC) contractor incorporating the terms and conditions of the *istisna* contract.[27] In return, Islamic banks/financiers make phased payments to the Project Company based on milestones reached as per the agreed predetermined schedule. These transactions are similar to conventional finance facilities. Ownership of the assets is delivered to the Islamic financiers upon project completion pursuant to the *istisna* contract.

In the operations phase, following project completion, the lease comes into effect. The *ijara* contract includes a promise from the Islamic financiers to transfer ownership of the leased asset to the borrower either at the end of the lease period or in stages during the term of the *ijara*. Once leasing commences, service arrangements become effective whereby the financiers appoint the Project Company as an agent to manage and maintain the assets. During this period, the Project Company pay periodical rents as per the terms of the lease agreement. On payment of the final lease rental, the financiers shall transfer the leased assets to the lessee (Project Company) in accordance with the terms of the sale undertaking.[28]

Another Islamic finance structure is *wakala-ijara/wakala-ijara mawsuf fi al dhimmah* structure, an alternate but comparable structure frequently used in financing projects.[29] In this case, the SPV acts as the owner's agent or *wakil* under a *Wakala* Agreement. Being an agency agreement, the contractual relationship between the Islamic financial institutions and the borrower is distinct from the *istisna* structure mentioned above. Everything else about the two designs is the same.[30]

A *murabaha* structure can also be utilised in specific situations. This type of financing includes the financial institution (which may or may not be Islamic) purchasing an asset and reselling it to the borrower on deferred payment terms at an

25 Davood Manzoor, Majid Karimirizi, and Ali Mostafavisani, "Financing Infrastructure Projects Based on Risk Sharing Model: Istisna Sukuk," *Journal of Emerging Economies and Islamic Research* 5, no. 3 (2017): 72–84, https://doi.org/10.24191/jeeir.v5i3.8832.

26 Manzoor, Karimirizi, and Mostafavisani, "Financing Infrastructure Projects Based on Risk Sharing Model," 72–84.

27 Manzoor, Karimirizi, and Mostafavisani, "Financing Infrastructure Projects Based on Risk Sharing Model," 72–84.

28 Manzoor, Karimirizi, and Mostafavisani, "Financing Infrastructure Projects Based on Risk Sharing Model," 72–84.

29 R. Sadikot, "Islamic Project Finance: Shari'a Compliant Financing of Large Scale Infrastructure Projects Rishad Sadikot," *Online Journal on Southwest Asia and Islamic Civilization* (2012): 1–9.

30 Sadikot, "Islamic Project Finance", 1–9.

agreed profit at the time of the contract.[31] Most assets are purchased with a down payment, and the rest of the money is paid in installments. Although the *murabaha* structure has the benefit of putting the property title in the borrower's hands, there are limits on prepayment.[32] Working capital or commodities (*tawarooq*)[33] are the standard Shari'ah-compliant form of *murabaha*.

An increase in the usage of *sukuk* financing for energy projects in the MENA region is also experienced in recent times.[34] Holders of *sukuk* own a hundred percent stake in the underlying asset. *Sukuks* can be compared to a bond in Western finance; the only difference is the *sukuk* complies with Shari'ah.[35] In other words, an issuer of *sukuk* sells certificates to a group of investors, who then use the money to buy assets. In *sukuk*, the issuer contractually agrees to purchase back the bond at face value on a future date.[36] *Sukuk* can be compared to asset-backed securities, which are essentially interest-free loans used to fund the acquisition of real estate. Green *sukuk* has been used to fund many initiatives, including the One SolarWatt Per Person in Indonesia and the Orasis in France.[37]

Multiple Islamic principles have also been employed to satisfy the needs of several other energy project financing transactions. For instance, the first was the USD 5.50 billion mining project in Saudi Arabia by the Ma'aden Phosphate Company, which involved power building and desalination.[38] The project incorporated

31 Hakan Kalkavan and Serkan Eti, "Determining Optimal Islamic Financing Methods for Small-Scale Sustainable Energy Investments Regarding Socio-Economic Welfare," in *Strategic Approaches to Energy Management*, ed. Serhat Yüksel and Hasan Dinçer (Cham: Springer 2021), 271–283.

32 Kalkavan and Serkan, "Determining Optimal Islamic Financing Methods", 271–283.

33 Amounts are lent to the SPV through the use of separate *Murabahas* for the acquisition by the lender (acting as the agent of the SPV) of amounts of commodity equal in value to the principal amount required, the immediate resale to the SPV at the purchase price of such commodity, plus an agreed return, and the immediate resale to the original seller of the commodity (normally for the price at which the original seller sold the commodity to the lender, plus a small transaction fee, which is passed on to the SPV). The profit portion owed to the lender is then in addition to the amounts lent to the SPV for the construction and/or operation of the project. While this form of Islamic financing is widely utilised, particularly in Saudi Arabia, it has been criticised by certain Islamic financial institutions, and borrowers in the GCC region are increasingly opting for other forms of *Sharia'ah*-compliant financing.

34 Nafis Alam, Meryem Duygun, and Rima Turk Ariss, "Green Sukuk: An Innovation in Islamic Capital Markets," in *Energy and Finance: Sustainability in the Energy Industry*, ed. André Dorsman, Özgür Arslan-Ayaydin and Mehmet Baha Karan (Cham: Springer 2016), 167–185.

35 Alam, Duygun, and Turk Ariss, "Green Sukuk", 167–185.

36 Alam, Duygun, and Turk Ariss, "Green Sukuk", 167–185.

37 Alam, Duygun, and Turk Ariss, "Green Sukuk", 167–185.

38 Saheed Adelekan, Sam Wamuziri, and Ben Binsardi, "Evaluation of Islamic Financing Products for Housing and Infrastructure Development," in *Proceedings 29th Annual Association of Researchers in Construction Management Conference, ARCOM 2013*, 2013.

sstisna-ijara mawsufah fi al-dhimmah here. The Al Dur project in Bahrain in 2009 is a recent example of another independent water and power project (IWPP).[39] Another independent power project (IPP) in the GCC area was the Oman Al Manah Power Project.[40] Similarly, over 20 IPP/IWPP energy projects will be implemented very soon in the UAE, Arabia, Oman, Qatar, Bahrain, and Indonesia.[41]

In the energy project, various reasons have contributed to the recent growth of Islamic finance. They include the establishment of new Islamic banks (for example, Alinma in Saudi Arabia and Abu Dhabi Islamic Bank and Dubai Islamic Bank in the UAE);[42] the development of more creative Islamic finance structures that can use the underlying assets of a project;[43] the growing number of conventional banks that are now willing to lend on an Islamic basis;[44] the willingness of credit funding agencies to work with Islamic financing structures and co-lenders;[45] and the preference for Islamic finance structures.[46]

The green economy will constantly advance in this scenario with the Islamic financing instruments to broaden the scope of many possible social and equitable models. In general, the usage of Islamic finance can improve the effectiveness of financial systems for all countries. It can also penetrate the markets and integrate foreign direct investments into the national economic structure.[47] With the involvement of Islamic and conventional institutions, it is feasible that Islamic financing may completely fund IPP/IWPP projects. With the advent of the market for *sukuk* and *istisna-ijara*, the energy project financing would revive with economic recovery induced by Covid-19.

---

39 Biancone and Radwan, "Sharia-Compliant Financing for Public Utility Infrastructure."
40 Biancone and Radwan, "Sharia-Compliant Financing for Public Utility Infrastructure."
41 Biancone and Radwan, "Sharia-Compliant Financing for Public Utility Infrastructure."
42 Momna Saeed and Marwan Izzeldin, "Examining the Relationship between Default Risk and Efficiency in Islamic and Conventional Banks," *Journal of Economic Behavior and Organization* 132 (2016): 127–154, https://doi.org/10.1016/j.jebo.2014.02.014.
43 Paolo Pietro Biancone and Maha Radwan, "Social Finance And Unconventional Financing Alternatives: An Overview," *European Journal of Islamic Finance*, no. 10 (2018): 1–5, https://doi.org/10.13135/2421-2172/2818.
44 Nosheen and Abdul Rashid, "Business Orientation, Efficiency, and Credit Quality across Business Cycle: Islamic versus Conventional Banking. Are There Any Lessons for Europe and Baltic States?," *Baltic Journal of Economics* 19, no. 1 (2019): 105–135, https://doi.org/10.1080/1406099X.2018.1560947.
45 Siong Choy Chong and Usman Olakunle Balogun, "Islamic Finance Professional Programme Structure: Development and Prospects," *International Journal of Islamic and Middle Eastern Finance and Management* 10, no. 2 (2017): 243–263, https://doi.org/10.1108/IMEFM-11-2016-0160.
46 Chong and Balogun, "Islamic Finance Professional Programme Structure, 243–263.
47 Hafezali Iqbal Hussain et al., "Sustainability of Leverage Levels in Response to Shocks in Equity Prices: Islamic Finance as a Socially Responsible Investment," *Sustainability (Switzerland)* 11, no. 12 (2019): 1–16, https://doi.org/10.3390/su10023260.

4.3 Standardisation of Islamic Financial Contracts for Energy Projects: Legal Challenges

The Shari'ah is a complex set of laws, and it is not only a legal system. Instead, it is a process that governs the lives of Muslims in practice. There is no absolute authority to oversee the determination of a judgment in the Islamic legal tradition since it is nonhierarchical.[48] Instead, judicial authority is vested upon the jurists (*mujtahid*), who issue rulings relating to different disputes.[49] Shari'ah is even referred to as a jurist's law because the function of a jurist is essential in determining the law.[50] It requires jurists to use their intellect to derive the law from the *Qur'an* and *Sunna*. Jurists do not claim to produce law; rather, they interpret God's law through *ijma* (consensus) and *qiyas* (analogical reasoning). The legal decision (*fatwa*) is deemed valid as long as the interpretation of legal principles is constructed with the most significant effort (*ijtihad*) and practice of Islamic philosophy.[51] A *fatwa* is nonbinding, allowing for dynamism in legal opinions.[52]

Most nations that offer Islamic finance and banking either have civil or common law systems. Hence, there is a lack of a comprehensive legal framework to appropriately regulate and enforce Islamic finance transactions. The lack of a sole legal system based on Islamic finance also raises issues with the enforceability of adequate principles and forms the lack of clarity on the Shari'ah compliance. The laws relating to Islamic finance vary from jurisdiction to jurisdiction and, indeed, from lender to lender.[53] As a result, only the Shari'ah board of a particular jurisdiction may determine whether a specific contract based on Islamic finance is Shari'ah-compliant or not. Contracts that have been determined to be Shari'ah-compliant should be subjected to a judicial system that will enforce them.

Hence, several not-for-profit organisations have been developed over the period to audit the Shari'ah standards for Islamic financial institutions and the industry. The Accounting and Auditing Organization for Islamic Financial Institutions (AAOIFI) is one in which Shari'ah scholars and economists serve on the standardisation process.[54]

---

48 Jonathan Breanbrack, "The Standardization of Islamic Financial Law: Lawmaking in Modern Financial Markets," *The American Journal of Comparative Law* 67, no. 4 (2019): 825–860, https://doi.org/10.1093/ajcl/avz010.

49 Breanbrack, "The Standardization of Islamic Financial Law", 825–860.

50 Breanbrack, "The Standardization of Islamic Financial Law", 825–860.

51 Nicholas H.D. Foster, "Islamic Finance Law as an Emergent Legal System," *Arab Law Quarterly* 21, no. 2 (2007): 170–188, https://doi.org/10.1163/026805507X214433.

52 Nicholas, "Islamic Finance Law", 170–188.

53 For instance, some lenders in Saudi Arabia only consider *Wakala-Ijara* structure to be compliant with Islamic law and not *Isitsna-Ijara. See*, Nicholas, "Islamic Finance Law", 170–188.

54 M. Kabir Hassan et al., "A Survey on Islamic Finance and Accounting Standards," *Borsa Istanbul Review* 19 (2019): 1–13, https://doi.org/10.1016/j.bir.2019.07.006.

In the process of interpreting the *fiqh*, scholars from AAOIFI take modern business conduct into account.[55] The interpretation of today's Islamic principles reflects an entirely new setup and is intended to mimic traditional market procedures. Nevertheless, Islamic laws require a legal discourse of standardisation of Islamic finance contracts into the hybrid legal system of different countries. Many hybrid legal systems of MENA nations, notably the UAE, require significant change if a high level of standardisation is to be achieved for Islamic finance contracts.[56]

The recent *Dana Gas*[57] dispute in respect to a USD 700 million *muduraba sukuk*, demonstrates the gap between Islamic finance law and UAE law and how this pluralistic legal interaction encourages complete standardisation of Islamic finance contracts.[58] UAE, Egypt, Algeria, and most other Arabic countries' legal systems derive from Napoleonic or French civil and penal codes but retain elements of the Shari'ah. The Constitution of UAE states that Shari'ah "shall be a main source of legislation in the Union."[59] This specifies that Shari'ah is just one of several sources, in addition to federal law, other basic legal principles, and customary practises. Nevertheless, article 2 of the 1985 Federal Civil Code carries a distinct rule concerning the Shari'ah: "The rules and principles of Islamic jurisprudence (*fiqh*) shall be relied upon in the understanding, construction and interpretation of these provisions."[60] According to the article, the application of Shari'ah in the UAE depends on civil law interpretation. Nevertheless, article 27 states, "it shall not be permissible to apply the provisions of a law specified by the preceding articles if such provisions are contrary to Islamic Shari'ah, public order, or morals."[61] These possible contradictions within the Constitution generate legal ambiguity in the application of Islamic law in UAE.

The UAE lawmakers have also opted to selectively apply the Shari'ah, as indicated by article 1 of the amended Civil Code, which excludes the Shari'ah applications in the Commercial Code. However, the Civil Code includes the applications of Shari'ah in the law of contract, which cannot be separated from commercial law. The Islamic contracts, such as the *istisna*, *ijara*, *salam*, and *mudaraba*, will be interpreted according to *fiqh* in financial transactions. On the other hand, the Commercial Code

---

55 Ercanbrack, "The Standardization of Islamic Financial Law: Lawmaking in Modern Financial Markets."

56 Jonathan George Ercanbrack, "Islamic Financial Law and the Law of the United Arab Emirates: Disjuncture and the Necessity for Reform," *Arab Law Quarterly* 33, no. 2 (2019): 152–178, https://doi.org/10.1163/15730255-12332011.

57 Dana Gas is an energy firm based in the United Arab Emirates.

58 Ercanbrack, "Islamic Financial Law and the Law of the United Arab Emirates: Disjuncture and the Necessity for Reform."

59 *Dustur Dawlat Al-Imarat Al-'Arabiya Al-Muttahida* [Constitution of the United Arab Emirates] art. 7 (1971) (translated by Jonathan George Ercanbrack in "The Standardization of Islamic Financial Law: Lawmaking in Modern Financial Markets.").

60 Law No. 5 of 1985 on the Civil Transactions Law (Civil Code) art. 2 (1985) (U.A.E.).

61 Law No. 5, 27.

indicates that Shari'ah will not apply to commercial affairs unless commercial custom reflects Shari'ah principles. In the absence of an agreement or applicable legislation, article 2 states that commercial custom and practices will apply to the particular situation, and where the custom is missing, civil law should apply as long as it does not conflict with broad commercial principles. As the Commercial Code excludes the application of Shari'ah, the Federal Supreme Court being the highest court of the United Arab Emirates, regularly enforces judgments that are lawful according to the Commercial Code; however, it touches on the religious sensitivity regarding the charging of interest and on other pertinent issues.[62]

Considering these sensitivities, Dana Gas demanded that their *Sukuk* be restructured and filed a case in the UAE court seeking to declare its USD 700 million *mudaraba sukuk* invalid under UAE law. They claimed that the restructuring is required "due to the evolution and continual development of Islamic financial instruments and their interpretation."[63] The *ad hoc* committee representing *sukuk* holders declined the exchange of the existing instruments with the new ones.[64] After a legal struggle with its *sukuk* holders in both the UK and the UAE, Dana Gas obtained a series of injunctions throughout the world, prohibiting the company from enforcing the exchange of restructured *sukuk*.[65]

Additionally, both the courts in the UK and UAE have found that divergences exist between the UAE's Civil Code provisions for Islamic contracts and the AAOIFI standards regarding the same.[66] This significant regulatory gap necessitates legislative ratification of the UAE's laws and the adoption of AAOIFI standards. The UAE Central Bank adopted the AAOIFI Shari'ah standards in the aftermath of the *Dana Gas* case, demonstrating a need for complete standardisation. However, the experts believe that the acceptance of AAOIFI standards by the UAE Central Bank is simply a first step toward standardising Islamic finance contracts, and it is still inadequate.[67]

On the other hand, the English courts encourage standardising the terms and conditions of Islamic finance transactions as it leads to a speedy resolution of

62 *See* Nabil Saleh, "Definition and Formation of Contract Under Islamic and Arab Laws," *Arab Law Quarterly* 5, no. 2 (1990): 101–116, https://doi.org/10.1163/157302590X00026.

63 Omair Haroon, Sameen Fatima Meenai, and Aun Raza Rizvi, "Dana Gas: The Sukuk Dispute," *Asian Journal of Management Cases* 17, no. 1 (2020): 42–54, https://doi.org/10.1177/0972820119884395.

64 Haroon, Sameen Meenai, and Rizvi, "Dana Gas", 42–54.

65 The English court decided in November 2017 in favour of Dana's creditors, rejecting the company's claims.

66 Ercanbrack, "The Standardization of Islamic Financial Law: Lawmaking in Modern Financial Markets."

67 Fulya Apaydin, "Regulating Islamic Banks in Authoritarian Settings: Malaysia and the United Arab Emirates in Comparative Perspective," *Regulation and Governance* 12, no. 4 (2018): 466–485, https://doi.org/10.1111/rego.12201.

disputes and creates trust in the Shari'ah authenticity of the market.[68] Nevertheless, in practice, the English court does not consider AOIFI standards when interpreting Islamic finance contracts/transactions.[69] The authenticity of Shari'ah is undermined as the English courts uphold parties' contractual agreements.[70] For instance, the case of *Islamic Investment Co. v. Symphony Gems N.V.*,[71] which is regarded as the first Islamic financial dispute in an English court, exhibited that courts would uphold parties' contractual agreements, even if they contradict Shari'ah principles, such as the prohibition of *riba*. The court did not decide the case in accordance with the Shari'ah compliance of the *murabahah* agreement; rather, it applied the mere terms of the agreement, which was indeed Shari'ah non-compliant. Similarly, *Shamil Bank v. Beximco Pharmaceuticals Ltd.*[72] was another important case that reiterated that English courts would not resolve the dispute based on Shari'ah.[73]

The English court's approach to Islamic finance contracts causes a credibility and trust gap.[74] Hence, to minimise complication, the parties of the contract in international commercial transactions choose the governing law they desire for dispute resolution. Investors also prefer a formal dispute resolution mechanism to avoid regulatory and legal gaps. Hence, investors often insist on using English law with the notion that it will reduce the legal risks. However, the sector cannot remain impervious to the lack of Shari'ah authenticity in Islamic financial transactions. Standardisation is required to fill the legal gap and bring public trust and confidence in Islamic financial transactions. It is a call for the time that the Islamic concepts or guidelines, such as the AAOIFI Shari'ah standards, be included in contracts by the parties. Shari'ah invalidity arguments will disappear if such integration and standardisation take place. The AAOIFI

---

68 *See* generally Syarah Syahira Mohd Yusoff and Umar A. Oseni, "Standardisation of Legal Documentation in Islamic Home Financing in Malaysia: A Literature Survey," *Journal of Islamic Accounting and Business Research* 10, no. 3 (2019): 448–465, https://doi.org/10.1108/JIABR-02-2017-0016.

69 Ercanbrack, "The Standardization of Islamic Financial Law: Lawmaking in Modern Financial Markets."

70 Historically, the interpretational *modus* of English common law takes a literalist approach to contractual interpretation. This is illustrated in the well-known *Lovell & Christmas Ltd. v. Wall* [1911] 104 LT 85 (CA) case. Lord Hoffmann enunciated the decisive shift towards a contextual approach to contractual interpretation in *Investors Compensation Scheme Ltd. v. West Bromwich Building Society* [1998] 1 WLR 896 (HL) 912–13. Lord Hoffmann outlined what earlier courts had already set in motion, namely, Lord Wilberforce in *Prenn v. Simmonds* [1971] 1 WLR 1381, 1381–86, and in *Reardon Smith Line Ltd. v. Hansen-Tangen* [1976] 1 WLR 989. *See* also Ercanbrack, "The Standardization of Islamic Financial Law: Lawmaking in Modern Financial Markets."

71 [2002] All ER (D) 171.

72 [2004] EWCA (Civ) 19.

73 The governing clause states, "Subject to the principles of the Glorious Sharia'a, this Agreement shall be governed by and construed in accordance with the laws of England." *See* Ercanbrack, "The Standardization of Islamic Financial Law: Lawmaking in Modern Financial Markets."

74 Jonathan Ercanbrack, "The Regulation of Islamic Finance in the United Kingdom," *Ecclesiastical Law Journal* 13, no. 1 (2011): 69–77, https://doi.org/10.1017/S0956618X10000827.

standards have been proved to conform to the highest level of uniformity. Malaysia is an example of such standardisation of Islamic finance contracts, which represents a state-led, top-down approach. Such an approach positively impacted Malaysia, and the country is now known for being the most standardised Islamic finance jurisdiction.[75] Standardisation requires interactive legal systems and state support, which Malaysia achieved through considerable aid from the Government.

4.4 The Way Forward

The economic character of energy trading seeks to reduce legal disparities by utilising market forces. Hence, the usage of standard-form documentation has become a norm in energy trading.[76] On the other hand, Islamic financial transactions are becoming popular, not only in Muslim countries but also in western societies. Nevertheless, it is experienced by scholars that the commercial market desire uniformity and harmonisation of Islamic principles through standardised contractual documents.[77] Standard-form contract is preferred by investors, mainly in the energy industry.[78] Standardised documents are also particularly popular among English law firms, which play a significant role in organising Islamic financial contracts. One such example is the London-based Loan Market Association (LMA), a prominent standard-setting organisation for international finance in Europe and the Middle East. The User's Guide to Islamic Finance Documents was prepared by English law firms to assist attorneys in writing Shari'ah-compliant loan arrangements.[79] Similarly, International Islamic Financial Market (IIFM) with the goal to "harmonise" Islamic capital and money markets by creating consistency in the cross-border transaction, has collaborated with traditional standard-setting bodies to develop nine standard-form contracts.

Although standardisation is viewed as a critical component of the commercial world, there are many criticisms of the usage of a standard form of document in Islamic financing. Islam encourages parties to innovate and address contractual obligations

---

75 Mufti Ismail Ebrahim Desai, "Islamic Finance–Opportunities and Challenges," *Journal of Islamic Banking and Finance* 33, no. 1 (2016): 86–90.

76 Ljiljana Rudic-Dimic and Zorana Stojkovic, "EFET Agreements on Energy Trading in PE EPS Pracitice," in *IET Conference Publications*, 2016, https://doi.org/10.1049/cp.2016.1030. *See* also Camilla Baasch Andersen, "Defining Uniformity in Law," *Uniform Law Review* 12, no. 1 (2007): 5–54, https://doi.org/10.1093/ulr/12.1.5.

77 Ercanbrack, "The Standardization of Islamic Financial Law: Lawmaking in Modern Financial Markets."

78 Farahdilah Ghazali et al., "Feed-in Tariff, Auctions and Renewable Energy Schemes in Malaysia: Lessons from Other Jurisdictions," *IIUM Law Journal* 28, no. 1 (2020): 113–137, https://doi.org/10.31436/iiumlj.v28i1.482.

79 Jonathan G. Ercanbrack, *The Transformation of Islamic Law in Global Financial Markets* (Cambridge University Press, 2015), 173–236.

from many perspectives, as long as the terms of the contract stay within the boundaries of Shari'ah. With all its remarkable qualifications and experience, the Shari'ah authority and Islamic financial auditing institutes, such as AAOFI, are not omniscient. Their interpretation relies on a literal application of the Qur'anic command, without taking many contemporary circumstances into account.[80] Hence, there is a possibility of unequal bargaining power for the customers if they standardise contractual terms of Islamic finance.[81] This is where the Islamic financing contract must be examined depending on the contemporary circumstances.[82] A contract or a contractual term that is significantly unjust simply cannot be Shari'ah-compliant, even if the Islamic scholars approve it. It is not appropriate to characterise something as "Islamic" if it is unjust and repressive. Ibn Qayyim, a well-known Shari'ah scholar, put it this way:

> The Shari'ah is entirely justice, compassion, wisdom, and prosperity. Therefore, any ruling that replaces justice with injustice, mercy with cruelty, prosperity with harm, or wisdom with nonsense, is a ruling that does not belong to the Shari'ah, even if it is claimed to be so according to some interpretations.[83]

Hence, the scholars still believe that the courts must have the judicial power to address both Shari'ah and conventional concerns in Islamic financial contracts.[84] Especially in the UK, judges should be aware of Shari'ah principles and make judgements considering them on the ground.[85] Referring exclusively to English law in Islamic financial contracts may disregard the whole purpose of the investment, which is an interest-free loan. Hence, the best workable solution is to include reference to the AAOIFI standards by the contractual parties with a term that states in case of any ambiguity as to the meaning of Islamic finance concept used, the parties agree that the meaning and interpretation proffered by the AAOIFI standards is to be adopted. In this way, the court will have the chance to enforce the AAOIFI standards by reference to the agreed terms of the contract.

80 Qur'an, Chapter 5: 1 where Allah says: "O ye who believe! fulfil (all) obligations." *See* also John Benson, Adnan Trakic, and Pervaiz K Ahmed, "Dispute Resolution in Islamic Finance: The Way Forward," in *Dispute Resolution in Islamic Finance*, ed. Adnan Trakic, John Benson, Pervaiz K Ahmed (London: Routledge, 2019).
81 Azeemuddin Subhani, "Structural Compliance of Islamic Finance with Qur'anic Exegesis," in *Handbook on Islam and Economic Life*, ed. M. Kabir Hassan and Mervyn K. Lewis (Cheltenham: Edward Elgar Publishing Limited, 2014), 153–172.
82 Subhani, "Structural", 153–172.
83 Ibn al-Qayyim, *I'lam al-Muwaqi'een*, Vol. 4, 1st edn (Dar Ibn al-Jawzi) 337.
84 John Benson, Adnan Trakic, and Pervaiz K Ahmed, "Dispute Resolution in Islamic Finance: The Way Forward," in *Dispute Resolution in Islamic Finance*, ed. Adnan Trakic, John Benson, Pervaiz K Ahmed (London: Routledge, 2019).
85 Benson, Trakic, and Ahmed, "Dispute Resolution in Islamic Finance".

4.5 Conclusion

Institutionalised risk-sharing in the form of Islamic finance can assist the energy market in resisting the shocks of Covid-19 and reviving the economy. With the increasing involvement of Islamic institutions, Islamic financing instruments such as *istisna-ijara*, *wakala-ijara*, *murabaha*, *sukuk*, and *tawarooq* may completely fund energy projects.

Nevertheless, a need is sensed by the energy industry for the standardisation of Islamic finance contracts. Energy markets require predictability, transparency, and stability. The AAOIFI standards relating to the contractual terms are flexible enough to address pertinent concerns relating to Islamic finance. Precise contractual provisions detailing the parties' rights and remedies are favourable to sustainable investment in the energy industry. As the amount of cross-border transactions in the energy industry has expanded tremendously, legal professionals encounter an ethical and professional obligation to reduce the risks and costs of such transactions.[86] As a result, the creation of a globally accepted set of standards may lend them the impression of neutrality. Furthermore, when a globally accepted set of standards can be adopted, confusion about how the laws will be applied is reduced. Such standardisation leaves a long trail behind them, allowing the effects of their implementation to be easily determined.

86 Ercanbrack, "The Standardization of Islamic Financial Law: Lawmaking in Modern Financial Markets."

Ashgar Ali Ali Mohamed and Muhamad Hassan Ahmad

5 Insubordination in Employment Law: The Common Law and Shari'ah Perspective

5.1 Introduction

In the interest of maintaining industrial harmony and, further, the trust and confidence between the parties to the contract of employment, it is a fundamental obligation for an employee to obey the lawful and reasonable orders or instructions of his superior. In *Laws v London Chronicle (Indicator Newspapers) Ltd*,[1] it was stated, inter alia, that any wilful disobedience of a lawful and reasonable order shows a disregard – a complete disregard – of a condition essential to the contract of service, namely the condition that the servant must obey the proper orders of the master, and that unless he does so the relationship is, so to speak, struck at fundamentally.

Undoubtedly, any refusal or disobedience of an order or instruction of a superior will bring a chaotic situation to any organisation in terms of discipline, performance, as well as industrial peace. The superior order must be lawful and reasonable and not *vice versa*. It is obvious that an employee need not obey the instruction of his superior if the order is manifestly wrong or illegal, such as to falsify the account books or refuse to take an unworthy vehicle onto the road or not covered by third-party insurance, among others. If the employee were to be dismissed merely for his refusal and/or failure to obey an illegal order of the superior, the dismissal would be deemed unlawful and, thus, without just cause and excuse.

It is noteworthy that an employee who defrauds the company, for example, by falsifying the accounts, the figures in the valuation reports, cash bill receipts, forging the signature of the chairman and treasurer, falsifying and manipulating documents, swiping the attendance card on behalf of his superior and divulging the company's business information to a third party without getting authorisation from the company's management are examples of acts of grievous nature and sufficient to warrant his dismissal if found guilty. The integrity of the employee in the above situation is seriously jeopardised as he had breached the very foundation of his employment contract. It would be difficult for any employer to repose trust and confidence in such an employee. Hence, this chapter explores the principle of insubordination in employment law from the common law and Shari'ah perspective with special emphasis on the employee's duty to obey the employer's lawful and reasonable order and instruction and the consequence of its failure therefrom.

1 [1959] 2 All ER 285.

https://doi.org/10.1515/9783110766707-005

5.2 Insubordination: The Common Law Perspective

At common law, the employment relationship is described as a close personal relationship.[2] In a broader sense, it is a relationship of mutual trust and confidence. It is trite law that an employee is expected to faithfully discharge the duties placed on him by the employer, which include the duty to render loyal service to the employer, duty to obey lawful instructions, duty to exert a reasonable degree of competence and skill, duty to protect employer's property, and exercise trust placed on him by the employer.[3] Further, the employee is expected to obey the legitimate directives or orders issued by the superior, provided that such orders are lawful and reasonable, and within the job scope. Failure to carry out a lawful and legitimate instruction would constitute a material or fundamental breach of contract or major misconduct.

In *Clouston & Co v Corry*,[4] Lord Hereford stated: "There is no fixed rule of law defining the degree of misconduct which will justify dismissal. Of course, there may be misconduct in a servant which will not justify the determination of the contract of service by one of the parties to it against the will of the other. On the other hand, misconduct inconsistent with the fulfilment of the express or implied conditions of service will justify dismissal."[5] Again, in *Laws v London Chronicle (Indicator Newspapers) Ltd*,[6] Lord Evershed M.R. stated: "Wilful disobedience of a lawful and reasonable order shows a disregard – a complete disregard – of a condition essential to the contract of service, namely the condition that the servant must obey the proper orders of the master, and that unless he does so the relationship is, so to speak, struck at fundamentally."[7] The propriety of the motive of the employer in giving out the instruction would, under the circumstances, be irrelevant. For example, in *Bouzourou v Ottoman Bank*,[8] a Christian employee was obliged to obey an order to work at a branch in Asia Minor, notwithstanding the well-known hostility of the Turkish Government to his religion.

The emphasis here is that the superior order must be lawful and reasonable. Whether the order of the employer was lawful and reasonable would depend very

---

2 *See Vorvis v Insurance Corporation of British Columbia* (1989) 58 DLR (4th) 193, 224 (SCC).

3 *See* JK Verma, *BR Ghaiye's Misconduct in Employment*(New Delhi: Eastern Book Company, 3rd ed, 2018). In *Kvaerner Petrominco Engineering Sdn Bhd v Virginia Jaqueline Chan* [2007] 1 ILR 494, the Industrial Court stated: "the relationship between an employer and an employee is of a fiduciary character. The employee is required at all times to act in a faithful manner and not to place himself in a position where his interest conflicts with his duties. If the employee does an act which is inconsistent with the fiduciary relationship, then it will be an act of bad faith for which his services can be terminated."

4 [1906] AC 122 (PC).

5 [1906] AC 122 (PC), 129.

6 *See* footnote 1.

7 [1959] 1 WLR 698, 699.

8 [1930] AC 271.

much on the terms and conditions of the contract and the character of employment and is to be determined with reference to the circumstances of the individual case. A dismissal for failure to obey an illegal order is obviously unlawful. In *Morrish v Henlys (Folkestone) Ltd*,[9] refusal to obey the superior order to falsify the account books at the garage where he worked was held not to be in breach of the contract. Again, in *Gregory v Ford*,[10] the refusal of the employee to take on the road a vehicle not covered by third-party insurance was held not to be in breach of the contract. An employee who is sick will only be excused from performing orders rendered impossible by the illness.[11]

Sometimes it would be difficult to decide what constitutes an unreasonable order of the employer. For example, is the employee obliged to obey the superior order to do work outside the strict confines of the contract? While it is accepted that an employee is not obliged to do more than what he/she has contracted to do, the courts seemed to suggest that an employee has a duty to be cooperative; that is, the employee can be expected to do more than the contractual requirement. Thus, refusal to obey the lawful and reasonable orders of the employer, though not being within the scope of his contract, may constitute a fundamental breach.

Having said the above, it is worth reviewing the Federal Court's decision in *Ngeow Voon Yean v Sungei Wang Plaza Sdn Bhd / Landmarks Holdings Bhd*,[12] a locus classicus case of insubordination at common law. In this case, Siti Norma Yaakob FCJ stated that an employee's most fundamental implied duty is to obey his employer's lawful and reasonable orders.

> Working as instructed is the employee's basic consideration under a contract of employment just as providing remuneration is the basic consideration of his employer. However, the employee's duty to comply is confined to all the lawful and reasonable orders of his employer in respect of the performance of such functions that fall within the scope of his contract of employment. Whether the employer's orders are lawful and reasonable would depend very much on the terms and conditions of the contract and the character of employment. The term "lawful and reasonable order" is often used to describe the order given and in this context it means primarily an order which is reasonable within the ambit of the employment in question so that, in any given dispute much or all will depend on the terms of the individual contract of employment. The employer cannot give an order outside the proper scope of the employment.[13]

Her Ladyship further stated:

> The duty of an employee at common law is also similar in that he is to comply with all lawful and reasonable orders given by his employer with respect to the performance of such functions within the scope of his employment. The duty is one of the fundamental obligations which are

9 [1973] ICR 482.

10 [1951] 1 All ER 121.

11 *See Marshall v Alexander Sloan & Co. Ltd.* [1981] IRLR 246.

12 [2006] 5 MLJ 113.

13 [2006] 5 MLJ 123.

> deemed to be impliedly undertaken in every contract of hiring. The duty of obedience at common law is subject to two qualifications, firstly that the employer may not order his employee to do something illegal or secondly order his employee to do anything dangerous. However, it may well be that an employee is caught in the situation that he is required to obey an order and he is doubtful whether the order is legal or not. Under those circumstances, the proper course is for the employee to obey the order first and to challenge its legality in separate proceedings. This distinction is made on the basis that if the law allows the employee to disobey any order he thinks is not legal, it would be impossible for the management to maintain discipline and industrial peace. On the other hand, if the employee takes upon himself to disobey the order which he thinks to be unlawful and unreasonable two courses are open to him. He can point out his difficulties, if any, to the superior and if the latter insists in the order being carried out, he can do the work and take the matter further in proceedings against his employer or to complain to his union. If he disobeys, he must take the risk if the court finds the order to be lawful and reasonable.[14]

Earlier, the Court Appeal had, through the judgment delivered by Richard Malanjum JCA, stated, inter alia, that:

> obedience is expected of an employee where he is in doubt of the legality or reasonableness of an order by a superior. But if it is obvious to an employee that an order given is manifestly wrong and he is very conscious of such fact, we are of the opinion that the general rule should not apply. In such a situation we do not think the issue of fear of dismissal should arise in the mind of the employee for if indeed such an event happens, his rights as an employee is assured.[15]

The Federal Court had, however, disapproved the Court of Appeal's observation. In its response, the Federal Court stated:

> duty of obedience is confined to compliance with the lawful and reasonable orders of an employer and as such the concept of an order being manifestly wrong has no part in the doctrine of superior orders. To that extent, the Court of Appeal erred when it made an exception to disobey the orders of his superior orders when stating that an employee is entitled to disobey the orders of his superior if he, the employee, is aware that such orders are manifestly wrong. However, that exception holds good in military or criminal law as seen from the case of *Public Prosecutor v Tenku Mahmood Iskandar* [1973] 1 MLJ 128 where it was held that "a soldier is not protected where the order is grossly illegal".[16]

The brief facts of *Ngeow Voon Yean*'s case are as follows. The claimant was dismissed from employment on the grounds of misconduct. The allegations against him were related to the misrepresentations in the two deeds of assignment in favour of two banks which stated that the price for all the units had been fully paid when in fact, that was not so. The appellant's contention was that he had endorsed and signed the two deeds of assignment on the instructions of Mr. Simon Chong, the then Executive Director of the respondent, who had assured him that everything was in order and

14 [2006] 5 MLJ 124.

15 *See Ngeow Voon Yean v Sungei Wang Plaza Sdn Bhd & Anor* [2004] 1 MLJ 512, 520–521 (CA).

16 Per Siti Norma Yaakob FCJ, 124.

that he, Mr. Simon Chong, would take the responsibility of collecting the purchase price of the properties sold. In fact, the appellant had inquired about the payment of the 10 percent deposit, and Mr. Simon Chong assured him that he, Mr. Simon Chong, would issue him with a comfort note to ally his fears. The comfort note was in fact, issued by Mr. Simon Chong at the time of the execution of the second sale and purchase agreement. The Industrial Court held in favour of the claimant on the basis that at the time of endorsing the two deeds, the appellant was merely carrying out the orders of his superior, Mr. Simon Chong. The High Court, however, quashed the Industrial Court's award on the ground that the Industrial Court had committed serious errors of law that went to its jurisdiction. The High Court arrived at the decision on the basis that merely carrying out superior orders is not a defence if the orders carried out are to do something illegal or wrongful.[17]

Against the High Court's decision, the appellant appealed to the Court of Appeal. The appeal was, however, dismissed. The appeal court noted that the Industrial Court's finding that had the appellant refused to comply with the instruction of Mr. Simon Chong, would have been an "open defiance of authority and insubordination that could jeopardize his position in the company" was in fact not in tandem with the stand of the appellant namely, that it was not out of fear of losing his job that he endorsed the deeds. The appellant knew that the instructions given were wrong. Nevertheless, he endorsed the two deeds on the instruction and assurance by Mr. Simon Chong that the money would be collected. It was, thus, obvious that the interest of the respondent was never the priority in the mind of the appellant.

Against the Court of Appeal's decision, the appellant appealed to the Federal Court. In allowing the appeal, the court stated that the Court of Appeal, in accepting the conclusion by the High Court, made the same error as the High Court.

> This is borne out by the statement of the Court of Appeal that although the appellant "knew of the true position of the transactions at the material time, he went on to endorse the deeds on the assurance given by his superior Mr Simon Chong". This statement cannot be right as the court alluding to finding based on facts that happened prior to the endorsements of the deeds of assignment to arrive at the conclusion that the appellant had the guilty knowledge at the time the two deeds were endorsed. This conclusion we say is erroneous as the guilty mind that requires to be established must be the guilty mind present at the time of the endorsements of the deeds and not at the time of executions of the two sale and purchase agreements. As I have indicated above, at the time of the endorsements, the Industrial Court had concluded that the appellant was not aware that the purchase price of the properties had been paid in full, a finding of fact, which we are not about to disagree as the evidence support such a finding and we *see* nothing perverse about it to warrant reversing it.[18]

17 *See Sungai Wang Plaza Sdn Bhd / Landmarks Holdings Berhad v Ngeow Voon Yean & Anor* [1997] 1 LNS 370 (HC).

18 Per Siti Norma Yaakob, 122.

As from the above, the Federal Court had declined to interfere with the finding of facts of the Industrial Court that at the time of the endorsements, the appellant was merely carrying out the superior order and that he was not aware that the purchase price of the properties had been paid in full. The Federal Court further added that the guilty mind to be established against two charges levelled on him is the guilty mind at the time of the endorsement of the Deeds of Assignment. The guilty mind at the stage of the execution of the Sales and Purchase Agreement should be disregarded because the charges laid against the claimant were not specifically related to the Sales and Purchase Agreement. The Federal Court had, thus, been careful to preserve the distinction between appeal and review. The duty of a judge in a judicial review application is merely to enquire into the decision-making process to be satisfied as to the correctness, legality, or propriety of any decision recorded or passed and as to the regularity of any proceedings of the Industrial Court.[19]

Although the Federal Court had disapproved the doctrine of manifestly wrong as propounded by the Court of Appeal, nonetheless, this doctrine is implied. This is in line with the Federal Court's view when the court stated: "The duty of obedience at common law is subject to two qualifications, firstly that the employer may not order his employee to do something illegal or secondly order his employee to do anything dangerous." Thus, the superior order must be lawful and reasonable. It cannot be an unlawful or unreasonable act, and therefore, an employee can decline the order if it is manifestly illegal or dangerous.

However, should an employee be caught in a situation where he is doubtful whether the order is legal or not, the proper cause is "for the employee to obey the order first and to challenge its legality in separate proceedings." The reason for this approach is that "if the law allows the employee to disobey any order he thinks is not legal, it would be impossible for the management to maintain discipline and industrial peace." But where an employee takes upon himself to disobey the order which he thinks to be unlawful and unreasonable there are two possible courses open to him. Firstly, the employee "can point out his difficulties, if any, to the superior and if the latter insists in the order being carried out, he [the employee] can do the work and take the matter further in proceedings against his employer or to complain to his union." Secondly, "if he disobeys [and thereby dismissed for insubordination], he must take the risk if the court finds the order to be lawful and reasonable." From the above proposition of law, it would still be possible for an employee to disobey the superior orders which he deemed to be unreasonable or unlawful, and in this situation, he takes the risk if the court were to subsequently find that the order to be lawful and reasonable.

---

19 The recent amendment to the Industrial Relations Act 1967, which came into effect on 1 January 2021, introduced, among others, a new section 33C that provides for an appeal against the Industrial Court award to the High Court.

5.3 Insubordination: The Shari'ah Perspective

In Islam, a worker who has accepted the job should perform his responsibility with honesty, trust, and concentration. He must discharge his duties and responsibility with sincerity, diligently, and with full responsibility. A worker who discharges his responsibility conscientiously shall get double rewards. The Prophet (SAW) was quoted as saying: "God wants that when a man accepts a responsibility he should develop a feeling of conscientiousness."[20] The Prophet (SAW) further stated: "Three kinds of people shall get double rewards. One of them is the worker, who is discharging his responsibilities towards his master and serving God as well."[21] The qualities of honesty, integrity, and accountability which reigned supreme during the tenure of Prophet Muhammad (SAW) has been emphasised in a number of Qur'anic verses as well as in the tradition of Prophet SAW as follows:

> O you who believe! Fear God, and be with those who are true (in word and deeds).[22]
> O you who believe! Keep your duty to Allah and speak straight, true words.[23]
>
> Be maintainers of justice and bearers of true witness for Allah, even if it (the truth) goes against your own selves or parents or relatives or someone who is rich or poor.[24]
>
> Truthfulness leads to righteousness, and righteousness leads to Paradise. In addition, a man keeps on telling the truth until he becomes a truthful person. Falsehood leads to wickedness and evil-doing, and wickedness leads to the (Hell) Fire, and a man may keep on telling lies till he is written before God, as a liar.[25]
>
> Honesty descended from the Heavens and settled in the roots of the hearts of men (faithful believers), and then the Quran was revealed and the people read the Quran, (and learnt it from it) and also learnt from the sayings and traditions. Both the Quran and the traditions strengthened their honesty.[26]
>
> Let he who believes in God and the Last Day either speak good or keep silent.[27]

Further, an employee must not betray the trust placed on them by the employer, such as being incompetent, inefficient, and complacent, nor giving in to their selfish needs like being greedy, unscrupulous, and unproductive. Many verses in the Qur'an[28] and

---

20 *Sahih Bukhari,* Vol 3 Book 46 No 727.
21 *Sahih Bukhari,* Vol 3 Book 46 No 727.
22 *Surah Tauba* (9): 119.
23 *Surah Ahzab* (33): 70.
24 *Surah An-Nisa* (4): 135.
25 *Sahih Al-Bukhari.*
26 *Sahih Muslim.*
27 *Sahih Muslim.*
28 "Allah doth command you to render back your trusts to those to whom they are due; and when ye judge between man and man, that ye judge with justice: verily how excellent is the teaching which He giveth you! For Allah is He who heareth and seeth all things" (*Surah Al Nisa* (4): 58). "O ye who believe! Betray not the trust of Allah and the Messenger nor misappropriate knowingly things entrusted to you" (*Surah Al Anfal* (8): 27). "If one of you deposits a thing on trust with another, let the trustee (faithfully) discharge his trust, and let him fear his Lord. Conceal not evidence;

hadith of the Prophet (SAW)[29] required, inter alia, that a person entrusted with certain duties or obligations must fulfil them regardless of what the situation may be.

> O ye who believe! Fear Allah and be with those who are true (in word and deed).[30]
> O ye who believe! Fulfil (all) obligations.[31]
> Fulfil every engagement, for every engagement will be enquired into, on the day of reckoning.[32]
> Also mentioned in the Book (the story of) Ismail: He was (strictly) true to what he promised, and he was a messenger (and) a prophet.[33]

On the authority of Abu Hurairah, the Prophet (SAW) said: "Hypocrites are known by their characteristics: if he talks he lies, if he promises he fails to keep his promise, and if he is trusted in any matter he proves to be untrustworthy."[34] In another tradition, the Prophet (SAW) said: "If one tells a lie, the angels stay a mile away from him for the rotten he has done."[35]

An untrustworthy or one who does not value *Amanah* is a person who lies when he speaks and the one who promises but never fulfils his promise, and further, he cannot be depended on because he will never deliver. It also encompasses those who do not carry out their promises. Hence, the concept of *Amanah* or trustworthiness implies honesty, compassion, responsibility, and accountability. These are the basic attitudes and approaches towards work. As the Qur'an provides: "And keep the promise; the promise is a responsibility."[36]

Aside from the above, indulging in deception, fraud, cheating, taking part in wrongful or illegal activities, to name but a few, are completely at odds with the Islamic faith. As the Qur'an proclaimed: "Oh ye who believe! Eat not up each other's property by unfair and dishonest means."[37] The involvement in an unethical trade practice, particularly in relation to tampering with measurements and weights, is

for whoever conceals it – His heart is tainted with sin. And Allah knoweth all that ye do" (*Surah Al Baqarah* (2): 283). "Now hath come unto you a clear (sign) from your Lord! Give just measure and weight, not withhold from the people the things that are their due; and do no mischief on the earth after it has been in order: that will be best for you, if ye have faith" (*Surah Al A'raf* (7): 85).

29 Prophet (SAW) stated that: "the hearts of true believers are the repositories of the quality of *amanat*" (*Iman Muslims Sahih)*. The trust held by the person in authority is for the benefit, and in the interests of the general public. Prophet (SAW) was quoted as saying; "God wants that when a man accepts a responsibility he should develop a feeling of conscientiousness" (*Sahih Bukhari*, Vol. 3 Book 46, No 727).

30 *Surah l-Tawbah* (9): 119.

31 *Surah Al Maidah* (5): 1.

32 *Surah Al Isra* (17): 34.

33 *Surah Maryam* (19): 54.

34 *Sahih Muslim* vol. 1 *Kitab Al-Iman*, 40.

35 *Sunan Tirmidhi, Hadith*: 197.

36 *Surah Al Isra* (17): 34.

37 *Surah An-Nisa* (4): 29.

specifically addressed by the Qur'an in *Surah Al Mutaffifin* (those who deal in fraud). A severe warning is given in the verse below to traders who cheat in weight: "Woe to those who deal in fraud, those who, when they have to receive by measure from men, exact full measure, but when they have to give by measure or weight to men give less than due. Do they not think that they will be called to account on a Mighty Day, a Day when (all) mankind will stand before the Lord of the Worlds?"[38]

Hence, neither the employee nor the employer is permitted to indulge in unclean and corrupt means of earning a livelihood, such as dishonest trading, embezzlement, gambling, speculation, and bribery. For example, the Apostle of Allah (SAW) cursed the one who pays bribes and the one who takes bribes.[39] The Prophet (SAW) had also despised those who cheat in business by saying: "He who cheats is not of us. Deceitfulness and fraud are things that lead one to Hell."[40] Again: "Whoever bears arms against us is not one of us, and whoever cheats us is not one of us."[41] The Messenger of Allah had uttered the above words after discovering that some persons were practising fraud, deception, and other dubious means when promoting their merchandise.

In other words, the parties to the employment relationship must be truthful by holding their faith dearer than any worldly gain. The earnings of the employer and employee must be from lawful sources. The unlawful earnings are devoid of *Baraka* (blessing). Abu Sa'eed Al-Khudree said: "The Messenger of Allah SAW delivered a speech to the people in which he said: 'No, By Allah! What I fear for you people is what Allah is going to bring out for you of the beauties of this world'–until he said: 'Whoever takes a wealth rightfully, it will be blessed for him and whoever takes it unlawfully his example is like someone who eats but is never satisfied'."[42] Although today there are many attractive things and different tricky avenues to get unlawful wealth, all this should be avoided by the parties to the contract of employment. As cheating, deception, fraud, gambling, speculation, and bribery, among others, are described as heinous sins, the employer must not compel their workers' to commit such despised acts.

What is apparent from the foregoing discussion with reference to the primary texts of Shari'ah is that an employee must discharge his duties and responsibilities faithfully for the benefit of the employer. He is expected to obey all the lawful and reasonable orders and instructions of the employer so long as they are within his job specification. It is also important to note that an essential characteristic of the Muslim faith is the desire to remove or want to remove evil or wrongdoing in society. It is the duty of every Muslim to correct every other Muslim who violated the commands of

---

38 *Surah Al-Mutaffifin* (83): 1–6.
39 *Sunan Abu Dawud.*
40 *Sahih Muslim.*
41 *Sahih Muslim.*
42 *Sahih Al-Bukhari* and *Sahih Muslim.*

Allah (SWT) and His Prophet (SAW). There are many verses that speak of enjoining what is good and forbidding what is evil.

> The believers, men and women, are *Awliyaa'* (helpers, supporters, friends, protectors) of one another; they enjoin (on the people) *Al-Ma'roof* (i.e. Islamic Monotheism and all that Islam orders one to do), and forbid (people) from *Al-Munkar* (i.e. polytheism and disbelief of all kinds, and all that Islam has forbidden).[43]
>
> Let there arise out of you a group of people inviting to all that is good (Islam), enjoining *Al-Ma'roof* (i.e. Islamic Monotheism and all that Islam orders one to do) and forbidding *Al-Munkar* (polytheism and disbelief and all that Islam has forbidden).[44]
>
> You (true believers in Islamic Monotheism, and real followers of Prophet Muhammad and his Sunnah) are the best of peoples ever raised up for mankind; you enjoin *Al-Ma'roof* (i.e. Islamic Monotheism and all that Islam has ordained) and forbid *Al-Munkar* (polytheism, disbelief and all that Islam has forbidden).[45]

The Prophet (SAW) said: "Whoever of you sees evil action, let him change it with his hand (by taking action); and if he is not able to do so, then with his tongue (by speaking out); and if he is not able to do so, then with his heart (by at least hating it and believing that it is wrong) – and that is the weakest of faith."[46] The above *hadith* outlines the way a Muslim employee should respond to wrongdoings or evil action in their organisation, namely: (i) Let him change it (i.e. the evil) with his hand (by taking action); (ii) If he cannot change the evil with his hands such as by taking appropriate action, then with his tongue (by speaking out); and (iii) And if he cannot (i.e. do either of the above), then with his heart – and that is the weakest of faith.

The command in the above *hadith* "whoever of you" is directed to each and every Muslim. Everyone has an obligation to forbid evil if they have the means to do so, and this would include the employee. However, "removing it" would depend on one's ability to do so. It should be done by the hand, if at all possible, and if not, then by the tongue or speech. If neither of the above two means is possible, then the last option is to hate the action with one's heart.

Obviously, the people in a position of authority over others, such as the head of the organisation have special responsibilities to forbid evil because they can remove it by enacting rules and imposing sanctions that would keep those under their care away from committing the evil. If one is not able to do it with his hand, the next level is to try removing it with their tongue. When the person is powerless to change an evil action or wrongdoings by his hand or tongue, he must denounce and detest the evil action in his heart. Preferably also that he must keep away from the places where that sin is being committed. Allah (SWT) says in the Glorious Qur'an:

---

43 *Surah al-Tawbah* 9:71.

44 *Surah al-'Imraan* 3:104.

45 *Surah al-'Imraan* 3:110.

46 An-Nawawi, *Forty Hadith* at 110.

> And when you (Muhammad) *see* those who engage in a false conversation about Our Verses (of the Qur'an) by mocking at them, stay away from them till they turn to another topic. And if *Shaitaan* (Satan) causes you to forget, then after the remembrance sit not you in the company of those people who are the *Zalimun* (polytheists and wrongdoers).[47]
>
> And it has already been revealed to you in the Book (this Qur'an) that when you hear the Verses of Allah being denied and mocked at, then sit not with them, until they engage in a talk other than that; (but if you stayed with them) certainly in that case you would be like them. Surely, Allah will collect the hypocrites and disbelievers all together in Hell.[48]

As from the above *hadith*, Islam allows a person to disclose the sin of others if the person has devoured or attempts to devour the property of another through illegal ways. Disclosure is also allowed if a fellow worker or the employer committed wrongdoings that affect the right of other persons. The purpose or wisdom behind the disclosure is to prevent the person from either committing the act or to correct the wrongdoings or misconduct. This principle is in line with the verse 104 in *Surah al Imran*, where Allah (SWT) says: "Let there arise out of you a band of people inviting to all that is good, enjoining what is right, and forbidding what is wrong: They are the ones to attain felicity."

The above verse explains that it is a duty of a Muslim to promote what is right and true and to forbid any wrong committed by others. A Muslim who stops enjoining the good and eradicating the evil, even though he has the ability to do so, would be answerable for his omission in the hereafter. The Prophet (SAW) said: "There is no people among which evil is committed and they have the ability to change that but they do not change it, except that Allah will soon afflict them with a punishment that will affect them all."[49] In another *hadith*, the Prophet SAW said: "By the One in whose hand is my soul, you must order the good and forbid evil or Allah will soon send upon you a punishment from Himself and then you supplicate to Him and He will not respond to you."[50] Based on the above *hadiths*, the eradication of evil is the duty of every Muslim who obeys Allah, detests all evil actions or conduct that Allah hates or dislikes, and has compassion for fellow Muslims in trying to guide them to what is good and forbidding evil. In other words, an employee can refuse to obey the superior order when he reasonably believes that the order or instructions of the employer are illegal, wrong, or violate the rights of others, among others.

It is worth adding that in Islam, a Muslim believes in life after death and that life in this world is only temporary, thus striving for the betterment in the hereafter is essential. Allah (SWT) proclaimed in the Qur'an: "Verily Allah has purchased from the believers their lives and their wealth in exchange for *Jannat* (ie the infinitely more

47 *Surah al-An'aam* 6: 68.
48 *Surah al-Nisaa'* 4: 140.
49 *Sunnan* Abu Da'ud.
50 *Musnad* of Ahmad Ibn Hanbal.

beautiful life yet to come)."[51] "Allah will not call you to account for what is futile in your oaths, but He will call you to account for your deliberate oaths."[52]

Therefore, Muslims are expected to keep to their solemn oath to the utmost of a person's ability. Allah (SWT) proclaimed: "And make not Allah's (name) an excuse in your oaths against doing good, or acting rightly, or making peace between person; for Allah is One who heareth and knoweth all things."[53] Further, Allah (SWT) has ordained believers to have faith and do good deeds. "And He will test you, which of you are best in actions."[54] Further, a Muslim's dealings are always with Allah (SWT), who sees him at all times and in all places. A person may hide from the whole world but not from Allah (SWT). Again, he may deceive everyone but cannot deceive Allah (SWT). In the same vein, he can flee from the clutches of anyone else but not from Allah (SWT). Thus, whatever man does in this life, he cannot escape from the fact that one day he will die and be compelled to account for what has passed. On that day, there will be no advocating, no favour, no impartiality, fraud, and deception, and justice will be done.

> O my son! (said Luqman), if there be (but) the weight of a mustard seed and it were (hidden) in a rock, or (anywhere) in the heavens or on earth Allah will bring it forth: for Allah understands the finer mysteries (and) is well-acquainted (with them).[55]
>
> It was We who created man, and We know what dark suggestions his soul makes to him: for We are nearer to him than his jugular vein. Behold, two (guardian angels) appointed to learn (his doings) one sitting on the right and one on the left. Not a word does he utter but here is a sentinel by him, ready (to note it).[56]
>
> And the Book (of deeds) will be placed (before you) and thou wilt *see* the sinful in great terror because of what is (recorded) therein; they will say, "Ah! Woe to us! What a book is this! It leaves out nothing small or great, but takes account thereof!" they will find all that they did, placed before them: and not one will thye Lord treat with injustice.[57]

In other words, Muslims believe that their salvation depends on the performance of good deeds and the observance of the laws enunciated by Allah (SWT) and Prophet (SAW). God-consciousness and piety make a believer do what pleases Him and refrain from what displeases Him. Allah (SWT) proclaimed in the Qur'an that He would judge human beings not by what they possess but on the basis of their belief and righteous conduct. For example, in *Surah Al Baqarah* (2): 62: "Any who believes in Allah and the Last Day, and works righteousness, shall have their reward with their Lord; on them shall be no fear, nor shall they grieve." In the Farewell Sermon, Prophet (SAW) reminded the Muslims by stating: "Remember one day you will meet

---

51 *Surah At-Taubah* (9): 111.
52 *Surah Al Maidah* (5): 89.
53 *Surah Al Baqarah* (2): 224.
54 *Surah Al Mulk* (67): 2.
55 *Surah Luqman* (31): 16.
56 *Surah Qaf* (50): 16–18.
57 *Surah Al Kahf* (19): 49.

Allah and answer your deeds. So beware do not go astray from the path of righteousness after I am gone."[58]

5.4 Conclusion

As seen from the foregoing discussion, it is obvious that both at common law and Shari'ah an employee has a duty to obey the superior order so long as they are lawful and reasonable. At common law, the employee's duty to obey the superior order was clearly outlined by the Malaysian Federal Court in *Ngeow Voon Yean*'s case. This duty, however, is subject to two qualifications, namely that the employer may not order his employee firstly, to do something illegal and secondly, anything dangerous. An employee who is caught in a situation where he is doubtful whether the order is legal or not, the proper cause for him is to obey the order first and thereafter to challenge or raise the matter with the management on its legality. The reason for this approach is that if the law allows the employee to disobey any order he thinks is not legal, it would be impossible for the management to maintain discipline and industrial peace. But if the employee is dismissed for his refusal to obey an order which is manifestly illegal or dangerous, the dismissal would be deemed unlawful and, thus, warrants the court's intervention to set aside the dismissal.

On the other hand, the Shari'ah contains explicit ruling on this subject which is derived from the Quran and Sunnah of the Prophet (SAW). As noted in the earlier discussion, the religion commands a Muslim to perform his duties and responsibilities with honesty, trust, and concentration. He must not betray the trust placed on him by the employer, for example, being incompetent, inefficient, and complacent, nor should he give in to his selfish needs like being greedy, unscrupulous, and unproductive, among others. Further, he is not supposed to condone or support illegal activity or anything contrary to religious doctrine in the workplace. In fact, he must have the desire to remove or want to remove evil or wrongdoing in the workplace and beyond that violates the commands of Allah SWT and His Prophet SAW. He is commanded to promote goodness (*amru bil maaruf*) and forbid wrongdoing (*wal nahyi anil munkar*). Hence, wrongdoings in the workplace such as dishonesty, misuse of company's property, workplace violence, and conflict of interest, among others, are conducts that are abhorred and must be eliminated. It ought not to be followed by the employee even if the order is from the superior, but its disclosure to the enforcement authority is an obligation imposed on every Muslim. Those who clearly abandoned the duty of forbidding evil or *munkar* in their organisation will be answerable for their omission in the hereafter as the Prophet SAW said: "You

58 *See* "The Farewell Sermon of the Prophet Muhammad (PBUH)," accessed March 24, 2022, https://humanappeal.org.uk/news/2020/07/the-farewell-sermon-of-the-prophet-muhammad-pbuh.

must command the good, forbid evil and prevent injustice, otherwise you will incur Allah's wrath."[59] As a final remark, it would be worthwhile to reflect on the Hadith of the Prophet (SAW) reported by Abdullah bin Abbas where the Messenger of Allah (SAW) said that Allah, the Glorious, said:

> Verily, Allah (SWT) has ordered that the good and the bad deeds be written down. Then He explained it clearly how (to write): He who intends to do a good deed but he does not do it, then Allah records it for him as a full good deed, but if he carries out his intention, then Allah the Exalted, writes it down for him as from ten to seven hundred folds, and even more. But if he intends to do an evil act and has not done it, then Allah writes it down with Him as a full good deed, but if he intends it and has done it, Allah writes it down as one bad deed.[60]

59 *Sunnan Abu Da'ud.*
60 *Sahih Bukhari and Muslim.*

Elsa Satkunasingam

6 Tabung Haji: A Missed Opportunity to Display Good Corporate Governance of an Islamic Institution?

6.1 Introduction

As the sole agency in charge of hajj operations in Malaysia, Lembaga Tabung Haji (TH) is perceived by Muslims and non-Muslims as the epitome of how an Islamic institution should be managed. However, the alleged mismanagement of TH's resources and the accounting irregularities resulting in a restructuring exercise to dispose of non-performing assets has damaged TH's reputation. This chapter examines the alleged mismanagement in TH, the changes from the subsequent restructuring exercise, and whether these will be lasting changes if the board and management do not uphold TH's operational independence and protect it from any type of external interference. The lessons in this chapter can be extended to any public sector institution regardless of whether it is secular or Islamic. This chapter will also demonstrate how principles of good governance are universal and do not require any harmonisation of common law and Islamic law.

6.2 Formation of Lembaga Tabung Haji

TH was established to enable Malaysian Muslims to deposit their savings to perform the hajj in Mecca. There was a general reluctance among Muslims in the first half of the twentieth century to place their savings in financial institutions due to the payment of *riba* (interest). This caused many Muslims to save incrementally for their pilgrimage by keeping cash under their pillows or mattresses or, at times, selling a few possessions in order to finance the trip.[1] Performing the hajj is one of the five pillars of Islam, but it is only a requirement for people who have the financial means to do so. Nevertheless, there were instances of Muslims in Malaysia getting into debt after performing the hajj as they had borrowed money for the trip.[2]

The concept of savings account for pilgrims that would enable them to save towards the hajj and increase their savings through investments was first mooted by

1 Joni Tamkin Borhan and Che Zarrina Sa'ari, "The Role of Tabung Haji as a Deposit Mobiliser of Muslims in Malaysia, 1969–1990: A Historical Approach," *Jurnal Al-Tamaddun* 1 (2005): 215.
2 Zainal Abidin Abd Wahid, Yusof Ibrahim, and Mohd Amin Hassan, *Sejarah Perkembangan Tabung Haji Malaysia: 30 Tahun* (Kuala Lumpur: Jabatan Perdana Menteri, 1993).

https://doi.org/10.1515/9783110766707-006

Royal Professor Ungku Abdul Aziz. He proposed an institution that would accept deposits from Muslims towards the hajj and share profits with the depositors, a practice which is permitted in Islam compared to *riba*, which is prohibited. The Pilgrims' Savings Corporation (as it was known) was first established in 1962 and subsequently merged with the Pilgrims Affairs Office which had been established in 1952 in Penang to form the Lembaga Urusan dan Tabung Haji under the Pilgrims Management and Fund Board Act 1969.[3] This was subsequently repealed by the Tabung Haji Act 1995 (Tabung Haji Act).

TH enabled Muslims to save in order to be able to perform the hajj, to participate in investments according to Islamic principles, and provided protection, control and welfare for Malaysian Muslims during the performance of the hajj. TH used the *wadiah yad dhamanah* (safe keeping with guarantee) principle, where the safety of depositors' savings is guaranteed by TH (through a government guarantee) as the custodian. TH has since 2019 used the *wadiah* principle (*wadiah al wakalah*) to invest depositors' savings into Shari'ah-compliant businesses. Profit is not guaranteed, but any profit from these investments will be distributed among depositors through bonuses or dividends.[4]

6.3 Key Provisions in the Tabung Haji Act 1995

TH is entrusted with powers to administer the fund and to administer all matters, including formulating policies concerning the welfare of the pilgrims. TH may enter into partnerships or joint ventures for profit sharing and may acquire or sell shares or securities. It may also establish a company to carry out its projects.[5] This provision empowers TH to invest and manage the pilgrims' deposits.

TH's Board of Directors comprises two *ex officio* members, namely a representative from the Prime Minister's Department and a representative from the Treasury, a chairman, and not more than seven (7) directors, appointed by the Minister.[6] The *ex officio* directors' appointment is to enable them to oversee the management of TH as an investment fund of public importance. The directors are not entitled to remuneration but may be paid an honorarium and travelling and subsistence allowances as determined by the Minister.[7]

3 Act No. 8 of 1969.
4 "Wakalah FAQ," Tabung Haji, accessed April 14, 2022, https://www.tabunghaji.gov.my/en/soalan-lazim-wakalah.
5 Tabung Haji Act 1995, s 4.
6 Tabung Haji Act 1995, s 6.
7 Tabung Haji Act 1995, s 7.

The directors, any committee member, officer, servant, or agent would not be personally liable for any loss or damage caused by their act or omission in carrying out their powers and duties unless it was caused by an intentionally wrongful act or omission on his part.[8] This protects the directors and employees of TH from legal action by depositors if there are losses from any investments or other losses such as injury or illness suffered by pilgrims when they are performing the hajj or umrah. However, directors and employees that have intentionally committed wrongful acts or omissions will not be protected by this provision.

While TH has an investment committee, it cannot exercise powers of investment without the approval of the Minister.[9] In relation to investments, TH has the absolute discretion to determine whether it is prudent to declare profits and, with the Minister's approval, to declare the sum of distributable profit in respect of the financial year. However, the Tabung Haji Act also lays down several conditions before profits can be declared. Among these are that the assets of TH must not be less than the aggregate liabilities of the fund, amounts due to depositors being calculated as if immediately payable.[10]

6.4 Financial Position Prior to the Restructuring Exercise

In December 2015, the Governor of Bank Negara Malaysia (BNM) wrote to TH to highlight that its reserves levels were in the negative. The Governor also highlighted that TH had only 98 sen in assets for every ringgit in liability which would hamper its ability to pay bonuses and dividends unless it liquidated its assets within a short period to pay the depositors. In all likelihood, this would mean liquidating the assets at a discount. TH had been paying out dividends of 6 percent to 6.5 percent, with a bonus ranging from 2 percent to 2.5 percent since 2011. The letter from BNM also highlighted that TH's deposits were concentrated among a small number of depositors as 5 percent of depositors contributed 75 percent of the total deposits.[11] One

8 Tabung Haji Act 1995, s 43.
9 Tabung Haji Act 1995, s 20.
10 Tabung Haji Act 1995, s 22.
11 The Malaysian Insider, "Tabung Haji Reserves in the Red, Warns Bank Negara," *The Edge Markets*, January 26, 2016, https://www.theedgemarkets.com/article/tabung-haji-reserves-red-warns-bank-negara.

depositor had RM190 million deposited in TH.[12] This made TH particularly vulnerable to risks associated with mass withdrawals.[13]

While the letter was not officially made public, it was leaked to the media. BNM subsequently, without any specific reference to TH, issued a statement that as part of its mandate to promote financial stability, it undertook surveillance on significant non-bank financial institutions that had important linkages with the financial system, and issued advice as a pre-emptive measure to promote the financial stability of such institutions and to avoid any systemic implication to the financial system.[14]

There were also concerns expressed by depositors and the public over some of TH's transactions, namely its decision in 2015 to purchase 0.64 hectares of land in the area known as Tun Razak Exchange (TRX) from 1MDB Malaysia Berhad (1MDB) at a price that was 43 times higher than the price that 1MDB paid when the company purchased it from the Federal Government in 2011.[15] The actual price paid was not clear as the Chief Executive Officer of TH stated that it had paid RM188.5 million for one plot of land at a discounted price and that the value of the land was based on an independent professional valuer's opinion, while politicians from the opposition stated that two plots of land had been purchased at RM772 million.[16] TH did not clarify its financial position in this matter in its 2015 Annual Report except to state that it had been heavily criticised by various quarters who had misinterpreted its actions and been misinformed about its activities. The lack of clarification was a missed opportunity to be transparent and earn public trust.

As a result of public discussions and questions from members of the opposition, TH reduced its dividend payouts to 5 percent for Financial Year Ended (FYE) 2015 but increased the hajj bonus payments from 2 percent in 2014 to 3 percent in 2015. The hajj bonus payments are only made to depositors who have not performed the haj.[17] Profits for FYE 2016 increased to 5.75 percent, and payments for FYE 2017, which were paid out as usual in March 2018, just before the 14th General Election, amounted to 6.25 percent, comprising 4.5 percent of dividends and 1.75 percent of hajj bonus payments.

The Auditor General's Report on TH's Financial Statements for FYE ended 31st December 2017 issued in July 2018 noted under "Emphasis of Matter" (EOM)

---

12 Farhan Gazi, "Tabung Haji Found to Have Been Illegally Paying Out Dividends," *imoney*, December 11, 2018, https://www.imoney.my/articles/tabung-haji-found-illegally-paying-dividends.

13 It should be noted that financial institutions with a similar profile would be categorised as high risk.

14 Bank Negara Malaysia, "*Surveillance of Non-Bank Financial Institutions,*" January 26, 2016, https://www.bnm.gov.my/-/surveillance-of-non-bank-financial-institutions.

15 Ram Anand, "TH Still Evaluating Offers for TRX Land, Says Chairman," *The Malaysian Insider*, July 28, 2015, https://www3.theedgemarkets.com/article/tabung-haji-still-evaluating-offers-trx-land-says-chairman.

16 Ram Anand, "Tabung Haji Admits to Land Deal with 1MDB," *The Malaysian Insider*, May 7, 2015, https://www.theedgemarkets.com/article/tabung-haji-admits-land-deal-1mdb.

17 Notes to the Financial Statements in Lembaga Tabung Haji, *Annual Report 2015:* 327.

that the Impairment Policy for TH's Financial Assets was inconsistent. There had been annual changes to the impairment policy, particularly in 2017, when the policy had been changed twice. The Auditor General also indicated that based on paragraph 8 of the Malaysian Financial Reporting Standards 136 – Impairment of Assets, provisions for impairment should be made if the carrying amount of the investments exceeded the recoverable amount. For FYE 31st December 2017, TH had not recorded impairment of RM227.81 million against investments in three associates and three subsidiaries, particularly in TH Heavy Engineering Berhad where impairment was RM164.58 million.[18]

A subsequent report by an independent auditor, PriceWaterhouseCoopers (PwC), entitled "Financial Position Review of TH" tabled in Parliament on 10 December 2018, indicated that TH had total assets of RM70.3 billion against RM74.4 billion in liabilities for FYE 2017. TH had in the Notes to the Financial Statements in its Annual Reports over past years, indicated that it had used the Financial Reporting Standards (FRS) framework.[19] However, according to PwC's report,[20] TH had not complied with the FRS in several instances by manipulating thresholds for impairments as noted in the Auditor General's report and also by selling and buying shares to show a profit that would enable TH to pay out profits to depositors.

Asset management fund entities and financial institutions deem a decline in fair value of investments below 20 percent of the original cost or a decline in fair value below the original cost for a period of more than nine to twelve months as significant impairment. TH did not disclose that it had departed from this practice and adopted a threshold of 70 percent decline in fair value of investments before recording it as an impairment. In 2017, TH, as indicated under the EOM in the Auditor General (AG)'s report, changed this threshold to 85 percent and subsequently to 90 percent. No explanation was provided for the original threshold, which went against market practice, or the subsequent changes in the threshold.

If TH had kept to its original threshold of 70 percent, the impairment loss impact reported would have been RM1.313 billion. If the threshold had remained at 85 percent, the impairment loss impact would have been RM171 million, whereas, at a threshold of 90 percent, the impairment loss impact was RM1 million. Had TH kept to the market practice of a threshold of 20 percent below market cost, the impairment loss impact would have been RM4.258 billion, and when offset against

18 Report of the Auditor General on the Financial Statements of Lembaga Tabung Haji for the Year Ended 31 December 2017.

19 Note 2(a) Statement on Compliance states that the financial statements of the Group and TH have been prepared in accordance with Financial Reporting Standards ("FRS") issued by the Malaysian Accounting Standards Board ("MASB") for entities other than private entities, modified to comply with Shari'ah principles and requirements.

20 "Azeez Insists on Tabung Haji Surplus, But Doesn't Reveal Creative Accounting," *Malaysiakini*, December 11, 2018, https://www.malaysiakini.com/news/455691.

retained earnings of RM162 million, the adjusted accumulated losses would have been RM4.096 billion. As these were material amounts, the AG should have issued a qualified opinion instead of an EOM. TH had also sold some of its shareholdings in BIMB Holdings Berhad (BIMB) for RM2.551 billion, which permitted it to record RM553 million as revenue. However, the shares were re-purchased from BIMB at a price of RM2.688 billion four days later from the same brokers.[21] This is tantamount to false trading or market rigging, which is an offence.[22] The sales and purchase of shares were not disclosed in TH's Group Financial Statements, which was contrary to the requirements in paragraph 18 of FRS 12.

TH's actions were taken to enable it to pay out profits. TH was noted for paying out high profits to depositors, which is one of the reasons why depositors preferred to place their savings with TH instead of other Islamic financial institutions which are subject to stricter supervision by BNM. The initial purpose of TH, which was to assist depositors to save and earn profits towards the costs of performing the hajj, has been subsumed under a different purpose which is to make investments that guarantee high profits.[23]

6.5 The Restructuring Exercise

The Government formulated a restructuring and rehabilitation plan in 2018 for TH, as the loss in investment and high impairment would continue if action was not taken, and this could impact the stability of the financial system. The purpose of the plan was to ensure that TH's liabilities did not exceed the value of its assets and that problematic and low-yielding assets would be isolated from TH's balance sheet.

A Government-owned Special Purpose Vehicle (SPV) company known as Urusharta Jamaah Sdn. Bhd (UJSB) was established, and TH's underperforming assets were transferred to UJSB. These comprised shares in 106 listed companies, one unlisted plantation where unrealised losses were greater than 20 percent or there was significant impairment, and twenty-nine properties and lands that generated less than 2 percent returns. The amount transferred to UJSB was assets with fair value of RM9.73 billion at a premium of RM10.17 billion, resulting in a transfer price of RM19.9 billion. UJSB issued *sukuk* to TH in two (2) tranches. The first tranche comprised RM10 billion zero coupon *sukuk* with nominal value of RM13.2 billion over a

21 PwC's Report as sighted in Malaysiakini indicated that the shares were re-purchased four days after the sale and the entire transaction had been entered into to recognise profits to meet the profit distribution targets for 2017.

22 Capital Markets and Services Act 2007, s 175(3).

23 Nur Hasnida Abdul Rahman, Fatimah Noor Rashidah, Mohd Sofian, Fadhilah Abdullah Asuhaimi and Farihana Shahari, "A Conceptual Model of Depositors' Trust and Loyalty on Hajj Institution – Case of Lembaga Tabung Haji Malaysia," *International Review of Management and Marketing* 10, no. 1 (2020): 99.

seven (7) year period with yield-to-maturity of 4.05 percent, and the second tranche comprised RM9.6 billion zero coupon *sukuk* with nominal value of RM14.3 billion over a 10-year period with yield-to-maturity of 4.10 percent. The *sukuk* was entirely subscribed by TH and was non-transferable with no secondary market value.

The Government had committed to set aside funding of RM500 million in 2020 and a sum of RM1.73 billion annually from 2021 onwards to UJSB for the purpose of repayment of the *sukuk*. UJSB could redeem the *sukuk* by way of cash payment and/or by transfer to TH of the transferred assets and/or any other assets to be mutually agreed upon between UJSB and TH. The redemption sum was an equivalent value to 100 percent of the outstanding nominal value of the *sukuk*. In addition, TH was also given the First Right of Refusal to take over any assets that had been transferred to UJSB should UJSB intend to sell those assets. This enabled TH to protect its interest if the assets recovered their value. TH would only take over recoverable and viable assets that would generate higher expected returns than its target investment return.[24]

The restructuring exercise placed TH's financials in a healthy position as its total assets stood at RM76.5 billion with liabilities of RM75.5 billion as at 31st December 2018. It had offloaded non-performing assets to UJSB and recorded revenue from the *sukuk*. However, it also had to recognise impairments of RM1.5 billion for FYE 31 December 2018.

6.6 Reducing Moral Hazard

The offloading of non-performing assets to an SPV is not unusual. Such measures are usually taken to prevent a systemic failure in the financial system. For example, an asset management company (AMC) may be established to take over non-performing assets to dispose or restructure those assets. Most AMCs established during the Asian Financial Crisis in 1998 were centralised and backed by government guarantees, which allowed them to purchase or take over non-performing assets, which in turn allowed financial institutions to have a healthier balance sheet. This contributed to maintaining the stability of the financial system. AMCs may pay above-market value to acquire assets if they are of the view that these assets will increase in value over time, while at other times, assets are acquired at a discount.

A prominent example of an AMC in Malaysia is Pengurusan Danaharta Nasional Berhad (Danaharta), a statutory body established under the Danaharta Act 1998 to deal with non-performing assets from financial institutions. Danaharta applied certain pricing models when acquiring loans. The price of secured loans was determined by referring to the value of the collateral. In cases where the collateral was property, the acquisition price was 95 percent of the property's market value as determined by an independent professional valuer. If the collateral was in the form of equities, the

24 Tabung Haji's Annual Report 2018, 38–42 and Tabung Haji's Annual Report 2019, 31.

price was based on the shares' market or net tangible asset value. Unsecured loans were purchased at 10 percent of the outstanding loan amount. Surplus recovery of these loans in excess of the purchase price and holding costs was shared at a ratio of 80:20 between the financial institution and Danaharta, with the amount receivable by the financial institution capped at the shortfall value. In this way, Danaharta not only "persuaded" financial institutions to sell their unsecured loans but shared the recovery amount with them.[25]

Danaharta's business model showed that it applied price discounts when it took over non-performing assets. Financial institutions had to bear losses ranging from 5 percent to 90 percent depending upon the type of collateral backing the loans and Danaharta's ability to obtain payment from borrowers. This reduced some of the moral hazard as the financial institutions had to be accountable for engaging in high-risk transactions. If the financial institutions had been permitted to transfer their losses to AMCs without any impact on them, there would have been no incentive for them to change their lending practices or manage their risks adequately.

Perbadanan Insurans Deposit Malaysia (PIDM), which insures deposits of individual depositors in its member financial institutions up to a maximum of RM 250,000 per account,[26] also works on the principle of reducing moral hazard. Financial institutions are required to pay an annual premium to PIDM based on the risk categories in which they have been classified under premium regulations.[27] This is dependent on criteria that comprises factors relating to the capital, profitability and asset quality, concentration, and growth of a financial institution, and among other things, BNM's supervisory rating of that financial institution. Financial institutions classified as high risk will have to pay higher premiums to PIDM than those classified as lower risk.[28] The premiums from all financial institutions (and insurance and takaful companies) are kept in a fund that is managed by PIDM and will be used to pay depositors in the event of failure of a financial institution.

The Tabung Haji Act has also incorporated the moral hazard principle by stating that any payment out of the Consolidated Fund is a debt by TH to the Government.[29] However, the restructuring exercise in TH was handled differently. The fair value of TH's non-performing assets amounted to RM9.73 billion. The transfer price was RM19.9 billion resulting in a premium of RM10.17 billion to TH. The Government and TH did not explain how they arrived at the transfer price and whether the price was based on the projected

25 Thomas Mathew, "Managing Turbulent Times, A Malaysian Experience," *Association of Professional Bankers, Sri Lanka*, 2008, https://apbsrilanka.com/wp-content/uploads/2021/01/2008_20th_conv_a_12_Thomas_Mathews.pdf.

26 Deposits in TH are not covered by PIDM.

27 PIDM Act 2011 (Amended 2022), ss 47, 48 and 49.

28 Malaysia Deposit Insurance Corporation (Differential Premium Systems in Respect of Deposit-Taking Members) Regulations 2011.

29 Tabung Haji Act 1995, s 24(2).

value of the transferred assets at the maturity period of the *sukuk*. Without such explanations, it would appear that the transfer price was fixed solely to resolve TH's liabilities. For example, the TRX land had a book value of RM196,096,930 million but was transferred at RM400,000,000. Land in Klebang Melaka with a book value of RM48,000,000 was transferred at RM72,947,169. A commercial building in Platinum Park with a book value of RM485,810,740 million was transferred at RM737,399,698 million, and another commercial building in Kota Bharu Kelantan with a book value of RM10,500,000 million was sold at RM15,957,193 million.[30]

Table 6.1 shows the difference in book value and transfer value for a selection of TH's investments in equities that were transferred to UJSB.

Table 6.1: Premiums for Equities.[31]

Description	Number of Shares	Book Value (RM)	Transfer Value (RM)
Adventa Berhad	14,335,900	6,236,117	38,787,042
Ahmad Zaki Resources	21,766,700	6,638,844	21,776,831
Alam Maritim	91,965,700	7,357,256	111,224,108
Bintulu Port	17,000,000	76,500,000	111,872,988
Bonia Corporation	18,749,300	4,124,846	17,755,445
Brahim Holdings	45,553,450	12,754,966	83,605,981
Bumi Armada	51,962,800	8,054,234	115,248,112
Dayang Enterprise	76,367,600	41,238,504	202,233,786
Felda Global Ventures Holdings Bhd	283,710,100	202,852,722	1,310,020,819
Icon Offshore Bhd	103,611,268	7,252,789	139,003,037
Ikhmas Jaya Group Bhd	24,261,700	2,426,170	17,046,476
Integrated Logistic Bhd (NS)	20,584,783	9,571,924	34,646,882
Lafarge Malaysia Berhad	13,450,100	24,344,681	83,867,207
Lion Industries Corporation Bhd	44,026,800	22,013,400	71,991,567
MCT Bhd	133,480,000	99,442,600	170,854,400
Mudajaya Group Bhd	53,865,500	15,620,995	154,947,016
NAIM Holdings Bhd	24,827,200	11,048,104	78,271,318
Parkson Holdings Bhd	105,908,219	25,947,514	331,645,737
Pelikan International Corporation Bhd	157,185,498	54,228,997	329,489,901
Puncak Niaga Holdings Bhd	44,073,600	15,425,760	139,266,369
Sapura Energy Bhd	120,428,700	34,924,323	212,660,769
Scomi Energy Services Bhd	108,317,600	4,332,704	87,123,728
Star Media Group Bhd	39,806,300	27,267,316	125,679,749
TH Heavy Engineering Bhd	334,162,107	10,024,863	380,349,719
TSR Capital Bhd	16,926,500	5,924,275	22,613,657

30 "Tabung Haji Assets Transferred at Double Its Worth to Government," *Malaysiakini*, March 15, 2019, https://www.malaysiakini.com/news/468076.

31 The full list of equities can be obtained at Malaysiakini, "Tabung Haji Assets Transferred at Double Its Worth to Government".

Table 6.1 (continued)

Description	Number of Shares	Book Value (RM)	Transfer Value (RM)
UZMA Bhd	26,263,200	15,101,340	66,694,838
Velesto Energy Bhd	410,247,380	73,844,528	289,075,730
Wah Seong Corporation Bhd	15,733,700	9,990,900	25,934,641
WCT Holdings Bhd	118,655,900	80,092,733	240,692,475
WTK Holdings Bhd	8,949,700	3,848,371	28,356,507
WZ Satu Bhd	43,498,672	8,264,748	33,214,351
YLI Holdings Bhd	9,312,300	1,909,022	30,575,371

6.7 Governance Issues as a Result of the Restructuring Exercise

6.7.1 Sharing of Risk

The manner in which TH offloaded underperforming assets raises some questions about whether it practised the concept of risk-sharing, which is one of the cornerstones of Islamic finance. It is unclear how TH justified protecting itself from the risk of further depreciation of the transferred assets while benefiting through the first right of refusal from any appreciation of the assets, in light of the Islamic legal maxim, which states that there is no reward without risk (*al-ghorm bil ghonm*).[32] As a result of the restructuring exercise, TH not only managed to have a healthy balance sheet but is also entitled to the nominal value of both tranches of the *sukuk* upon maturity amounting to RM27.5 billion, which is far higher than the book value of RM9.73 billion. Did TH bear any of the risk when it transferred its losses to UJSB? Has this increased the moral hazard in relation to TH?

The huge discrepancy in the transfer value compared to the book value in some of these underperforming assets, as shown in Table 6.1, makes it unlikely that UJSB will benefit from these assets. For example, UJSB obtained 334,162,107 shares in TH Heavy Engineering (THHE) with a book value of RM 10,024,863 million, while the transfer value was RM380,349,719 million. This represents a premium of almost 3700 percent, although THHE was classified as a PN17 company at that time.[33]

32 Obiyathulla Ismath Bacha and Daud Vicary Abdullah, "The Risk Sharing Philosophy of Islamic Finance," *SEACEN Financial Stability Journal* 7 (2016): 63.

33 THHE's securities were suspended in December 2021 when Bursa Malaysia rejected its application to grant a further extension of time to submit a regularisation plan. It has appealed to Bursa Malaysia and is awaiting its decision.

TH explained that the assets were transferred at a premium that would cover the deficit gap between the value of its assets and liabilities as a result of the impairment of its investments. This ensured that its financial position could be restored immediately. However, the impact on the SPV was that it acquired TH's assets that were declining in value and becoming less competitive. The gap between the book value and transfer value for most of the transferred assets, ranging from 20 percent to 90 percent, was too high, making any recovery of the assets at transfer value highly unlikely. UJSB indicated that upon valuation of the assets, further impairments had to be undertaken, which meant that the actual value of some of those assets was lower than the book value. The equities portfolio transferred to UJSB concentrated on small-cap stocks that were illiquid and not covered by analysts. This made it difficult for UJSB to offload those stocks to buy better-performing stocks on Bursa Malaysia.[34]

TH stated that it was the Government's responsibility under section 24 of the Tabung Haji Act 1995 to ensure that TH's financial position could be restored immediately. It added that if the assets were not transferred, TH's liabilities would exceed its assets, and it would not be able to distribute profits to depositors for a few years. TH also stated that this would cause a potential liquidity crisis or bank-run.[35] It would appear that the payment of profits was also an important consideration in the decision to transfer non-performing assets to UJSB. Should TH's priority be to provide high profits to depositors?[36]

TH's annual report states that "It was only prudent for TH to transfer the underperforming assets because by successfully transferring them to the SPV, the total assets value is normalised and any further deterioration of the transferred asset market value will not continue to affect TH future performance."[37] In addition to not disclosing how risks were shared in the restructuring exercise, TH has not disclosed why it could be considered ethical to pass the entire risk of its poor business decisions to the Government via UJSB and, consequently, the Malaysian public without any real consequences to TH.

Although the *sukuk* issued by UJSB was unrated and non-transferable, there is no real risk to TH as the *sukuk* is backed by the Government. The transfer of non-performing assets to UJSB and commitment by the Government to pay RM1.73 billion per annum to service the *sukuk* until maturity means that TH has transferred the risk

---

34 Jose Barrock, "Urusharta Jemaah Explains Its Role and Strategy," *The Edge Markets*, May 12, 2020, https://www.theedgemarkets.com/article/urusharta-jamaah-explains-its-role-and-strategy.

35 "TH Restructuring and Rehabilitation Plan," accessed April 14, 2022, https://www.tabunghaji.gov.my/en/corporate/faq/taxonomy-th-restructuring-and-rehabilitation-plan.

36 Nur Hasnida Abdul Rahman, Fatimah Noor Rashidah, Mohd Sofian, Fadhilah Abdullah Asuhaimi and Farihana Shahari, "A Conceptual Model of Depositors' Trust and Loyalty on Hajj Institution – Case of Lembaga Tabung Haji Malaysia", *International Review of Management and Marketing* 10, no. 1 (2020): 99.

37 Tabung Haji's Annual Report 2018, 32.

to a third party, UJSB, and indirectly, the Malaysian public, who were not a party to the contract between TH and its depositors or its fund managers. Third-party government guarantees for *sukuk* are acceptable under Islamic law to spur economic development in the country.[38] However, in this case, it was also to rescue TH from its poor investment decisions.

Since the restructuring exercise, UJSB's *sukuk* has been a significant contributor to TH's income and generates revenue of RM800 million per annum.[39] It is difficult to *see* how TH's actions can be justified when it offloaded non-performing assets that were the result of poor investment decisions and poor risk management in a manner that not only allowed it to have a clean balance sheet but also a guaranteed revenue from those non-performing assets.

6.7.1.1 Lack of Transparency and Accountability

TH operated on the *wadiah* (safekeeping) principle which is based on a trust (*amanah*) covenant where depositors entrust TH with their deposits. Parties receiving the deposits entrusted to them under this covenant are not responsible for any loss or damage unless it is due to their negligence or deliberate actions. TH was made aware in 2015 by BNM that its liabilities exceeded its assets. It continued to pay profits and bonuses, which it was not entitled to do under the Tabung Haji Act. The sale and repurchase of shares in BIMB Holdings, the amendments to the asset impairment policy to have extraordinarily high thresholds for decline in fair value investments, transfer of shares in TH's companies to companies that had only paid 2 percent of the purchase price, were indications of possible mismanagement of TH's assets.

Accountability and transparency are acknowledged in Islam as fundamental principles of good governance. TH should therefore hold those who were responsible for its losses accountable as they have breached the trust covenant.[40] TH has replaced the assets through the restructuring exercise. However, this should not absolve the former board members and senior management from their responsibility to manage the funds properly. To suggest otherwise would be to overlook their conduct simply because the assets were replaced, and this could encourage future board members and senior management to act in a similar manner, knowing that they will not be held accountable. To date, TH has not taken any action to hold its board

---

38 Chaibou Issofou, "The Islamic Capital Market and the Concept of Third Party Guarantee" in *Islamic Banking and Finance: Principles, Instruments and Operations*, ed. Adnan Trakic and Hanifah Haydar Ali Tajuddin (Selangor: Current Law Journal, 2012), 214.

39 Tabung Haji's Annual Report 2019, 48.

40 Imam Taufiq, "Transparency and Accountability in the Qur'an and Its Role in Building Good Governance," *International Journal of Business, Economics and Law* 6, no. 4 (April 2015): 73.

members or senior management accountable.[41] Due to this, it is difficult to distinguish TH's restructuring exercise from a government bailout. Furthermore, as indicated, previous government bailouts incorporated moral hazard and risk-sharing, which is not evident in TH's restructuring exercise.

Section 24 of the Tabung Haji Act states that if any expenditure in relation to withdrawals by depositors cannot be met by TH, then it shall be charged and payable out of the Consolidated Fund. Section 24 goes on to state that any payment out of the Consolidated Fund shall be repaid by TH and will be considered owing to the Government until it is repaid. However, there is no indication in TH's financial statements that it owes any debt to the Government via UJSB.

The restructuring exercise is akin to cherry-picking. By TH's own admission, the Government was responsible to ensure that TH's financial assets could be restored immediately, but there is no accountability to repay the amount as required under section 24(2). In other words, TH has passed the burden of its alleged mismanagement to the Malaysian public without complying with its statutory responsibilities.

6.8 Governance Framework Post Restructuring

TH has been under BNM's supervision since 2019, which covers areas such as governance and financial audits. The power to do this is provided under section 223 of the Islamic Financial Services Act 2013. This arrangement will continue until the Royal Commission of Inquiry into the alleged mismanagement of TH's affairs is completed.[42]

TH has revised its governance structure and the terms of reference of its board of directors and its committees. TH has also developed strategic building blocks comprising cost management discipline, sustainable income generation, prudent management and to drive business synergies. It revised and improved its Strategic Asset Allocation (SAA) to reflect its risk appetite and focused on stable and sustainable returns. The SAA sets out clear investment strategies for TH and thresholds stipulating that 55 percent of TH's investments must be in fixed income assets, 25 percent in equities, 15 percent in real estate, and the balance 5 percent in Islamic money market instruments.[43]

---

41 TH has delegated this responsibility to the Royal Commission of Inquiry which has compromised its operational independence.

42 Bernama, "King Consents to Setting Up of RCI to Investigate Tabung Haji Issues – Wan Junaidi," *The Edge Markets*, January 19, 2022 https://www.theedgemarkets.com/article/king-consents-setting-royal-commission-inquiry-rci-investigate-tabung-haji-management-and.

43 Tabung Haji's Annual Report 2019, 49.

TH's key investment directions, among other things, are to replenish the equity portfolio by disposing of low yielding assets and reinvesting in assets with better returns, to optimise its tenancy rate and rental income, and to move towards a more environment, social and governance (ESG) compliant portfolio. TH has also adopted a more robust risk management policy, such as a cut-loss policy which would minimise the downside risks of underperforming equity investments.[44] This would prevent a recurrence of situations such as TH's refusal to dispose of its FGV Berhad shareholdings even when the value of the shares was clearly on a downward trend.

TH also established the Hibah Equalisation Reserve to set aside profit on reserve for the future. It also resolved to make quarterly announcements as part of its efforts towards greater transparency. TH also focused on a Liquidity Risk Management Framework by ensuring that it had high-quality liquid assets in the event of high withdrawals.

These efforts have paid off, resulting in lower operational expenditure in 2019 and higher net assets and net profits.[45] Nevertheless, TH needs to strengthen its governance and internal processes as this is not the first time that TH has been embroiled in controversy. It had faced financial difficulties in 1997 during the Asian Financial Crisis,[46] and in 2001, RM9 million, an amount equivalent to 10 percent of TH's revenue at that time, had been fraudulently withdrawn.[47] The management of TH was subsequently professionalised, and the organisation was restructured. However, this did not prevent a similar recurrence of alleged mismanagement at TH, which resulted in the current restructuring exercise.

6.9 Strengthening the Foundations of TH's Governance

TH embarked on a comprehensive integrity plan in 2015. While most organisations then had various codes and policies and provided some form of training to staff to familiarise them with the same, TH went a step further to complete the full cycle of implementation by educating staff about integrity, taking steps to reduce the risk of poor ethical practices such as corruption, and most importantly, focusing on rewarding good behaviour. TH's integrity plan was part of its strategic plan, which was an important step in inculcating and embedding a culture of integrity, as a

44 Tabung Haji's Annual Report, 24.

45 Tabung Haji's Annual Report, 20.

46 Nor Mohamed Yakcop, *Pushing the Boundaries: Stories from the Putrajaya Years (May 2000 – May 2013)* (Petaling Jaya: MPH Group Publishing, 2016), xvii.

47 Wong Sulong, *Notes to the Prime Minister: The Untold Story of How Malaysia Beat the Currency Speculators* (Petaling Jaya: MPH Group Publishing, 2011), 413.

strategic plan usually has key performance indicators to enable senior management and the board to have visibility as to whether targets have been achieved.

TH's ethical framework focused on ethical policies such as the Code of Business Conduct that applied to its board and employees, a Supplier Code of Conduct, and a whistleblower policy to enable employees, suppliers, and third parties to report any wrongdoing by TH's employees. TH also put in place processes to assess the plan's implementation, such as including the assessment of compliance with these codes in the internal audit plan and report. It also had a finance and internal control manual to guide employees on proper processes and required employees to complete their annual asset declaration (a process that had been in place since 2008). TH also addressed the role of people in building an ethical culture by providing protection for whistleblowers and appointing "integrity ambassadors" to promote a culture of integrity throughout the organisation. In an unusual step, they also specially recognised employees who displayed a high level of integrity.[48] TH's integrity plan also highlighted that as holders of public office, employees were required to avoid any conflict of interest and ensure that they carry out their duties and exercise their powers in the interests of the public.[49]

In spite of this plan which was more comprehensive than similar plans in the majority of public and private sector organisations, TH allegedly engaged in transactions such as using Yayasan Tabung Haji funds which were meant for the underprivileged, poor and needy, totalling over RM22 million for politically linked activities in 2017, purchasing TRX land from 1MDB at a higher price than market value in 2015, transferring 95 percent of the shares of PT TH Indo Plantations (THIP), owned by two (2) of TH's subsidiaries, to PT Borneo Pacific, although the latter had only paid an earnest deposit of USD 18.2 million for the shares,[50] selling and repurchasing their shares in BIMB to record profit, and adjusting the Impairment Policy annually and subsequently twice, in 2017 to reflect levels there were far below acceptable levels of decline in fair value of investments. This was probably to pay high profits before the 14th General Election,[51] presumably to keep depositors satisfied with the Government and its management of the economy.

TH has revised its governance structure since 2018 and recently launched its Stewardship Framework, which has the objective of embracing Maqasid Shariah to conduct operations in compliance with Shariah principles and to uphold strong

48 Tabung Haji's Annual Report, 2015, 95–105.

49 "Integrity Plan," Tabung Haji, accessed April 13, 2022, https://www.tabunghaji.gov.my/en/corporate/integrity/integrity-policy.

50 "TH Lodges Police Reports Against Former Chairman, CEOs and Senior Management," *New Straits Times*, November 30, 2018, https://www.nst.com.my/business/2018/11/436156/th-lodges-police-reports-against-former-chairman-ceos-and-senior-management.

51 "Tabung Haji Umum Bonus 6.25%," *Berita Harian Online*, February 7, 2018 https://www.bharian.com.my/berita/nasional/2018/02/385825/tabung-haji-umum-bonus-625-peratus.

corporate governance with integrity.[52] It propounds four (4) governance principles: Islamic values and principles, effective ethical leadership, effective internal controls and risk management, and accountability to stakeholders.

How can TH ensure that the post-restructuring initiatives remain in place, especially when it is no longer subject to BNM's supervision? Will the Stewardship Framework be able to prevent financial mismanagement and poor governance in future?

6.10 Operational Independence

TH is a "gateway" for Malaysian Muslims to perform the hajj, and therefore, as an organisation it is closely linked to the Muslim population, many of whom are also voters. This makes it particularly vulnerable to influence by political parties seeking to advance their own agenda. Therefore, as a public sector organisation, TH must be able to navigate political, economic and social objectives, and put in place governance arrangements accordingly. TH's integrity Plan was a step in the right direction. However, it was unable to counter the influence of top management in making decisions that were not in TH's or the public's interest. The Stewardship Framework may not be able to protect TH as while it is comprehensive, it does not address a difficult question: how TH intends to withstand external pressure in the future.

If TH is to avoid a repeat of the mismanagement that led to the restructuring exercise, it must ensure that it exercises operational independence, which is the ability to carry out its mandate without interference from external parties. This will require TH to be independent of any external body, including political parties as well as its depositors, who may apply political pressure on the Government in order for the Minister to approve high dividends and bonuses payouts. While the Minister's approval is required under the Tabung Haji Act for many of TH's initiatives and the Minister appoints members of the board, it does not preclude TH from being operationally independent and fulfilling its mandate.

TH can achieve operational independence in the following ways:

Tone from the Top

One of the fundamental concepts underlying Islamic leadership is that a leader is expected to be a caretaker and guardian of the people that he or she leads, will not dodge responsibility for his or her actions, has strong moral values, and must be a

52 "TH Stewardship Framework" Tabung Haji, accessed February 23, 2022, https://www.tabunghaji.gov.my/en/corporate/corporate-information/th-stewardship-framework.

strong role model.[53] The board and senior management should comprise people who are prepared to uphold TH's operational independence. This will require strong mental commitment and courage from the board. They are not in a unique position as public sector organisations in other jurisdictions face similar issues.[54] The board and senior management should set the example in TH, as the "tone from the top determines the echo from the bottom." If the board is prepared to act as role models and defend TH's operational independence, employees will be encouraged to do the same.

One of the ways the board can uphold operational independence is for all board members to be aligned and speak with one voice. Although appointments to the board of TH are made by the Minister, TH should take the opportunity to have more input into the appointment of non *ex officio* new members of the board and senior management under the Government's recently launched People's Investments (PERKUKUH) initiative. PERKUKUH comprises 20 key initiatives, including sharpening the purpose, mandate, and objectives of the government-linked investment companies (GLICs) and enhancing governance, especially in the nomination process for boards, investment panels, and senior management. TH as a GLIC is subject to these initiatives.[55]

TH should conduct a board skills gap analysis, set the criteria for new appointees based on the skills required, and adopt BNM's "Fit and Proper" criteria for the board and senior management appointments, which will ensure that only individuals with the highest level of probity are appointed to the board.[56] It should also have in place an annual evaluation of the board, board committees, and individual directors and provide an overview of the outcome of the evaluation and areas for improvement on TH's website and in its annual report, as this will provide more transparency on the quality and capability of its board members. These practices have been adopted by other statutory bodies in Malaysia.[57] Such practices ensure that board members are people of high integrity, perform their roles effectively, carry out their roles responsibly, and are independent of external influence.

---

53 Mohamed Alabed, *Exploring Islamic Principles on Leadership and Its Implementation between Muslims Leaders in Sweden* (2017) Master of Science Thesis, Chalmers University of Technology Sweden, 7–18.

54 "Pursuit of Transparency and Accountability," Australian Government Productivity Commission, accessed April 14, 2022, https://www.pc.gov.au/news-media/speeches/transparency-accountability and "The Role and Powers of Police and Crime Commissioners," at Parliament UK, accessed February 20, 2022, https://publications.parliament.uk/pa/cm201011/cmselect/cmhaff/511/51106.htm.

55 Perkukuh Pelaburan Rakyat, *Strategic Transformation of GLICs for Enhanced Resilience and Socioeconomic Impact* (Putrajaya: Ministry of Finance, Malaysia, 2022).

56 Tabung Haji should adopt BNM's Fit and Proper Criteria regardless of whether it continues to remain under BNM's supervision in future.

57 For example, PIDM's Statement on Governance, the Securities Commission's Annual Report and Employees Provident Fund Annual Report discloses some of the processes involved in board appointments and evaluations.

Transparency

As indicated earlier, transparency is an important fundamental principle of good governance in Islam. Without it, there would be no accountability. The board should act with professionalism and be prepared to counter any Ministerial or Government action that is not in TH's interests. It may be difficult to do so in an environment where political parties use GLICs to further their political agenda.[58] This, however, can be achieved if the board and senior management are prepared to be transparent about their investment decisions and their profits and losses, as transparency is an "antidote" to external interference. Transparency requires TH to communicate information clearly and accurately, enabling it to withstand public scrutiny. This is necessary to obtain the trust and confidence of stakeholders.[59]

Greater transparency can be achieved if the board and senior management ally themselves with civil society groups, the media, and members of the academia to communicate information and answer queries about TH's operations and investments, as this will be able to counter external influences.[60] In this, TH should bear in mind that non-Muslims are also its stakeholders, albeit indirectly, due to the Government guarantee to TH, which is paid from the Consolidated Fund, and also because non-Muslims are not conversant with Islam and gain their understanding from how Muslim-led organisations like TH conducts itself.

The release of data-driven quarterly financial reports would also be a step towards greater transparency.[61] In addition, TH should release balanced information about its non-financial activities, similar to listed companies that not only disclose their successes during the financial year but also the challenges that they have faced.

TH should also openly address how it has dealt with the governance issues raised by the way the restructuring exercise was carried out.

---

58 Edmund Terence Gomez, Thirshalar Padmanabhan, Norfaryanti Kamaruddin, Sunil Bhalla and Fikri Fisal, *Minister of Finance Incorporated: Ownership and Control of Corporate Malaysia* (Kuala Lumpur: Palgrave Macmillan, 2018).

59 International Federation of Accountants, *Governance in the Public Sector: A Governing Body Perspective* (2001).

60 Firoz Abdul Hamid and Jeevakumar Govindasamy, "Malaysia's Approach to Fighting Corruption: Evolution, Failures and Successes of Malaysia's Anti-Corruption Efforts" in *Enhancing Government Effectiveness and Transparency: The Fight Against Corruption*, World Bank (September 2020), accessed February 20, 2022, https://documents1.worldbank.org/curated/en/235541600116631094/pdf/Enhancing-Government-Effectiveness-and-Transparency-The-Fight-Against-Corruption.pdf.

61 Tabung Haji's latest report on its financial position was released on 8 September 2021. It should emulate listed companies that release quarterly reports.

Accountability

Accountability is the process by which organisations and the individuals within them are responsible for their decisions and actions and subject themselves to adequate scrutiny. When power and responsibility are given to an organisation, it must be accountable for the way it exercises that power and carries out that responsibility.[62]

TH had lodged police reports against its former chairman, CEO, and senior management for alleged mismanagement and abuse of power. However, there have been no updates on the results of these investigations, and over three (3) years later, no action has been taken against these parties by TH. Instead, the Government has established a Royal Commission of Inquiry (RCI), a process that has only recently begun due to the coronavirus (Covid-19 pandemic).

Without taking accountability for the mismanagement that allegedly occurred, it is unlikely that TH will be able to preserve its strong governance structure for long, as it has missed the opportunity to send the message to external parties and its own employees that TH is prepared to act against its former board members and employees. In other words, TH has missed the opportunity to assert its operational independence by holding those responsible for its losses to account.

6.11 Conclusion

As the sole agency in charge of hajj operations in Malaysia, TH is perceived by Muslims and non-Muslims as the epitome of how an Islamic institution is managed. The poor investment decisions resulting in the transfer of its assets to UJSB in 2018 has affected its reputation and standing. Since then, TH has strengthened its governance framework. However, its lack of operational independence means that despite the governance framework, TH may continue to be subject to external influence. To counter this, it should take steps to be more transparent and accountable to its stakeholders.

If TH is to stand out over and above other institutions as a symbol of good governance and sound management, it needs to drive the basic governance principles of integrity, accountability, and transparency together with moral courage throughout the organisation. The first step will be to explain the governance issues arising from the restructuring exercise so that the exercise is not viewed as a bailout, and the second step will be to act against the board members and employees who had oversight of TH's investment decisions resulting in the losses suffered. The final step will be for the senior management and board to uphold the recently implemented risk management

62 International Federation of Accountants, *Governance in the Public Sector: A Governing Body Perspective* (2001).

and investment profile as well as the Stewardship Framework and to ensure that they are prepared to assert TH's operational independence against third parties who seek to use it to further their own agenda. If TH is prepared to take these steps, it will stand out as an example of good governance for public sector institutions regardless of whether they are secular or Islamic institutions.

Farheen Baig Sardar Baig and Ashgar Ali Ali Mohamed

7 Defamation from Common Law and Shari'ah Perspective: The Convergence and Divergence

Woe to every kind of scandalmonger and backbiter. (Qur'an, Al Humazah (104):1)

7.1 Introduction

Freedom of speech and expression is a valuable and cherished right possessed by a citizen, and this right is enshrined in article 10(1)(a) of the Federal Constitution (Malaysia). However, no person is entitled under the guise of freedom of speech and expression to make irresponsible accusations against another. To allow absolute and unfettered freedom to defame another in the name of freedom of speech and expression would only allow lawlessness to prevail. Hence, the domestic laws on defamation, sedition, and offensive language impose reasonable restrictions on the citizen's right to freedom of speech and expression in the interest of public order, security of the state, decency or morality, and impartial justice. The statutes relating to the above are the Defamation Act 1957 (Malaysia), Sedition Act 1948 (Malaysia), Printing Presses and Publications Act 1984 (Malaysia), and the Penal Code (Malaysia), in particular, section 499.[1]

Where a defendant recklessly defames the plaintiff, the plaintiff has a right to protect his or her reputation, and this includes filing a defamation action in tort against the defendant unless the defendant can establish any of the defences available in a defamation action. The burden is on the plaintiff, who must show not only that the impugned statements or words were defamatory but also that the words complained of referred to the plaintiff and that the words had been published.

In Islam, freedom of expression or speech can be considered as an essential interest (*masalih daruriyah*) in maintaining the stability of the socio-political order. As such, this freedom should be exercised according to the guidelines and limitations as mentioned under the protection of five principles of Shariah (*maqasid as*-shari'ah), i.e. protection of faith, life, intellect, lineage, and property. Freedom of expression or speech is not a matter of privilege in Islam, but it is one of the fundamental rights which is respected, revered, and protected by Islamic law. The term

1 The Penal Code, s 499 provides: "Whoever, by words either spoken or intended to be read or by signs, or by visible representations, makes or publishes any imputation concerning any person, intending to harm, or knowing or having reason to believe that such imputation will harm the reputation of such person, is said, except in the cases hereinafter excepted, to defame that person."

https://doi.org/10.1515/9783110766707-007

"freedom of opinion" refers to the right of the individual to express his or her own opinion as long as he or she does not violate the Islamic teachings, as contained in the Quran and Prophetic teachings.

In light of the above, this chapter discusses the law on defamation from the conventional and Islamic law to find a common thread between the two systems, particularly in relation to the remedy and mechanism for settlement of such disputes. At this juncture, it is worthwhile noting that the main divergence between civil and Shari'ah is that when a person defames another and gets away with it, he will nevertheless be accountable for his actions in the next life. At common law, the matter ends during the lifetime of the defamer. However, divine laws await the defamer in the hereafter for his final judgment. It would be emphasised that both systems perceive this act as weighty and of profound significance.

7.2 Defamation: The Common Law Perspective

The law assumes that a person is of good character unless proven otherwise. If a statement about a person is defamatory and affects the reputation of that person in the eyes of the public, that person may have a claim for defamation against the maker of that defamatory statement. A defamatory statement is a statement by any communication (verbal or non-verbal, oral or written, temporary or permanent, or an unprivileged false statement) that tends to lower a person in the estimation of right-thinking members of society; causes a person to be shunned or avoided or to expose him to hatred, contempt, or ridicule; or conveys an imputation on a person disparaging or injurious to his office, profession, calling, trade or business. Having said the above, it is useful at the outset to lay down the basic elements of defamation from the common law perspective.

The tort of defamation aims to protect a person's dignity and reputation. Hence, where the defendant makes an unfounded statement that is defamatory about the plaintiff, the latter will have a right of action against the former. The exception, however, is if the defendant can establish any one or more of the defences available in a defamation suit. The court will then be tasked to balance the interest of the individual in the protection of his dignity and reputation against the freedom of speech of the person who makes the alleged defamatory statement.

7.2.1 Categories of Defamation

Basically, defamation is categorised into two, namely libel and slander. In the former, a defamatory statement is contained in a form commonly commissioned by writing and usually in a permanent record. It also constitutes a libel when the same is contained in a statute, caricature, effigy, or chalk marks on a wall or pictures as was decided in *Monson v Tussauds Ltd.*[2] In *Monson*'s case, the waxworks of a plaintiff in the "Chamber of Horrors" has been held to be a libel. Meanwhile, in slander, the defamatory statement is in spoken word, not in permanent form. In *Luk Kai Lam v Sim Ai Leng,*[3] it was noted inter alia that libel is actionable per se while slander is only actionable where the plaintiff can show that he has suffered special damage that can be estimated in money.

While it is true that in a slander action, the plaintiff must generally prove that he has suffered special damage, there are some exceptions to this rule. This includes the situation where the defendant implicated the plaintiff for having committed a serious criminal offense. The plaintiff in such a situation need not show that he has suffered special damage.[4] Again, where the imputation is that the plaintiff is a lesbian[5] or that the plaintiff has been raped[6] is actionable without proof of special damage. Likewise, where the imputation against the plaintiff is that he is suffering from an infectious or contagious disease, such as a venereal disease, which is likely to prevent other persons from associating with the plaintiff, such slander is actionable without proof of special damage.[7] Lastly, where the imputation is that of unfitness in one's trade or profession as provided by section 5 of the Defamation Act 1957.[8]

7.2.2 Elements of Defamation

Further to the above, to establish defamation, the burden is on the plaintiff where he has to establish that the written or spoken words were defamatory, the impugned words refer to the plaintiff, and that the words had been published to a person other than the plaintiff himself.[9] According to Lord Atkin in *Sim v Stretch,*[10] defamatory words are words that tend to lower the plaintiff in the estimation of

2 [1894] 1 QB 671.
3 [1978] 1 MLJ 214.
4 *Hecking v Mitchell* [1910] 1 KB 609.
5 *Kerr v Kennedy* [1942] 1 KB 609.
6 Defamation Act 1957 (Malaysia), s 5 provides: "In an action for slander in respect of words calculated to disparage the plaintiff in any office, profession, calling, trade or business held or carried on by him at the time of the publication, it shall not be necessary to allege or prove special damage whether or not the words are spoken of the plaintiff in the way of his office, profession, calling, trade or business." *See* also *Yousoupoff v MGM* (1930) 50 TLR 581.
7 *Bloodworth v Gray* (1844) 7 Man & G 334.
8 *Luk Kai Lam v Sim Ai Leng* [1978] 1 MLJ 214 and *Wan Abdul Rashid v S Subramaniam* [1984] 1 MLJ 385.
9 Per Varghese George JCA in *Dr Syed Azman bin Syed Nawawi & Ors v Dato' Seri Haji Ahmad bin Said* [2015] 5 MLJ 141, 146.
10 [1936] 2 All ER 1237.

right-thinking members of society. The statement may lower the plaintiff in the estimation of right-thinking people by exposing him to "hatred, contempt or ridicule."[11] The words may be defamatory in their ordinary and natural meaning or may carry a secondary meaning (known as innuendo) or both.[12] In considering whether a statement is defamatory, the words must be interpreted in the context in which they were written or spoken. In *Fields v Davis*,[13] the defendant called the plaintiff, a married woman, a "tramp". The word was held not to be defamatory because they were uttered by the defendant in a fit of temper and were understood by those around as mere vulgar abuse. Again, in *C Shivanathan v Abdullah bin Dato' Haji Abdul Rahman*,[14] the words spoken by the defendant were that the plaintiff was "dishonest, cheat, liar."[15] They were uttered in anger and understood in their context as not imputing a crime but as mere general abuse. Likewise, in *Mohamed Azman v System TV (M) Bhd*,[16] it was held that the words spoken in jest were not to be defamatory.

Further, the defendant's word or statement must refer to the plaintiff. In *Knupffer v London Express Newspaper Limited*,[17] Viscount Simon LC stated: "Where the plaintiff is not named, the test which decides whether the words used refer to him is the question whether the words are such as would reasonably lead persons acquainted with the plaintiff to believe that he was the person referred to."[18] In *Hulton v Jones*,[19] the defendant published an article in their newspaper that described a motor show in Dieppe. In the article, they described the activities of one Artemus Jones, who was a churchwarden in Peckham and who was described as "life and soul of a gay little band that haunts the casino and turns night into day, besides betraying a most unholy delight in the society female butterflies."[20] The plaintiff, who was called Artemus Jones but was a barrister rather than churchwarden at Peckham, brought a libel action against the defendants. Neither the writer of the article nor the editor of the paper had heard of the plaintiff, and neither intended to refer to him, but the plaintiff brought witnesses who said that they thought that the article referred to him. The House of Lords held that if reasonable people understood the language of the article as being defamatory of the plaintiff, it was irrelevant that the defendant did not intend to defame the plaintiff. A defendant may be liable if his statement is true of one

11 *Parmitern v Coupland and Another* (1840)151 ER 340.

12 All these common law principles have been adopted in Malaysia in many cases such as *Syed Husin Ali v Syarikat Perchetakan Utusan Malayu Bhd* [1973] 2 MLJ 56; *Chok Foo Chow v The China Press* [1999] 1 MLJ 371; *DP Vijendran v Karpal Singh* [2000] 3 MLJ 22.

13 (1955) CLY 1543.

14 [1984] 1 MLJ 62.

15 [1984] 1 MLJ, 63.

16 [2000] 4 MLJ 120.

17 [1944] AC 116.

18 [1944] AC, 119.

19 [1910] AC 20 (HL).

20 [1910] AC, 21.

person but is, in fact, defamatory of another person, not known to the defendant and who suffered injury as a result of the publication of the statement.

Again, in *Newstead v London Express Newspapers Ltd*,[21] an article in the defendants' newspaper entitled "Why Do People Commit Bigamy" referred to a self-confessed bigamist called "Harold Newstead, a thirty-year-old Camberwell man." The plaintiff who was of the same name and lived in Camberwell, brought a libel action against the defendants. The defendants argued that they had not intended to refer to the plaintiff but to another Harold Newstead who lived in Camberwell. The defendants were nevertheless held liable to the plaintiff because they should have taken extra care to ensure that the article could not have been taken as referring to someone else. The Malaysian cases that expressed similar sentiments are *Ummi Hafilda bte Ali v Karangkraft Sdn Bhd*,[22] *Dato' Annas Bin Khatib Jaafar v Sharifuddin Mohamed & Ors*,[23] *Muzdalifah bt Abu Bakar lwn Nora Sidah bt Abd Hamid*,[24] and *Utusan Melayu (Malaysia) Berhad & 3 Ors v Tjanting Handicraft Sdn Bhd & Anor.*[25]

In relation to the last-mentioned paragraph, it is observed that there is no requirement that the plaintiff is expressly referred to by the defendant. It can also be satisfied where the defendant's statement does not make an obvious but an implied reference to the plaintiff. In *Morgan v Odhams Press Ltd*,[26] the plaintiff claimed that he had been libelled by the defendants in an article concerned with a dog-doping gang that had allegedly kidnapped a certain Miss Murray. At the time, Miss Murray was staying in the plaintiff's flat, and the plaintiff produced six witnesses who testified that they thought that the article was referring to the plaintiff and that he was involved with this dog-doping gang. The House of Lords held that there was sufficient evidence to go to the jury because the ordinary reader who had special knowledge of the circumstances would conclude that the article referred to the plaintiff. If the aforementioned elements are established by the defamed person to the satisfaction of the court, damages may be awarded accordingly.

Besides, the other requirement to establish defamation is that the defendant must publish the defamatory statement about the plaintiff. The defendant need not have intended that the defamatory statement be communicated to any particular person but is sufficient that the publication to that person could have been reasonably anticipated. In *Theaker v Richardson*,[27] the defendant wrote a defamatory letter to the plaintiff accusing her of being a whore and a brothel-keeper. The plaintiff was a married woman and was a fellow local councillor with the defendant. The defendant put

21 [1940] 1 KB 377.
22 [2003] MLJ 684.
23 [2014] MLJU 1770.
24 [2021] MLJU 2266.
25 [2005] 1 AMR 624.
26 [1971] 1 WLR 1239.
27 [1962] 1 WLR 151.

the defamatory letter through the plaintiff's letterbox in a manila envelope, similar to the type used for election addresses. The plaintiff's husband picked up the envelope, and believing it to contain an election address, he opened it and read its contents. The defendant was held liable because it was a natural and probable consequence of the defendant's method of delivery of the letter that the plaintiff's husband would open it and read it.[28] Again, in *Huth v Huth,*[29] the defendant sent a defamatory letter to his wife, from whom he was separated, stating that they were not married and that their children were illegitimate. The letter was opened by a curious butler who read its contents. It was held that there was no publication of the letter because the defendant could not reasonably have anticipated that an inquisitive butler would open his wife's mail.

7.3 Who Can Sue?

Having considered the elements that must be shown to sustain a defamation suit, it is also important to state here that only a living person can bring an action in defamation. A dead person cannot be defamed, no matter how distressing the defendant's statement is to the deceased's relatives. In relation to corporations, as they have a legal personality, they can for this purpose sue for defamatory statements made affecting their business.[30] The defamatory rule thus applies to all plaintiffs regardless of their nature.[31] Even a local authority was initially allowed by the English common law to sue for defamation. In *Bagnor Regis UDC v Campion,*[32] it was ruled that "just as a trading company has a trading reputation which it is entitled to be protected by bringing an action for defamation, so the plaintiff as a local government, has a governing reputation which they are equally entitled to protection in the same way . . . bearing in mind the vital distinction between defamation of a corporation and defamation of its individual officers or members."[33]

The House of Lords in *Derbyshire County Council v Times Newspapers Ltd and others,*[34] however, made a major dent into this common law principle. They overruled

28 In *Saharudin bin Abd Jabar v Bank Islam Malaysia Bhd* [2016] 7 MLJ 293 where it was stated, inter alia, that "it would be perfectly reasonable, to presume that a letter addressed to a UMNO office would most likely be opened and read by the staff. Other than the staff that works there, a political organisation's office will normally attract scores of visitors."

29 [1915] 3 KB 32. *See* also *Tan Sri Abdul Rahim bin Datuk Thamby Chik v John Marcom* [2000] 5 MLJ 191.

30 *Metropolitan Saloon Omnibus Co. v Hawkins* (1859) 4 H & N 87.

31 *South Helton Coal Co Ltd. v North Eastern News Association* [1894] 1 QB 133.

32 [1972] QB 94.

33 [1972] QB, 98.

34 [1993] AC 534.

the *Campion* case and held inter alia that the government bodies, whether central or local, do not have the right to maintain an action for damages for defamation as it would be contrary to the public interest for the organs of government (whether central or local) to have that right because it is of the highest importance that a government body should be open to uninhibited public criticism, and the right to sue for defamation would not only have a chilling effect but would also place an undesirable fetter on the freedom of speech.

It was fortunate that in Malaysia, the Federal Court in *Chong Chieng Jen v Government of State of Sarawak & Anor*,[35] rejected the application of *Derbyshire*'s case. In this case, the defamatory statements attributed to the respondent, a Member of Parliament and State Assemblyman, concern the alleged mismanagement of the state's financial affairs. The apparently libellous statement was published in two publications, the *Sin Chiew Daily News* on 3 January 2013 and the online news portal *Malaysiakini*. The issue raised for the court's determination, inter alia, was whether the first appellant, the State Government of Sarawak, and/or the second appellant, a government department and a government organ, have the right to sue and maintain an action for damages for defamation against the respondent. In affirming the Court of Appeal's decision, the Federal Court held, among other things, that the respondents had the right to sue and maintain an action for damages for defamation. The court's refusal to receive the common law *Derbyshire* principle was largely based on section 3 of the Government Proceedings Act 1956, which does not exclude proceedings in defamation by or against the government, and section 3(1)(c) of the Civil Law Act 1956, which sets the cut-off date for the reception of the English law in Sarawak namely, up to 12 December 1949. The case of *Derbyshire* was decided way after the above cut-off date.[36]

7.3.1 Remedies

It is important to note that an essential feature of the Common Law system is that when a civil action for defamation is brought to court, it is common for the aggrieved party to seek monetary relief for the injury or the harm done to him. It is also common for certain public figures to bring the defamation suit to claim for an exorbitant sum as damages such as RM100 million. However, the amount that may be recovered would very much be based on the specific facts of each case. The factors that the court normally considers in determining the quantum of damages include the gravity of the alleged defamatory statement; mode and extent of its publication; the plaintiff's

35 [2019] 3 MLJ 300, FC.

36 *See* Ashgar Ali Ali Mohamed, Mohd Akram Shair Mohamed and Farheen Baig Sardar Baig, "Application of English Common Law in Malaysia: With Reference to *Derbyshire County Council v Times Newspapers Ltd & Ors*," *Malayan Law Journal* 1 (2017): lix.

position and standing in society; whether the defendant received any benefit or advantage from the defamatory statement and the absence or refusal of retraction or apology. The following cases illustrate the quantum of damages that have been awarded by the court in a defamation suit. In *Ling Wah Press (M) Sdn Bhd & Ors v Tan Sri Dato Vincent Tan Chee Yioun*,[37] a sum of RM7,000,000.00 was awarded to the plaintiff. Again, in *Nurul Izzah binti Anwar v Tan Sri Khalid bin Abu Bakar & Anor*,[38] the first and second defendants were ordered to pay the plaintiff damages a sum of RM400,000.00 and RM600,000.00, respectively. Likewise, in *Dato' Seri Anwar bin Ibrahim v Khairy Jamaluddin*,[39] a sum of RM150,000.00 was awarded to the plaintiff. While, in *Dato' Seri Anwar bin Ibrahim v The New Straits Times Press (M) Sdn Bhd & Anor*,[40] the plaintiff was awarded a sum of RM100,000. Again, in *Lim Guan Eng v New Straits Times Press (M) Bhd*,[41] a sum of RM300,000 was awarded to the plaintiff. Lastly, in *Raub Australian Gold Mining Sdn Bhd v Mkini Dotcom Sdn Bhd & Ors*,[42] a sum of RM150,000 was awarded.

As stated earlier, defamation can also constitute an offence under sections 499 to 520 of the Penal Code (Malaysia). This caters for serious libels, including breaches of public peace. Criminal defamation, however, is not discussed here as it is beyond the scope of this chapter.

7.3.2 Defences

To escape liability for defamation, there are various defences under the Defamation Act 1957, such as justification (section 8), fair comment (section 9), privilege (absolute and qualified) (sections 11 and 12), apology (section 10), and unintentional defamation (section 7). Even if a statement is spread with malice, the defendant will succeed in his defence if he can prove the truth of his statement. For the defence of fair comment, if the comment of the defamer is based on true facts and is fair, his defence will succeed. However, it must not be spiked with malice and is only for issues of public interest. Privilege defences are of two: absolute and qualified in which persons are allowed to communicate defamatory words to seek justice. Unintentional defamation is where the words are published innocently, and the defamer makes an offer of amends. An apology can work to mitigate damages.

37 [2000] 4 MLJ 77.
38 [2018] MLJU 472.
39 [2017] MLJU 1495.
40 [2010] 2 MLJ 492.
41 [2017] 9 MLJ 622.
42 [2018] MLJU 34.

7.3.3 Settlement

Finally, it is worthwhile adding that a defamation action may be commenced in the High Court or the Sessions Court, depending on the quantum of damages sought by the plaintiff. Basically, a claim below RM1 million would come within the civil jurisdiction of the Sessions Court pursuant to section 65(1)(b) of the Subordinate Courts Act 1948 (Malaysia). While any amount in excess of RM1 million would come within the jurisdiction of the High Court *vides* the Courts of Judicature Act 1964 (Malaysia). In addition to damages, the plaintiff may also ask for an injunction against the defendant from repeating the defamation. And the procedure for a defamation claim is governed by Order 78 of the Rules of Court 2012 (Malaysia). It is worth adding that at common law, an aggrieved party who filed a civil action for defamation in court would seek, inter alia, monetary relief for the injury or the harm done to him, and it is often rare for an out of court settlement to be arrived at. The case will go up to and until completion of the full trial, where either the award is made in favour of the plaintiff or the case is dismissed.

7.4 Defamation: From Shari'ah Perspective

Islamic Law approaches defamation from a different perspective. Its aim is not to punish but is preventive. The Quran touched the heart of man in that a true believer who understands, appreciates and praises his Creator would abide by the rules laid down in the divine revelation. This will prevent a person from uttering defamatory words and spreading defamatory messages about another person unless it is necessary to forbid evil and enjoin good. This principle is in line with the verse 104 in *Surah al Imran*, where Allah (SWT) says: "Let there arise out of you a band of people inviting to all that is good, enjoining what is right, and forbidding what is wrong: They are the ones to attain felicity." The wisdom behind that is to correct wrongdoings. The above verse explains that it is a duty of a Muslim to promote what is right and true and to forbid any wrong committed by others. A Muslim who stops enjoining the good and eradicating the evil, even though he has the ability to do so, would be answerable for his omission in the hereafter.

The Prophet (SAW) said: "There are no people among which evil is committed and they have the ability to change that but they do not change it, except that Allah will soon afflict them with a punishment that will affect them all."[43] In another *hadith*, the Prophet SAW said: "By the One in whose hand is my soul, you must order the good and forbid evil or Allah will soon send upon you a punishment from

43 *Sunnan* Abu Da'ud.

Himself and then you supplicate to Him and He will not respond to you."[44] Based on the above *hadiths*, the eradication of evil is the duty of every Muslim who obeys Allah, who detests all evil action or conduct that Allah hates or dislikes, and one who has compassion for fellow Muslims in trying to guide them to what is good and forbidding evil. It is obvious therefrom that the Defamation Act 1957 can never be compared to the superiority of these divine verses in view of harmonisation.

7.4.1 The Verses

There are many verses regarding slander in the Quran and Hadith (prophetic teachings).[45] These are the rules that govern the law of defamation in Islam. In essence, it warns about the tarnishing of the honour that has been bestowed upon man by Allah, to the extent that Muslims are encouraged to conceal the wrongdoings of another, which will entail a generous reward in the hereafter. A true believer understands and appreciates how these are divine verses that seek to protect a person's honour and the wrath of Allah that comes with non-adherence to it. As these verses are universal and applicable through time, it is seen how perfect these verses are when it comes to social media, where fake messages can go around the world instantly. Some of these messages are so well done that no one will know the real truth except for the defamer, the defamed, and, most important, Allah himself. This is the power that does not exist in defamation law. These verses on the prohibition of this form of expression and the severe punishment that goes with it conform to the collective Shari'ah objective of protecting people's honour and reputation from hurtful and derogatory statements and false rumours. Without these provisions, there would be greater social corruption on earth.

---

44 *Musnad* of Ahmad ibn Hanbal.

45 The Quran proclaimed to be the words of Allah (SAW) (*see Surah Al Hijr* (15): 9). It is a revelation from the All-Wise and Praiseworthy Allah (SWT) (*see Surah Fatir* (35): 8). It is also explicit and unequivocal teaching for mankind (*See Surah Al Asra* (17): 9). It confirms what has been revealed before and calls human beings to the life of virtue, morality, law, and order.*Hadith* is the tradition of Prophet Muhammad (SAW). Prophets (SAW) mission as a messenger was twofold: first, he was to transmit whatever revelation was communicated to him; the second task was to interpret the will of Allah (SWT) by preaching, teaching and counselling people in the practical steps of religious, ethical, and legal matters. Allah (SWT) says, "(We sent them) with clear signs and scriptures and we have sent down unto thee (also) the Message: That thou may est explain clearly from them, and that they may give thought" (*Surah Al Nahl* (16): 44). Again, "O ye who believe! Obey Allah, and obey the Messenger, and those charged with authority among you. If you differ in anything among yourselves, refer it to Allah and His Messenger, if you do believe in Allah and the Last Day: that is best, and most suitable for final determination" (*Surah Nisa* (4): 59). In his last sermon given in the Uranah Valley of Mount Arafat on the 9th day of the Dhul Hijjah 10 AH, the Prophet (SAW) said to the believers: "O people, no prophet or apostle will come after me and no new faith will be born. I leave behind two things: the Quran and my example, the Sunnah; if you follow these you will never go astray."

7.4.1.1 Honour of the Son of Adam

To defame a person or falsely accuse a person is viewed seriously in Islam as it flames spite, hatred, and revenge in the hearts of people and is usually motivated by malice, envy, mockery, or to blame another for committed sins. Islam strongly upholds the honour and dignity of another irrespective of their religious faith. Unlike the secular concept, in Islam, the Creator has ordained humans with dignity and honour. As Allah's vicegerent on earth, man has been created in a position of honour above the other creations. The Quran, *Surah Al Isra* (17): 70 provides: "We have honoured the sons of Adam." As Allah (SWT) has honoured mankind, it is also incumbent upon mankind to observe the same among themselves, to preserve its integrity and avoid its violation.[46] Aside from the above, there are several passages in the Quran affirming Allah's love and compassion onto mankind,[47] and this sets a basic framework of the relationship between mankind. Hence, dignity, restraint, politeness, and amicability have always been regarded as virtues as opposed to snobbery, arrogance, and discourteousness, which have never been recognised as good moral values in Islam.

7.4.1.2 Do Not Harm or Insult

Further, Islam stresses the concept of brotherhood, where Muslims are urged not to oppress, humiliate, insult, backbite, or look down on one another. Abu Huraira reported the Prophet (SAW) as saying: "A Muslim is the brother of a Muslim. He neither oppresses him nor humiliates him nor looks down upon him. It is a serious evil for a Muslim that he should look down upon his brother Muslim. All things of a Muslim are inviolable for his brother in faith: his blood, his wealth and his honour".[48] Again, "Do not harm your fellow Muslims, do not impute evil to them, and do not try to uncover their nakedness. For behold, if anyone tries to uncover the nakedness of his Muslim brother, God will uncover his own nakedness."[49]

---

46 Mohammad Hashim Kamali, *The Dignity of Man: The Islamic Perspective* (Kuala Lumpur, Iimiah Publishers: 1999), 30.

47 For example, in *Surah Al-Tawbah* (Chapter 9) verse 4 and 7 "Allah (SWT) truly loves those who are conscious of Him"; in *Surah Al-Baqarah* (Chapter 2) verse 195 "Allah (SWT) loves those who are good to others"; *Surah Ali-Imran* (Chapter 3) verse 159 "Allah (SWT) loves those who place their trust on Him"; *Surah Al-A'rfah* (Chapter 7) verse 156 " My mercy engulfs everything and extent beyond everything" and *Surah Al-Zumar* (Chapter 39) Verse 53 "O my servants who transgressed against their souls! Do not despair of the mercy of God. For God forgives all sins. He is most forgiving, most merciful."

48 *Sahih Muslim*, translated into English by Abdul Hamid Siddiqui, 1361.

49 Tirmidhi, *Sunan* III, 255. It was reported that the Holy Prophet (SAW) was quoted as stated that: "No harm is to be inflicted on another and no unjustifiable harm is to be inflicted in recompense." (Reported in Imam Malik's "*Al-Muwatta*" Vol. 1 (Beirut: Al-Maktabah Al-Thaqafiah, 1988) 745.)

Every man has a duty to appreciate the other and not to lower his honour and dignity, which necessarily includes not insulting or humiliating. Insulting a person to humiliate and tarnish the good name of the person by the utterance of words, gestures, cursing, and backbiting, among others, is prohibited. In the same vein, calling a person immoral, maliciously accusing another person of criminal is equally prohibited. The Quran and the *Sunnah* of the Prophet (SAW) repeatedly warn against violating human dignity and remind the believers to observe justice in their dealings. Allah (SWT) says:

> O believers, let not people ridicule other people, perchance the latter may be better than the former, nor let women ridicule other women, perchance the latter may be better than the former. Neither find fault with your own people nor call one another by nicknames.
>
> And defame not one another behind your backs. Does any one of you like to eat the flesh of his dead brother? Surely you would abhor it.[50]
>
> Avoid aggression, for Allah loves not the aggressors.[51]

Further, the Prophet (SAW) said:

> It is not for a believer to indulge in insults, sarcasm or cursing.[52]
>
> Whoever saved the honour of his brother, God will save his countenance against the blaze of fire in the day of judgment.[53]
>
> Do not annoy the Muslims, nor defame them, and do not expose their nakedness, for one who exposes the nakedness of his Muslim brother, Allah (SWT) will expose his own nakedness.[54]

What is apparent from the above is that the honour and dignity of each individual have been regarded as sacred. Further, Islam enjoins the believers to uphold justice and kindness, which call for just standards of behaviour to all irrespective of whether they belong to the fold of Islam. As Allah (SWT) said: "Allah does not love evil talk in public unless it is by someone who has been subjected to injustice (and cruelty)."[55] Equally, as mentioned earlier, abusive language or strong words of condemnation are equally prohibited. As from the above, the religion commands a believer to refrain from backbiting another, and worst still defame the person, be it in the form of libel or slander. Allah (SWT) said: "Woe to every kind of scandalmonger and backbiter."[56] According to Ibnu Kathir, there are two divisions of defamation (*fitnah*), i.e. *Al-Hammaaz* as the acts of spreading the news without concerning of

50 *Surah Al Hujurat* (49): Verse 11–12.
51 *Surah Al-Baqarah* (Chapter 2) verse 190.
52 Al Tabrizi "*Mishkat*" Vol 1 Hadith No 4847.
53 Cited in Mohammed Hashim Kamali, *Freedom of Expression in Islam* (Kuala Lumpur: Berita Publishing Sdn Bhd: 1994), 119.
54 Tirmidhi *Sunna al Tirmidhi* III 255 Hadith 84.
55 *Surah Al-Nisa* (4): 148.
56 *Surah al Humazah* (104): 1.

its truthfulness orally, and *Al-Lammaaz* as the act of is the act of spreading the news without concerning of its truthfulness in written or through documentation.

7.4.1.3 Punishment

Backbiting of another and worst still to defame the person, be it in the form of libel or slander, is completely forbidden and would incur sin which account will be shown in the next world. It is worthwhile adding that Muslims believe in life after death and that life in this world is only temporary thus, striving for the betterment in the hereafter is essential. Allah (SWT) proclaimed in the Qur'an: "Verily Allah has purchased from the believers their lives and their wealth in exchange for *Jannat* (i.e. the infinitely more beautiful life yet to come)."[57] Again, "Allah will not call you to account for what is futile in your oaths, but He will call you to account for your deliberate oaths."[58] Therefore, Muslims are expected to keep to their solemn oath to the utmost of a person's ability. Allah (SWT) proclaimed: "And make not Allah's (name) an excuse in your oaths against doing good, or acting rightly, or making peace between-person; for Allah is One who heareth and knoweth all things."[59] Further, Allah (SWT) has ordained believers to have faith and do good deeds: "And He will test you, which of you are best in actions."[60]

Further, a Muslim dearly upholds that his dealings are always with Allah (SWT), who sees him at all times and in all places. A person may hide from the whole world but not from Allah (SWT). Again, he may deceive everyone but cannot deceive Allah (SWT). In the same vein, he can flee from the clutches of anyone else but not from Allah (SWT). Thus, whatever man does in this life, he cannot escape from the fact that one day he will die and be compelled to account for what has passed. On that day, there will be no advocating, no favour, no impartiality, fraud, and deception, and justice will be done.

> O my son! (said Luqman), if there be (but) the weight of a mustard seed and it were (hidden) in a rock, or (anywhere) in the heavens or on earth Allah will bring it forth: for Allah understands the finer mysteries (and) is well-acquainted (with them).[61]
>
> It was We who created man, and We know what dark suggestions his soul makes to him: for We are nearer to him than his jugular vein. Behold, two (guardian angels) appointed to learn (his doings) one sitting on the right and one on the left. Not a word does he utter but here is a sentinel by him, ready (to note it).[62]

57 *Surah At-Taubah* (9): 111.
58 *Surah Al Maidah* (5): 89.
59 *Surah Al Baqarah* (2): 224.
60 *Surah Al Mulk* (67): 2.
61 *Surah Luqman* (31): 16.
62 *Surah Qaf* (50): 16–18.

> And the Book (of deeds) will be placed (before you) and thou wilt *see* the sinful in great terror because of what is (recorded) therein; they will say, "Ah! Woe to us! What a book is this! It leaves out nothing small or great, but takes account thereof!" they will find all that they did, placed before them: and not one will thye Lord treat with injustice.[63]

Lastly, on the day of reckoning, the only thing that helps a person is his own good deeds, the rewards that he has earned through doing righteous deeds, including helping others, enjoining goodness, and forbidding and resisting evil. However, the rewards and the good deeds he earned in this life could be lost easily in the hereafter, where they may be consumed by others for his transgressions and bad manners to them. Abu Hurairah (r.a.) reported:

> Messenger of Allah (SAW) asked the companions, "Do you know who is bankrupt?" They replied: "The bankrupt among us is one who has neither money with him nor any property." The Prophet said, "The real bankrupt of my *Ummah* would be he who would come on the Day of Resurrection with prayers, fasting, and *Sadaqah* (charity), (but he will find himself bankrupt on that day as he will have exhausted the good deeds) because he reviled others, brought calumny against others, unlawfully devoured the wealth of others, shed the blood of others and beat others; so his good deeds would be credited to the account of those (who suffered at his hand). If his good deeds fall short to clear the account, their sins would be entered in his account and he would be thrown in the (Hell) Fire."[64]

From the above, these are clear warnings of punishments for those who do evil deeds. For defamation, in particular, there are three. One comes under criminal law under the *hudud* offence of *qazf* (slander of chaste women of unlawful sexual intercourse), the other is discretionary punishment, and the third is a punishment that will be given to the evildoers in the hereafter. *Qazf* literally means throwing out. It is a crime of accusing another person of committing *zina* (unlawful sexual intercourse). The person making the accusation (the slenderer) has the right to prove his case by producing the required evidence. Otherwise, his accusation will be malicious, false, defamatory, and constitutes a gross offence punishable by eighty lashes. He also loses his status in society as a trustworthy person and will be branded as *fasiq* until he makes real repentance. As the Quran proclaims: "And those who launch a charge against chaste women and produce not four witnesses (to support their allegations) – flog them with eighty stripes, and reject their evidence ever after for such men are wicked transgressors unless they repent thereafter and mend (their conduct); for Allah is All-Forgiving, Most Merciful."[65]

In fact, during the lifetime of the Prophet (SAW), a slanderous charge was spread about the wife of the Prophet (SAW), Saidatinah Aiysha and this put not only her but also her husband and her father Abu Bakar in the most painful

63 *Surah Al Kahf* (19): 49.
64 *Sahih Muslim.*
65 *Surah Nur* (24): 4–5.

predicament. Allah (SWT) exposed the falsehood of the accusation through the revelation of the abovementioned verse. In another verse, Allah (SWT) says: "Those who slander chaste women, indiscreet but believing, are crushed in this life and in the Hereafter: For them is a grievous penalty."[66] The Prophet (SAW) expressed his views on *qazf* as follows:

> It is reported by Abu Hurairah that the Prophet (SAW) said: "Keep away from seven abominable acts: association of partners with Allah (SWT), the magic; killing someone which is forbidden by Allah (SWT) except when it is with the injunction, eating of the usury, devouring the property of the orphans, turning away from the day of *jihad* in the path of Allah (SWT) and the slander of chaste but indiscreet women."[67]
>
> If anyone says something about a person which is not true in order to defame him, Allah will confine him in the fire of Hell until it extinguishes his utterance.[68]

As from the above, it is clear that Muslims are advised to dispel gossip and shun such news and give the benefit of the doubt to the person who is being defamed. To utter that which a person has no knowledge of is a great wrong, especially if it turns out to be untrue (slander). The requirements of evidence are also given importance in that failure of which the defamer would be deemed a liar. Even the warnings of punishment are severe, a painful punishment. Meanwhile, as for the defamed, it can be learnt from the story of Aishah (r.a) that such situations are to be handled with patience (*sabr*), which is means of entry into paradise.

As for the punishment for those who participated in the slander of Aishah (r.a.), they were forgiven. This all-encompassing event, and the verses that were revealed that vindicated Aishah, and the other verses on defamation cited above, is an embodiment of the laws that govern defamation in Islam. It is complete, it focuses not only on the defamed and defamer but on the receivers of the information as well. As the Quran and sunnah are universal laws, they will apply even to current events like spreading malicious gossip on social media that enables news to spread like wildfire. Nobody knows the truth, pictures are doctored, lies, fake news, a lot of slanders, cyberbullying, etc., and it disseminates at the touch of a button. It is submitted that if the rule of law applied is Islamic law, there would be less corruption and false accusations spread.

7.4.2 Defences

This would come under the understanding of when a person is allowed to speak. As long as words have been spoken abiding by Allah's commands and prohibitions in

66 *Surah Nur* (24): 23.
67 *Sahih* Bukhari.
68 Reported by Al-Tabarani.

the Quran and prophetic teachings (i.e. for upholding justice and forbidding evil), they will be excused. However, if it is done maliciously, even if it is true, it will amount to backbiting for which the defamer is answerable in the hereafter. Having said the above, defences like justification and fair comment will not be available in Islam if the news has been maliciously spread, even if it is true. Defences like privilege are circumstances in which a person is allowed to speak with honesty and with the intention of seeking justice. An apology is applicable in both systems. Abu Hurairah (r.a.) reported that the Prophet (SAW) said: "Whosoever believes in Allah and the Last Day, then let him speak good or remain silent."[69] Lastly, as Allah (SWT) says: "Not a word does one utter, except that there is an (angel) Watching, Ready to record it."[70]

7.5 Conclusion

Freedom of speech is allowed in both systems, and at the same time, they are subject to certain restrictions. It does not extend to making irresponsible accusations of another person but is allowed for certain reasons like to establish justice. At common law, defamatory words must pass the test of defamation. The words must tend to make people look down, shun, or avoid the plaintiff; examples of offensive words are like adulteress, prostitute and those that are not actionable are like calling politicians "frog" and words said in jest, among others. However, in Islam, human honour and dignity is regarded as inviolable and sacred. We are commanded not to defame, laugh at others, be sarcastic, call each other by offensive nicknames, to avoid suspicion for suspicion in some cases becomes a sin, also not to speak ill of each other behind their backs for all these would be a sin, the punishment of it of which is "eating the flesh of his dead brother."[71]

Further, the concept of defamation is the same in both systems, with a little difference as to the terms. At common law, there is liable and slander, permanent form or spoken, which in Islam there are terms like *hammaz* (oral) and *lammaz* (documentation) that also mean the same thing. In a different perspective, the Arabic term *buhtan* in the Quran refers to slander, i.e. spreading a lie, that which is untrue or fabricated. Therefore, backbiting would mean spreading statements to others that are not true of a person, and this undoubtedly constitutes a sin.

Besides, in both systems, punishment is harsh as defamation has serious repercussions. This is one of the main threads that are similar in both legal systems. As far as the scope and concept are concerned, there can be a convergence between the two

69 *Sahih Al-Bukhari.*
70 *Surah Qaf* (50): 18.
71 *See* footnote 51.

systems. However, on the issue of punishment, it is not seen in Islamic Law that damages, i.e. monetary compensation, are awarded. This is unlike at common law, where it has become a trend for the courts to grant handsome awards into millions of ringgit, depending on who brings the action. These awards have stimulated more litigation of defamation actions to clear their names and become richer at the same time. Lastly, in Islamic Law, the most serious slander is that of a chaste woman for which 80 lashes is prescribed (*hudud*). If the slander does not meet the level of the *hadd*, the discretionary punishment can be carried out depending on the discretion of the judge. Punishment in the Qur'an for these acts that are considered sinful is more concentrated in the hereafter. Especially in current times because many people escape the clutches of the law after sending defamatory material on social media. If a person thinks he is safe under the common law if he has not been found liable for defamation, he is still not free from it in the next world. As a final remark, it is worthwhile to quote the Prophet (SAW) addressed during the Farewell Pilgrimage: "Your lives, your honour, and your property are as sacred to each other as the sacredness of this your day, in this your month, and in this your city."[72]

72 *See* "The Farewell Sermon of the Prophet Muhammad (PBUH)," accessed March 24, 2022, https://humanappeal.org.uk/news/2020/07/the-farewell-sermon-of-the-prophet-muhammad-pbuh.

Ridoan Karim and Normann Witzleb

8 "Trust" and "Self-Accountability" in the Protection of Privacy: Responding to the Rise of International Data Protection Standards in Muslim Countries

8.1 Introduction

The world over, people seek to guard their personal privacy against wrongful invasion by state power, commercial actors, and intrusive neighbours. The value of privacy has taken its legal manifestation as the right to privacy. Following the Universal Declaration of Human Rights, a range of international legal instruments[1] and an ever-increasing number of domestic legal systems acknowledge and protect this right in one form or another.

Nevertheless, the universal nature of privacy does not imply it is perceived similarly everywhere.[2] In fact, there are widely acknowledged differences of opinion regarding the significance, analysis, components, and extent of privacy in different jurisdictions.[3] While the strongest influence on privacy jurisprudence and scholarship has been Western legal thought, the importance of respecting the privacy of others is also recognised in Islam, as is evident in both the *Qur'an* (sacred scripture of Islam) and *Sunnah* (tradition of the Prophet Muhammad). Some scholarship has been exploring the extent to which privacy is protected by Islam and the kinds of privacy recognised by Shari'ah.[4] A closer analysis of the extent to which Islamic legal

1 Oliver Diggelmann and Maria Nicole Cleis, "How the Right to Privacy Became a Human Right," *Human Rights Law Review* 14, no. 3 (2014): 443, doi.org/10.1093/hrlr/ngu014. *See* also Lorna Woods, "Digital Privacy and Article 12 of the Universal Declaration of Human Rights," *Political Quarterly* 90, no. 3 (2019); 422–429, doi.org/10.1111/1467-923X.12740.

2 Kristian P. Humble, "International Law, Surveillance and the Protection of Privacy," *International Journal of Human Rights* 25, no. 1 (2021): 1–25, doi.org/10.1080/13642987.2020.1763315. *See* also Salwa Ahmed Medan, "Violation of the Right to Electronic Privacy in Public International Law," *Opción* 36, 27 (2020); 663–83.

3 The task of identifying these differences is made more complex by the fact that no universal definition of the term "privacy" has emerged in the philosophical, political and juridical debates: Daniel J. Solove, "Conceptualizing Privacy," *California Law Review* 90, no. 4 (2002): 1087, doi.org/10.2307/3481326.

4 Prominent discussions include: Muhammad Aslam Hayat, "Privacy and Islam: From the Quran to Data Protection in Pakistan," *Information and Communications Technology Law* 16, no. 2 (2007): 137–148, doi.org/10.1080/13600830701532043; Ali Alibeigi, Abu Bakar Munir and Md Ershadul Karim, "Right to Privacy, a Complicated Concept to Review," *Library Philosophy and Practice* (2019), doi.org/10.2139/ssrn.3537968; Ahmad Atif Ahmad, *Islam, Modernity, Violence, and*

https://doi.org/10.1515/9783110766707-008

thought endorses data protection and privacy could have considerable practical significance. Shari'ah, being the formal legal system in many Muslim countries, promises to uphold the moral and religious values among its citizens and governs issues pertaining to social trust among political institutions. At present, a number of countries following Shari'ah have enacted data privacy laws.[5] However, the main objective of data protection laws in these countries is not to enshrine the principles of Islam, but to emulate international legal standards, in particular those of the European Union's General Data Protection Regulation (GDPR). Doing so follows predominantly a commercial objective: when domestic laws achieve a respectable level of data protection, international data flows are facilitated, making the countries potentially attractive markets for data exports and the provision of data-reliant services. It is notable that none of the Muslim states have yet claimed that their privacy laws are Shari'ah-compliant, which stands in marked contrast to banking and financial laws, where Muslim countries have made significant efforts to establish Shari'ah-compliant products and services.

This chapter explores the extent to which the right to privacy has been recognised in the laws of certain key Muslim countries. In this process, several aspects of data protection laws will be investigated from both Islamic and Western perspectives, the latter with a focus on the common law. The purpose of this chapter is neither to extol the virtues of, nor excoriate, one legal tradition over another but to explore how different jurisprudential systems approach a similar societal issue. Keeping in mind the ultimate objective of law to establish justice, equity, and fairness in society, positive features of a legal system regarding any issue can provide valuable learnings for the development of law and legal practice. Islamic thoughts and ideas have for centuries penetrated the global legal discourse and furnished thought-provoking and beneficial insights into principles of international trade governance and commerce.[6] It is a fascinating reminder that the desire to safeguard data protection and privacy rights, which has been given significant attention under both common law and Shari'ah, may lead to the formulation of robust laws and policies that are compatible with both legal systems.

Everyday Life (New York: Palgrave Macmillan, 2009), ch "The Right to Privacy", doi.org/10.1057/9780230619562_8.

5 *See* Hayat, "Privacy and Islam: From the Quran to Data Protection in Pakistan." *See* also Sattam Eid Almutairi, "The Islamic and Western Cultures and Values of Privacy," *Muslim World Journal of Human Rights* 16, no. 1 (2019): 51–80, doi.org/10.1515/mwjhr-2019-0004. Also *see* A. Rasheed, "Prioritizing Fair Information Practice Principles Based on Islamic Privacy Law," *Berkeley J. Middle E. & Islamic L.* 11, no. 1 (2020): 1, doi.org/10.15779/Z38P843W74.

6 R. Karim and I.M. Sifat, "Treatment of Silence as Misrepresentation in Contracts: A Critical Comparative Analysis of Common Law and Islamic Jurisprudence," *International Journal of Law and Management* 60, no. 1 (2018): 69–78, doi.org/10.1108/IJLMA-08-2016-0073.

8.2 Conceptions of Privacy in Islamic Thought

Before addressing the status of privacy in Islamic law, it will be useful to explain the structure and sources of Shari'ah. Shari'ah is the way of living by a Muslim to achieve the desired adherence to Islam in worldly existence and the afterlife. While Shari'ah is the Islamic law revealed in the *Qur'an*[7] and the *Sunnah*,[8] the *fiqh* is the human reasoning to discern the practical consequences of Islam.[9] *Fiqh* expands and develops Shari'ah through interpretation (*ijtihad*)[10] of the Qur'an and Sunnah by Islamic jurists (*ulama*) and is implemented by the rulings (*fatwa*) of jurists on questions presented to them. As *Qur'an* and *Sunnah* do not explicitly deal with every problem of today's world, interpretations by Islamic jurists are necessary for the development of Shari'ah. Islam's basic principle is steadfast devotion to God's precepts. The *Qur'an* is the divine message from Allah, and the *Sunnah* refers to the practices of the Prophet Muhammad of Islam. *Sunnah* are compiled and codified in *Hadiths*, known as Prophetic traditions. The *Qur'an* and *Sunnah* reside at the top of Islamic jurisprudence, and all the Shari'ah principles derive from them.[11]

Under Islamic belief, a pious person submits himself to God and is obligated to enhance the good of humankind as God instructed.[12] Since its inception, Islamic

---

7 The *Qur'an* is replete with conditions to ordain good and forbid evil. The Arabic term is: *Amr bi al-Maruf wa'l-Nahy an al-Munkar*, meaning commanding right and forbidding wrong.

8 The *Sunnah/Hadiths*, or Prophetic traditions, are the model behaviours as demonstrated by the Prophet. It is a method, practice or manner of living for a good Muslim. The *Sunnah* were compiled through Prophet Muhammad's communications in the form of *Hadiths*, which are religious or secular communications, stories, or discussions of history and philosophy. The *isnad*, or narrators of the *Hadith*, convey the *matn*, or content, of the Prophet's actions or statements. The Sunnah's accuracy came under scrutiny over time by Muslim scholars as most of them are compiled after the Prophet's demise; hence, concerns remain about their falsification and dilution. Nevertheless, many Sunnah are invariably accepted by Muslim scholars and considered the most important source of Islamic law, after the Qur'an. *See* Vidushi Marda and Bhairav Acharya, "Identifying Aspects of Privacy in Islamic Law," The Centre for Internet & Society, 2014, cis-india.org/internet-governance/blog/identifying-aspects-of-privacy-in-islamic-law.

9 *See* generally, Mohd Yusri Bin Ibrahim, "Maqasid Al-Shariah: Sejarah Perkembangan Serta Sumbangan Para Ulama Usul Al-Fiqh Awalin Dan Muta'akhirin [Maqasid Al-Shariah: The History of the Development and Contribution of the Scholars of Usul Al-Fiqh Awalin and Muta'akhirin" *International Research Journal of Shariah, Muamalat and Islam* 1, no. 2 (2019): 18–30, doi.org/10.35631/irjsmi.12003.

10 *Ijtihad* presupposes a range of secondary sources such as analogic reasoning (*Qiyas*), logical interpretations in the public interest (*Isthihsan*), unanimous consensus (*Ijma*), and the continuity presumption (*Istishab*). *Ijtihad* implies a persistent attempt to infer the law from the primary sources (*Qur'an* and *Sunnah*) that are not clear enough to implement in the contemporary world.

11 Ahmed Gad Makhlouf, "Evolution of Islamic Law in the 20th Century: The Conception of Collective Ijtihād in the Debate between Muslim Scholars," *Oxford Journal of Law and Religion* 9, no. 1 (2020): 157, doi.org/10.1093/ojlr/rwaa019.

12 Marda and Acharya, "Identifying Aspects of Privacy in Islamic Law".

law has maintained a separation of the private and public realms. For example, rights (*huqq*) in Islam are divided into two domains, with the rights of God (*huqq Allah, huqq al-Shar*) and the rights of men (*huqq al-ibd, huqq an-ns*).[13] The rights of men correspond to the interests between individuals, such as the right of ownership. The rights of God do not deal with any individual but rather address the interest of all human beings. A satisfactory answer to the question of how Islamic law should deal with the right to privacy in today's era is that privacy can be regarded both as a right of men and a right of God.

In Islam, the right to privacy is considered a fundamental and sacred human right. For instance, the Universal Islamic Declaration of Human Rights of 1981, the Cairo Declaration of 1990, and the Arab Charter on Human Rights of 1994 recognised privacy as a human right. The Universal Islamic Declaration of Human Rights, in its article XXI, mentions that "every person is entitled to the protection of his privacy."[14] The Universal Islamic Declaration of Human Rights of 1981 is the second fundamental document proclaimed by the Islamic Council to mark the beginning of the fifteenth century of the Islamic era, the first being the Universal Islamic Declaration announced at the International Conference, held in London in April 1980. The Universal Islamic Declaration of Human Rights is based on the *Qur'an* and the *Sunnah* and has been compiled by eminent Muslim scholars, jurists, and representatives of Islamic movements and thought. In addition to the Universal Islamic Declaration of Human Rights, article 19(b) of the Cairo Declaration states that "[e]veryone shall have the right to privacy in the conduct of his private affairs, in his home, among his family, with regard to his property and his relationships. It is not permitted to spy on him, to place him under surveillance or to besmirch his good name. The State shall protect him from arbitrary interference."[15] Additionally, article 21(1) of the Arab Charter on Human Rights states that "no one shall be subjected to arbitrary or unlawful interference with his privacy, family, home or correspondence, or to unlawful attacks on his honor and reputation."[16] In 1994, the League of Arab States adopted the first version of the Arab Charter on Human Rights at the League's 50th anniversary. The adoption of the Charter symbolised the importance of respect for human rights both to the Arab world and the League.

Islamic law thus recognises a duty on the state/community to safeguard matters relating to privacy, as the state is under an obligation to protect the human rights of its citizens.[17] The believers in Islam are obliged to respect the privacy of others, considering it an integral part of their faith and religious duty to establish

13 Mashood Adebayo Baderin, "Modern Muslim States Between Islamic Law and International Human Rights Law" (PhD diss., The University of Nottingham, 2001), 48–64.

14 Universal Islamic Declaration of Human Rights (1981), art XXI.

15 Cairo Declaration of the Organisation of Islamic Cooperation on Human Rights (2020), art 19(b).

16 Arab Charter on Human Rights (2004), art 21(1).

17 Arab Charter on Human Rights (2004), art 21(1).

social conscience and trust.[18] Hence, it falls under the rights of God. However, the right to privacy should also be regarded as a right of men as it establishes the protection of the honour and repute of an individual, including the prohibitions of any interference or encroachment on an individual's life and property.

Islamic law also acknowledges social rules and norms beyond the religious one and sets out punishments for breaching both rights of men and rights of God.[19] The distinction also has implications for the question of punishment for sins committed, with Islamic law accepting a division of sins against humankind and sins against God.[20] Islamic law recognises contemporary modern laws as long as they conform with *Qur'an* and *Sunnah*.[21] As such, the contemporary enactments in privacy law are compatible with Islamic laws as long as they do not violate, vary, or subtract from the Shari'ah principles of *Qur'an* and *Sunnah*.

Today's understanding and references relating to the term "privacy" cannot be derived directly or solely from the *Qur'an* and *Sunnah*, due to the difference in social and historical contexts. However, there are several aspects of our modern understanding of privacy that can be correlated to the historic texts. The *Qur'an* contains several prescriptions relating to the sanctity of the home, the prohibition on meddling and spying, and the protection of honour, reputation, and private correspondence. These can all be understood as early recognitions of the need to protect personal space and privacy.

In Islam, the sanctity of the home is of significant importance, as is apparent from the *Qur'anic* verse: "Do not enter any houses except your own homes unless you are sure of their occupant's consent."[22] On several occasions, the Prophet also instructed his disciples not to enter other people's dwellings unexpectedly.[23] The *Qur'an*, in addition to *Sunnah*, reprimands persons who pry for no good reason or harbour suspicions about others, and it acknowledges that some such acts or slanders may even be deemed a crime.[24] As regards unwanted meddling and spying,

18 Hayat, "Privacy and Islam: From the Quran to Data Protection in Pakistan".

19 Baderin, "Modern Muslim States Between Islamic Law and International Human Rights Law", 48–64.

20 Baderin, "Modern Muslim States", 48–64.

21 *See* generally Gamal Moursi Badr, "Islamic Law: Its Relation to Other Legal Systems," *The American Journal of Comparative Law* 26, no. 2 (1978): 187–198, doi.org/10.2307/839667. *See* also Asasriwarnia Asasriwarnia and M. Jandra, "Comparison Of Legal System: Islamic Law System, Civil Law, and Common Law," *UMRAN – International Journal of Islamic and Civilizational Studies* 5, no. 2–1 (2018): 3–10, doi.org/10.11113/umran2018.5n2-1.304.

22 Surah An-Nur, Al-Qur'an, 24:27.

23 Hayat, "Privacy and Islam: From the Quran to Data Protection in Pakistan".

24 Al-Qur'an, 49:12: "Do not spy on one another." *See* Almutairi, "The Islamic and Western Cultures and Values of Privacy".

the Prophet requested not to interfere with others' personal matters that do not concern the larger community.[25] The Prophet reportedly said that the non-interference of individuals in matters that do not concern them is a sign of their good faith.[26] The Prophet, according to the hadith of *Amir Mu'awiyah* remarked: "If you try to find out the secrets of the people, then you will definitely spoil them or at least you will bring them to the verge of ruin."[27] Hence, many Muslim scholars believe that private information is safeguarded in Shari'ah, giving individuals significant protection of their private domain.[28]

Islam aims at establishing its society on the clearness of conscience and mutual trust. In Islam, the basic assumption concerning people is that they are innocent. A mere suspicion should not be allowed to result in the accusation of an innocent person. In *Qur'an*, it is clearly stated: "O ye who believe! Avoid suspicion as much (as possible): for suspicion in some cases is a sin: and spy not on each other, nor speak ill of each-other behind their backs."[29] Connecting the basic assumption of innocence to a prohibition on spying and slander, Shari'ah extends the concept of privacy of communications. The Prophet once said, "He, who looks into a letter belonging to his brother, looks into the Hellfire,"[30] indicating that private communications shall not be interfered with. This is also evident from another saying of the Prophet, "private encounters result in entrustment,"[31] which entails a restriction on communications arising out of private meetings. A reasonable conclusion from reading these *Hadiths* is that Islam mandates respect for the privacy of communications between individuals, guaranteeing that a faithful believer will not show disrespect by disclosing it.

Islam also prohibits the dissemination of information where it leads to injustice and destruction.[32] In this respect the *Qur'an* states: "When there comes to them some matter touching (public) safety or fear, they divulge it. If they had only referred it to the Messenger, or to those charged with authority among them, the proper investigators would have tested it from them (directly)."[33] Therefore, information may be

25 Sunan Abu Dawud, Hadith No. 4890. Additionally, Qur'an provides the similar connotations in Sura'ah Al-Hujurat: 12.

26 *See* also Marda and Acharya, "Identifying Aspects of Privacy in Islamic Law".

27 Sunan Abu Dawud, Hadith No. 4888.

28 *See* generally, Almutairi, "The Islamic and Western Cultures and Values of Privacy". *See* also Marda and Acharya, "Identifying Aspects of Privacy in Islamic Law". *Also* Hayat, "Privacy and Islam: From the Quran to Data Protection in Pakistan".

29 Al Qur'an, Sura'ah Al-Hujurat: 12.

30 The quote is taken from Ahmad Atif Ahmad, *Islam, Modernity, Violence, and Everyday Life* (New York: Palgrave Macmillan, 2009), 178. *See* also Marda and Acharya, "Identifying Aspects of Privacy in Islamic Law".

31 *See* Marda and Acharya, "Identifying Aspects of Privacy in Islamic Law."

32 *See* Al Qur'an, ch. 12:5; and ch. 2:195.

33 Al Qur'an, ch. 4:83.

disseminated in Islam as long as this serves the public interests and promotes justice. Islam does not prevent Muslims from accessing knowledge or collecting information, as long as it is done in good faith, with good intentions, and for clear benefit.[34]

In Islam, information that is useful to society and Ummah (the community of Muslims) can be approved, used, and disseminated after the proper verification. The Prophet Sulayman (Solomon) was reported to have made efforts to verify intelligence information brought to him regarding the activities of the people of Saba.[35] A well-established Islamic principle is that information that is essential in social and religious life must come from authentic sources.[36] This is divine guidance to be followed by Muslims when they receive information. In fact, the *Qur'an*[37] outlines that a stringent approach is especially critical when information comes from a sinful (*jasiq*): "O ye who believe! If a wicked person comes to you with any news, ascertain the truth, lest ye harm people unwittingly, and afterwards become full of repentance for what ye have done."[38] Under the precepts of the *Qur'an*, verification is essential if the validity of information is in doubt so as to avoid harm to the person it concerns.

Shari'ah not only recognises the sensitivity of private information and communications in the abstract, but also sanctions infringement of personal privacy through civil or criminal liability.[39] One general category of crime consists of those offences revealed in the Holy *Qur'an* with specified punishments that cannot be modified or altered.[40] Another category of crimes is punishable by *tazir*, which are crimes not specifically indicated in the Holy *Qur'an* or in the Prophet's *Sunnah*; however, they are punishable because they represent acts of disobedience to God's commandments and lead to wrongdoing.[41] As the importance of privacy has been directly and indirectly revealed in the *Qur'an* and *Sunnah*, breach of privacy under specific Islamic

---

34 Hadith narrated by *al-Turmudhi*, *Ibn Majah*, *al-Baihaqi*, *al-Tabrani*, and *Ibn Abi Shaiban*.

35 Al Qur'an, ch. 27:27. *See* also Sonny Zulhuda, "Information Security in the Islamic Perspective: The Principles and Practices," in *Proceeding of the 3rd International Conference on Information and Communication Technology for the Moslem World: ICT Connecting Cultures, ICT4M 2010*, 2010, doi.org/10.1109/ICT4M.2010.5971936.

36 A.D. Al-'Amili, *Mawsu'al Al-Istikhbiirat Wa Al-Amn [The Documents of Intelligence and Security]* (Beirut: Dar al-Amfr li al-Thaqafah wa al-'Uliim, 1993). Similar discussions can be found in A.F. Yousif, *Islam & Science* (Kuala Lumpur: IIUM Press, 2004) and in Zulhuda, "Information Security in the Islamic Perspective: The Principles and Practices". Al Qur'an, ch. 27:27.

37 Al Qur'an, ch. 49:6.

38 Al Qur'an, ch. 49:6.

39 Hayat, "Privacy and Islam: From the Quran to Data Protection in Pakistan".

40 Muhammad Afzal and Muhammad Khubaib, "Flexibility in the Implementation of Islamic Criminal Law in Modern Islamic Society in the Light of Qur'ān and Sunnah," *Journal of Islamic Thought and Civilization* 11, no. 1 (2021): 396–410, doi.org/10.32350/JITC.111.21.

41 Afzal and Khubaib, "Flexibility in the Implementation of Islamic Criminal Law", 396–410.

rules can be considered information theft, which may be considered a *tazir* offence.[42] In such cases, the sentence may vary according to the nature of the offence and the harm caused.

Islamic law does not equate personal data with the property.[43] Interestingly, civil liability attached to a privacy breach is based on the *fiqh* (juristic principle) of Islam, which shares similarities with torts in the common law (and civil wrongs in the civil law tradition). The infringement of information rights creates civil liability; for example, several Islamic legal maxims (*qawaid fiqhiyyah*) reflect these liability principles as referred to in the *Mejelle*, the Islamic civil law code (1877–1926) utilised in the Ottoman Califate. The legal maxims impose obligations to pay monetary compensation for economic losses to the innocent parties, and such principles are equally applicable to the privacy breach or wrongful interference with personal information, including online data of today's digital age.

In summary, Islam recognises privacy as a sacred right through different commands and principles of the *Qur'an* and *Sunnah* mentioned above. The believers in Islam are obliged to respect the privacy of others, considering it an integral part of their faith and a religious duty. Islam safeguards privacy against the state as well as against private parties. Shari'ah recognises the sensitivity of private information and communications, and the violation of privacy is considered a sin. The breach of privacy also creates civil liability, and the legal liability can be imposed to pay monetary compensation for economic losses to the innocent parties.

8.3 Privacy and Data Protection in the Common Law System

Traditionally, the common law did not recognise a right to privacy. An invasion of privacy was actionable only where it fell within the confines of an established tort, constituted a breach of confidence, or breached a contractual agreement.[44] However, today's situation is, albeit with significant jurisdictional variations, quite different. Many common law jurisdictions recognise one or more privacy torts, in addition to the protection of data privacy rights under public law. While some juris-

42 In Islamic Law, the punishment of *tazir* offences is at the discretion of the judge (*qadi*) or ruler of the state.

43 However, some Muslim scholars consider personal information to be a form of intangible property: *See* Hayat, "Privacy and Islam: From the Quran to Data Protection in Pakistan", 31.

44 Tort actions to protect privacy interests include defamation, trespass, nuisance and intentional infliction of harm. In some contexts, copyright legislation can also provide some protection.

dictions have created statutory torts,[45] others rely on protections developed at common law.

While the United States has the longest history of recognising distinct privacy torts, the strong protection of free speech in the First Amendment of the US Constitution has hampered the development of comprehensive privacy protections in that country.[46] Other common law jurisdictions, such as Canada, New Zealand, and the United Kingdom, adopted their bills of rights in more recent times. While not all these instruments expressly protect the right to privacy,[47] they provide the foundation for privacy protections in these jurisdictions. In the United Kingdom, the courts have developed a new tort of misuse of private information, initially building on the equitable action for breach of confidence. This jurisprudence was prompted by the enactment of the Human Rights Act 1998, which incorporated the European Convention on Human Rights in domestic law. Responding to domestic human rights protections, courts in New Zealand and the Canadian provinces without statutory privacy torts have also recognised common law actions against the invasion of privacy and unlawful disclosure of private facts. The protection of privacy is never absolute; it requires the balancing of privacy with competing public and private interests.[48]

One important recent example of a constitutional right to privacy developed through judicial law-making can be found in India. In the case of *Puttaswamy v Union of India*, a nine-judge bench held that the right to privacy is protected as a fundamental right under articles 14, 19, and 21 of the Constitution of India.[49] There are also some dicta that suggest the existence of a tort of invasion of privacy,[50] although the position is not clear. In other common law jurisdictions, such as Hong Kong,

45 The Canadian provinces of British Columbia (1968), Manitoba (1970), Saskatchewan (1974) and Newfoundland and Labrador (1981) enacted statutory privacy torts for the unauthorised disclosure of private facts and for unreasonable intrusion into seclusion: Chris DL Hunt and Nikta Shirazian, "Canada's Statutory Privacy Torts in Commonwealth Perspective" *Oxford U Comparative L Forum* (2016): 3. *See* Normann Witzleb, "A Statutory Cause of Action for Privacy? A Critical Appraisal of Three Recent Australian Law Reform Proposals," *Torts Law Journal* 19 (2011): 104–34, doi.org/10.13140/2.1.3159.1684.

46 Edward J. Bloustein, "Privacy, Tort Law, And The Constitution: Is Warren And Brandeis' Tort Petty And Unconstitutional As Well?," in Edward J. Bloustein, *Individual & Group Privacy* (Boca Raton: Routledge, 2017), doi.org/10.4324/9781351319966-2. *See* also Lior Jacob Strahilevitzt, "Reunifying Privacy Law," *California Law Review* 98, no. 6 (2010), doi.org/10.15779/Z38RX2P.

47 Petra Butler, "The Case for a Right to Privacy in the New Zealand Bll of Rights Act," *New Zealand Journal of Public and International Law* 11, no. 1 (2013).

48 *See* generally, Daniel J. Solove and Neil M. Richards, "Rethinking Free Speech and Civil Liability," *Columbia Law Review* 109, no. 7 (2009): 1650–1707.

49 Justice K. S. Puttaswamy (Retd.) v Union of India, Writ Petition (Civil) No 494 of 2012; (2017) 10 SCC 1; AIR 2017 SC 4161.

50 Secretary General, Supreme Court of India v Subhash Chandra Agarwal (2010) INHCD 40, para. 110.

Malaysia, Singapore, and Australia, law reform efforts to create a privacy tort are also yet to bear fruit. The perceived difficulty of formulating the elements of a privacy action and a belief that incidental protections might be sufficient create formidable obstacles to privacy law reform.[51] Accordingly, the established equitable doctrine of breach of confidence remains the main mechanism for the protection of privacy in these jurisdictions.[52]

These general protections of privacy are supplemented through specific protection of information privacy via data protection statutes. Most such laws can trace their intellectual roots to the beginning of the modern information age in the 1970s. Notwithstanding some jurisdictional variation, many of the laws in the common law jurisdictions were intended to follow and adopt the 1980 Privacy Guidelines, issued by the Organisation for Economic Co-operation and Development (OECD) for the fair, lawful, and transparent usage of personal data.[53] Within the European Union, the 1998 EU Directive required Member States to harmonise their data protection principles further. This trend towards general data protection laws did not extend to the United States, which has preferred sectoral privacy legislation, albeit there is now an increasing interest at the US state level to enact European-style data protection laws. In 2018, the General Data Protection Regulation (GDPR), replacing the EU Data Protection Directive, has modernised the law, created a largely uniform set of European data protection standards, and strengthened the enforcement of these standards. Additionally, the European Charter recognises data protection as a distinct fundamental right (article 8) alongside the right to respect for private life (article 7).[54] Providing a high level of data protection through the GDPR and related enactments remains a signature initiative of the European Union.

Several important cases demonstrate the vitality and strength of European data protection principles. In *Digital Rights Ireland v Minister of Communications*,[55] an

---

51 *See* Normann Witzleb, "Another Push for an Australian Privacy Tort: Context, Evaluation and Prospects," *Australian Law Journal* 94 (2020): 765–76.

52 *See* also Megan Richardson, "Whither Breach of Confidence: A Right of Privacy for Australia," *Melbourne University Law Review* 26 (2002): 381. *Also* Gavin Phillipson and Helen Fenwick, "Breach of Confidence as a Privacy Remedy in the Human Rights Act Era," *Modern Law Review* 63, no. 5 (2000): 660–93, doi.org/10.1111/1468-2230.00286. *And* Daithi Mac Sithigh, "Beyond Breach of Confidence: An Irish Eye on English and Scottish Privacy Law," *Juridical Review*, 2014, 27–36.

53 OECD, Recommendation of the Council concerning Guidelines Governing the Protection of Privacy and Transborder Flows of Personal Data, 1980, legalinstruments.oecd.org/en/instruments/OECD-LEGAL-0188.

54 European Union, Charter of Fundamental Rights of the European Union, OJ 2012 C 326/391.

55 Digital Rights Ireland Ltd v. Minister for Communications, Marine and Natural Resources (Cases C-293/12 and C-594/12) EU:C:2014:238 (08 April 2014).

Irish civil society group successfully challenged the validity of the EU Data Retention Directive.[56] The Court of Justice of the EU (CJEU) struck down certain provisions of the EU Data Retention Directive as invalid because they fell short of the requirements under the Charter of Fundamental Rights of the European Union. In the case of *Data Protection Commission v. Facebook Ireland Ltd. and Maximillian Schrems*, the CJEU invalidated the US/EU Privacy Shield, which formed the basis for data transfers between both trading blocs, because the court found that the sweeping nature of the measures permitted by US surveillance laws infringed on EU citizens’ data rights.[57] The ruling required the EU and the US to work on a new framework for transatlantic data transfers that provided more robust protection of EU citizens’ data.[58]

These cases, as well as others,[59] have been identified “as yet another sign of the possibility of convergence around legal standards of privacy protection in the future [. . .] for all the legal, social-cultural and political differences that remain and for all the new challenges to privacy that we can expect to *see*.”[60] Principles of Islamic law are another potential force in shaping future privacy protection around a set of shared values but have yet to be recognised as developing impact on contemporary debates.

8.4 Privacy and Data Protection Laws in Muslim Countries

The majority of Muslim nations are characterised by legal pluralism, administering civil and Islamic law in the same jurisdiction. As data privacy is a comparatively modern legal concept, the traditional principles of Islamic law need to be re-interpreted and developed before they can be applied to contemporary data processing practices. Hence, in this section, we consider selected recent legal developments relating to the right to privacy in the Shari’ah-based Muslim states.

56 Directive 2006/24/EC of the European Parliament and of the Council of 15 March 2006 on the retention of data generated or processed in connection with the provision of publicly available electronic communications services or of public communications networks and amending Directive 2002/58/EC, OJ 2006L 105/54.

57 Data Protection Commission v. Facebook Ireland Ltd. and Maximillian Schrems (Case number C-311/18) ECLI:EU:C:2020:559 (16 July 2020).

58 The successor pact, the Trans-Atlantic Data Privacy Framework, has been agreed upon in principle: European Commission, European Commission and United States Joint Statement on Trans-Atlantic Data Privacy Framework, Press Release (25 March 2022), ec.europa.eu/commission/press corner/detail/en/ip_22_2087.

59 Megan Richardson, “A Common Law of Privacy?,” *Singapore Journal of Legal Studies*, 2021, 6–18, also referring to *Vidal-Hall v Google Inc* [2016] QB 1003 (CA); *In re Facebook, Inc., Consumer Privacy User Profile Litigation*, 402 F Supp 3d 767 (ND Cal 2019).

60 Richardson, “A Common Law of Privacy?,”6–18.

Let us start the discussion with countries that have a majority Muslim population and, due to their colonial past, follow the common law tradition. In multi-ethnic Malaysia, Islam is the official religion, but Islamic law only applies to Muslims, primarily in the context of family matters. The Federal Constitution of multi-ethnic Malaysia makes no mention of privacy. Nevertheless, in the case of *Sivarasa v Badan Peguam Malaysia*,[61] the Federal Court stated, without elaborating, that the right to personal liberty under article 5(1) of the Federal Constitution encompasses a right to privacy.[62] However, the percolation of this constitutional protection into private law is still underway. The case of *Ultra Dimension Sdn. Bhd v Kook We Kuan*[63] explored whether an invasion of privacy was actionable in tort under Malaysian law. Referring to the UK decision in *Kaye v Robertson*,[64] the judge held that, as English common law does not recognise the right to privacy, it also does not exist in Malaysian law. While subsequent decisions have shown more willingness to recognise a common law right to privacy, the law continues to be in flux, yet decisions considering a privacy action do not refer to Islamic principles.[65]

The absence of general protections in the law as well as the rise of data processing in the information age bolstered the need for a separate data protection law in Malaysia. Consequently, Malaysia enacted its Personal Data Protection Act, generally known as PDPA, in 2010. The PDPA's purpose is to protect the personal data of individuals, but its coverage is limited to information privacy in the commercial context. It does not apply to data processing by public authorities. The protection standards enacted in the PDPA also fall short of the international benchmarks on personal data protection, in particular the (subsequently enacted) GDPR.[66] Hence,

---

61 [2010] 3 CLJ 507.

62 Gopal Sri Ram FCJ (for the Court) referred to the decision of the Supreme Court of India in *Govind v State of Madhya Pradesh* AIR 1975 SC 1378 for this extension. *See* discussion in Normawati Hashim and Abd Shukor Mohd Yunus, "Right to Privacy and Malaysian Practice: A Step Further in Recognising Another Aspect of Human Rights," *Environment-Behaviour Proceedings Journal* 5, no. SI3 (2020): 289–295, doi.org/10.21834/ebpj.v5isi3.2570.

63 [2004] 5 CLJ 285.

64 [1991] FSR 62.

65 The tort was considered in: *Ultra Dimension Sdn Bhd v. Kook Wei Kuan* [2004] 5 CLJ 285; *Maslinda Ishak v. Mohd Tahir Osman* [2009] 6 CLJ 653; *Dr Bernadine Malini Martin v MPH Magazine Sdn Bhd* [2010] 7 CLJ 525 (CA). The tort was recognised in: *Lee Ewe Poh v. Dr Lim Teik Man* [2011] 4 CLJ 397. Further discussion in Usharani Balasingam & Saifullah Qamar Bin Siddique Bhatti, "Between Lex Lata and Lex Ferenda: An Evaluation of the Extent of the Right to Privacy in Malaysia," *Malayan Law Journal* 4 (2017): 29–55.

66 For an extension to cover predictions: Tay Pek San, "Predictions from Data Analytics: Does Malaysian Data Protection Law Apply?," *Information and Communications Technology Law* 29, no. 3 (2020): 291–307, doi.org/10.1080/13600834.2020.1759276.

privacy scholars advocate legislative reforms to the PDPA to enhance its scope of protection.[67]

In the Islamic Republic of Pakistan, article 14(1) of the 1973 Constitution recognises the "dignity of man and, subject to law, the privacy of home" as inviolable. Other aspects of privacy are not explicitly guaranteed, although the general provision in article 4(1) states that life, liberty, body, reputation, and property can only be interfered with in accordance with law. Specific data privacy laws have been discussed for many years.[68] Recently, the Ministry of Information Technology and Telecommunications released a draft of the Personal Data Protection Bill 2020 for further consultation,[69] which still awaits further debate and adoption.

Bangladesh is essentially a secular country. The Constitution of Bangladesh secures the home against entry, search, and seizure, and protects communications privacy. Although there are no general data protection laws in Bangladesh, there are several statutes that protect privacy interests in different situations, including the Telecommunications (Amendment) Act 2006, Information and Communication Technology Act 2006, the Right to Information Act 2009, and the Digital Security Act 2018.[70]

Indonesia, home to the world's largest Muslim population, has a different colonial history and does not follow English common law tradition. Yet, similarly to Bangladesh and Pakistan, Indonesia does not have a single personal data protection law or any Islamic principles that imply data privacy through the legal and regulatory framework.[71] The regulations on personal data protection are scattered in several sectoral laws. Many of the laws and regulations overlap, resulting in the absence of a comprehensive and integrated concept of personal data protection.[72] At present, the provisions on personal data protection can be found in Law 11/2008 on Electronic Information and Transactions; Government Regulation 71/2019 on Implementation of Electronic Systems and Transactions; Ministry of Communication and

67 *See* Ali Alibeigi and Abu Bakar Munir, "Malaysian Personal Data Protection Act, a Mysterious Application," *University of Bologna Law Review* 5, no. 2 (2020): 362–74, doi.org/10.6092/ISSN.2531-6133/12441.

68 Naseem Razi and Rashida Zahoor, "Analyzing the Cyberspace Laws to Protect Data Privacy in Pakistan," *Revista de Direito, Estado e Telecomunicacoes* 13, no. 2 (2021): 42–55.

69 Graham Greenleaf, "Pakistan and Sri Lanka's Data Privacy Bills Move Forward," *Privacy Laws & Business International Report* 24 (2021): 173.

70 Greenleaf, "Pakistan and Sri Lanka's Data Privacy Bills," 173; Muhammad Omar Faruque and Sk. Habibullah, "Privacy as a Human Right in the Digital Age: In Quest of a Safer Protection Regime in Bangladesh," in Mizanur Rahman et el (eds), *ELCOP Yearbook of Human Rights 2018* (Dhaka, Bangladesh: ELCOP, 2018).

71 Danny Kobrata and Rahma Atika, "The Privacy, Data Protection and Cybersecurity Law Review: Indonesia," *The Law Reviews* (2021), thelawreviews.co.uk/title/the-privacy-data-protection-and-cybersecurity-law-review/indonesia.

72 Kobrata and Atika, "The Privacy, Data Protection and Cybersecurity Law Review".

Informatics Regulation No. 20 of 2016 on Personal Data Protection in Electronic Systems; and Ministry of Communications and Informatics Regulation No. 5 of 2020 on Electronic System Provider amended by Ministry of Communications and Informatics Regulation No. 10 of 2021 (MCI 5/2020).[73] However, the Indonesian Government and Parliament are currently discussing the enactment of a Personal Data Protection Bill that is inspired by the GDPR.[74]

In the Middle East, with the exception of Kuwait, all countries of the Gulf Cooperation Council (GCC), consisting of Bahrain, Kuwait, Oman, Qatar, Saudi Arabia, and the United Arab Emirates, have over recent years enacted data protection laws at the national level.

Following the enactment of the GDPR, Qatar was the first nation in the GCC to introduce a data protection statute. The Personal Data Protection Law (DPL), issued at the end of 2016, has established a new legal framework to protect information privacy.[75] The enactment introduced several provisions to ensure lawful and transparent processing of personal data – violation of the law may result in heavy fines of up to USD 1.350 billion.[76]

Bahrain, being another economic hub in the Gulf Region, followed with the enactment of the Personal Data Protection Law No. 30 of 2018, which is modelled on the EU's GDPR.[77] The law applies to residents and firms operating in Bahrain and also to those who use any means accessible in Bahrain to process personal details without having a commercial location in the nation.[78] While the law does not create a general right to privacy, it imposes special consent requirements for data processing and establishes a personal data protection authority.[79]

In the United Arab Emirates (UAE), a new Federal Data Protection Law No. 45 of 2021 came into effect on 2 January 2022.[80] The law has extra-territorial scope, applying to any company established in the UAE and processing personal data overseas or a company established outside of the UAE and processing personal data

73 Kobrata and Atika, "The Privacy, Data Protection and Cybersecurity Law Review".

74 Kobrata and Atika, "The Privacy, Data Protection and Cybersecurity Law Review".

75 *See* Graham Greenleaf, "Global Data Privacy Laws 2017: 120 National Data Privacy Laws, Including Indonesia and Turkey," *Privacy Laws & Business International Report* (2017) 145, 10–13.

76 Law No. (13) of 2016 on Protecting Personal Data Privacy.

77 Maria Casoria and Eman Mahmood AlSarraf, "The Impact of the GDPR on Extra-EU Legal Systems: The Case of the Kingdom of Bahrain," in Maria Tzanou (ed), *Personal Data Protection and Legal Developments in the European Union* (IGI Global, 2020), 224–37, doi:10.4018/978-1-5225-9489-5.ch011.

78 Casoria and Mahmood AlSarraf, "The Impact of the GDPR on Extra-EU Legal Systems", 224–37.

79 Casoria and Mahmood AlSarraf, "The Impact of the GDPR on Extra-EU Legal Systems", 224–37.

80 *See* Alexandre Brazeau and Charlotte Wright, "United Arab Emirates: New UAE Federal Decree Law On Personal Data Protection: What You Need To Know," *Mondaq* (February 2022), www.mondaq.com/data-protection/1158520/new-uae-federal-decree-law-on-personal-data-protection-what-you-need-to-know.

inside the UAE.[81] The law does not apply to Government entities and Government data, nor to personal data already regulated by the Abu Dhabi Global Market (ADGM) or Dubai International Financial Centre (DIFC) data protection laws or covered by special legislation (e.g. personal health data and banking and credit personal data).[82] In addition to this newly enacted law, a number of civil and criminal laws create liability for breaches of privacy, including the Cyber Crimes Law and the Electronic Transactions and Commerce Law.[83] The Abu Dhabi Global Market (ADGM) – an International Financial Centre – adopted its own Data Protection Regulation 2021.[84] The 2021 Regulation is designed to be aligned with the international standards, particularly the GDPR, and enforced by an Office for Data Protection.[85]

Saudi Arabia and Oman have also recently enacted general data protection laws. These appear likewise to be modelled on protections contained in the GDPR, although their practical effect will only become evident after some time of operation. The constitutions of these countries guarantee aspects of the right to privacy, in particular the sanctity of the home and the confidentiality of communications, albeit not a general right to privacy.[86] For example, article 36 of the Constitution of the Kingdom of Saudi Arabia protects the sanctity of the home, and article 40 guarantees the privacy of telegraphic, postal telephone, and other means of communication. It prohibits interference with such communications, except as provided by law. Based on this framework and elaborating on basic Shari'ah that create a right of action (*masouliya taqsiriya*) for the wrongful disclosure of a person's private information,[87] Saudi legislation has focused on privacy violations relating to telecommunications and information technology. For example, the Electronic Transactions Law guarantees data protection in electronic transactions, and the Anti-Cyber Crime Law penalises individuals who illegally access and intercept data transferred over data networks.[88] The code of healthcare practice also limits sharing of health

---

81 Brazeau and Wright, "United Arab Emirates".

82 Brazeau and Wright, "United Arab Emirates".

83 Sagee Geetha Sethu, "Legal Protection for Data Security: A Comparative Analysis of the Laws and Regulations of European Union, US, India and UAE," in *2020 11th International Conference on Computing, Communication and Networking Technologies, ICCCNT 2020*, 2020, doi.org/10.1109/ICCCNT49239.2020.9225488.

84 *See* Sayid Madar, "ADGM: Data Protection Regulations 2021 and what they mean for businesses," *Data Guidance* (March 2021), www.dataguidance.com/opinion/adgm-data-protection-regulations-2021-and-what-they.

85 Sayid Madar, "ADGM".

86 Ali Polat, "Effects of GDPR on the Financial Services Sector in the Kingdom of Saudi Arabia," *Journal of Data Protection and Privacy* 4, no. 3 (2021): 273–82.

87 Simon Elliott, Amgad T. Husein and John Balouziyeh "Privacy and Data Interception in Saudi Arabia," 2012, www.lexology.com/library/detail.aspx?g=ac7a9ca2-367e-4e12-8c14-e513d05db4b1.

88 Tareq Saeed Alshammari and Harman Preet Singh, "Preparedness of Saudi Arabia to Defend Against Cyber Crimes: An Assessment with Reference to Anti-Cyber Crime Law and GCI Index," *Archives of Business Research* 6, no. 12 (2018): 131–46, doi.org/10.14738/abr.612.5771.

data with third parties and imposes penalties for violations.[89] A new Personal Data Protection Law, scheduled to come into full effect in 2023, governs the practices of organisations that collect, process, and store the personal data of individuals.[90] Identified as a significant step forward, the law is heavily modelled on European Union data protection legislation and incorporates internationally accepted principles of data protection law.[91] The unlawful disclosure of sensitive data is sanctioned with the imprisonment for up to two years and/or a fine of up to SAR3,000,000 (about USD 800,000).[92] Failure to comply with the requirements relating to transfers of personal data also attracts significant penalties, namely imprisonment for up to one year and/or a fine of up to SAR1,000,000 (about USD 270,000).[93]

With the promulgation of the Personal Data Protection Law 2022, Oman has become the latest country in the Middle East to adopt data protection legislation.[94] Similar to Saudi Arabia, it requires that data should be processed with "transparency, honesty and human dignity . . . and subject to the Personal Data Subject's express prior consent."[95] At the time of writing, Kuwait thus remains the only GCC country that does not have a stand-alone personal data protection law. However, Law No 20 of 2014 (Electronic Activities) safeguards the right to privacy and includes a dispute resolution process arising from personal data usage, mainly in economic and administrative transactions.[96] In addition, the Kuwaiti Communication and Information Technology Regulatory Authority released Data Privacy Protection Regulation No. 42 of 2021, which adopts rules for the processing of personal data by communication and information technology service providers.

Despite the precarious human rights situation in many Arab countries, strategic partnerships with the West have prompted most Gulf countries to make greater efforts to improve privacy and data protection in the region. As in other regions, the standards adopted in the GDPR have proven particularly influential. While the new regulations share concepts of the GDPR and other international data protection standards, practices and procedures, it is generally not evident that Shari'ah principles are a major influence in determining the newly created data protection laws. The civil wrong of disclosing a person's private information (*masouliya taqsiriya*),

---

89 Hana Alharthi, "Healthcare Predictive Analytics: An Overview with a Focus on Saudi Arabia," *Journal of Infection and Public Health* 11, no. 6 (2018): 749–756, doi.org/10.1016/j.jiph.2018.02.005.

90 *See* Royal Decree M/19 of 9/2/1443H (16 September 2021).

91 Nick O'Connell, "An Overview of Saudi Arabia's New Personal Data Protection Law," *Al Tamimi & Co* www.tamimi.com/law-update-articles/an-overview-of-saudi-arabias-new-personal-data-protection-law/, accessed January 23, 2022.

92 O'Connell, "An Overview of Saudi Arabia's New Personal Data Protection Law".

93 O'Connell, "An Overview of Saudi Arabia's New Personal Data Protection Law".

94 Royal Decree 6/2022 Promulgating the Personal Data Protection Law (2022).

95 Personal Data Protection Law (2022), art 10.

96 *See* Hebah Nassar Alkhaldi, "Legal Challenges of E-Commerce in Kuwait during the COVID-19 Pandemic," *Kilaw Journal* 8, no. 6 (2020): 125.

standing outside the statutory data protection regime, is an example of traditional laws protecting personal privacy on the basis of Shari'ah.

8.5 The Missing Principle in Conventional Data Protection Laws: A Need for Self-Accountability (*Muhasabah*) to Preserve Trust (*Amanah*)

Conventional data protection laws and Islamic principles concerning privacy have a lot in common. The discussion in the earlier section allows us to conclude that the Islamic principles relating to personal information promote lawful, fair, and transparent handling, as do the conventional data protection laws. Islam is also concerned with data accuracy and integrity. Additionally, the Islamic privacy principle seeks to protect personal data from unauthorised or wrongful interference, destruction, or damage, similar to the conventional data protection principles of "integrity and confidentiality," which require that personal data be safeguarded with appropriate technical or organisational measures. Against the background of shared values in the handling of personal information, this section will explore whether the Islamic principle of self-accountability (*muhasabah*) has the potential to be a useful addendum to existing principles enshrined in conventional data protection laws, at least in Muslim countries.

The *Qur'anic* verses clearly emphasise that every Muslim must show self-accountability in all earthly matters.[97] This principle is particularly apposite when applied to data protection. Often, injustices relating to data protection go unobserved by worldly processes and will not be caught under the existing laws and enforcement processes. Furthermore, many questionable data practices in modern information societies lack transparency or are so complex that it is difficult for ordinary individuals to tell how their data was handled and what adverse consequences may flow from misuse. Lastly, even if relevant laws are in place and consumers are aware of their data rights, regulators are often under-resourced to investigate all breaches of data protection laws. This demonstrates the weakness of modern data protection regimes that build solely on legal standards and regulatory enforcement.

The present legal and regulatory settings emphasise accountability towards a regulator rather than attempting to protect privacy as an inherent obligation of each

---

97 Dina M. Abdelzaher, Amr Kotb, and Akrum Helfaya, "Eco-Islam: Beyond the Principles of *Why* and What, and Into the Principles of *How*," *Journal of Business Ethics* 155, no. 3 (2019): 623–43, doi.org/10.1007/s10551-017-3518-2.

data controller.[98] A system for self-accountability, leveraging both public and private responsibility through a combination of legal, regulatory, and technical means, could make a real contribution to tackling contemporary privacy concerns, particularly in jurisdictions where expertise in privacy protection and enforcement is still developing.[99] In addition, we suggest that there is potential for a co-regulation strategy based on a corporate social responsibility model,[100] a trust between the data processor and the data subject, therefore placing a more significant duty on the data controller for compliance. Additionally, self-accountability in data processing will improve society and human lives.

Allah states in the *Qur'an* that "no human action goes unaccounted: And whoso doeth good an atom's weight will *see* it then. And whoso doeth ill an atom's weight will *see* it then."[101] Additionally, the Qur'an mentions: "And say (unto them): Act! Allah will behold your actions, and (so will) His messenger and the believers, and ye will be brought back to the Knower of the Invisible and the Visible, and He will tell you what ye used to do."[102]

In modern data protection regimes, the notion of accountability is already established as a part of data governance. For example, the GDPR has codified the accountability principle in article 5(2), under which a controller shall be responsible for, and be able to demonstrate, compliance with the fundamental data protection principles in article 5(1). Furthermore, article 24 mandates data controllers to "implement the necessary technological and organisational measures" to comply demonstrably with the regulatory standards.[103] This includes reviewing their adopted measures as necessary and implementing an appropriate data protection policy.[104] It means that businesses are accountable to demonstrate their fundamental privacy practices through data protection plans and management systems. However, the

98 Jenna Lindqvist, "New Challenges to Personal Data Processing Agreements: Is the GDPR Fit to Deal with Contract, Accountability and Liability in a World of the Internet of Things?," *International Journal of Law and Information Technology* 26, no. 1 (2018): 45–63, doi.org/10.1093/ijlit/eax024.

99 *See* also Abdulaziz Almebrad, "The Sufficiency of Information Privacy Protection in Saudi Arabia" (SJD thesis, Indiana University, 2018) www.repository.law.indiana.edu/etd/56/.

100 *See* Aviva Geva, "Three Models of Corporate Social Responsibility: Interrelationships between Theory, Research, and Practice," *Business and Society Review* 113, no. 1 (2008): 1–41, doi.org/10.1111/j.1467-8594.2008.00311.x.

101 Al Qur'an, ch. 99:7–8.

102 Al Qur'an, ch. 9:105.

103 Article 24 of the General Data Protection Regulation (GDPR). *See* Lachlan Urquhart, Tom Lodge and Andy Crabtree, "Demonstrably Doing Accountability in the Internet of Things," *International Journal of Law and Information Technology* 27, no. 1 (2019): 1–27, doi.org/10.1093/ijlit/eay015. *See* also Regina Becker et al., "DAISY: A Data Information System for Accountability under the General Data Protection Regulation," *GigaScience* 8, no. 12 (2019): 1–10, doi.org/10.1093/gigascience/giz140.

104 Urquhart, Lodge and Crabtree, "Demonstrably Doing Accountability", 1–27.

precise data protection measures required or expected are not one-size-fits-all.[105] The measures will depend on the circumstances of the data processing, including the risks arising for data subjects.

In practical terms, the accountability principle means that a business acting as a controller may need to implement some of the following key practices: demonstrate appropriate record management, ensure effective and transparent communication with data subjects, conduct a comprehensive review of subscription and application forms, and review the manner in which any consents are collected from data subjects.[106] The principle also incorporates ensuring the implementation of appropriate technical and organisational measures, reviewing data processing agreements, and, if applicable, appointing a Data Protection Officer to oversee their compliance.[107] Accountability is an ongoing obligation of data controllers. Data controllers must observe compliance with data protection rules in the long term and establish a proactive and comprehensive strategy to ensure the right to privacy for its stakeholders. This is where self-accountability comes into play.

It is important to note that self-responsibility should be but one feature of a regulatory system. As in other fields of economic activity, data-driven business practices cannot be regulated through reliance on self-responsibility alone. Economic pressures all too often create temptations to circumvent, water down, or disregard self-regulatory standards. Ultimately, the moral responsibility of "self-accountability" must be backed up by legal responsibility for privacy compliance. The interplay of legal and moral responsibilities may create the virtue of fair treatment of data subjects. Legal responsibilities arising from data protection laws create public law obligations enforceable by regulatory authorities, while moral responsibility seeks to achieve adherence through a commitment to ethical guidelines. Ideally, legal responsibility and ethical accountability are mutually connected for the effective discharge of functions.

Indeed, the nexus between legal responsibility and self-accountability is not new, as can be seen in recent initiatives to move from corporate social responsibility to corporate accountability.[108] To ensure social responsibility, a corporation must first be accountable to itself and its stakeholders. In treating such a responsibility with a private regulatory system, the legal features of "self-accountability" need to be determined. If data protection also relies in part on a private self-

105 Luca Marelli, Elisa Lievevrouw and Ine Van Hoyweghen, "Fit for Purpose? The GDPR and the Governance of European Digital Health," *Policy Studies* 41, no. 5 (2020): 447–67, doi.org/10.1080/01442872.2020.1724929.

106 Hannah Crowther, "The GDPR's Accountability Principle: A Shift in Mindset," *Dropbox Product Tips* (2018) blog.dropbox.com/topics/product-tips/gdpr-accountability-principle.

107 Crowther, "The GDPR's Accountability Principle".

108 *See* Min Yan and Daoning Zhang, "From Corporate Responsibility to Corporate Accountability," *Hastings Business Law Journal* 16, no. 1 (2020): 43–64. *See* also Jau-Yang Liu, "An Internal Control System That Includes Corporate Social Responsibility for Social Sustainability in the New Era," *Sustainability (Switzerland)* 10, no. 10 (2018): 3382, doi.org/10.3390/su10103382.

regulatory system, then the problem of data regulation compliance can be resolved in several ways. Public commitment to engage in self-regulation may form a building block in achieving overall compliance. It is, therefore, a moment for deepened consideration of the value of data privacy, ethics, and social responsibility, which are presently often given low importance in the pursuit of both personal and organisational gains. Religious spirituality, particularly Islamic self-accountability philosophy, might enhance the range of ethical data use, at least in Muslim nations, so that contemporary businesses adopt more responsible and more compassionate practices.

When corporations and societies explore new methods to utilise personal data, it is vital to establish a moral framework in addition to the legal one to ensure that personal data are used responsibly, transparently and ethically, under adequate privacy controls. Secular western societies now seem more concerned with ethical obligations that combine morality and personal values. According to Islam, whatever leads to social and individual welfare is morally good and whatever is injurious is morally bad.[109] Thus, the ethical system prescribed in Islam is eternally divine and forms the foundation of Islamic society, placing great emphasis on social responsibility, trust, and justice.[110] Islamic principles on data use are not fundamentally different from contemporary ethical philosophies; they impose a duty on an individual to reflect God's divine commandments, permeate every aspect of society, including privacy, and guide each person to behave in a socially responsible and just manner. Self-accountability provides a mechanism to demonstrate adherence to these values. It requires an assessment of the potential risks and benefits of specific data use and defines the intended benefits and possible trade-offs between companies and individuals so that all the stakeholders derive benefit from the data practices. This may create a new paradigm of trust (*Amanah*) in the data protection regime.

Amanah is a fundamental virtue associated with all aspects of human actions. Its fulfilment is a command of the Almighty Allah and His Messenger. Interpretations of *amanah* are attached to religious, individual and social responsibilities and to establish justice in every sector.[111] *Surah An-Nisa* in *Qur'an* states: "Surely, Allah commands you to deliver trust to those entitled to them, and that, when you judge between people, judge with justice. Surely, excellent is the exhortation Allah gives you. Surely, Allah is All-Hearing, All-Seeing."[112] The *Qur'an* mentions that trust is

---

109 Jawed Akhtar Mohammed, "The Ethical System in Islam – Implications for Business Practices," in Christoph Luetge (ed), *Handbook of the Philosophical Foundations of Business Ethics* (Dordrecht: Springer, 2013), doi.org/10.1007/978-94-007-1494-6_3.

110 Jawed Mohammed, "The Ethical System in Islam".

111 Muharman Lubis and Mira Kartiwi, "Privacy and Trust in the Islamic Perspective: Implication of the Digital Age," in *2013 5th International Conference on Information and Communication Technology for the Muslim World, ICT4M 2013*, 2013, doi.org/10.1109/ICT4M.2013.6518898

112 Al-Qur'an, Surah An-Nisa 4:58.

the first requirement to be called *mu’min* (believer of Islam).[113] Trust is mainly concerned with personal boundaries, confidentiality, ownership, and ethics from the Islamic perspective. If the trust is breached, it should be dealt with as betrayal (*khiyiiniit*), which is considered a sin.[114]

Muslim scholars emphasise the vast dimension of *Amanah*, which transcends all areas and stages of human life.[115] Hence, humans should be thoughtful and act with responsibility in order to uphold the values of trust. Privacy and trust are closely related to each other. The rapid expansion of information technology revolutionised communication processes and created multiple ethical issues within society and its members. Infringement of privacy expectations can occur not only during the collection of personal data but also in their subsequent use, especially when it involves attempts to profit from illegitimate practices that fall outside a data subject’s consent or expectations. Studies of interpersonal information exchange confirm that trust is a precondition for self-disclosure because it reduces perceived risks involved in revealing private information.[116]

The implementation of fundamental principles relating to the collection and proper use of personal data, authentication of its accuracy, assessments of the impact of data usage on the person concerned, the need for proper custody of information and preservation of confidentiality can all be found in many *Qur’anic* injunctions and Prophetic traditions. Therefore, it is accurate to conclude that Islam encourages, adopts, and practices fair information and privacy principles. Additionally, embracing the concept of self-accountability and trust in data protection may help to improve compliance and reduce perceived privacy risks involved in modern data-driven business models.

8.6 Conclusion

The modern right to privacy has historic antecedents and religious support in Islam, as is evident in both the *Qur’an* and *Sunnah*. In recent years, there has been a growing global trend to enact or reform data protection laws that reflect principles enshrined in the GDPR and other international data protection laws. Countries following Islamic law in the Middle East and elsewhere do not make specific recourse to Islamic principles in drafting their data laws. Instead, data privacy and protection laws are adopted

113 Al Qur’an, Surah Al Mu’menun: 8.
114 Zulhuda, “Information Security in the Islamic Perspective: The Principles and Practices”.
115 Lubis and Kartiwi, “Privacy and Trust in the Islamic Perspective: Implication of the Digital Age”.
116 Tracy Ann Kosa, “Vampire Bats: Trust in Privacy,” in *PST 2010: 2010 8th International Conference on Privacy, Security and Trust* (2010), doi.org/10.1109/PST.2010.5593227.

and enhanced to accommodate a developing global consensus on the need for the effective protection of personal information. This allows these jurisdictions to access data flows from Western economies and reap the economic benefits of providing data-driven services in the international marketplace. The continued development of the right to data protection and privacy, both in common law and in conventional human rights perspectives, has growing significance in the digital age. There are no fundamental disparities between these secular laws of data protection and Islamic legal principles. Hence, as long as data protection laws encourage and require the fair, just, and equitable use of personal data, they may be regarded as Shari'ah-compliant.

Secular laws on data protection can be supported with well-established Islamic principles relating to the sanctity of the home, the prohibition on meddling and spying, and the protection of honour, reputation, and private correspondence. In addition, there is untapped potential to draw on the Islamic notion of self-accountability in support of enhancing compliance with modern data privacy laws. Demonstrated self-accountability can engender trust between data processor and data subject, which in turn facilitates data practices that are sustainable, legitimate and beneficial for all parties. Especially agencies and organisations operating in societies adhering to Shari'ah principles and values are invited to consider the advantages of self-accountability to acknowledge and protect the interests of their clients and consumers.

Indeed, without building public trust through self-accountability, the legal protection of privacy may leave undesirable gaps, in particular where public knowledge about secular data protection laws is still developing. When corporations and societies seek new methods to utilise personal data, it is vital to establish a moral framework in addition to the legal one to ensure that personal data are used responsibly.

Maizatun Mustafa

9 Enhancing Environmental Sustainability Through the Harmonisation of Common Law and Shari'ah

9.1 Introduction

For several decades, countries globally have been dealing with environmental problems, including air and water pollution, depletion of natural resources, and climate change.[1] The primary cause of these problems is human disturbance. Starting from the nineteenth century's industrial revolution, which mechanised the production and manufacturing of goods and utilised fuels as a source of energy, the industrial sector continues to become one of the main factors in the deteriorating quality of the environment.[2] Additionally, factors such as urbanisation, population and energy consumption increase, and agricultural intensification also contribute to environmental pollution.[3] The World Health Organization[4] and the United Nations Environment Programme[5] have confirmed that pollution has accounted for nearly 25 percent of global mortalities, including 7 million deaths per year due to poor air quality and 3.5 million deaths as a result of poor water quality. In 2020 and 2021, the United Nations published the World Water Development Report, which highlighted the impacts of climate change on water quality in many parts of the world[6] and the deteriorating water quality due to pollution.

Continued environmental degradation necessitates countries to set up their legal framework to provide for long-term measures toward environmental protection. Throughout several decades, the importance of having a national environmental policy and law has been well documented. In 2019, the United Nations' first-ever "Global Assessment of Environmental Rule of Law" highlighted the dramatic growth of

1 United Nations Environmental Programme, *Annual Report 2021* (Nairobi: UNEP, 2022), 1–13.
2 M.A. Kuddus, E. Tynan & E. McBryde, "Urbanization: A Problem for the Rich and the Poor?," *Public Health Rev* 41, no. 1 (2020): 1–4.
3 United Nations, *Global Environment Outlook – GEO-6: Healthy Planet, Healthy People* (Nairobi: University Printing House, Cambridge, 2019), 3–17.
4 "Policy Brief: Priority Environment and Health Risks, 2021," WHO, accessed April 1, 2022, https://www.who.int/heli/risks/en/.
5 United Nations Environmental Programme, *Annual Report 2021.*
6 UNESCO, *United Nations World Water Development Report 2020: Water and Climate Change* (Paris: UNESCO, 2020), 10–37.

Notes: This chapter is funded by the IIIT Strategic Research Project (SRP) 2020 "Applied Maqasid Studies."

https://doi.org/10.1515/9783110766707-009

environmental laws worldwide and noted that 176 countries had established their national laws which are pertinent in slowing or reversing environmental degradation.[7]

The beginning of the "modern" national-level environmental legal framework started in 1972 following the United Nations Conference on the Human Environment in Stockholm.[8] It was during this Conference that, for the first time, countries across the world came together to identify and address environmental issues affecting the world. This Conference was founded on the central issue of conflict between economic development and environmental protection, and it was during this time that the idea of "sustainable development" was born.[9] Following the Stockholm Conference, many countries, including Malaysia, made a concerted effort to enact environmental laws, establish environmental agencies, and introduce policy directives on the matter. In 1992, the United Nations held another Environment and Development Conference attended by a much bigger world community to clearly address the environment development nexus of both developed and developing nations.[10] The resulting 1992's Conference was the Rio Declaration on Environment and Development and the elaboration of the sustainable development concept.[11] Until now, sustainable development and other related international law principles continue to be the foundation for countries all over the world in framing their national framework on environmental protection, including Malaysia.

As an outcome of the Stockholm Conference, Malaysia developed its environmental legal framework, which adheres to international law principles. However, despite the establishment of such a framework, challenges towards environmental protection remain a major concern, especially in achieving its sustainability targets.[12] As an upper-middle-income country, it is obvious that Malaysia's ongoing economic development

7 UNEP, *Environmental Rule of Law: First Global Report* (Nairobi: United Nations Environment Programme, 2019), 1–33.

8 "Conference 48/14. Report of the United Nations Conference on the Human Environment. A/CONF.48/14/ Rev.1," United Nations General Assembly 1972, accessed April 1, 2022, http://www.un-documents.net/aconf48-14r1.pdf.

9 "Conference 48/14. Report of the United Nations Conference on the Human Environment. A/CONF.48/14/ Rev.1," United Nations General Assembly 1972, accessed April 1, 2022, http://www.un documents.net/aconf48-14r1.pdf.

10 "The Rio Declaration on Environment and Development, Conference in Rio de Janeiro, Brazil, 3–14 June 1992, (A/CONF.151/26 Vol. I)," United Nations General Assembly 1992, accessed April 1, 2022, http://www.un.org/documents/ga/conf151/aconf15126-1annex1.htm.

11 "Agenda 21. United Nations Conference on Environment & Development, Rio de Janeiro, Brazil, 3 to 14 June 1992," United Nations Sustainable Development, accessed April 1, 2022, https://sustainabledevelopment.un.org/content/documents/Agenda21.pdf.

12 Maizatun Mustafa, "Environmental Quality Act 1974: A Tool Towards the Implementation and Achievement of Malaysia's Environmental Policy," *IIUM Law Journal* 19, no. 1 (2011), 1–34.

has enabled the country to better its socioeconomic standing and living standards.[13] Nevertheless, in most situations, economic growth has frequently been blamed for environmental problems as well as for the increased anthropogenic greenhouse gases.[14] In as much as Malaysia is putting serious efforts into environmental protection and pollution control, and despite being guided by fundamental international environmental principles, the existing legal framework has not been able to provide sufficient solutions to environmental pollution or to effectively inculcate environmental responsibility of the various sectors.[15]

Being a Muslim majority country, it is pertinent that Malaysia's direction in environmental protection is examined from the context of Islam. There are a number of Islamic principles which can offer significant points of reference in environmental management.[16] The necessity of clearly articulating environmental protection objectives from the perspective of Islam cannot be overstated. Throughout this discussion, it will be obvious that Islamic values, particularly pertaining to environmental governance, play a critical role in supporting the current environmental legal framework. Protecting the environment from an Islamic perspective has regained prominence in the face of the ongoing climate and environmental crises and has received support from prominent international bodies such as the United Nations.[17] As a result of today's environmental issues, there has been a number of research on environmental principles in Islam that can be applied to support the present standards and regulations, as will be illustrated later in this article. There are some similarities between Shari'ah and contemporary international principles, including sustainable development, which demonstrate the compatibility and importance of drawing on Shari'ah legal traditions to enhance and promote the protection of the environment within Malaysia's policy and law.[18]

The chapter is organised as follows: in the next sections, the status of Malaysia and its environmental quality are presented, followed by the position of the present legal framework relating to environmental protection. Then the application of international law principles is examined to trace the foundation of environmental policy targets and law compliance. Thereafter, to ascertain the position of Islam towards environmental governance, relevant Islamic principles are examined, and their added values within the

13 Ministry of Environment and Water, *Third Biennial Update Report to the UNFCCC 2020* (Putrajaya: Ministry of Environment and Water, 2020), 1–24.

14 Department of Environment, *Annual Report 2019* (Putrajaya: Department of Environment, 2020), 42–170.

15 Department of Environment, Annual Report 2019, 42–170.

16 Abubakr Ahmed Bagder et al., "Environmental Protection in Islam," *IUCN Environmental Policy and Law Paper*, no. 20 Rev (1994):1–29.

17 "Al-Mizan: A Covenant for the Earth," UNEP, accessed April 1, 2022, https://www.unep.org/al-mizan-covenant-earth.

18 "Islamic Declaration on Sustainable Development 2012," The Islamic World Educational, Scientific and Cultural Organization, accessed April 1, 2022, https://www.icesco.org/en/.

Malaysian legal frameworks are identified. This chapter argues that Malaysia should incorporate the perspective of Islam within its policy directives which can enhance environmental quality and secure stakeholders' responsibility toward the environment.

9.2 Malaysia in General

Malaysia is a tropical country situated in Southeast Asia with an equatorial monsoon climate with rainforests rich in plant and animal species and extremely complex ecosystems. The geographic facts of Malaysia, combined with species richness, validate its place in the world as one of the seventeen megadiverse countries.[19] Natural resources play an important role in providing social benefits, ecosystem services, and environmental stability, including their contribution toward economic development and poverty eradication. Since the 1980s, Malaysia's economy has progressed rapidly, and in 2022, its economic performance is ranked 8th among 39 countries in the Asia–Pacific region, and its overall score is above the regional and world averages.[20]

The current population of Malaysia of over 30 million[21] consists of a multiracial society with a myriad of religions. Although other faiths such as Christianity, Buddhism, and Hinduism are widely practiced, Islam is considered the official religion which is currently being observed by over 50 percent of the population. As a Muslim majority country, Islamic law has its position under the Federal Constitution and plays certain roles within the legal system. While there are parallel systems of civil law and Islamic law in Malaysia,[22] the application of the latter is narrowly confined to the personal law of the Muslims, such as succession, marriage and divorce, and guardianship, as well as that relating to *waqf*, charitable institutions, *zakat*, *baitulmal*, and mosque. Matters relating to environmental protection are not governed by Islamic law but by civil law through the enactment of legislation at the federal level by the Parliament or at the state level through the State Legislative Assembly.[23] In relation to a regulatory agency, the most prominent is the Ministry of Environment and Water which was formed in 2020 to replace the Ministry of Energy, Science, Green Technology, and

---

19 Ministry of Natural Resources and Environment, *National Policy on Biological Diversity 2016–2025* (Putrajaya: Ministry of Natural Resources and Environment, 2016), 1–116.

20 "Index of Economic Freedom 2022," The Heritage Malaysia, accessed April 1, 2022, https://www.heritage.org/index/country/malaysia.

21 "Population & Demography," Department of Statistics Malaysia, accessed April 1, 2022, https://www.dosm.gov.my/v1/index.php?r=column/cthemeByCat&cat=117&bul_id=akliVWdIa2g3Y2VubTVSMkxmYXp1UT09&menu_id=L0pheU43NWJwRWVSZklWdzQ4TlhUUT09.

22 Farid S. Shuaib, "The Islamic Legal System in Malaysia," *Pacific Rim Law & Policy Journal* 21, no. 1 (2012): 85–113.

23 Maizatun Mustafa, *Environmental Law in Malaysia, 4th ed.* (The Netherlands: Kluwer Law International, 2019), 23–32.

Climate Change.[24] The Department of Environment, established under the new Ministry, is the primary agency responsible for environmental protection as well as for developing rules and enforcing legislation throughout the country.[25]

9.3 Environmental Pollution

Controlling pollution is an uphill battle for Malaysia due to various factors, including conflicting policy goals of economic growth and environmental protection and issues within the law such as that of enforcement and compliance.[26] Since the 1970s, Malaysia has started to give focus on economic development, with industrialisation as its primary growth target.[27] As a result, the industrial sector has expanded at a considerable pace. Over five decades, Malaysia has transformed itself from a country with an over-reliant on agriculture and tin mining to one dominated by industrial development and a high growth rate.[28] Malaysia is currently classified by the World Bank as an upper-middle-income country on the verge of reaching the high-income threshold between 2020 and 2024.[29] Within the Muslim world, Malaysia continues to be the most developed Islamic economy ecosystem for the eighth consecutive year according to the Global Islamic Economy Indicator, which tracks the development of the Islamic economy in 73 countries.[30]

While Malaysia is gaining benefits from rapid economic and technological advancements, pollution and ecological destruction continue to be major issues. Similar to many other upper-middle-income countries, industrialisation has been identified as the primary source of pollution, with manufacturing and agro-based industries accounting for a large share of pollutant emissions[31] in addition to urbanisation, and land-use change. At present, the main environmental issues for the country include:[32]

- inland water and marine pollution from various sources;

24 "Corporate Information," Ministry of Environment and Water Malaysia, accessed April 1, 2022, https://www.kasa.gov.my/ms/.

25 "About DOE," Department of Environment, accessed April 1, 2022, https://www.doe.gov.my/.

26 Maizatun Mustafa, "*Environmental Law in Malaysia*".

27 Sir Robert Aiken et al., *Development and Environment in Peninsular Malaysia* (Singapore: McGraw-Hill International, 1982), 228–239.

28 Ministry of Environment and Water, *Third Biennial Update Report.*

29 "Malaysia," The World Bank, accessed April 1, 2022, https://www.worldbank.org/en/country/malaysia.

30 "Malaysia Leads Global Islamic Economy Indicator for Eighth consecutive Year Driven by Strong Islamic Finance Initiatives and Ecosystem," Salaam Gateway, accessed April 1, 2022, https://www.salaamgateway.com/story/malaysia-leads-global-islamic-economy-indicator-for-eighth-consecutive-year-driven-by-strong-islamic.

31 Ministry of Environment and Water, *Third Biennial Update Report.*

32 Department of Environment, *Annual Report 2019.*

- contamination of air quality from traffic, industry, and agricultural activities;
- haze pollution due to open burning and pollution emissions;
- dangerous discharge of hazardous and toxic wastes; and
- natural resources degradation and depletion of biological diversity due to land-use conversion, infrastructure development, and other factors.

Malaysia's legal framework relies mainly on conciliatory and punitive styles of securing compliance with the law.[33] Most environmental cases were brought to court based on criminal sanctions due to the violation of environmental law. Every year, the regulatory agency such as the Department of Environment would be prosecuting numerous pollution cases as an outcome of monitoring and surveillance activities as well as through public complaints. In 2019, a total of 291 polluting offences were prosecuted by the Department of Environment under the Environmental Quality Act 1974, with a total fine of RM 5,253,500. During the same year, criminal actions were taken against 55 non-compliance industries with a collected fine of RM 8,046,500, besides the issuance of 2,109 notices and 3,032 compounds to such industries for them to take appropriate actions to comply with the law.[34] In addition, the Department of Environment also received a total of 11,127 environmental pollution complaints for the year 2019 from the public. Most of the complaints received involved air pollution 9,085 (81.7 percent), followed by water pollution (976 complaints), noise pollution (278 complaints), illegal dumping of scheduled or toxic wastes (189 complaints), and other types of environmental harms such as oil spillage and land pollution.[35]

Despite efforts undertaken to prosecute environmental offenders, compliance with the law remains one of the biggest challenges in legal enforcement, especially for the industrial sector. The increasing number of industries discharging pollutants into various mediums of the environment continues to impact the quality of the environment and public health. For example, in 1987, the volume of toxic wastes generated from the industries was 400,000 tonnes for the whole of Malaysia.[36] However, about 24 years later, the volume had increased to 1.6 million tonnes for the year 2011 and to two million tonnes for the year 2017.[37] The 2020's data from the Compendium of Environment Statistics Malaysia indicates a further increase in scheduled waste,

---

33 Maizatun Mustafa and Nurah Sabahiah Mohammed, "The Development of Environmental Crime and Sanction in Malaysia," *European Scientific Journal* 11, no. 25 (2015): 29.

34 Department of Environment, *Annual Report 2019*.

35 Department of Environment, Annual Report 2019.

36 Goh K.S, "Developing Hazardous Waste Programmes in Malaysia," *Waste Management & Research* 8 (1990): 151–156.

37 "Compendium of Environmental Statistics, Malaysia 2018/2019," Department of Statistics Official Portal, accessed April 1, 2022, https://www.dosm.gov.my/.

which was four million tonnes in 2019.[38] Weaknesses of legal strategy here relate to enforcement and compliance with the law, especially in curbing illegal dumping of toxic wastes.[39] One of the most serious incidents happened in 2019 when about 20 to 40 tonnes of chemical waste containing benzene, acrylonitrile, and acrolein were dumped into the Kim Kim River in the state of Johor by an illegal tyre recycling company.[40] This incident has affected the health of thousands of residents due to the exposure to hazardous gaseous emissions. As a result of this occurrence, around 6,000 people were impacted, the majority of whom were children, and 2,775 were hospitalised. As the number of persons affected increased, the Education Ministry had to order the closure of over 100 surrounding schools to avoid severe health implications.[41]

Another example of an environmental threat facing Malaysia is the issue of haze pollution.[42] Every year, the highest type of complaints made by the public is air pollution which is over 80 percent of the total number of complaints received by the Department of Environment in the year 2019.[43] For Malaysia, haze is a major issue that affects air quality, which is primarily a man-made problem resulting from unsustainable agricultural, industrial, and transportation activities.[44] In recent years, several "Haze Emergencies" have been declared due to severe haze episodes.[45] During such episodes, schools and facilities were shut down to minimise public exposure to haze, which can contribute to health issues, including increased mortality and hospital admissions, especially for respiratory outcomes. As a result of haze pollution from local and transboundary sources, Malaysia's Ministry of

---

38 "Compendium of Environment Statistics, Malaysia 2020," Department of Statistics Official Portal, accessed April 1, 2022, https://www.google.com/url?sa = t&rct = j&q = &esrc = s&source = web&cd = &ved = 2ahUKEwiCt5-Er_r2AhUozTgGHfZhARYQFnoECAMQAQ&url = https%3A%2F%2Fwww.dosm.gov.my%2Fv1%2Findex.php%3Fr%3Dcolumn%2FpdfPrev%26id%3DTjM1ZlFxb3VOakdmMnozVms5dUlKZz09&usg = AOvVaw0b6C_hQM46ZzT0ZK2aku9g.

39 Maizatun Mustafa & Zuraini Ab. Hamid, "Evaluating Current Practices of Disaster Management under Environmental Law Towards Sustainable Development," in *2019 International Conference on Climate Change, Disaster Management and Environmental Sustainability*, ed. Rawshan Ara Begum et al (Kumamoto: Center for Water Cycle, Marine Environment and Disaster Management, Kumamoto University, 2019), 738–746.

40 Kathy Xu, "Pasir Gudang Dumping – What Happened and Who is Responsible?," *Eco Business*, May 7, 2019, https://www.eco-business.com/news/pasir-gudang-dumping-what-happened-and-who-is-responsible/.

41 Azura Abas, "Health Ministry: Almost 6,000 Sought Treatment over Sungai Kim Kim Pollution," *The Straits Times*, March 20, 2019, https://www.nst.com.my/news/nation/2019/03/41277/health-ministry-almost-6000-sought-treatment-over-sungai-kim-kim.

42 "Chronology of Haze Episodes in Malaysia," Department of Environment, accessed April 1, 2022, http://www.doe.gov.my/portalv1/en/info-umum/info-kualiti-udara/kronologi-episod-jerebu-di-malaysia/319123.

43 Department of Environment, *Annual Report 2019*.

44 Maizatun Mustafa, "Legal Solutions to Air Pollution Control in Malaysia," in *Handbook of Sustainable Development in Asia*, ed. S. Hsu (Oxon: Routledge, 2018), 566–580.

45 "Chronology of Haze Episodes in Malaysia".

Education had to close 4,778 schools in 2015, affecting roughly 2.7 million pupils countrywide,[46] in addition to aircraft cancellations, disruptions in tourism industry, and numerous enterprises.[47] From the examples of these pollution incidences, it can be construed that the implications of environmental threats have gone far beyond harm to the ecosystem. In fact, these impacts are challenging the essence of human wellbeing, which is the core of sustainable development. The growing evidence of the linkage between human health, economic activities, and pollution means that there is an obligation on the policymaker to review the law to protect the environment and safeguard the public from environmental consequences. The subsequent discussion is to identify national policy directives and their connections to international principles on environmental protection, particularly in upholding the essence of sustainable development within the legal strategies.

9.4 Policy, Law, and International Principles

Policies and laws, along with their implementation, play a crucial role for Malaysia in regulating environmental and climate change issues and dealing with their impacts, as well as ensuring society's best interests are upheld and protected in all aspects. Malaysia implements the top-down approach methodically through policies that demonstrate consistent goals articulated at the top and law enforcement that is aligned with the policy.[48] As a result of Malaysia's strong parliamentary tradition, environmental issues are primarily governed by federal law such as the Environmental Quality Act. This and other related laws are necessary to put into effect many of the objectives of national policy directives.[49] As already mentioned, administratively, environmental matters are administered by the Ministry of Natural Resource and Environment through its enforcement arm, the Department of Environment. Within the environmental-related legislations, various strategies have been applied to protect the environment from a regulatory system through criminal penalties to a self-regulated strategy that permits polluters to determine the best way to comply.[50] For Malaysia, the most important driver for its environmental

46 E.S. Heng, "Haze Forces 4,778 Schools to Close Today; 2,696,110 Students Affected" *the Borneo Post*, October 22 2015, http://www.theborneopost.com/2015/10/22/haze-forces-4778-schools-to-close-today-2696110-students-affected/#ixzz41jDpOSMb.

47 T.L. Cheng, "Haze Will Affect Tourism Arrivals and Retail Sector," *The Star*, March 15, 2014, http://www.thestar.com.my/business/business-news/2014/03/15/haze-will-affect-tourism-arrivals-and-retail-sector/.

48 Maizatun Mustafa, "Environmental Quality Act 1974: Development and Reform," 2 *MLJ* (2009): lv.

49 Maizatun Mustafa, "*Environmental Law in Malaysia*".

50 Maizatun Mustafa, "Environmental Quality Act 1974: A Tool Towards the Implementation and Achievement of Malaysia's Environmental Policy".

policy objectives is international commitment. As a member state of numerous United Nations environmental conventions, Malaysia is heavily influenced by and committed to the United Nations' sustainability agendas. It was as a result of participation in the United Nations Conference on the Human Environment in Stockholm in 1972 that Malaysia introduced its first environmental policy, enacted the Environmental Quality Act in 1974, and set up the Department of Environment to enforce the law.

Malaysia's legal strategies for the environment are being guided by policy directives which can be found in several documents. One of the most important ones is the Malaysia Plan, starting from the Third Malaysia Plan (1976–1980)[51] until the present Twelfth Malaysia Plan (2021–2025).[52] Generally, the Malaysia Plan is a five-year national development initiative containing comprehensive outlines of government development policies and strategies, which also include that of environmental protection. In addition to the Malaysia Plans, a number of environmental-related policies continue to be introduced. For example, in 2002, the National Policy on the Environment was formally launched to establish a framework for economic, social, and cultural advancement through environmentally sound and sustainable development.[53] The Policy takes a broad strategic approach to critical areas such as pollution prevention and control. It also serves as a foundation for implementing environmental strategies within the legal framework and emphasises the importance of environmental sustainability as a component of a comprehensive socio-economic development strategy.[54] The National Climate Change Policy, which was launched in 2009, is another national policy created to guide public and private sectors as well as major groups in addressing the challenges of climate change in a holistic manner based on the principle of sustainable development.[55]

Malaysia has long benefitted from the concept of sustainable development, which establishes guidelines for environmental and economic compatibility. The United Nations defines sustainable development as "development that meets current needs without jeopardising future generations' ability to meet their own."[56] This principle has been further developed by the United Nations, which has resulted in the adoption of the Rio Declaration on Environment and Development by

51 Jabatan Perdana Menteri, Unit Pemodenan Tadbiran dan Perancangan Pengurusan, *Third Malaysia Plan 1976–1980* (Kuala Lumpur: Jabatan Percetakan Negara 1976), 69.

52 Jabatan Perdana Menteri, Unit Perancang Ekonomi, *Twelfth Malaysia Plan 2021–2025* (Putrajaya: Jabatan Percetakan Negara 2021), Chapter 8, 8–2, 8–31.

53 The full policy statement is available at the Department of Environment's official website. *See* http://www.doe.gov.my/portalv1/wp-content/uploads/2013/01/dasar_alam_sekitar_negara.pdf.

54 The full policy statement is available at the Department of Environment's official website. *See* http://www.doe.gov.my/portalv1/wp-content/uploads/2013/01/dasar_alam_sekitar_negara.pdf.

55 Ministry of Natural Resources and Environment Malaysia, *National Climate Change Policy 2009* (Putrajaya: Ministry of Natural Resources and Environment Malaysia, 2010), 1–32.

56 World Commission on Environment and Development, *Our Common Future* (Oxford: Oxford University Press, 1987), 11–27.

Table 9.1: Summary of the Rio Declaration on Environment and Development.

1. Human beings are at the centre of concerns for sustainable development.	10. Environmental issues are best handled by citizens through access to information and participation. States shall facilitate access to public awareness and participation.	19. States shall notify affected states on activities having an adverse transboundary environmental effect.
2. States have the right to exploit resources and the responsibility to ensure no damage is caused to the environment of other states.	11. States shall enact environmental legislation and reflect the environmental and developmental context to which they apply.	20. Women have a vital role in environmental management and development.
3. Right to development must meet the environmental needs of present and future generations.	12. States should cooperate to promote a supportive and open international economic system.	21. The youth should be mobilized to forge a global partnership.
4. To achieve sustainable development, environmental protection shall constitute an integral part of development.	13. State shall develop national law on liability and compensation for the victims of pollution.	22. Indigenous people and local communities have a vital role in environmental management and development.
5. Eradicating poverty is required for sustainable development.	14. States should discourage other states from activities that cause environmental degradation.	23. Environment and natural resources of people under oppression shall be protected.
6. Special needs of developing countries shall be given special priority.	15. States shall apply a precautionary approach according to their capabilities.	24. Warfare is inherently destructive of sustainable development.
7. States shall cooperate to conserve, protect and restore the health and integrity of the ecosystem.	16. National authorities should promote internalization of environmental costs. The polluter should bear the cost of pollution.	25. Peace, development, and environmental protection are interdependent and indivisible.
8. To achieve sustainable development, states should reduce and eliminate unsustainable production and consumption patterns.	17. Environmental impact assessment shall be undertaken for activities that are likely to have a significant adverse impact on the environment.	26. States shall resolve environmental disputes peacefully in accordance with the UN Charter.
9. States should cooperate on capacity building for sustainable development.	18. States shall notify other states of natural disasters causing harmful effects on the environment of those states.	27. States and people shall cooperate in good faith and in a spirit of partnership to fulfil the Declaration's principles.

Source: The Rio Declaration on Environment and Development.

member states. This Declaration is composed of a preamble and 27 principles relating to environmental protection,[57] as summarised in Table 9.1, all of which are centred on humans and their rights to live healthy, productive lives in harmony with nature.

The Rio Declaration promotes principles such as the centrality of human beings to sustainable development concerns, the primacy of poverty eradication, and the importance of the environment for current and future generations.[58] The United Nations' most recent progress on sustainable development occurred in 2015 when nations worldwide agreed on a set of Sustainable Development Goals (SDGs) as a new approach to resolving development issues faced by all countries, regardless of their level of development, and aimed to be achieved by 2030.[59] The SDGs comprise 17 high-level goals, as illustrated in Table 9.2, with 169 specific targets that address development's social, economic, and environmental dimensions.

Table 9.2: The 17 Sustainable Development Goals.

GOAL 1: NO POVERTY End poverty in all its forms.	GOAL 7: AFFORDABLE AND CLEAN ENERGY Ensure access to affordable, reliable, sustainable and modern energy for all.
GOAL 2: ZERO HUNGER End hunger, achieve food security and promote sustainable agriculture.	GOAL 8: DECENT WORK AND ECONOMIC GROWTH Promote inclusive and sustainable economic growth, productive employment and decent work for all.
GOAL 3: GOOD HEALTH AND WELL-BEING Ensure healthy lives and promote well-being for all.	GOAL 9: INDUSTRY, INNOVATION AND INFRASTRUCTURE Build resilient infrastructure, promote inclusive and sustainable industrialization and foster innovation.
GOAL 4: QUALITY EDUCATION Ensure inclusive and equitable quality education and promote lifelong learning opportunities for all.	GOAL 10: REDUCED INEQUALITY Reduce inequality within and among countries.

57 United Nations Conference on Environment and Development, *Report of the United Nations Conference on Environment and Development* (New York: United Nations, 1993), Resolution I, annex I, Resolution I, annex II.
58 United Nations Conference on Environment and Development, Report of the United Nations Conference on Environment and Development (New York: United Nations, 1993), Resolution I, annex I, Resolution I, annex II.
59 "Transforming Our World: The 2030 Agenda for Sustainable Development," United Nations, accessed April 1, 2022, https://sustainabledevelopment.un.org/content/documents/.

Table 9.2 (continued)

GOAL 5: GENDER EQUALITY Achieve gender equality and empower all women and girls.	GOAL 11: SUSTAINABLE CITIES AND COMMUNITIES Make cities and human settlements inclusive, safe, resilient and sustainable.
GOAL 6: CLEAN WATER AND SANITATION Ensure availability and sustainable management of water and sanitation for all. GOAL 13: CLIMATE ACTION Take urgent action to combat climate change and its impacts.	GOAL 12: RESPONSIBLE CONSUMPTION AND PRODUCTION Ensure sustainable consumption and production patterns. GOAL 16: PEACE, JUSTICE AND STRONG INSTITUTIONS Promote peaceful and inclusive societies for sustainable development, provide access to justice and build effective, accountable and inclusive institutions at all levels.
GOAL 14: LIFE BELOW WATER Conserve and sustainably use the oceans, seas and marine resources for sustainable development.	GOAL 17: PARTNERSHIPS TO ACHIEVE THE GOAL Strengthen the means to implement and revitalize the global partnership for sustainable development.
GOAL 15: LIFE ON LAND Protect, restore and promote sustainable use of terrestrial ecosystems, sustainably manage forests, combat desertification, and halt and reverse land degradation and halt biodiversity loss.	

Source: United Nations General Assembly Resolution on Agenda 2030.

When the overall objectives of sustainable development are considered, including the current SDGs, it becomes clear that many of the principles, such as "the right to development," were established to address development concerns and emphasise the unique needs of developing countries or emerging economies such as Malaysia.[60] However, in the overall context of sustainable development, the right to development should be guided by an ethical sense of obligation and moral responsibility. This is particularly important for Malaysia, which has a strong tendency towards prioritising economic development, which can threaten environmental quality.[61]

Despite being voluntary in nature, it is necessary to highlight that both sustainable development and SDGs contain some moral principles to guide policymakers based on

60 Maizatun Mustafa, "Indicators for Sustainable Development: Criteria for a Successful Sustainability Relevant to Environmental Law in Malaysia," *International Journal of Engineering & Technology*, 7 (3.30) (2018):141–147.

61 A.A. Hezri, and M.N. Hasan, "Towards Sustainable Development? The Evolution of Environmental Policy in Malaysia," *Nat. Resour. Forum*, 30 (2006): 37–50.

three interconnected environmental, economic, and social pillars. In order to secure the "balanced achievement of sustained economic development, improved social equity and environmental sustainability" the Rio Declaration proposed guiding principles such as shared but differentiated responsibilities, polluter pays, and the precautionary principle.[62] Other ethical-related principles such as institutional and policy integration, public participation, accountability, and easy access to justice are meant to guide nations on the critical role of public participation in achieving sustainable development, as well as the requirement for nations to establish legal instruments to address environmental issues.[63] Similar to sustainable development, SDGs can also be looked at from an ethical perspective in the context of balancing economic development and environmental protection. While the SDGs are based on development aspirations and are expected to contribute to the realisation of the good life and a good society, there are underlying fundamental principles to guide policymakers and lawmakers, such as inequality, social justice, and human rights.[64] Many of the seventeen SDGs and their associated targets are directly related to environmental protection, particularly in terms of public health, living conditions, and the ecosystem.[65]

From the scrutiny of sustainable development and SDGs already highlighted, it can be construed that the concept of sustainable development does not simply concern with taking care of one's environment, but it opens up much more complex and interrelated social and ethical dimensions of the problem. Sustainable development, therefore, touches on a very wide issue of economic and legal processes as well as ethical. While Malaysia requires continued economic growth, ethical values inspired by sustainable development and SDGs should be integrated and enhanced within the related strategies to seek an equitable level of economic and environmental well-being.[66] Thus, values such as accountability, transparency, access to justice and information, and public participation need to be applied more extensively within the policy and law. This is to support legal strategies to be more effective in combatting pollution and ensuring continuous environmental protection.[67] Understanding these ethical criteria would enable Malaysia to address the ongoing challenge of balancing present and future needs. Because of the transformative nature of the sustainable development and SDGs commitments, Malaysia needs to mobilise all possible resources to succeed in meeting the targets. Thus, the potential for Islamic principles to play a

62 World Commission on Environment and Development, *Our Common Future.*

63 Maizatun Mustafa, "Indicators for Sustainable Development".

64 Magdalena Bexell & Kristina Jönsson, "Responsibility and the United Nations' Sustainable Development Goals" *Forum for Development Studies* 44, no.1 (2017):13–29.

65 Jerome Singh, "The Sustainable Development Goals: The Role of Ethics" *Sight and Life* 29, no. 2 (2015): 56–63.

66 "Malaysia Sustainable Development Goals Voluntary National Review 2017," Economic Planning Unit, accessed April 1, 2022, https://www.epu.gov.my/.

67 "Malaysia Sustainable Development Goals Voluntary National Review 2017," Economic Planning Unit, accessed April 1, 2022, https://www.epu.gov.my/.

role in supporting Malaysia's existing environmental protection targets based on international commitment needs to be identified and explored.

9.5 Environmental Protection in Islam

In order to articulate the position of Islam on the environment, and whether the concept of sustainable development has its place in Shari'ah which can provide guidance to the Muslim countries, especially Malaysia, on environmental protection, it is necessary to examine the teachings of the Quran and Hadith of the Prophet (SAW) on the matters. The Islamic perspective on the environment is founded on the belief that Allah is the universe's sole Creator and Sustainer, and He has created it with perfect wisdom (*hikmah*) and perfect balance (*mizan*).[68] Thus, from this perspective, environmental protection is considered a fundamental part of faith in Islam. This is established in the Qur'an, *Surah al-Furqan* 25:2, when Allah says, "It is He Who created All things, and ordered them In due proportions." The same can be observed in *Surah al-Jathiya* 45:3–5, which commands:

> Verily in the heavens and the earth, are Signs for those who believe. And in the creation of yourselves and the fact that animals are scattered (throughout the earth) are Signs for those of assured Faith. And the alteration of Night and Day, and the fact that God sends down Sustenance from the sky, and revives therewith the earth after its death, and in the change of the winds, -are Signs for those that are wise.

As the main source of reference in Islam, these verses of the Qur'an, which emphasise that every living thing, including human beings, animals, and plants, have been created with their respective functions to create harmonisation among each other, can provide guidance on how natural resources should be managed.[69] Such harmonisation is important to ensure stability and balance, while misuse or abuse of nature is forbidden in Islam as it can bring negative effects to the ecosystem. In emphasising the role of the human as the vicegerent or *khalifah* on earth, everything that is accomplished by human beings needs to take into account the concept of *mizan*.[70] In Islam, duties towards environmental protection have been entrusted upon the mankind by the Creator based on *Surah al-An'am*, 6:165 when Allah says "It is He who hath made you (His) agents inheritors of the earth: He hath raised you in ranks some above others: that he may try you in the gifts He hath given you."

---

68 Mohammad Hashim Kamali, "Environmental Care in Islamic Teaching: A Qur'anic Perspective," *ICR Journal* 3, no. 2 (2012): 261–283.

69 Abubakr Ahmed Bagder et al., "Environmental Protection in Islam".

70 I. Ozdemir "Towards an Understanding of Environmental Ethics from a Qur'anic Perspective," In *Islam and Ecology*, ed. R.C. Foltz, F. M. Denny, & A. Baharuddin (Cambridge: Harvard University Press, 2003), 3–38.

This verse is a reminder to human beings that since they are sharing the earth with the other living species, it is, therefore, their responsibility to respect nature and protect the earth with utmost care.

The balance or *mizan* provides stability through being orderly and in harmony with one another. Such balance would not be put at risk if humans could refrain from indiscriminately exploiting the environment through pollution and natural resources degradation. In this regard, God-fearing and accountability in Islam can be associated with the appreciation of the surrounding environment, which is an ultimate creation of the Creator.[71] Allah commands in *Surah al-Qasas*, 28:77: " But seek, with the (wealth) Which God has bestowed on thee, The Home of the Hereafter, Nor forget thy portion in this World: but do thou good, As God has been good To thee, and seek not (Occasions for) mischief in the land: For God loves not those Who do mischief." In another *Surah al-Maidah*, 5:87 Allah says "O ye who believe! make not unlawful the good things which God hath made lawful for you but commit no excess: for God loveth not those given to excess." Islam, as evidenced by these two verses, forbids actions that endanger the earth.

Even though mankind is encouraged to take advantage of God's blessings, they are cautioned against acts that would cause harm. The Islamic perspective on environmental protection can be further understood through a large number of Prophetic sayings. For example, it has been reported by Anas ibn Malik that Prophet Muhammad (SAW) said, "If the Resurrection were established upon one of you while he has in his hand a sapling, then let him plant it." This hadith sends a strong message about the importance of sustainability, emphasising the significance of sustaining nature's growth even when all hope for humanity is lost. The Prophet (SAW) believed that even when the world is ending, human beings should persist in what good deeds they can do and finish what efforts they can.[72] Another hadith can also be used to emphasise the importance and benefit of environmental conservation that transcends economic gain. As narrated by Al-Bukhari, the Prophet (SAW) said: "There is none amongst the believers who plants a tree, or sows a seed, and then a bird, or a person, or an animal eats thereof, but it is regarded as having given a charitable gift for which there is great recompense." This hadith illustrates the Islamic perspective of planting and conservation of vegetation, which is considered an act of worship as well as a charitable deed.[73] In fact, in Islam, any other

71 Mohammad Hashim Kamali, "Environmental Care in Islamic Teaching".

72 D. Abdelzaher, A. Kotb & A. Helfaya "Eco-Islam: Beyond the Principles of Why and What, and Into the Principles of How," *Journal of Business Ethics* 155 (2019): 623–643.

73 D. Abdelzaher, A. Kotb & A. Helfaya "Eco-Islam", 623–643.

environmental preservation activity that has a sustainable impact in the long term would be regarded as a perpetual charity in which the reward continues to flow.[74]

While the Qur'an contains many warnings that the world is likely to be overwhelmed with environmental issues of the sort it is now facing if human beings do not resist acts of selfishness and greed, there is ample guidance for the Muslims in resolving the current issues through the broad framework of *Maqasid* Shari'ah.[75] Generally, the environmental worldview in Islam is based on the vision of peace, progress, and continuity, which are founded by the Shari'ah's higher purposes (*Maqasid* Shari'ah) and centred on a set of essential goals namely, the protection of life (*nasf*), faith (*deen*), mind (*aql*), property (*maal*), and family (*nasl*).[76] From this perspective, the question of whether Islam supports the concept of sustainable development finds an immediate answer in the principle of *Maqasid of* Shari'ah which upholds critical components of sustainable development upon which responsibility is imposed on the Muslim countries as well as on individual Muslims to safeguard these values and to uphold their protection at all times.[77] These five main objectives of Shari'ah entail wisdom and justice to guide the Muslims towards fulfilling basic needs and avoiding excessiveness as main priorities within the strive for economic growth.[78] For example, safeguarding life implies that society can resist natural resources degradation, which can lead to detrimental impacts on human health and welfare.[79] Whereas the insistence of Islam on the preservation of the family or progeny is meant to ensure inter-generational equity through fair distribution of wealth and prosperity, which in turn is linked to resources conservations and sustenance of the environment.[80] The World Commission on Environment and Development in 1987 presented the definition of sustainable development focusing on inter-generational equity, whereby it is the "development that meets the needs of the present without compromising the ability of future generations to meet their own needs." It implies that economic development should be balanced with environmental conservation and calls for a fair utilisation of

---

74 A. H. Ansari, P. Jamal, and U. A. Oseni, "Sustainable Development: Islamic Dimension with Special Reference to Conservation of the Environment," *Adv. Nat. Appl. Sci.* 6, no. 5 (January 2012): 607–619.

75 Ali Ali Saged et al, "The Role of the Maqasid al-Shariah in Preserving the Environment," *Humanomics* 33, no. 2 (2017): 125–132.

76 Ali Ali Saged et al, "The Role of the Maqasid al-Shariah", 125–132.

77 Mohammad Hashim Kamali, "Environmental Care in Islamic Teaching".

78 M Ashraf Al Haq & Norazlina Abd Wahab, "The Maqasid Al Shariah and the Sustainability Paradigm: Literature Review and Proposed Mutual Framework for Asnaf Development," *Journal of Accounting and Finance in Emerging Economies* 5, no. 2 (June 2019): 179–196.

79 Muhammad Hashim Kamali, "Maqasid Al-Shari'ah and Ijtihad as Instruments of Civilizational Renewal: A Methodological Perspective," *Islam and Civilisational Renewal* 2, no. 2 (2011): 1–46.

80 Muhammad Hashim Kamali, "Maqasid Al-Shari'ah and Ijtihad as Instruments of Civilizational Renewal", 1–46.

natural resources across generations. In sum, the Commission's approach to sustainable development is in consonance with the *Maqasid* Shari'ah.[81]

Earlier examinations of the sustainability principles based on the Rio Declaration indicate that while these principles have not been developed on a religious basis, most of the principles are founded on ethical grounds that align with the spirit of Islam based on the framework of *Maqasid* Shari'ah.[82] Whereas the goals within the SDGs reflect a set of universal values similar to Islam as they intend to guide humanity in the right direction.[83] These include addressing local challenges such as environmental sustainability, poverty, food insecurity, the availability of safe drinking water, and closing opportunity gaps between rural and urban areas, as well as between rich and poor people.[84] A prominent jurist, Hashim Kamali,[85] when examining the broader scope of Islamic environmental protection, noted some parallels between its applications and the 1987 World Commission on Environment and Development's concept of sustainable development. According to Kamali, "the overall understanding of sustainability and sustainable development in the Islamic context has much in common with how they are understood in the mainstream literature, especially with regard to inter-generational equity and enhancement of the quality of life."[86] In this context, sustainable development is understood to be a long-term perspective that takes into account both intra-generational and inter-generational equity in order to ensure a sustainable future. This notion is further supported by the International Union for Conservation of Nature which expands the understanding of sustainable development to include the overall quality of life in addition to the carrying capacity of supporting ecosystems.[87] The in-depth research by several authors has identified the compatibility of the modern concept of sustainable development with *Maqasid* Shari'ah.[88] On this basis, the environmental policy directives of Malaysia, which are formulated based on the said concept, can also be considered fitting with that of Islam.

While sustainability principles are consistent with Islamic teaching since they are founded on a common goal of environmental practises that benefit, not harm, future

81 A. H. Ansari, P. Jamal, and U. A. Oseni, "Sustainable Development".

82 Salwahiddah Abu Bakar, Azila Ahmad Sarkawi &Alias Abdullah, "Environmental Planning Policy and Development Strategies in the Context of Maqasid Al-Shari'ah," *Journal of Computational and Theoretical Nanoscience* 23, no. 7 (July 2017): 6381–6385.

83 Sohaib Mukhtar, Zinatul Ashiqin Zainol, & Sufian Jusoh, "Islamic Law and Sustainable Development Goals," *Tazkia Islamic Finance and Business Review* 12, no. 1 (2018): 81–99.

84 "Transforming Our World: The 2030 Agenda for Sustainable Development".

85 Mohammad Hashim Kamali, "Islam and Sustainable Development," *ICR Journal* 7, no. 1 (2016): 8–26.

86 Mohammad Hashim Kamali, "Islam and Sustainable Development," 8–26.

87 Abubakr Ahmed Bagder et al., "Environmental Protection in Islam".

88 Mehdi Shabannia Mansour, Kamal Halili Hassan, & Parviz Bagheri, "Shari'ah Perspective on Green Jobs and Environmental Ethics," *Ethics, Policy & Environment* 20, no. 1 (2017): 59–77; Dariah, Atih Rohaeti, Muhammad Syukri Salleh, & Hakimi M. Shafiai, "A New Approach for Sustainable Development Goals in Islamic Perspective," *Procedia-Social and Behavioral Sciences* 219 (2016): 159–166.

generations, it is still necessary to identify additional values that Islam can offer to the Muslim countries in enhancing their environmental framework. All along, the debate on sustainable development has been centred on the issues of environmental quality degradation and climate change which are facing all countries globally. Thus, an important question remains: how can Islam contribute to addressing environmental sustainability in developmental issues? In the case of Malaysia, since the 1970s, its legal framework on environmental protection based on United Nations' universal principles has been established and continued to be enhanced to deal with environmental and climate change challenges.[89] Thus the inability of the present framework to effectively deal with the said challenges supports the idea of finding another source of guidance and commitment, namely that of Islam.[90]

Despite their compatibility, there are some fundamental differences and clear gaps in the existing sustainable development concept in the light of Islamic teachings, as highlighted by some authors.[91] The Islamic perspective contains an additional but crucial need for sustainable development that is on the spiritual aspect of sustainability, which is vital towards the realisation of Allah's worship (*ibadah*) and the formation of equality in humanity as a whole.[92] Thus, the concept of sustainable development in Islam is based on a value system that views human life as having a specific purpose: worshiping his Creator as his servant and trustee for the reward in the hereafter.[93] These are highlighted in the following Qur'anic verses: "I have only created Jinns and men, that They may serve Me" (*Surah al- Zariyat* 51:56); "I will create a vicegerent (*khalifah*) on earth" (*Surah al-Baqarah* 2:30); and "That to thy Lord Is the final Goal" (*Surah an-Najm* 53:42).

Compared to the modern ideas of development and acquiring of wealth, which promotes material accumulation or consumption, sustainable development in Islam entails human actions and intentions strictly guided by divine teachings.[94] The hereafter (*akhirah*) concept is significant in the context of sustainable development because the associated environmental problems were exacerbated in the first place by humans who discounted the future in favour of immediate gratification.[95] Rather than maximising consumption and wealth accumulation, the Islamic worldview

89 Sir Robert Aiken et al., "*Development and Environment in Peninsular Malaysia*".

90 Dariah, Atih Rohaeti, Muhammad Syukri Salleh, & Hakimi M. Shafiai, "A New Approach for Sustainable Development Goals in Islamic Perspective".

91 Mohammad Hashim Kamali, "Islam and Sustainable Development"; Zubair Hasan, "Sustainable Development from an Islamic Perspective: Meaning, Implications and Policy Concerns," *Journal of King Abdulaziz University-Islamic Economics* 19, no. 1 (2006): 3–18.

92 Asyraf Hj Ab Rahman et al, "Sustainable Development from Islamic Perspective," *International Journal of Civil Engineering and Technology* 9, no. 4 (April 2018): 985–992.

93 Mohammad Hashim Kamali, "Islam and Sustainable Development".

94 Zubair Hasan, "Sustainable Development from an Islamic Perspective."

95 Junaid Qadir Zaman, "Sustainable Development Viewed from the Lens of Islam," *International Journal of Pluralism and Economics Education* 10, no. 1 (June 2018): 1–12.

advocates reducing one's desires and consumption in the present, sacrificing short-term benefits for long-term gains. The recognition that protecting the environment is considered an act of worship as well as a responsibility of each individual, who is a trustee of Allah, can act as a strong motivator for human beings to tread lightly on the earth and to take actions that promote harmonious co-existence of human and nature. This does not, however, imply that Islam discourages development in society, as Muslims are encouraged to seek the good of both this world and the hereafter (*Surah al-Baqarah* 2:201). *Surah al-Qasas* (28:77) can again be referred to for guidance: "But seek, with the (wealth) Which God has bestowed on thee, The Home of the Hereafter, Nor forget thy portion in this World: but do thou good, As God has been good To thee, and seek not (Occasions for) mischief in the land: For God loves not those Who do mischief."

In any decision on environmental protection and economic development, Islam provides that public interests take precedence over the individual, and all actions are assessed in terms of their outcomes as social benefits (*masalih*) or social evils (*mafasid*).[96] These principles can be used as guidance by the Muslim countries when promoting the public welfare of the society. Thus, any environmental-related policy and decision-making must always seek the maximisation of public welfare with priority to be given to preserving the universal public interest over particular interests.[97] According to Islam, a government's primary responsibility is to promote justice and prohibit wrongdoing. For policymakers, because Islam views all actions in terms of their consequences as social goods and benefits or social detriments, the goal of environmental protection should therefore be the society's universal common good.[98] As a result, the authority should impose liability on any person or entity responsible for causing environmental damage that adversely affects the community's welfare.[99] Similarly, the authority has the power to penalise any individual or entity for violating environmental law.[100] Simultaneously, the authority must bear responsibility for preventing or mitigating damage by prohibiting certain activities that may cause environmental harm or by imposing specific measures to mitigate environmental impact.[101]

96 Raudha Md Ramli, "The Principle of Natural Resources Management Based on Maqasid Al-Shari'ah: A Conceptual Framework," *International Journal of Islamic Economics and Finance Research* 3, no. 1 (2020): 57–74.

97 Muhammad Hashim Kamali, "Maqasid Al-Shari'ah and Ijtihad as Instruments of Civilizational Renewal: A Methodological Perspective," *Islam and Civilisational Renewal* 2, no. 2 (2011): 1–46.

98 Muhammad Hashim Kamali, "Maqasid Al-Shari'ah and Ijtihad as Instruments of Civilizational Renewal", 1–46.

99 Junaid Qadir Zaman, "Sustainable Development Viewed from the Lens of Islam".

100 Junaid Qadir Zaman, "Sustainable Development Viewed from the Lens of Islam".

101 Jens Koehrsen, "Muslims and Climate Change: How Islam, Muslim Organizations, and Religious Leaders Influence Climate Change Perceptions and Mitigation Activities," *WIREs Climate Change* 12, no. 3 (May/June 2021): 1–19.

9.6 Integration of Islamic Principles

In Malaysia, several attempts have been made by policymakers to integrate Islamic principles within the legal framework for environmental protection. One of which is through the inclusion of the Islamic development concept, known as *Islam Hadhari* within the Ninth Malaysia Plan (2006–2010).[102] This concept which was based on Qur'anic teachings sought to "enjoin progress and advancement as an imperative for the people while remaining firmly rooted in Islam's universal values and injunctions" and aimed to achieve certain objectives that Muslim nations must demonstrate, including environmental protection.[103] More importantly, this concept, which was promoted as part of institutional reform, was intended to guide Malaysia as a Muslim country toward fulfilling its obligations and demonstrating its capacity to fully participate in the globalisation and modernisation processes, including environmental protection.[104]

Malaysia has taken an additional step to incorporate and uphold Islamic principles in its environmental policy directives through the establishment of the world's first Shari'ah Index, with the goal of ensuring continuous improvement in government performance on issues such as environmental protection.[105] This index, which was launched in 2015, is intended to serve as a benchmark for assessing whether a country is meeting the five objectives of the *Maqasid* Shari'ah. Apart from the environment, this benchmarking process takes into account the judicial, economic, educational, and infrastructure, as well as the health, culture, politics, and social sectors. Essentially, this index employs a scientific measurement technique to quantify two critical functions: assessing the government's commitment to meeting Islamic standards for government policies and programmes on an annual basis and identifying areas for improvement to maximise the benefits of Islam's universal values adoption.[106] For 2017, the index gave the environmental aspect an 86.7 percent score. This score was calculated based on waste management policies that consistently prioritise environmental sustainability and community well-being.[107] The

102 Jabatan Perdana Menteri, Unit Perancang Ekonomi, *Ninth Malaysia Plan 2005–2010* (Putrajaya: Jabatan Percetakan Negara 2005), 42.

103 Ahmad Atory Hussain, "Islam Hadhari: Suatu Kesinambungan Dasar Penerapan Nilai-Nilai Islam selepas Era Tun Dr. Mahathir Mohamad," *REKAYASA–Journal of Ethics, Legal and Governance* 2 (2006): 1–10.

104 Ratna Roshida Abd Razak & Muhammad Hasru Zakariah, "Islam Hadhari: Apa Dan Kenapa (Islam Hadhari Approach: What is it and Why)," *Jurnal Hadhari: An International Journal* 2, no. 1 (2010): 1–21.

105 Bernama, "Najib Launches Malaysian Syariah Index," *Astro Awani*, February 10, 2015, https://www.astroawani.com/berita-malaysia/najib-launches-malaysian-syariah-index-20710.

106 "Indeks Syariah Malaysia: Model Tadbir Urus Berteraskan Maqasid Syariah" Jabatan Kemajuan Islam Malaysia, 2015, accessed August 22, 2021, https://www.islam.gov.my/en.

107 Tasnim Lokman, "Malaysian Syariah Index Score Goes up to 76.06 Pct for 2017," *New Straits Times*, August 3, 2017, https://www.nst.com.my/news/nation/.

index assessed three primary stakeholders, namely policymakers, enforcement agencies, and society, to ascertain the extent to which laws, policies, and programmes can be successfully realised and implemented in accordance with the five aspects of *Maqasid* Shari'ah.

9.7 Concluding Remarks

There are several points to be considered from this discussion and the resultant effects of the teaching of Islam on environmental protection. From the assessment, it can be construed that for Malaysia, the incorporation of Islamic principles within its environmental policy directive and the introduction of the Shari'ah Index are the right steps forwards toward enhancing its legal framework on environmental protection. However, more needs to be done to ensure that the existing framework can achieve its sustainability targets. While environmental governance is granted a high profile by Malaysia, given the severity of the climate and pollution threats, and growing public concern, it is necessary that improved measures are introduced within the existing legal framework. There is a growing recognition of the linkages between compliance and enforcement and a host of other factors.[108] To achieve the objectives of environmental protection, the adoption of ethical and spiritual principles within the policy and law plays a central role in conjunction with sustainable development.[109] Apart from that, the application of Islamic principles can guide Malaysia towards its environmental compliance as well as in establishing action priorities, tracking progress, and ensuring accountability.[110]

It is further stressed that the need for intervention to environmental threats received enhanced support from Islam through the concept of *Maqasid* Shari'ah which should be integrated within the existing legal framework to make it more dynamic. Earlier practice on the inclusion of Islamic values for environmental protection under the previous Malaysia Plan through the concept of *Islam Hadhari* can be emulated by the present policymaker. Similarly, the application of Shari'ah Index to benchmark and assess Malaysia's achievement of the *Maqasid* Shari'ah within various sectors, including that of environmental protection should be revived. In addition to incorporating the spirit of *Maqasid* Shari'ah, basic Islamic principles such as the concept of the human being as a trustee on earth should be embraced.

---

108 A. Heyes, "Implementing Environmental Regulation: Enforcement and Compliance" *Journal of Regulatory Economics* 17 (2000): 107–129; James Alm, "Environmental Enforcement and Compliance: Lessons from Pollution, Safety, and Tax Settings," *Foundations and Trends in Microeconomics* 10, no. 4 (January 2014):209–274.

109 Maizatun Mustafa, "Indicators for Sustainable Development".

110 Sabariyah Yaakub & Nik Ab Halim Nik Abdullah, "Towards Maqasid Shariah in Sustaining the Environment Through Impactful Strategies," *IJIB* 5, no. 1 (2020): 36–45.

This is to support the law in enhancing legal compliance by injecting the accountability principle as stipulated in Islam towards equity and justice for the sake of environmental quality, economic growth, and human well-being. These include laws on the prevention of wastage or overutilisation of natural resources, where public rights are prioritised over individuals.

Malaysia's rapid economic and social development over the last few decades has resulted in natural resources degradation impacting socio-economic wellbeing. While environmental regulation is primarily governed by federal law based on policy directives targeting sustainable development, the status of environmental quality has revealed that pollution and climate change issues are getting more serious due to non-compliance, accountability, and various other governance weaknesses. In principle, the concept of sustainable development has its basis in the Islamic tenet, which teaches humanity to conserve air, land, water, and other living things while also pursuing just economic needs and positive social interactions based on certain ethical values.[111] To have an effective legal framework for environmental protection, similar values should be secured as a foundation for an environmental action plan. In Islam, environmental stewardship and nature care are considered necessary demands of God that all must observe. Islamic teaching reminds the followers to maintain the delicate balance of the earth and promote moderation in consumption and avoidance of excessive usage of natural resources. As already illustrated, numerous verses of the Qur'an provide humans with a framework on matters relating to sustainability, besides examples from Prophet Muhammad's life. As a result, Islam views environmental protection as a critical ethical and moral issue. At the individual, institutional, and social levels, moral consciousness and religious knowledge can inspire individuals to consider the common good rather than focus exclusively on their own interests. These ethical standards should be incorporated into environmental legislation and regulation, and the resulting consequences should be effectively implemented. It would be the responsibility of the government to uphold environmental justice and equity through equitable resource allocation and distribution. Current alarms about environmental incidences indicate that now is the time to implement the concepts of environmental protection embedded in the Shari'ah to support and complement the existing framework to steer Malaysia's policy and law to address these concerns better.

111 Dariah, Atih Rohaeti, Muhammad Syukri Salleh, & Hakimi M. Shafiai, "A New Approach for Sustainable Development Goals in Islamic Perspective," *Procedia-Social and Behavioral Sciences* 219 (2016): 159–166.

Sridevi Thambapillay

10 Selected Issues in Family Law: Towards the Harmonisation Between Shari'ah and Common Law

10.1 Introduction

A family, comprising a man, woman, and their children, forms the basic unit of society. Society's strength and stability depend on the family unit. When families disintegrate, society's harmony and well-being collapse. Hence, it is of utmost importance to safeguard the family institution.[1]

Malaysia practises a dual system of family law, one for Muslims and one for non-Muslims. This is clearly provided under article 74 of the Federal Constitution read together with the State List in the Ninth Schedule therein, which lists down Islamic family law matters that fall within the jurisdiction of the States. This is further strengthened by the amendment to the Federal Constitution in 1988, *via* the Constitution (Amendment) Act 1988,[2] which added a new clause (1A) to article 121 of the Federal Constitution. Article 121(1) generally confers the jurisdiction to the civil courts in Malaysia. The new clause 1(A) reads as follows: "The courts referred to in clause (1) shall have no jurisdiction in respect of any matter within the jurisdiction of the Syariah Courts."

The above amendment could be said to have uplifted the status of the Shari'ah[3] Courts in Malaysia as it has theoretically clearly demarcated the jurisdiction between the civil courts and the Shari'ah Courts. The said amendment to the Federal Constitution in 1988 seems to have settled the conflicting jurisdiction between the Shari'ah Courts and the Civil Courts, where if the parties are Muslims, they are subjected to the Shari'ah Courts, and if the parties are non-Muslims, they are subjected to the Civil Courts. Nevertheless, one major problem that still remains unsettled is when one of the parties to the marriage has converted to Islam while the other party has not. The question that arises following the conversion of one of the parties to Islam is which court has jurisdiction to deal with the family matters that arise between them or concerning their children? Is it the Shari'ah Court or the Civil Court? At this juncture, it is to be noted that the Shari'ah Court does not possess jurisdiction over the non-Muslim spouse.

1 Mimi Kamariah Majid, *Family Law in Malaysia* (Kuala Lumpur: Malayan Law Journal Sdn Bhd, 1999), 1.

2 Act A704.

3 The spelling of "Syariah," which is used in the Malay language, is replaced with "Shari'ah" in this chapter for consistency and ease of reference.

https://doi.org/10.1515/9783110766707-010

Hence, this chapter aims to examine three selected issues that arise as a result of the conversion to Islam by one of the spouses, i.e., divorce, unilateral conversion of the children of the marriage to Islam, and the custody of the children. The writer would also attempt to suggest some recommendations to resolve these issues, which actually threaten the harmonisation between Shari'ah and Common Laws in Malaysia.[4]

10.2 The Law Reform (Marriage and Divorce) Act 1976: Pre- and Post-2017 Amendments

Prior to examining the three issues as aforesaid, it is pertinent to discuss the relevant statute that applies to non-Muslim Family Law, i.e., the Law Reform (Marriage and Divorce) Act 1976 (LRA).[5] This Act governs matters such as marriage, divorce, and ancillary matters, for example, maintenance, custody, and division of property upon divorce. The LRA was gazetted in 1976 but only enforced throughout Malaysia from 1 March 1982.[6] The long title to the LRA provides as follows: "An Act to provide for the monogamous marriages and the solemnization and registration of such marriages; to amend and consolidate the law relating to divorce; and to provide for matters incidental thereto."

Prior to the enactment of the LRA, there was no single statute that governed marriage and divorce laws for non-Muslims throughout Malaysia. There were various Ordinances in force for marriages and divorces, respectively, such as the Civil Marriage Ordinance 1952, Registration of Marriages Ordinance 1952, and Divorce Ordinance 1952. The need for a particular statute for marriage and divorce for non-Muslims was first suggested by Thomson LP in the case of *Re Ding Co Ca, Deceased*[7] as follows:

> . . . the whole question of personal law in the country, particularly as regards questions of marriage, divorce and succession, calls for the attention of the legislature. As regards persons professing Islam the position is tolerably clear. But as regards persons of Chinese race the law the courts are administering is probably different from any law that exists or ever has existed in China. . . . The same sort of position may well arise in relation to persons professing the Hindu religion by reason of the enactment in India of the Hindu Marriage Act 1955. The questions involved are questions which go to the very root of the law relating to the family, which, after all, is the basis of society at least in its present form, and the existence of a civilised

4 It is to be noted herein that the writer would be referring to the common law as civil law in this chapter, because when compared with Shari'ah law, the term civil law is more apt.

5 Act 164.

6 *Supra* n 1.

7 [1966] 1 LNS 157; [1966] 2 MLJ 220.

> society demands that these questions be settled beyond doubt by legislation which will clearly express the modern mores of the classes of persons concerned and put the rights of individuals beyond the chances of litigation.[8]

As a result of the calls by the bench, the Royal Commission on Non-Muslim Marriage and Divorce Laws was appointed on 4 February 1970 to study the existing laws on marriage and divorce which were applicable to non-Muslims. The said Commission was also tasked with the duty to reform and unify the non-Muslim marriage and divorce laws. In 1972, the Royal Commission published its report and drafted the Law Reform (Marriage and Divorce) Bill.[9] The Bill was debated in Parliament and finally was passed in 1976.

Section 3(3) of the LRA provides that it does not apply to Muslims as follows:

> This Act shall not apply to a Muslim or to any person who is married under Islamic and no marriage of one of the parties which professes the religion of Islam shall be solemnized or registered under this Act; but nothing herein shall be construed to prevent a court before which a petition for divorce has been made under section 51 from granting a decree of divorce on the petition of one party to a marriage where the other party has converted to Islam, and such decree shall, notwithstanding any other written law to the contrary, be valid against the party to the marriage who has so converted to Islam.

Upon perusing the above provision, it could be noted that generally, the LRA is not applicable to Muslims. However, there is an exception, i.e., where one of the parties to the marriage converts to Islam and the non-converting spouse petitions for divorce on the ground of conversion to Islam under section 51. In such an instance, the civil court has the jurisdiction to hear the divorce petition, although one of the parties is a Muslim. Further thereto, the decree of divorce, if granted by the said court, is valid against the Muslim party. Hence, the LRA is only applicable to a Muslim convert in a divorce proceeding brought by the non-converting spouse under section 51.

In addition to the granting of a decree of divorce under section 51(1), section 51(2) further provided that the court may also make provisions on spousal and child maintenance as well as child custody. This provision led to problems, especially in a situation where one of the spouses converted to Islam after the filing of the divorce petition or granting of the decree of divorce. If the non-converting spouse tried to use section 51(2) to claim the ancillary matters mentioned therein, the converting spouse would raise the argument that the said subsection does not apply to him or her as the divorce was not petitioned or the decree granted under section 51(1) (on the ground

---

8 MacIntyre J echoed Thomson LP's call in the same case. A few years later Mohamed Azmi J repeated the call in the case of *Mary Ng & Anor v Ooi Gim Teong* [1972] 1 LNS 85; [1972] 2 MLJ 18.

9 Mehrun Siraj, "Women and the Law: Significant Developments in Malaysia," *Law and Society Review* 28, no. 3, *Law and Society in Southeast Asia* (1994): 561–572.

of conversion to Islam). Further discussion on the cases pertaining to this issue will be provided later in this chapter under the sub-topic "Divorce."

In 2017, the LRA underwent several major amendments ("the 2017 amendments") via the Law Reform (Marriage and Divorce) (Amendment) Act 2016.[10] Two of the provisions that were amended were section 3(3) and section 51. The new section 3(3) reads as follows:

> This Act shall not apply to a Muslim or to any person who is married under Islamic law and no marriage of one of the parties which professes the religion of Islam shall be solemnized or registered under this Act; but nothing herein shall be construed to prevent a court from having exclusive jurisdiction over the dissolution of a marriage and all matters incidental thereto, including granting a decree of divorce or other orders under Part VII and Part VIII on a petition for divorce under section 53 where one party converts to Islam after filing of the petition or after the pronouncement of a decree, or a petition for divorce under either sections 51, 52 or 53 on the petition of either party or both parties to a marriage where one party has converted to Islam, and such decree and orders made shall, notwithstanding any other written law to the contrary, be valid against the party to the marriage who has so converted to Islam.

The amendment to section 3(3) has, in fact, extended the application of the LRA to the spouse who has converted to Islam. Prior to the amendment, as explained above, the LRA only applied to the Muslim convert when his or her non-converting spouse applies for a divorce on the ground of conversion to Islam under section 51. The converting spouse is not given any right to petition for divorce. The amendment to section 3(3) now enables the converting spouse to also petition for divorce under section 51. In addition to the ground of divorce stated in section 51, the converting spouse is also given the right to petition for divorce with his or her non-converting spouse under section 52 (on the ground of mutual consent) or petition under section 53 (on the ground of irretrievable breakdown of the marriage). Hence, it could be summed up that the 2017 amendments have conferred the same right to the converting spouse to petition for divorce as the non-converting spouse. This could be observed in the Explanatory Statement to the Law Reform (Marriage and Divorce) (Amendment) Bill, which provides as follows:

> *Clause 2* seeks to amend subsection 3(3) of Act 164 to enable a party to a marriage who has converted to Islam or both parties to present a petition for divorce before a civil court under Act 164. At present, the right to present a petition for divorce is only given to the party who has not converted to Islam. Those who have converted to Islam cannot apply for divorce under Islamic Family Law Act or Enactment because the Syariah Court does not have jurisdiction to hear any case where a non-Muslim is involved.

In addition to the above, the amendment to section 3(3) has also resolved the issue that the writer raised earlier, i.e., does the civil court have jurisdiction to hear applications for ancillary matters such as maintenance and child custody when one of

10 Act A1546.

the parties to the marriage converts to Islam after the filing of a divorce petition or after the granting of a decree of divorce? The amendment to section 3(3) answers the above question in the affirmative.

Hence, it is submitted that the above amendment to section 3(3) has not only conferred the right to the converting spouse to file a petition for divorce under section 51 (on the ground of conversion to Islam), sections 52 and 53, it has also cleared the issue as to whether the court has jurisdiction pertaining ancillary matters over a party to a marriage, who converts after the filing of a divorce petition or after the granting of a decree of divorce.

10.3 Legal Issues

Having examined the application of the LRA to Muslim coverts (both pre- and post-2017 amendments), the writer will next examine the three legal issues that arise when one of the parties to a marriage converts to Islam.

10.3.1 Divorce

The first legal issue is pertaining to divorce. Although this sub-issue was addressed earlier in this chapter, the writer would delve in depth on this issue with cases and commentaries in this segment. This issue would be further divided into three sub-issues, which are:

(a) Right of a converting spouse to petition for divorce;
(b) Jurisdiction of the court to order ancillary matters where the converting spouse converts after the filing of the divorce petition or after the granting of a decree of divorce; and
(c) The court's jurisdiction to grant damages for adultery where the co-respondent is a Muslim (though this issue does not directly arise from the conversion of one of the parties to the marriage to Islam, the writer is of the opinion that this is an important issue when discussing the application of the LRA to Muslims).

(a) Right of a converting spouse to petition for divorce

Prior to the 2017 amendments, as discussed above, only the non-converting spouse had the right to petition for divorce on the ground of conversion to Islam under section 51 of the LRA. The former section 51(1) of the LRA provides as follows: "[w]here one party to a marriage has converted to Islam, the other party who has not so converted may petition for divorce."

Hence, the converting spouse had no right whatsoever to petition for divorce. This provision came under severe criticism from academic scholars.[11] There were two criticisms raised against section 51. First, the right to file a petition is only given to the non-converting spouse, as the converting spouse is treated as the person at fault. Secondly, the converting spouse is also not given the right to petition for divorce under the ground of irretrievable breakdown of marriage under section 53, due to section 3(3) (as discussed earlier in this chapter), which generally provides that the LRA does not apply to Muslims save in divorce proceedings under section 51.

The above situation could be observed in the case of *Pedley v Majlis Ugama Pulau Pinang & Anor*,[12] where the court observed as follows: " . . . under the law, a non-Muslim marriage is not dissolved upon one of the parties converting to Islam. It only provides a ground for the other party who has not converted to Islam to petition for divorce."[13]

The call to amend section 51 in order to give the right to the converting spouse to file a petition for divorce was also made by the learned judge Abdul Hamid Mohamed J in the case of *Ng Siew Pian v Abd Wahid bin Abu Hassan, Kadi Daerah Bukit Mertajam & satu lagi*.[14] In this case, the husband, who converted to Islam, applied to the Shari'ah court for a decree of divorce on the ground that he had converted to Islam. The Shari'ah court granted a decree of divorce in the wife's absence. The wife made an application to the High Court for a declaration that the Shari'ah court had no jurisdiction to grant the decree of dissolution. The High Court agreed that the Shari'ah court had no jurisdiction to hear the husband's application in the wife's absence. Further thereto, the relevant Shari'ah Enactment requires both parties present before the court to be Muslims. The High Court judge then looked at whether such a petition by the husband could be brought under section 51 of the LRA. Unfortunately, the answer was in the negative. Hence, the learned judge suggested that section 51 of the LRA be amended in order to allow a converting spouse to petition for divorce.

The 2017 amendments amended section 51 to overcome the weaknesses that existed. The new section 51(1) reads as follows: "[w]here one party to a marriage has converted to Islam – (a) either party may petition for a divorce under this section or section 53; or (b) both parties may petition for a divorce under section 52." Thus, perusing the above amendment, it is submitted that it has laid to rest the weaknesses surrounding section 51(1). First, it extends the right to file a petition for divorce on the ground of conversion to Islam to the converting spouse. In addition, the converting spouse is also given the right to petition for divorce either under

---

11 Ahmad Ibrahim, "Seksyen 51 Akta Membaharui Undang-Undang (Perkahwinan dan Perceraian) 1976 Perlu Dipinda," *KANUN*, no. 2 (1990): 32.

12 [1990] 2 MLJ 307.

13 [1990] 2 MLJ, 308.

14 [1991] 1 CLJ 391.

section 52 (on the ground of mutual consent together with the non-converting spouse) or section 53 (on the ground of irretrievable breakdown of the marriage). It is further submitted that the said amendment would also avoid a situation that existed before, i.e., where the converting spouse files a divorce petition in the Shari'ah court, thereby resolving the issue of conflict of jurisdiction between the Shari'ah court and the civil court.[15]

(b) Jurisdiction of the court to order ancillary matters where the converting spouse converts after the filing of the divorce petition or after the granting of a decree of divorce

The second issue pertaining to the old section 51 (as was discussed earlier) is the power of the court to grant ancillary relief under section 51(2), where one of the parties converts to Islam after the filing of the divorce petition or after the decree of divorce is granted. The former Section 51(2) of the LRA provided as follows: "[t]he court upon dissolving the marriage may make provision for the wife or husband, and for the support, care and custody of the children of the marriage, if any, and may attach any conditions to the decree of dissolution as it thinks fit."

In the case of *Tan Sung Mooi v Too Miew Kim*,[16] the Supreme Court held that the High Court does have jurisdiction to order ancillary relief despite the fact that one of the parties to the marriage had converted to Islam after the dissolution of marriage. According to Mohamed Dzaiddin SCJ, there were two reasons for this decision. First, the court held that the petitioner applied for the ancillary matters under sections 76 (a division of matrimonial property) and 77 (spousal maintenance) of the LRA, which concerned matters affecting both parties' legal obligations as non-Muslims. The High Court would have jurisdiction to hear or determine the ancillary proceedings, despite the fact that the respondent had converted to Islam after the divorce but before the hearing of the ancillary application. The High Court in the present matter exercised its jurisdiction under section 24(a) of the Court of Judicature Act 1964, which states that the High Court's jurisdiction shall include "jurisdiction under any written law relating to divorce and matrimonial causes." The learned judge further explained that "written law" in the above provision must include the LRA.

15 Najibah Mohd Zin, Hidayah Mohamed Jani, Abdul Ghafur Hamid, and Nora Abdul Hak, "Jurisdictional Conflict in Interfaith Child Custody Disputes: A Legal Discourse in Malaysian Courts," *Al Shajarah* 24, no.1 (2019): 1–24, 20, https://journals.iium.edu.my/shajarah/index.php/shaj/article/view/851.

16 [1994] 3 MLJ 117.

Secondly, the learned judge stated as follows:

> from the wording of s51(2), the legislature clearly intended to provide ancillary reliefs for non-Muslim spouses and the children of the marriage as a result of one party's conversion to Islam. In our opinion, by implication from s51(2) above, the High Court, in the present reference, has jurisdiction to hear and determine the ancillary issues . . . It would result in grave injustice to non-Muslim spouses and children whose only remedy would be in the civil courts if the High Court no longer has jurisdiction, since the Syariah Courts do not have jurisdiction over non-Muslims. In the context of the legislative intent of s3 and the overall purpose of the Act, the respondent's legal obligations under a non-Muslim marriage cannot surely be extinguished or avoided by his conversion to Islam.

The 2017 amendments also amended section 51(2). The new section 51(2) reads as follows:

> The Court upon dissolving the marriage or at any time, may make provision for the wife or husband, and for the support, care and custody of the children of the marriage, if any, under Part VII and Part VIII and may attach any conditions to the decree of the dissolution as it thinks fit.

It is submitted that the above amendment has resolved the dilemma that existed as stated aforesaid. Two observations could be made upon perusing the new section 51 (2). First, the amendment has added the phrase "at any time." This means that the court is given the flexibility to order the ancillary relief at any time. This would then enable the parties to the marriage to request ancillary relief at any time. Secondly, the new section 51(2) specifically makes reference to Part VII and Part VIII of the LRA. Part VII of the LRA refers to the division of matrimonial property upon divorce and judicial separation as well as wife maintenance. Part VIII provides for child custody and maintenance. The new amendment has indeed paved the way for the parties to a marriage to claim ancillary relief at any time and do not have to submit the claim when the petition of divorce on the ground of conversion to Islam filed. It could also be said that the amendment ensures that a Muslim convert fulfils his or her obligations to the family.[17]

(c) The court's jurisdiction to order a co-respondent who is a Muslim to pay damages for adultery

As mentioned earlier in this chapter, although this issue does not arise as a result of the conversion of one of the parties to Islam, the writer submits that as there was a new development in the law on this issue at the time of writing this chapter, which attracted the attention of the media and the public, it would be interesting to

17 Daleleer Kaur Randawar, Nur Ehzan Rahmat, Akbar Kamarudin @ Abduk Shukor, *Family Law in Malaysia* (Petaling Jaya: LexisNexis, 2018), 162.

examine it. Further thereto, this issue had also raised the question of which court had jurisdiction: the Shari'ah or the civil court?

The relevant provision regarding this issue is section 58 (1) and (2) of the LRA, which reads as follows:

> On a petition for divorce in which adultery is alleged, or in the answer of a party to the marriage praying for divorce and alleging adultery, the party shall make the alleged adulterer or adulteress a co-respondent, unless excused by the court on special grounds from doing so.
>
> A petition under subsection (1) may include a prayer that the co-respondent be condemned in damages in respect of the alleged adultery.

In the case of *AJS v JMH & Another Appeal,*[18] the appellant had filed a petition for judicial separation against her husband on the ground that their marriage had irretrievably broken down due to the adulterous relationship with the respondent. The appellant cited the respondent, who is a Muslim, as a co-respondent and claimed damages from her under section 58 of the LRA. The respondent applied to strike out the petition on two grounds, i.e., 1) section 3(3) of the LRA excludes the application of the LRA to Muslims; and 2) section 58 of the LRA, which enables a petitioner to claim damages against a co-respondent only applies in divorce proceedings and not judicial separation proceedings. Pertaining to the first issue as to the application of the LRA to Muslims by virtue of section 3(3), both the High Court and Court of Appeal dismissed the appellant's claim and appeal, respectively, on the ground that the wordings in section 3(3) is clear in providing that the LRA does not apply to Muslims. Hence, the co-respondent cannot be named as a party in the current proceeding. On appeal to the Federal Court, Tengku Maimun Tuan Mat CJ, delivering the majority judgment, observed as follows: "[s]ection 3(3) of the LRA paints a clear picture of the intention of the Parliament to exclude Muslims entirely from the application of the LRA and the only exception for this exclusion is as stipulated in section 3(3) of the LRA itself (where a non-Muslim spouse subsequently converts to Islam after his or her civil marriage)."[19]

Her Ladyship further stated as follows on the effect if the court agrees with the appellant to condemn in damages a Muslim co-respondent:

> Further, the power of the court to condemn in damages a co-respondent such as the respondent in this case under section 58 of the LRA is also a specific power conferred unto the court as a part of non-Muslim personal law. Allowing a non-Muslim petitioner to condemn a Muslim co-respondent is tantamount to enforcing non-Muslim personal law on a Muslim.
>
> Similar options are not and cannot be legally made available to Muslim parties in litigation with each other in the Syariah Court but which might involve a non-Muslim as well. It follows

18 [2022] 1 CLJ, 331.
19 [2022] 1 CLJ, 360.

> that just as a non-Muslim cannot be brought to a Syariah Court, a Muslim co-respondent cannot be brought to a civil court – in light of the clear demarcation of jurisdictions under art.121(1A).[20]

Hence, the above statement by Her Ladyship clearly lays down the principle that a Muslim co-respondent cannot be condemned in damages for adultery in a divorce petition in the civil court.

The appellant then raised the issue that the above ruling would lead to an unjust result as the said Muslim co-respondent will escape liability. Her Ladyship replied to this concern as follows:

> Firstly, a Muslim if found to engage in the immoral act of committing adultery is answerable to the criminal side of the Syariah system. This is not the same with non-Muslims who do not generally face criminal penalty for adultery under the personal laws on morality. It remains open for the non-Muslim party to lodge a complaint with the religious authorities that the Muslim co-adulterer or adulteress has committed an offence under Syariah law. *See* for example sections 24 and 27 of the Syariah Criminal Offence (Federal Territories) Act 1997 which respectively outlaw intercourse out of wedlock and *khalwat* (close proximity between men and women who are otherwise married or who are within the categories of prohibited relationships for marriage or "*mahram*").[21]

Upon perusing the above dictum, it is submitted that Her Ladyship has provided recourse for the appellant in the current case, where instead of condemning the co-respondent in damages under the LRA, the appellant could instead lodge a complaint with the Islamic religious authorities. In such a situation, adultery then becomes an offence under Muslim law.

The second issue that was discussed by the Federal Court was whether the claim for damages could be made against an alleged co-adulterer or adulteress in a petition for judicial separation. This is due to the fact that the wordings in section 58(1) start with "on a petition for divorce." There is no mention of a petition for judicial separation therein.

The appellant argued that section 58(1) does not prohibit a joinder in the case of a petition for judicial separation. The Federal Court, in the current case, agreed with the Indian case of *Rajendra Prasad Gupta v Prakash Chandra Mishra*[22] which held that a procedural provision is to be taken to permit anything that is not expressly prohibited. In addition, the Federal Court referred to section 64(1) of the LRA, which provides as follows: "A petition for judicial separation may be presented to the court by either party to the marriage on the ground and circumstances set out in s.54 and that section shall, with the necessary modification, apply in relation to such a petition for divorce."

20 [2022] 1 CLJ, 360.
21 [2022] 1 CLJ, 361.
22 (2011) 2 SCC 705.

Therefore, since the respondent's adulterous conduct is one of the grounds for a breakdown of marriage under section 54, the Federal Court held that sections 64 and 54 should not be read in segregation with section 58. Her Ladyship, Tengku Maimun Tuan Mat CJ, stated as follows:

> Given that section 54 is not only applicable to a divorce petition but also to a petition for judicial separation, with necessary modifications, I hold that s.58(2) does not limit a claim or prayer that a co-respondent be condemned in damages in respect of an alleged adultery to a divorce petition. A petitioner in a petition for judicial separation may also include a prayer that a co-respondent be condemned in damages in respect of the alleged adultery. In simpler words, sections 64(1) and 54(1) must be read harmoniously with the specific procedure and regime on damages contained in sections 58 to 60 of the LRA.[23]

It is submitted that though the Federal Court here took a liberal interpretation of sections 64(1) and 54(1) by extending the right of a petitioner in a judicial separation matter to condemn in damages a co-respondent under section 58 of the LRA, the appellant in the current case did not gain anything out of the interpretation as the court had already decided that section 58 does not apply to the respondent here as she is a Muslim. Nevertheless, this principle could be applied by the courts in the future when a similar claim to condemn a co-respondent in damages under section 58 is brought in a petition for judicial separation.

Having examined the development pertaining to divorce matters when one of the parties converts to Islam, it is submitted that the law has minimised the conflict of jurisdiction between the Shari'ah courts and the civil courts in Malaysia, thereby paving the way towards the harmonisation between Shari'ah and Common Law.

10.3.2 Unilateral Conversion of Children to Islam

The second legal issue that will be examined is the unilateral conversion of the children to Islam by the converting spouse. This issue has been in the limelight since the High Court decision in the case of *Chang Ah Mee v Jabatan Hal Ehwal Agama Islam & Ors.*[24] The main issue in the above case as well as the cases that were decided thereafter, is whether the converting spouse has the right to unilaterally convert his or her children to Islam without obtaining the consent of the non-converting spouse. As can be seen in the cases discussed below, the courts referred to article 12(4) of the Federal Constitution in deciding this issue. Article 12(4) provides as follows: "For the purposes of Clause (3) the religion of a person below the age of eighteen years shall be decided by his parent or guardian."

23 *Supra* n 15, 366.
24 [2003] 1 CLJ 458.

In deciding the above issue, the real question that has to be addressed by the courts is whether the word "parent" that appears in article 12(4) refers to a single parent or to both the parents. An examination of a few major cases that had to decide on the interpretation of the word "parent" in article 12(4) in relation to the issue of the unilateral right to convert the children to Islam is made below.

In the case of *Chang Ah Mee v Jabatan Hal Ehwal Agama Islam & Ors*,[25] the plaintiff sought a declaration from the court that the conversion of her two-year child to Islam was solemnised by the first defendant with the consent only of her husband was null and void under section 68 of the Sabah Administration of Islamic Law Enactment 1992 (Sabah Enactment). The defendants contended that as the word "parent" in article 12(4) of the Federal Constitution referred to a single parent, hence the word "parents" in section 68 of the Sabah Enactment referred to either the father or mother of the infant. The learned High Court judge, Ian HC Chin, disagreed with the defendants and stated:

> The Constitution does not discriminate against the sexes and since the father and the mother have equal right over the person and property of an infant, the term "parent" in art 12(4) must necessarily mean both the father and the mother if both are living. To construe otherwise would mean depriving, for example, a mother of her right as a parent to choose the religion of the infant under art. 12(4), if the father alone decides on the religion to be followed by the infant. To allow just the father or the mother to choose a religion would invariably mean depriving the other of the constitutional right under art. 12(4).[26]

Therefore, the learned judge in the above decision took a liberal interpretation of the term "parent" and applied it to both parents.

However, the above interpretation was not followed by the High Court in the case of *Shamala Sathyaseelan v Dr Jeyaganesh C Mogarajah & Anor.*[27] In this case, the wife sought a declaration from the court that the unilateral conversion of her two minor children to Islam by her converted husband as being null and void. She also contended that the said conversion was done without her knowledge and consent. In the present case, the wife referred to article 12(4) as well as section 5(1) of the Guardianship of Infants Act 1961[28] (GIA), which confers equal parental rights in guardianship and custody issues concerning children. The wife also cited the case of *Chang Ah Mee v Jabatan Hal Ehwal Agama Islam & Ors*[29] in support of her argument.

Unfortunately, the learned High Court judge, Faiza Tamby Chik, did not agree with the interpretation given by the former case to article 12(4). The learned judge preferred to apply the plain meaning rule, i.e. "If the meaning of the Act is plain, it

25 [2003] 1 CLJ 458.
26 [2003] 1 CLJ, 462.
27 [2004] 2 CLJ 416.
28 Act 351.
29 *Supra* n 21.

is to be given that plain meaning. Where the language of an Act is clear and explicit, we must give effect to it, whatever may be the consequences, for in that case the words of the statute speak the intention of the legislature."[30] The High Court judge explained that article 12(4) provides "be decided by his parent or guardian." As both nouns "parent" and "guardian" are singular and the determiner used is "his," it is sufficient if either his parent or his guardian consents to his conversion. Further thereto, his Lordship observed that the noun "parent" is either a father or a mother. Hence, there is no need for both parents to consent to the child's conversion to Islam.

Perusing the above interpretation of article 12(4) by the High Court judge in the above case, it is submitted that the learned judge had applied the literal rule and had thereby narrowed the scope of the term "parent" provided in article 12(4). It is also respectfully submitted that as the wife in the above case cited section 5 of the GIA, which gives equality of parental rights in guardianship matters in support of her argument, the High Court should not have bypassed this argument and instead preferred to look at section 6 of the GIA, which basically provides what happens to the guardianship of a child when one of the parents dies. Section 5, instead, is a pertinent provision to refer to in the instant case, where it is clearly provided that both the parents have equal rights in the upbringing of the child. Hence, the said provision should be referred to in order to strengthen the argument that both parents need to consent to the conversion of the child to another religion.

The unilateral conversion of the child to Islam issue was raised a few years later in the case of *Subashini a/p Rajasingam v Saravanan a/l Thangathoray*.[31] In this case, the wife raised article 12(4) of the Federal Constitution as well as section 5 of the GIA. However, the Federal Court did not agree with her that the husband had no right to convert the children of the marriage without the wife's consent. His Lordship held that the word "parent" in article 12(4) of the Federal Constitution means a single parent. Howsoever, at the end of the case, the court decided that article 12(4) is not relevant here as the child concerned was no longer an infant.

It is submitted that although the Federal Court in the above case applied a narrow interpretation to the word "parent" in article 12(4) of the Federal Constitution, on the brighter side, it is to be noted that the remarks by his Lordship are merely obiter and are not binding on later cases. This is due to the fact that the court held that article 12(4) does not come into question here as the subject in question was no longer an infant.

About ten years later, the Federal Court was faced with the same issue in the landmark decision of *Indira Gandhi Mutho v Pengarah Jabatan Agama Islam Perak*

30 *Supra* n 24, 423.
31 [2008] 2 CLJ 1.

& Ors and Other Appeals.[32] Her Ladyship Zainul Al FCJ (delivering the judgment of the court) held that the interpretation of article 12(4) of the Federal Constitution by the Federal Court in *Subashini's* case was unsupported and erroneous. In contrast to the literal interpretation applied by the court in *Subashini's* case, the Federal Court in the present case applied the purposive approach of article 12(4) read with the Eleventh Schedule of the Federal Constitution,[33] which promotes the welfare of children. The Federal Court here also applied sections 5 and 11 of the GIA, which confers equal parental rights in child custody matters. Thus, the Federal Court unanimously declared that the conversion of the three children to Islam in the present case was unlawful as the consent of both parents was needed to convert a child.

The above decision could be described as having settled the issue of unilateral conversion of children, which had been an ongoing issue in Malaysia for the past nearly two decades. The Federal Court, which comprised five judges, unanimously agreed that the word "parent" in article 12(4) of the Federal Constitution refers to both the parents, thereby declaring that any unilateral conversion of the children of the marriage by either parent would be unlawful and against the Federal Constitution. Therefore, it is submitted that the above decision has laid to rest the dilemma that had existed from the case of *Chang Ah Mee*[34] as discussed earlier.

A few years after the Federal Court's decision in *Indira Gandhi,* the Court of Appeal was faced with a similar issue in the case of *Pendaftar Muallaf Wilayah Persekutuan v L.C.Y., Ketua Pengarah Jabatan Agama Islam, Ketua Pengarah Kementerian Pelajaran Malaysia & Kerajaan Malaysia.*[35] The appellant argued that the Federal Court decision in *Subashini* should be followed and that the Federal Court decision in *Indira Gandhi* is *per incuriam* and, as such, is not binding upon the High Court and the Court of Appeal. The Court of Appeal here referred to the doctrine of *stare decisis* and stated as follows:

> The Federal Court in *Indira Gandhi* in answering a specific question of law, had considered the relevant facts and applied the law as can be seen from paragraphs 142 until 181 of the grounds of judgment. All relevant statutory provisions and previous Federal Court decisions on the same issue including *Subashini* has been analysed and considered before the decision on the issue was decided. As such, the decision in *Indira Gandhi* that the consent of both parents are required before the Certificate of Conversion to Islam can be issued, is in our view, the *ratio decidendi* of the case.[36]

32 [2018] 3 CLJ 145.
33 Para 2(95) of the Eleventh Schedule defines words in the "singular" to include plural.
34 *Supra* n 21.
35 [2021] 1 LNS 2079.
36 [2021] 1 LNS 2079, para 28.

The Court of Appeal further added:[37]

> it is trite law that the latest decision of the Federal Court supersedes its earlier decision as explained in Dalip Bhagwan Singh's case (*supra*):
>
> If House of Lords and by analogy, the Federal Court, departs from its previous decisions when it is right to do so in the circumstances set out above, then also by necessary implication, its decision represents the present state of the law. When two decisions of the Federal Court conflict on a point of law, the later decision therefore, for the same reasons, prevails over the earlier decision.[38] (emphasis added)

The Court of Appeal, in the instant case, therefore, upheld the Federal Court's decision in *Indira Gandhi* and held that the children's conversion to Islam was without the consent of the father and that the High Court was correct in granting the order of *certiorari* to quash the said conversion, the issuance of the Certificate of Conversion and an order of **mandamus** to compel the *Pendaftar Muallaf Wilayah Persekutuan* and Ketua Pengarah Jabatan Agama Islam to cancel the registration of the conversion of the children to Islam.

At the time of writing this chapter, a recent case of unilateral conversion to Islam of the children was highlighted in the media. The mother of three children Loh Siew Hong, a Hindu Chinese, was awarded sole custody of all her children upon divorce from her husband, Nageshwaran Muniandy, in March 2019. Thereafter, the husband converted to Islam, took the children away, and unilaterally converted them to Muslims in Perlis. She was unable to *see* her children since then. Between 2017 and 2019, she had lodged numerous police reports against her husband for causing her injuries. The husband was later arrested for a drug-related offence and was serving a jail sentence in Kelantan.[39]

The children were then placed under the care of the Social Welfare Department (JKM). The wife filed a *habeas corpus* application for the release of her children, who were under the care of the JKM. On 21 February 2022, the High Court allowed the *habeas corpus* application. According to Justice Datuk Collin Lawrence Sequerah:

> Pursuant to an order of the High Court dated March 31, 2021, the applicant was granted the sole custody, care and control of the children. There was also earlier an interim ex parte order dated Dec 20, 2019 granting sole custody, care and control of the children to the applicant.
>
> The court orders still stand and are valid and are not to be treated with impunity upon the pain of contempt to court. By the reasons of the court orders therefore, I allowed the application to the habeas corpus as per enclosure one in the notice of motion.

---

37 [2021] 1 LNS 2079, para 34.

38 [2021] 1 LNS 2079, para 34.

39 Imran Hilmy, "Single Mum Hopes to Bring Kids Home, Files Judicial Review to Challenge Unilateral Conversion," *The Star*, February 22, 2022, https://www.thestar.com.my/news/nation/2022/02/20/single-mum-hopes-to-bring-kids-home-files-judicial-review-to-challenge-unilateral-conversion.

> The three children are to be released forthwith into the sole custody, care and control of the applicant.[40]

The applicant had also filed a separate court action to nullify the Islamic conversion of her three children by way of judicial review.[41] The Perlis Religious Department claimed that unilateral conversion is allowed under state laws, although the Federal Court, in the case of *Indira Gandhi*[42] ruled that pursuant to the Federal Constitution, both parents must consent to the conversion.[43] At the time of writing this chapter, the application to challenge the conversion of the children had not been decided by the court yet.

Nevertheless, the writer wishes to highlight the views expressed to the media by a leading academic scholar on constitutional law, Emeritus Professor Datuk Dr Shad Saleem Faruqi, on the issue of unilateral conversion. His views on the Loh Siew Hong's case are as follows:

> First, a custody order from the court is binding on all persons and any defiance of the judicial order may amount to contempt of court. Nobody is immune from this law.
>
> Second, the Federal Constitution is the supreme law of the land and it is superior to all other written laws, including state enactments. Any state law that violates the Constitution can be struck down by the superior civil courts.
>
> Thirdly, whenever there is a conflict between any laws or ambiguity in any law, as is almost always the case, the superior courts are the ultimate arbiters of what the law says and means.
>
> Fourthly, the *Indira Gandhi* Federal Court decision was the binding authority that unilateral conversion of minors to another religion without consent of both parents was unconstitutional. The said case is also the authority for the ruling that the word "parent" or "guardian" in Art 12(4) means "parents" and "guardians." This is due to the fact that para 2(95) of Schedule 11 provides "words in the singular include the plural."
>
> Finally, if the Perlis State Enactment 2016 provides otherwise, it needs to be amended and updated to conform to the decision in *Indira Gandhi.*[44]

He also added that all authorities are bound by the Federal Court decision in *Indira Gandhi*. It is submitted that the above views expressed by Emeritus Professor Datuk

---

40 *Loh Siew Hong v Nazirah Nanthakumar Abdullah & Anor* [2022] 4 CLJ 467, 484.

41 _N Trisha, "Single Mother Loh Challenging Conversion of Her Three Children," *The Star*, March 25, 2022, https://www.thestar.com.my/news/nation/2022/03/25/single-mother-loh-challenging-conversion-of-three-children.

42 *Supra* n 29.

43 *Supra* n 35.

44 Austin Camoens, "Single Mum Case: Federal Court Decision Overrides State Law, Says Constitutional Expert," *The Star*, February 18, 2022, https://www.thestar.com.my/news/nation/2022/02/18/single-mum-case-federal-court-decision-overrides-state-law-says-constitutional-expert.

Dr Shad Saleem Faruqi are commendable as it safeguards the rights enshrined in the Federal Constitution, especially the right of the parents to decide on the religion of their child. It is to be noted that article 12(4) falls under Part II of the Federal Constitution, entitled Fundamental Liberties. Hence, the right of the parents to decide on the religion of their child or children is a fundamental right that cannot easily be denied by state laws.

The writer hopes that Loh Siew Hong's application to nullify the unilateral conversion of her children is successful and that the court decides in her favour, as was done by the Federal Court in the case of *Indira Gandhi.*

10.3.3 Custody of Children

The third legal issue that arises as a consequence of the conversion of one of the parties to the marriage to Islam is pertaining to who has the right to obtain custody of the children. The relevant statutes that are applicable are the GIA and the LRA.

As mentioned earlier in this chapter, section 5 of the GIA confers equality of parental rights to the parents. In addition, when it comes to the claim of custody over the child, section 11 of the GIA provides as follows: "The court or judge, in exercising the powers conferred by this Act, shall have regards primarily to the welfare of the infant and shall, where the infant has a parent or parents, consider the wishes of such parent or both of them, as the case may be."

Nevertheless, the issue that arises is whether the above provisions apply to a Muslim convert. Reference pertaining to this issue is provided in section 1(3) of the GIA, which states:

> Nothing in this Act shall apply in any state to persons professing the religion of Islam until this Act has been adopted by a law made by the Legislature of that State; and any such law may provide that –
> (a) nothing in this Act which is contrary to the religion of Islam or the custom of the Malays shall apply to any person under the age of eighteen years who professes the religion of Islam and whose father professes or professed at the date of his death that religion or, in the case of an illegitimate child, whose mother so professes or professed that religion; and
> (b) in the case of any other person, this Act, so far as they are contrary to the religion of Islam, shall cease to apply to such person upon his professing the religion of Islam, if at the date of such professing he has completed his age of eighteen years or, if not having completed such age, he professes the religion of Islam with the consent of the person who under this Act is the guardian of the person of the infant.

At this juncture, reference could be made to section 3(3) of the LRA (pre-2017 amendments), which provided that the LRA does not apply to Muslims save in relation to a divorce petition where one of the parties to the marriage has converted to Islam. Nevertheless, the issue that arises is pertaining to ancillary matters, such as the custody of the children of the marriage, when one of the parties to the marriage converts after the filing of the divorce petition or after the granting of the decree of divorce. Would the civil court still have jurisdiction over the concerted spouse to hear the applications for ancillary matters?

This matter was settled by the case of *Tan Sung Mooi v Too Miew Kim*[45] (as discussed in-depth earlier). The Supreme Court held that the High Court still has the jurisdiction to grant ancillary relief under the LRA to a wife where the husband had converted to Islam after the marriage was dissolved. The court added that the converting spouse's "legal obligations under a non-Muslim marriage cannot be extinguished or avoided by his conversion to Islam."[46]

The Federal Court, in the case of *Subhashini*[47] agreed with the above principle, where the court held that:

> The husband could not shield himself behind the freedom of religion clause in Article 11(4) of the Federal Constitution to avoid his antecedent obligations under the 1976 Act on the ground that the civil court has no jurisdiction over him. It must be noted that both the husband and wife were Hindus at the time of their marriage. Therefore, the status of the husband and wife at the time of registering their marriage was of material importance, otherwise the husband's conversion would cause injustice to the unconverted wife including the children. A non-Muslim marriage does not automatically dissolve upon one of the party's conversions to Islam. Thus, by contracting the civil marriage, the husband and wife were bound by the 1976 Act in respect of divorce and custody of children of marriage, and thus, the civil court continues to have jurisdiction over him, notwithstanding his conversion to Islam.[48]

At this juncture, it is submitted that although the above decision received criticisms on the court's narrow interpretation of the word "parent" in article 12(4) of the Federal Court, it is commendable that the same court was flexible in stating that though one of the parties to the marriage has converted to Islam, his obligations and responsibilities under his civil marriage still continue. If the court were to decide otherwise, it would cause injustice to the non-Muslim wife and their children. Thus, it is clear that the civil court still has jurisdiction over the converted spouse in issues of custody of children.

The above decision was endorsed by the Federal Court in the case of *Viran Nagappan v Deepa Subramaniam & Other Appeals.*[49] The Federal Court, in the case of

45 *Supra* n 13.
46 *Supra* n 123–125 (MLJ).
47 *Supra* n 28.
48 *Supra* n, para 19.
49 [2016] 3 CLJ 505; [2016] 1 MLJ 585.

Indira Gandhi,[50] agreeing with the above decisions, added that the conversion to Islam of one of the parties to the marriage does not only not oust the court's jurisdiction under the LRA but also under the GIA. The Federal Court held as follows:

> Under the GIA, both the parents have equal rights in relation to the custody and upbringing of the infant children and the wishes of both are to be taken into consideration. The conversion of the husband to Islam does not alter the antecedent legal position, nor does it bring the children out of the ambit of the GIA.[51]

The decision in *Indira Gandhi* above resolved the dilemma as to whether the court has jurisdiction to decide issues concerning custody of the child of the marriage under the GIA where one of the parties had converted to Islam.

In addition to the above cases, which had held in favour of the civil court having jurisdiction to decide child custody matters despite the fact that one of the parents had converted to Islam, it is also heartening to note that the legislature had taken the initiative to codify this principle by way of the 2017 amendments to the LRA. As discussed earlier in this chapter, the 2017 amendments to section 3(3) of the LRA enables the court to have jurisdiction to decide on child custody issues, be it in a situation where one of the parties to the marriage converted to Islam prior to the divorce petition was filed in court or thereafter. Therefore, it is submitted that issues pertaining to child custody matters where one of the parents has converted to Islam have also been settled, especially after the amendment to section 3(3) of the LRA.

10.4 Findings and Recommendations

Based on the above three legal issues that arise as a result of the conversion of one of the parties of the marriage to Islam, it is submitted that two of the said issues have been amicably settled with the amendment to section 3(3) of the LRA via the 2017 amendments. The said amendment takes care of the court's jurisdiction over parties who have converted to Islam in divorce and custody issues. In divorce matters, it could be observed that not only has the amendment to sections 3(3) and 51 of the LRA gives the right to the converted spouse to file a petition for divorce on the ground of conversion to Islam, it also extends the right to the said person to file the divorce petition under the two other grounds, i.e., mutual consent and irretrievable breakdown of the marriage. Hence, it could be said that this would now enable the Muslim spouse to directly file the divorce petition in the civil court, rather than in the Shari'ah court, as was previously done prior to the 2017 amendments. This, in turn, raised two issues.

50 *Supra* n 29.
51 *Supra* n 210.

First, the converted spouse could only file the divorce petition in the Shari'ah court as he or she had no right to do so in the civil court. Secondly, although the converting spouse was able to file the divorce petition in the Shari'ah court, the non-converting spouse could not be made a party to the divorce matter as the Shari'ah Court does not have jurisdiction over non-Muslims. This led to a non-harmonious situation between the Shari'ah law and civil law. Howsoever, with the 2017 amendments, the above problem has been resolved. The same could be said for custody matters too.

Nevertheless, the issue that seems to be unresolved is the unilateral conversion of children to Islam, though the Federal Court, in the landmark case of *Indira Gandhi*[52] had already made a decision on the said issue. At this juncture, the writer would recommend two alternative measures to overcome the conflict in the application of the Shari'ah law or the civil law. First, it is respectfully submitted that a special tribunal on the unilateral conversion of children should be formed to decide this issue. The tribunal should comprise members who possess knowledge in both areas of laws: common law and Islamic law. As the issue of unilateral conversion of children touches on the principle of the best interests of the child, these experts who sit on the tribunal would have a better understanding of the best interest of the child concept, both under common law as well as the Islamic law.[53]

Secondly, or in the alternative, it is also submitted that the parties could also possibly settle the issue through a mediation process. This would be less costly than going through a litigation process, which is also time-consuming. It is also suggested that there should be two mediators, one a Muslim and the other a non-Muslim, so that there is no issue of bias. In addition, the mediation process will be less vindictive and can preserve the good relationship between the parties. At the end of the day, the parties should bear in mind that they should always place their child's best interest as the paramount consideration in their custody tussle.

In addition to the two measures suggested above, the writer submits that the best measure to overcome this issue lies in the hands of the legislature. So long as there is no written law to regulate the issue of unilateral conversion of children, the Shari'ah courts and civil courts will continuously be burdened with such cases in the future, thereby prolonging the conflict of jurisdiction between these two courts. Thus, it is fervently hoped that the legislature will take immediate action to amend the current law (as was done *via* the 2017 amendments to the LRA) to resolve the aforesaid issue.

---

52 *Supra* n 29.

53 *See* also Nur Syakirah Binti Mohd Adnan, "Resolving Conflict of Laws Issues Arising Out of Conversion in Malaysia," [2020] 1 *LNS(A)* xcv.

10.5 Conclusion

In conclusion, it is observed that the jurisdictional conflict between the civil and Syariah Courts has been an unsettled issue in Malaysia, especially after the amendment to article 121(1A) of the Federal Constitution. This could be seen especially in family law matters, where one of the parties to the marriage converts to Islam. The party, who converts to Islam, as could be observed in the cases discussed earlier in this chapter, tries to escape his or her responsibilities that arise from the non-Muslim marriage, stating that the civil laws do not apply to him or her anymore as he or she comes under the purview of the Shari'ah court, and not the civil court. This led to injustice to the non-converting spouse, especially if the Muslim spouse files a divorce petition or a custody claim in the Shari'ah court or unilaterally converts their children to Islam. The former would not be able to appear in the Shari'ah court to contest any of the said three issues as the Shari'ah court does not have jurisdiction over non-Muslims.

Bearing in mind that the above situation poses a threat to the harmonisation between Shari'ah and Common laws in Malaysia, the legislature took the bold step to amend sections 3(3) and 51 of the LRA, which have been extensively discussed in this chapter. Howsoever, the amendments to these two sections have only taken care of two of the three issues, i.e., divorce and custody. The issue of the unilateral conversion of children is in dire need of swift action by the legislature. Although the Federal Court in the case of *Indira Gandhi*[54] has clearly stated that both the parents need to consent to decide the religion of their child, it is respectfully submitted that until and unless this decision is codified in black and white by the legislature, future Federal Courts may not want to follow the said judgment. Hence, the writer reiterates that the ball is in the legislature's court to take immediate action to overcome this issue so that there is no longer any threat to the harmonisation of Shari'ah and Common laws in Malaysia in the interest of the nation.

54 Supra n 29.

Hanifah Haydar Ali Tajuddin and Nasimah Hussin

11 Harmonising Criminal Justice System

11.1 Introduction

Malaysia's historical background before the British intervention proves that Islamic criminal law is not alien to the Malay Peninsula. The history confirms that Islamic criminal law was extensively enforced in the community with the application of all the three categories of crimes and punishments: *hudud*, *qisas*, and *ta'zir*. Unfortunately, the British succeeded in setting aside Islamic law until it was only applied in a very limited scope, as it is today.

After the colonisation, many items that were originally under the Shari'ah court's purview were taken away by the British's common law system. The common law was made as the general law applicable throughout the Federation, while the Shari'ah was put under the jurisdiction of the states, covering only matters affecting the Muslims.[1]

The fact that Islam remains the religion of the Federation as provided in article 3(1) of the Federal Constitution, and the states have the power to legislate and enforce Islamic law through their Shari'ah courts preserved the importance of the law to a certain extent until today. Nevertheless, the extent of the application of Islamic criminal law in the Shari'ah courts is limited. There and there are more to the law which is yet to be harmonised into the Malaysian criminal justice system.

The effort of harmonising is especially relevant and important in order to come up with a better criminal justice system that can cater to the existing problems in the country relating to the increase in the number of crimes and increase of recidivism among the offenders who have completed their sentence. Today, many developed countries have transformed their criminal justice from punitive to a more holistic justice, i.e., restorative justice. Rather than the state being the main stakeholder, restorative justice has made victims, offenders, and society the main stakeholders, i.e., the parties directly affected when a crime is committed. Recent research has proved that the concept of restorative justice is similar to that of Islamic criminal law, especially in the concept of *qisas* and *diyyah* where victims are involved in the prosecution. It is also observed in its underlying objective of punishing, focusing on the offenders' reform through repentance. Other concepts in Islamic criminal law that are similar to that of restorative justice will be examined in this chapter.

The chapter will look into the development of the Malaysian criminal justice system, civil and Shari'ah, for the purpose of examining the grounds of harmonisation with the idea of shifting the Malaysian criminal justice system from that of punitive

---

1 Ashgar Ali Ali Mohamed, "The Syariah Court's Criminal Jurisdiction," *Malaysiakini*, October 1, 2020, https://www.malaysiakini.com/letters/544802.

https://doi.org/10.1515/9783110766707-011

to restorative. It is hoped that the analysis can help authorities and experts to focus more on the possibilities of harmonising the country's criminal justice system with Islamic criminal law.

11.2 Harmonising Two Laws

Harmonisation is translated as *tawfiq* in Arabic, which means "to bring one thing into harmony or agreement with another, or to make one thing harmonious with another."[2] According to Muhammad Hashim Kamali, harmonisation is necessary for bringing together different things or ideas, and if things or ideas are similar or identical, there is no need for harmonisation.[3] Regardless, the process of harmonising itself identifies the differences and similarities between the two things or ideas. Harmonising the laws does not, as usually thought, mean the replacement of the already established laws. In harmonising the laws, though the focus is more on creating common standards between them, the process could as well identify the best practices from both laws, and as a result, better harmonised law can be formulated.

11.3 History and Development

It is an established fact that Islam, which is the source of Islamic criminal law, came to the land as early as the tenth century.[4] The *Batu Bersurat* (lettered rock) evidenced the coming of Islam to the region documented in the year 1303.[5] The history also records that Islamic law was fully implemented in Malacca through its *Undang-undang Melaka,* and the implementation included every aspect of its civil and criminal laws in the fourteenth century.[6]

---

2 Muhammad Amanullah, "Principles to Be Followed in Partial Harmonization between Islamic Fiqh and Man-Made Law," *IIUMLJ* 16, (2008): 244.

3 Mohamad Hashim Kamali, Shari'ah *and Civil Law: Towards a Methodology of Harmonization,* cited by Muhammad Amanullah, "Principles to Be Followed in Partial Harmonization between Islamic Fiqh and Man-Made Law," *IIUMLJ* 16, (2008): 244.

4 Shamrahayu A. Aziz, "Islamic Criminal Law in the Malaysian Federal Structure: A Constitutional Perspective," *IIUMLJ* 15, (2007): 104–105.

5 Syed Naquib al-Attas, *The Correct Date of the Trengganu Inscription,* cited by Arba'iyah Mohd Noor, "Perkembangan Pensejarahan Islam di Alam Melayu," (Development of Islamic Historiography in Malay Archipelago) *Jurnal al-Tamaddun* 6, (2011): 37.

6 Hanifah Haydar Ali Tajuddin, Nasimah Hussin and Majdah Zawawi, "Restorative Justice in Islamic Law: Application in Malaysian Legal History and the Criminal Justice System," in *Research Handbook on Islamic Law and Society,* ed. Nadirsyah Hosen (Cheltenham: Edward Elgar, 2020), 250–269, 260.

Although there are differences in opinion as to when Islamic law was introduced and implemented in the region, it is indisputable that Islamic law was indeed applied in the region, way before the British colonisation, which brought the common law.[7] Respecting the local law, the British were documented to have passed several Islamic criminal law legislation and the punishment for breaching it. Some of the legislation passed during the colonisation included:[8]

i) 1885 – *Muhammadan to Pray in Mosque on Friday* law in 1885 in Perak, which obliged the Muslims and even provided punishment for those who did not perform their Friday prayer.
ii) 1894 – *Adultery by Mohammadan* in Perak and *Prevention of Adultery Registration* in Selangor
iii) 1904 – *Muhammadan Laws Enactment* in the Federated Malay States and *Muslim Law Enactment* in Pahang
iv) 1935 – *Offences (by Muhammadans) Enactment* in Johor
v) 1938 – *Muslim Offences Order in Council* in Negeri Sembilan
vi) 1939 – *Muhammadan (Offences) Enactment* in Perak

These enactments criminalised various actions by Muslims, such as not performing Friday prayers and adultery. Although these enactments enforced the already existing Islamic law, the British wanted the enactments to be understood as English law relating to the personal matters of the Muslims.[9]

The Islamic law was implemented and administered by Kathis Court before and after the colonisation.[10] Before the colonisation, the position of the court was special in that the Sultan himself heard the highest appeal.[11] Nevertheless, after the colonisation, through the passing of the Courts Enactment in 1905, the hierarchy of the court was positioned lower than the Second-Class Magistrate Court. Appeals from the Kathis Court were heard before the civil court, which the English or English law-trained judges staffed. Having these judges preside over these appeals is tantamount to disregarding Islamic law principles.[12]

Later, the Courts Enactment 1905 was repealed in 1919 and placed the Kathis Court under state jurisdiction that only decided cases relating to "Muhammadan religion, marriage and divorce, and all other matters regulated by Muhammadan

7 Shamrahayu A. Aziz, "Islamic Criminal Law in the Malaysian Federal Structure: A Constitutional Perspective," *IIUMLJ* 15, (2007): 105.
8 Aziz, "Islamic Criminal Law in the Malaysian Federal Structure," 105–106.
9 Mahmood Zuhdi bin Abdul Majid, *Pengantar Undang-Undang Islam di Malaysia* (Introduction to Islamic Law in Malaysia) (Kuala Lumpur, University of Malaya Press, 1997), 62–63.
10 The Kathis Court was later on, renamed as Syariah Court (spelled as Shari'ah court in this book).
11 Farid. S. Shuaib, "The Islamic Legal System in Malaysia," *Pacific Rim Law & Policy Journal* 21, no. 2 (2012): 89.
12 Shuaib, "The Islamic Legal System," 89.

law."[13] Afterward, the Court Ordinance passed in 1948 omitted the Kathis Court from the federal court system. This remains until today.

By limiting the application of Islamic criminal law, the British have made their English common law the law of the Federation. The English law was formally introduced into the region by the Charter of Justice in 1826 when Penang and Malacca became British colonies. The Charter and some other treaties agreed to and signed by the Sultans have conditioned the Sultans to accept British Residents or Advisers as their advisors in matters including enacting the laws in the States. The laws include the penal law and the procedures. The penal law and the procedures were enacted based on the Indian model. The British Residents also advised the Sultans in setting up the court system presided by the British judges and judges trained in English law. These judges then referred to the English law of torts and rules of equity in deciding cases before them. Eventually, the English law replaced the Islamic law in many matters, and the application of the latter was limited, as discussed earlier.

The problem with having a dual legal system is that one would somehow overtake the other jurisdiction, whether intentionally or not. This is especially true when one is the prevalent legal system or has a stronger hold at the federal level. Throughout the development of the Malaysian criminal justice system, there were cases where issues involving Shari'ah matters between Muslims were heard and decided by the civil court. There were also decisions by the Shari'ah courts that were overruled.[14] The issue that led to the overtaking of jurisdiction was due to the lack of clear delineation of the Shari'ah court's jurisdiction in the Federal Constitution. Article 121(1) of the Federal Constitution initially mentioned only the jurisdiction of the civil courts. Later on, however, clause 121(1A) was inserted, which resolved the jurisdictional issues. Article 121(1A) states: "The Courts referred to in Clause (1) shall have no jurisdiction in respect of any matter within the jurisdiction of the Syariah courts."

13 Courts Enactment 1919, s 63. Shamrahayu A. Aziz, "Islamic Criminal Law in the Malaysian Federal Structure: A Constitutional Perspective," 107.

14 For example, in *Ainan bin Mahmud v Syed Abu Bakar* [1939] MLJ 209 where Syariah court's decision in the case involving the determination of legitimacy of a child made based on Islamic rule of legitimacy was overruled the civil court applying section 112 of the Evidence Act (based on the Indian Evidence Act).

11.4 Islamic Criminal Law Equivalence with Restorative Justice

Conceptually, what is called Islamic criminal law is inclusive of three types of punishment and crimes prescribed in Islam; those are *hudud*, *qisas*, and *ta'zir*.[15] Currently, it is *ta'zir* that is being applied in Malaysia's Shari'ah criminal law. Unlike *ta'zir*, *hudud*, and *qisas* are clearly mentioned in the Quran and Hadith, and both crimes and punishments are fixed. *Ta'zir* comprises crimes and punishments that are not provided for in the Quran and Sunnah, and the authority to decide on what form its crimes and punishment is left with the rulers.

The concept of restorative justice was introduced as an alternative to punitive justice and is practiced by many developed countries. The idea came as experts noticed that victims are not made part of the process under punitive justice. If allowed, they only play minimal roles and frequently suffer mentally and financially due to crimes committed against them. Furthermore, there was also concern about the effect of prisonisation on offenders as the rate of recidivism increased among offenders who have completed the sentence. The earlier proponents of restorative justice hold that its concept originated from the early humans, as early as the ancient humans.[16] However, few researchers have sparked the idea that restorative justice might have also found its root in Islamic criminal law. Research by the first author of this chapter is one of the few research that aimed at finding the roots or origins of restorative justice in Islamic criminal law.[17] The following discussion highlights the restorative features of Islamic criminal law.

11.4.1 Hudud

Hudud are crimes and punishments that are fixed. The crimes are basically the actions that go against the rights of God, and so the punishments are specifically set in the Quran and Sunnah. Going against the rights of God is understood as affecting the public right to live in a safe and tranquil ambiance. *Hudud* crimes include *zina* (adultery), *sariqah* (theft), and *syurb al-khamr* (drinking alcoholic drinks). Proving

---

15 Mark Cammack, "Islamic Law and Law in the Contemporary Courts," *Berkeley Journal of Middle Eastern & Islamic Law* 4, no. 1 (2011): 2.

16 The Acephalous which means the stateless society. For further reading, *see* Theo Gavrielides, "Restorative Practices: from the Early Societies to the 1970s," *Internet Journal of Criminology*, (2011): 1–20, accessed June 3, 2022, www.internetjournalofcriminology.com.

17 Hanifah Haydar Ali Tajuddin, "Incorporating Restorative Justice into the Malaysian Criminal Justice System by Examining the Position in Islamic Law and Australia," (PhD Dissertation, International Islamic University Malaysia, 2021).

hudud crimes require strict adherence to rules of evidence, and it has to reach a very high standard of evidence before one can be convicted and punished.

Though many seem to look at *hudud* as a set of harsh punishment, due to the "popularised" cutting of hands for the crime of theft or whipping for the crime of adultery, the central principle in the application of the *hudud* punishments is actually to maximise mercy.[18] This was formulated clearly in a hadith reported from Prophet Muhammad (peace be upon him), where he said: "Ward off the hudud from the Muslims as much as you all can, and if you find a way out for the person, then let them go. For it is better for the authority to err in mercy than to err in punishment."[19] A Hadith also set another principle in convicting and punishing offenders of hudud crime: "From Abdullah Ibn Abbas, the Prophet (pbuh) said: Avoid the punishments with doubts."[20] The stringent requirement of evidence and the slightest doubt would drop *hudud* charge, making conviction for *hudud* crime almost impossible. In Saudi Arabia, for example, of 4925 convictions for theft in a period of one year, only two cases where the punishment of cutting of hand took place.[21] Many may wonder then what is the purpose of *hudud* as although it sets the harsh punishment, convicting one with its crime is very difficult, or some phrased it as "impossible."[22] It is not meant to punish the offender with the harshest of its punishment. Referring back to the Prophet's Hadith, as cited above, proves this particular logic. What then is the purpose of hudud? As Malise Ruthven stated in his book that love is the "central theme" of Christianity, and justice is the central theme of Islam.[23] Thus, through its law, Islam aims to uphold justice in society. This is important to ensure law and order in society. This is done through clear deterrence by setting harsh punishment for those who violate the law.[24]

---

18 Mohamed bin Ali, "Shariah Law and Hudud: Understanding Its Objectives and Spirit," RSIS Commentaries, no. 204/2013 (1 November 2013), S. Rajaratnam School of International Studies, Nanyang Technological University, accessed June 3, 2022, https://www.files.ethz.ch/isn/172845/RSIS2042013.pdf.

19 (Sunan Ibn Majah).

20 (Reported by Tirmizi) شرح حديث: ادرؤوا الحدود بالشبهات, accessed June 3, 2022, https://binbaz.org.sa/fatwas/20054/%D8%B4%D8%B1%D8%AD-%D8%AD%D8%AF%D9%8A%D8%AB-%D8%A7%D8%AF%D8%B1%D9%88%D9%88%D8%A7-%D8%A7%D9%84%D8%AD%D8%AF%D9%88%D8%AF-%D8%A8%D8%A7%D9%84%D8%B4%D8%A8%D9%87%D8%A7%D8%AA.

21 Jonathan Brown, "Stoning and Hand-Cutting – Understanding the Hudud and the Shari'ah in Islam," (updated January 8, 2021), accessed June 3, 2022, https://yaqeeninstitute.org/read/paper/stoning-and-hand-cutting-understanding-the-hudud-and-the-shariah-in-islam#ftnt21.

22 Brown, "Stoning and Hand-Cutting."

23 Susan C. Hascall, "Restorative Justice in Islam: Should *Qisas* be Considered a Form of Restorative Justice?" Berkeley of Middle Eastern & Islamic Law 4, no.1 (2011): 46.

24 Mohamed bin Ali, "Shariah Law and Hudud: Understanding Its Objectives and Spirit."

11.4.2 Qisas

Foundationally, *qisas* treats crimes that fall under its category as a violation against rights of individual or private rights. *Qisas* is commonly made synonymous with the law of retaliation, or *lex talionis*. However, it is argued that the translation "retaliation" is inaccurate in illustrating the juridical scope of *qisas*.[25] This is because *qisas* in Islamic law bears the aspects of proportionality and equality to ensure justice for the victim, his family, and the criminal himself.[26] These aspects in Arabic are synonymous with the term "*al-Musaawah*," which means "making a thing equal to another thing."[27] Therefore, the correct translation of *qisas* in English could be equitable or just retribution.[28]

The concept of *qisas* complements the just nature of Islam, where it acknowledges the loss on the part of the victim or his family by giving them three optional solutions; retaliate, forgive, and compensate (*al-diyah*) or forgive in total (*al-'afw*). The three options, whichever the parties opt for, could end the endless cycle of resentment and retaliation. The Qur'an mentions *qisas* and the three recourses.[29] The Prophet (pbuh) also mentioned the three options:

> Abu Shuraih al-Khuzai r.a reported that the Prophet (pbuh) said: "if a relative of anyone is killed, or if he suffers *khabl* (i.e., wound), he may choose one of the three things: he may retaliate; receive compensation (*al-diyah*); or forgive. But if he wishes a fourth, i.e., something more, hold his hands. After this whoever exceeds the limits shall be in grave penalty."[30]

However, pardon (*al-'afw*) is strongly encouraged, and this too is mentioned in the Qur'an and evident from the practices of the Prophet (pbuh).[31] Based on the following hadith, it is clear that although the first two options, retaliation and compensation, are offered to the victims and their families, the Prophet (pbuh) encouraged them to forgive. In a number of Hadith in Sunan Abu Dawud:

25 The use of the term "retaliation" would connote the negative meaning of returning evil for evil, when the major aspects of Qisas involve positive and constructive outcome between parties, i.e. through pardoning with or without compensation (*al-diyah*). *See* Sayed Sikandar Shah Haneef, *Homicide in Islam, Legal Structure and the Evidence Requirements* (Kuala Lumpur: A.S Noordeen, 2000), 87.

26 Muhammad Iqbal Siddiqi, *The Penal Law of Islam*, 145.

27 Muhammad Iqbal Siddiqi, *The Penal Law of Islam*, 145.

28 Sayed Sikandar Shah Haneef, *Homicide in Islam, Legal Structure and the Evidence Requirements*, 87.

29 Al-Quran (As-Shura) 42:40.

30 Abu Dawud, *Sunan Abu Dawud*, Book 41 Number 4481, accessed June 3, 2022, https://sunnah.com/abudawud/41.

31 Al-Quran (Al-Baqarah) 2: 17.

> Narrated by Anas bin Malik: "I never saw the Messenger of Allah that some dispute which involved retaliation that was brought to him but he commanded regarding it for remission and pardon."[32]
>
> Narrated by Wa'il ibn Hujr: "I was with the Prophet (pbuh) when a man who was a murderer and had a strap around his neck was brought to him. He (the Prophet) then called the legal guardian of the victim and asked him: do you forgive him? He said: no. He (the Prophet) asked: will you accept blood money? He said: no. He (the Prophet) asked: Will you kill him? He said: yes. He (the Prophet) said: take him (the murderer). When he (the Prophet) turned his back, he said: do you forgive him? After repeating all this (four times), he said: if you forgive him, he will bear the burden of his own sin and the sin of the victim. He (the guardian) then forgave him."[33]

Another example of the Prophet (pbuh) encouraging a show of mercy on an offender is when he was reported to have said: "The disputants should refrain from taking retaliation. The one who is nearer should forgive first and then the one who is next to him, even if the one (who forgives) were a woman."[34] Principally, *qisas* shares similarities with restorative justice as it fundamentally involves the victim in the prosecution. The above hadith proves that principles of *qisas* as practiced by the Prophet (pbuh).

Besides that, there are as well a number of hadith that reported the Prophet (pbuh) himself acted as a mediator, taking the role of calming disputants down and then leading them to peacefully settle their matters. The Prophet (pbuh), in carrying out his duties as a judge and a mediator, has always applied justice and encouraged the disputants to observe the principles of moral values, tolerance, and show of mercy so they can reach peaceful settlements.

The Prophet (pbuh) is also reported to set the amount of compensation in cases of *qisas*. It is noticeable that he was very specific in setting the amount of compensation. This is because Islam appreciates the life of human beings while promoting good and fair settlement between parties, especially the family of the victim who suffered due to the loss of their family member. In Sunan Abu Dawud:

> Narrated by Abdullah ibn Amr ibn al-'As that the Prophet (pbuh) gave judgment that if anyone killed accidentally, his blood wit should be one hundred camels: thirty she-camels which had entered their second year, thirty she-camels which had entered their third year, thirty she-camels which had entered their fourth year and ten male camels which had entered their third year.[35]

---

32 Abu Dawud, *Sunan Abu Dawud*, Book 41, Number 4482, accessed June 3, 2022, https://sunnah.com/abudawud/41.

33 Abu Dawud, *Sunan Abu Dawud*, Book 41, Hadith Number 4484.

34 Abu Dawud, *Sunan Abu Dawud*, Book 41, Hadith Number 4523.

35 Abu Dawud, *Sunan Abu Dawud*, Book 39, Number 4526, accessed June 3, 2022, http://quranmalayalam.com/hadees/abudawud/039.sat.html.

The empowerment of victims in *qisas* shows the flexibility in the administration of Islamic criminal justice. Nevertheless, such empowerment is regulated so as to prevent individuals from taking the laws into their own hands.

11.4.3 Reconciliation, Negotiation, and Mediation (al-Sulh)

Widened research on the area revealed that reconciliation and mediation in Islamic criminal law have long since been prescribed in the sources of Shari'ah; the Qur'an and the Sunnah. Reconciliation or mediation is formally known in Shari'ah as *al-Sulh*. It originates from the word *salaha,* which means "to do good deeds."[36] The process of *al-sulh* itself can be defined as a process of restoring something, be it a relationship or loss suffered.[37]

In criminal cases, *al-sulh* is an agreement between two disputants to reach a settlement or an agreement to compromise between two disputing parties.[38] Unlike litigation, where one of the parties wins and the other losses, reconciliation or mediation is a platform where it is possible for both parties to win, be it monetarily or emotionally. In Islamic criminal law, reconciliation or mediation is viewed as a mechanism that enables parties to achieve positive outcomes by compromising, reconciling, and forgiving each other.[39]

As Islam is a religion of peace, *al-sulh* is basically one of the main dispute resolution mechanisms in the religion. It resonates with the objective that it holds, which is forgiveness between the disputing parties and finding the best solution to solve the dispute at hand.

11.4.4 Repentance (At-Taubah)

Repentance or *at-Taubah* is principally defined as deciding not to do an evil deed again and return to Allah. Al-Qurtubi defined repentance as "having a feeling of penitence to God with good faith and sincere piety by performing good deeds to

---

36 Ramizah Wan Muhammad, "*Sulh* (mediation) in the Malaysian Syariah Courts," in *Mediation in Malaysia: The Law and Practice,* ed. Mohammad Naqib Ishan Jan and Ashgar Ali Ali Mohamed (Kuala Lumpur: Lexis Nexis, 2010), 416.

37 Raihanah Haji Azhari, "Sulh dalam Perundangan Islam: Kajian di Jabatan Kehakiman Syariah, Selangor Darul Ehsan" (PhD Dissertation, Universiti Malaya, 2005), 57, cited by Hanis Wahed, "Sulh: Its Application in Malaysia," *IOSR Journal of Humanities and Social Science* 20, no. 6 (2015): 71.

38 Muhammad Iman Jabiri, *As-Sulh ka Sabab li Inqida' ad-Da'wa al-Jina'I* (Dar al-Jami'ah al-Jadidah, 2011), 17.

39 Norjihan Ab Aziz and Nasimah Hussin, "The Application of Mediation (*Sulh*) in Islamic Criminal Law," 116.

counteract the effect of bad deeds."[40] It is interesting to note that Islamic criminal law is the only criminal law that accepts repentance as a factor in remitting one's punishment.[41]

Repentance is regarded as one of the factors that remit punishments in Islamic criminal law. The difference between repentance and pardon is that repentance is applicable in crimes affecting public rights, while pardon is applicable in crimes affecting private or personal rights. Thus, remittance of punishment due to repentance can only be granted by a judge or a ruler.

11.5 Restorative Elements in the Malaysian Criminal Justice

Though the country's criminal justice system is mainly based on punitive justice, it is observed that there are a few restorative elements that are in practice. This proves the constant development that happens in the legal system by harmonising a few aspects based on other legal systems. The restorative elements in the country's criminal justice, if not much, improve the delivery of service and also uphold the justice for the parties affected by crimes, especially the victims.

Restorative elements are noticeable in the practice of Victim Impact Statement,[42] where the victim is allowed to have a say before a judge sentences the offender, and the practice of plea bargain,[43] which allows the offender to bargain his plea by including certain act or payment in the bargain that can restore loss suffered. In sentencing, the practice of non-custodial sentencing, which includes community service,[44] compulsory attendance order, and parole, is also deemed as restorative as it can rehabilitate the offender, not by locking them away but by including them into the society in the course of undergoing their punishment.

In the Shari'ah court, these restorative elements are also traceable at the sentencing stage. In its recent development, the court has worked hard to adapt to the practice of its counterpart, the civil court, particularly in carrying out non-custodial sentencing. The effort was led by the Shari'ah Judiciary Department of Malaysia,

---

40 Al-Qurtubi, *Al-Jami' li Ahkam al-Quran*, cited by M.Shokry El-Dakkak, *Repentance as a Defence Comparative Study under Islamic Law, Common Law and Continental Law* (Kuala Lumpur: A.S Noordeen, 1994), 3.

41 M.Shokry El-Dakkak, *Repentance as a Defence Comparative Study under Islamic Law, Common Law and Continental Law*, 3.

42 Criminal Procedure Code, ss 173(m) and 183A.

43 Criminal Procedure Code, s 172C.

44 Criminal Procedure Code, s 293, Child Act 2016, chapter 3A, and Drug Dependants (Treatment and Rehabilitation) Act 1983.

where research and engagement were conducted to develop a set of guidelines for compulsory attendance order as a reference for the Shari'ah courts in sentencing the offenders.[45] The guidelines is mainly based on the Compulsory Attendance Act 1954, referred to by the civil court in sentencing. Besides that, the department has approached the Shari'ah courts in the states in order to encourage alternative punishment, mainly the non-custodial sentencing in setting the punishment for the offenders. Currently, the issue of treatment of child offenders in the Shari'ah court has been highlighted, and research is being conducted by looking into the practices of the judges and civil court experience in dealing with and sentencing child offenders.

11.6 Conclusion

This chapter proposes the examination of the concepts of Islamic criminal law as a whole with the idea of harmonising it into the Malaysian criminal justice system. This is by no means an effort to "Islamise" the law, as many contended. It is about coming up with a better practice of criminal justice, and as the Islamic criminal law existed in the *Tanah Melayu* legal system, it is worth exploring it. Restorative justice, as the literature depicts, would be able to resolve some recurrent issues in the criminal justice system in the country. The existence of some practices in the courts, civil and Shari'ah that are restorative is seen to be a good base for a future shift in the system. Moreover, as the roots are also found in the Islamic criminal law, this makes restorative justice more relevant to be considered and harmonised in the Malaysian criminal justice system.

45 *Refer* Garis Panduan Perintah Kehadiran Wajib (PKW) Bagi Pesalah Syariah (*Guidelines of Compulsory Attendance Order for Syariah Offenders*), prepared by Syariah Judiciary Department of Malaysia and States' Syariah Judiciary Departments.

Muhamad Hassan Ahmad, Mohammad Naqib Eishan Jan
and Ashgar Ali Ali Mohamed

12 Human Rights and the Rule of Law: The Common Law and Shari'ah Perspective

12.1 Introduction

The Qur'an is one of the most detailed and complex human manuals in the world. This glorious book was in existence for more than 1400 years. It contains rights that have been granted by Allah (SWT) in preserving the dignity of man and woman without them having to fight for it. It lays down every angle of human rights, such as right to equality, right to life and property, security of personal freedom, justice, and women's rights. Its purpose is to achieve peaceful human existence and harmony between the different races and diversity in which humans were created. Hence, the first constitution in Islamic history, i.e., the Medina Constitution, guaranteed the protection of human rights.

For the West, the concept of basic human rights came from the Magna Carta of Britain, though the Magna Carta itself came into existence a few hundred years after the advent of Islam. Unlike the divine decree of human rights in the Qur'an, which remains unchanged since its revelation, the western concept of human rights that kings and legislative assemblies had granted were conferred and withdrawn as they pleased. In this process, new concepts and understanding of human rights have arisen. Accordingly, the struggles to protect these newly found human rights have never ceased to continue. Some of these rights may not necessarily be in line with divine laws. Are Islam and the West speaking the same language when it comes to the topic of human rights? This chapter, therefore, aims to look into the concept of human rights from the Islamic and western viewpoints and the possibility of harmonisation between the two.

12.2 Rule of Law and the Protection of Human Rights: The Nexus

At the international level, the United Nations (UN) was established to achieve three predominantly vital objectives, i.e., to maintain international peace and security, to ensure human rights, and to bring about development for the global population. The collective endeavours of all Members of the UN in meeting these objectives are to be guided by the "rule of law." Members are required to take measures "to ensure adherence to the principles of supremacy of the law, equality before the law, accountability

https://doi.org/10.1515/9783110766707-012

to the law, fairness in the application of the law, separation of powers, participation in decision-making, legal certainty, avoidance of arbitrariness, and procedural and legal transparency."[1] In this sense, the rule of law is mainly a principle of governance that requires everyone – regardless of whether it is a sovereign state, a public institution, a private entity, or a natural person – to be accountable for promulgated laws and ensure that they are enforced equally, and adjudicated independently in accordance with international human rights standards. Hence, it can be observed that the rule of law is essential in protecting human rights and ensuring people's fundamental freedoms and liberties.[2]

The nexus between the "rule of law" and "protection of human rights" are strongly interconnected. The relationship between these two is intrinsic and indivisible in nature.[3] This is reflected in the Universal Declaration of Human Rights (UDHR), which recognises that: "the inherent dignity and of the equal and inalienable rights of all members of the human family is the foundation of freedom, justice and peace in the world."[4] Again, the members of the UN pledged in the United Nations Millennium Declaration that they would not spare any effort "to promote democracy and strengthen the rule of law, as well as respect for all internationally recognised human rights and fundamental freedoms, including the right to development."[5] In addition, the Sustainable Development Goals (SDGs)[6] dedicate "Goal 16: Peace, Justice and Strong Institution" mainly to promoting peaceful and inclusive societies in attaining sustainable development by providing "access to justice

1 United Nations, "United Nations and the Rule of Law: What Is the Rule of Law?," accessed April 4, 2022, https://www.un.org/ruleoflaw/what-is-the-rule-of-law/.

2 United Nations, "United Nations and the Rule of Law."

3 United Nations, "United Nations and the Rule of Law: Rule of Law and Human Rights," accessed April 4, 2022, https://www.un.org/ruleoflaw/rule-of-law-and-human-rights/#:~:text=As%20defined%20by%20the%20Secretary,%2F2004%2F616%2C%20para.

4 The Preamble of the Universal Declaration of Human Rights.

5 United Nations, "United Nations Millennium Declaration," General Assembly Resolution 55/2, September 8, 2000, available at: accessed April 4, 2022, <https://www.ohchr.org/en/instruments-mechanisms/instruments/united-nations-millennium-declaration. > (accessed on 04 April 2022).

6 "The Sustainable Development Goals (SDGs), also known as the Global Goals, were adopted by the United Nations in 2015 as a universal call to action to end poverty, protect the planet, and ensure that by 2030 all people enjoy peace and prosperity. The 17 SDGs are integrated – they recognise that action in one area will affect outcomes in others, and that development must balance social, economic and environmental sustainability." United Nations Development Programme, "The SDGs in Action: What Are the Sustainable Development Goals?," accessed April 4, 2022, https://www.undp.org/sustainable-development-goals?utm_source=EN&utm_medium=GSR&utm_content=US_UNDP_PaidSearch_Brand_English&utm_campaign=CENTRAL&c_src=CENTRAL&c_src2=GSR&gclid=CjwKCAjwxZqSBhAHEiwASr9n9HY-lectv0IpRjOlUCdxTJqNnivCAbLgXwLNrpY-P0RatEZhtuHS7hoC6eQQAvD_BwE.

for all and build effective, accountable and inclusive institutions at all levels."[7] Accordingly, it can be said that there can be no rule of law in a given society if there is no protection of human rights, and human rights cannot be protected without the rule of law. Thus, the rule of law is an important tool in promoting and protecting human rights. It is the mechanism that ensures the implementation of human rights principles at both international and national levels.[8]

12.3 Human Rights under International Instruments

A man was created with rights and duties, which means that "human rights" have existed since the creation of man. For this reason, human rights are inherent to all human beings regardless of nationality, residence, sex, national or ethnic origin, colour, religion, language, or any other status. Hence, natural rights have deep roots in Islam and other religions, and people, at least theoretically, are equally entitled to human rights without discrimination. Nonetheless, human rights have been violated under various pretexts. Before World War II, the concept of human rights was a disgrace to the West. The United States (US) practiced racism and segregation, Britain and France colonised other Asian and African countries, and Germany, under Hitler, because of religious or racial differences, committed massacres against its citizens. The international community at that time did not even bother about such incidents as they did not consider an act of colonisation to be illegal, nor did they bother to improve the relationship between states and citizens, for they considered this relationship to be an internal matter for each state. So, it was impossible to talk about the universal concept of human rights in a climate such as this.

The end of World War II marked the beginning of the realisation of human rights. In 1945, the Charter of the United Nations was signed, which made the promotion and protection of human rights the organisation's main goal.[9] In its preamble, the Charter "reaffirms faith in fundamental human rights, in the dignity and worth of the human person, in the equal rights of men and women and of nations

7 United Nations Development Programme, "Peace, Justice and Strong Institution," available at: accessed April 4, 2022, <https://www1.undp.org/content/singapore-global-centre/en/home/sustainable-development-goals/goal-16-peace-justice-and-strong-institutions.html?utm_source=EN&utm_medium=GSR&utm_content=US_UNDP_PaidSearch_Brand_English&utm_campaign=CENTRAL&c_src=CENTRAL&c_src2=GSR&gclid=CjwKCAjwxZqSBhAHEiwASr9n9Ju4aHl7_e-JmUB82rcDmoR2KtOk5aZPVVAfbDbFPSXRtM60QaNywxoC-1UQAvD_BwE.> (accessed on 04 April 2022).

8 United Nations, "United Nations and the Rule of Law: Rule of Law and Human Rights," accessed April 4, 2022, https://www.un.org/ruleoflaw/rule-of-law-and-human-rights/#:~:text=As%20defined%20by%20the%20Secretary,%2F2004%2F616%2C%20para.

9 The Charter of the United Nations, arts 1(3), 55 and 56.

large and small." Article 1(2) of the Charter provides that: "The achievement of international co-operation in resolving international problems of an economic, social, cultural or humanitarian nature, and in promoting and promoting respect for human rights and fundamental freedoms for all without distinction, in terms of race, gender, language or religion."

With regard to the establishment of "the conditions of stability and prosperity necessary for peaceful and friendly relations between nations on the basis of respect for the principle of equal rights and the determination of the destiny of the people," article 55 of the Charter provides that the UN "promotes universal respect for human rights and fundamental freedoms for all without distinction as to race, sex, language or religion." Again, article 56 of the Charter states: "All members pledge themselves to take joint and separate action in co-operation with the Organisation (UN) for the achievement of the purposes set forth in Article 55." The term "pledge" implies a legal obligation on the parts of member states.

However, the obligation is said not to observe human rights immediately but to work toward their fulfilment in the future. Nevertheless, states must not go backward and deliberately violate human rights. In its advisory opinion in the *Namibia case*,[10] the International Court of Justice (ICJ) has pointed out that, under article 2 (7) of the Charter, the UN cannot interfere in internal matters of a sovereign state on the pretext of protecting human rights, but it can do so if human rights violation in the state is such that endangers world peace and security.

In 1948, the UDHR, which consists of 30 articles, was adopted by the UN General Assembly[11] and declared that all human beings are free and equal, regardless of gender, colour, religion, or other characteristics. As a turning point, the UDHR sets out rights and freedoms for all, including the right to freedom from torture; the right to freedom of expression; the right to education; the right to asylum; other civil and political rights such as the right to life, liberty, and privacy; economic, social, and cultural rights such as social security, health, and housing rights.

Although the rights and freedoms mentioned in the UDHR apply to all people in all states around the world, they are restricted in the sense that they have to be exercised in a way not to violate the rights of others and must not adversely affect public order, welfare or moral of the society. The UDHR is not a treaty but is based on the UN General Assembly Resolution, which is a recommendation and thus not binding. However, "human rights are foreign to no culture and intrinsic to all nations. They belong not to a chosen few but to all people. It is this universality that

10 [1971] ICJ Rep 16.

11 Adopted by the UN General Assembly on 10th December 1948 [UN GA Res. 217A (III), Dec. 10, 1948].

endows human rights with the power to cross any border and defy any force."[12] Hence, it is generally agreed that some, although not all, provisions of the UDHR are crystallised into norms of customary international law binding on all states. This may be true with regard to certain civil rights, but the same is doubtful with regard to economic rights. Nevertheless, the UDHR has served as a yardstick and base for the development of various international human rights laws.

The UDHR also inspired the adoption of international human rights treaties, including the International Covenant on Civil and Political Rights (ICCPR)[13] and the International Covenant on Economic, Social and Cultural Rights (ICESCR).[14] The ICCPR, which was adopted in 1966, and came into force in 1976, is a treaty that incorporates the civil and political rights provisions of the UDHR. As a treaty, ICCPR is binding upon its parties. It requires each state party "to take the necessary steps to adopt such legislative or other measures as may be necessary to give effect to the rights recognised in the present Covenant."[15] There are two Optional Protocols to the ICCPR granting additional rights *vis-à-vis* the ratifying states. The First Optional Protocol[16] allows individuals to directly bring complaints before the Human Rights Committee, which is composed of 18 members elected by the states parties to the ICCPR. All that this committee can do is call upon the state concerned for an explanation and make recommendations. The Second Optional Protocol[17] requires the ratifying states to abolish the death penalty, but few states have ratified it.

Meanwhile, the ICESCR, which was adopted in 1966 and came into force in 1976, generally incorporates the economic, social, and cultural rights provisions of the UDHR. A multilateral treaty, but unlike ICCPR, is not directly binding, as its implementation depends on the goodwill and resource of states. Article 2 of the ICESCR makes it clear that the state party undertakes "steps to the maximum of its available resources, with a view to achieving progressively the full realisation of the rights recognised in the present Covenant." This provision makes the legal

12 Kofi A. Annan, "Foreword," in *The Universal Declaration of Human Rights: Fifty Years and Beyond*, ed. Yael Danieli, Elsa Stamatopoulou and Clarence J. Dias (New York, CRC Press, Routledge: 1999).

13 Adopted and opened for signature, ratification and accession by General Assembly Resolution 2200 A (XXI) of 16 December 1966. Entry into force: 23 March 1976, in accordance with art 49.

14 Adopted and opened for signature, ratification and accession by General Assembly Resolution 2200 A (XXI) of 16 December 1966. Entry into force: 3 January 1976, in accordance with art 27.

15 The International Covenant on Civil and Political Rights, art 2 (2).

16 Optional Protocol to the International Covenant on Civil and Political Rights, adopted and opened for signature, ratification and accession by General Assembly Resolution 2200 A (XXI) of 16 December 196. Entry into force: 23 March 1976, in accordance with art 9.

17 Second Optional Protocol to the International Covenant on Civil and Political Rights, aiming at the abolition of the death penalty, Adopted and proclaimed by General Assembly Resolution 44/128 of 15 December 1989. Entry into force: 11 July 1991, in accordance with art 8(1).

obligation rather weak, and it could be for this reason that the covenant does not make any provision for the individual petition.

There are a number of other international human rights treaties that have been adopted under the auspices of the UN. These treaties include the Convention on the Prevention and Punishment of the Crime of Genocide, the International Convention on the Elimination of All Forms of Racial Discrimination (CERD),[18] the Convention on the Elimination of All Forms of Discrimination Against Women (CEDAW),[19] Optional Protocol to the Convention on the Elimination of All Forms of Discrimination Against Women,[20] the Convention on the Rights of the Child (CRC),[21] Optional Protocol to the Convention on the Rights of the Child on the sale of children, child prostitution, and child pornography,[22] Optional Protocol to the Convention on the Rights of the Child on the involvement of children in armed conflicts,[23] Convention Against Torture and Other Cruel, Inhuman or Degrading Treatment or Punishment (CAT),[24] Optional Protocol to the Convention Against Torture and Other Cruel, Inhuman or Degrading Treatment or Punishment,[25] and the International Convention on Protection of the Rights of All Migrant Workers and Members of Their Families (ICMRW),[26] among others.

All the above-cited treaties, which have been ratified by the majority of the UN member states, are designed to provide universal respect for human rights. However, the gap between the laudable rhetoric of international human rights treaties and the reality of human rights actions or implementation remains wide. Violations of human rights are rampant, but there is no proper human rights enforcement body at the international level. For instance, the ICJ is inactive in the area of human rights simply because of the limitations of its jurisdiction and the firm desire of

18 Adopted and opened for signature and ratification by General Assembly Resolution 2106 A (XX) of 21 December 1965. Entry into force: 4 January 1969, in accordance with art 19.

19 Adopted and opened for signature, ratification and accession by General Assembly Resolution 34/180 of 18 December 1979. Entry into force: 3 September 1981, in accordance with art 27(1).

20 Adopted by General Assembly Resolution 54/4 of 6 October 1999 and opened for signature, ratification and accession on 10 December 1999. Entry into force: 22 December 2000, in accordance with art 16.

21 Adopted and opened for signature, ratification and accession by General Assembly Resolution 44/25 of 20 November 1989. Entry into force: 2 September 1990, in accordance with art 49.

22 Adopted and opened for signature, ratification and accession by General Assembly Resolution 54/263 of 25 May 2000. Entry into force: 18 January 2002, in accordance with art 14.

23 Adopted and opened for signature, ratification and accession by General Assembly Resolution 54/263 of 25 May 2000. Entry into force: 12 February 2002, in accordance with art 10.

24 Adopted and opened for signature, ratification and accession by General Assembly Resolution 39/46 of 10 December 198. Entry into force: 26 June 1987, in accordance with art 27(1).

25 Adopted by General Assembly Resolution 57/199 of 18 December 2002. Entry into force: 22 June 2006, in accordance with art 28(1).

26 Adopted by General Assembly Resolution 45/158 of 18 December 1990. Entry into force: 1 July 2003, in accordance with art 87(1).

most states to preclude it from hearing human rights cases. Further, although all the core international human rights treaties have monitoring bodies to oversee the implementation of the treaty provisions, these bodies have no teeth to bite, for they merely consider state parties' yearly reports as well as individual complaints or communications and make recommendations reminding states to be observant of their human rights obligations.

12.4 Human Rights under Domestic Laws

As mentioned above, the notion of the protection of human rights perceived today is relatively contemporary as it was formally acknowledged only after the formation of the UN in 1945. It has begun with the recognition of some principles of human rights under the UDHR,[27] which, as stated earlier, contains thirty articles of rights of universal applications to all people. Nevertheless, since it is not a treaty signed and ratified by the members of the UN but merely a declaration, it does not create any legal obligation on the state members to adhere. Although that is the case, UDHR still paves the way for the adoption of more than seventy human rights treaties at global and regional levels. All of those human rights treaties make references to the UDHR in their preambles.[28] This includes the Convention relating to the Status of Refugees 1951,[29] the Convention on the Elimination of All Forms of Racial Discrimination 1965 (ICERD), the International Covenant on Civil and Political Rights 1966 (ICCPR), the International Covenant on Economic, Social, and Cultural Rights 1966 (ICESCR), the Convention on the Elimination of All Forms of Discrimination against Women 1979 (CEDAW), the Convention on the Rights of the Child 1989 (CRC), among others.[30] Of course, all of the above human rights conventions are binding upon the respective parties. Some international law commentators even argue that principles of fundamental and universal human rights enshrined in the UDHR could be construed as well-established customary international laws as many countries have invoked those principles in various international treaties and legal instruments since the establishment of the UN.[31]

---

27 United Nations, "Where Can I Find UN Information on the 'Cylinder of Cyrus' a.k.a. 'Edict of Cyrus'?," June 7, 2021, https://ask.un.org/faq/194027.
28 United Nations, "Universal Declaration of Human Rights," accessed April 4, 2022, https://www.un.org/en/about-us/universal-declaration-of-human-rights.
29 *See* also Mohammad Naqib Ishan Jan, Ashgar Ali Ali Mohamed, and Mohamad Hassan Ahmad, *International Refugee Law: Practice and Procedure* (Kuala Lumpur: IIUM Press, 2017), 19–20.
30 Syed Hamid Albar, "Human Rights: High Time to Enforce Seriously," *MLJ*, no 3 (2021): ccclxix–ccclxxii.
31 Mohammad Naqib Ishan Jan, *Principles of Public International Law: A Modern Approach* (Kuala Lumpur: IIUM Press, 2011), 29–40.

With regard to the implementation of international human rights standards in the national jurisdiction, parties to the respective international treaties and legal instruments are obliged to incorporate those standards into their relevant domestic laws. Article 26 of the Vienna Convention on the Law of Treaties 1969 (VCLT) reflects the notion of "*pacta sunt servanda*" by stating that: "Every treaty in force is binding upon the parties to it and must be performed by them in good faith." The subsequent article 27 provides: "A party may not invoke the provisions of its internal law as justification for its failure to perform a treaty." However, there is no prohibition on a state which is not a party to a particular convention from adopting the principles of human rights mentioned in that convention in its national legislation. Therefore, the national laws of the states pertaining to human rights are varied from one jurisdiction to another.

12.5 Protection of Human Rights at Common Law

Generally, in most countries, some fundamental human rights and freedoms are promulgated mainly in the constitution and governed under the respective domestic legislations. Nevertheless, the UK has an uncodified constitution that confers Parliament the power to enact and repeal any law. For that reason, the British judiciary needs to categorise the statutes enacted by Parliament into two such as the constitutional statutes – laws with substantial constitutional content but passed by following the ordinary legislative process in the British Parliament – and the ordinary statutes.[32] Nevertheless, the Parliament is the highest authority in the law-making process, and it can repeal any statute regardless of whether it is constitutional in nature.[33] Dicey even went on to say: "It is fundamental principle of English lawyers, that Parliament can do everything but make a woman a man, and a man a woman."[34] He further explained the term "Parliament" by equating it to "the King, the House of Lords, and the House of Commons."[35] In the same vein, Peter Leyland expressed that – despite the fact that the courts should naturally and inherently have an interpretative function

32 Graziella Romeo, "The Conceptualization of Constitutional Supremacy: Global Discourse and Legal Tradition," *German Law Journal* 21, no. 5 (2020): 904–923.

33 Muhamad Hassan Ahmad, Ashgar Ali Ali Mohamed, and Chithra Latha Ramalingam, "Constitutional Supremacy and the Rule of Law: The Emergence of Constitutional Oath Doctrine," *MLJ*, no. 3 (2021): lvi.

34 Jutta Limbach, "The Concept of the Supremacy of the Constitution," *The Modern Law Review*, vol 64, no. 1, (2001): pp. 1–10.

35 A. V. Dicey, *Introduction to the Study of the Law of the Constitution* (8th ed.) (Liberty Fund, 1915) as cited in Jutta Limbach, "The Concept of the Supremacy of the Constitution," *The Modern Law Review*, vol 64, no 1, (2001), p. 1, fn 2.

with regard to the application of legislation – it is not the case in the UK as only the Parliament has the final word in determining the law.[36]

In the case of *Public Prosecutor v Aluma Mark Chinonso (Negerian) and Another Appeal*,[37] the court observed that since the UK practices parliamentary supremacy, the Parliament has the decisive position to administer what is good for the public and the power to make a law to that effect. Hence, the judiciary has to give effect to the will of the Parliament, and judges have to be submissive to the legislation while judicial activism is not encouraged. It can be observed that, in the UK, the rule of law requires the judiciary to be subservient to the Parliament and thus cannot go against the legislature.[38] Nevertheless, under the common law tradition, courts still reserve significant power to protect human rights except in situations where domestic legislation specifically prohibits or limits such power.

Despite the lack of a constitution enumerating what is considered human rights, the constitutional dimension of recognising these rights is reflected in the vein of common law. In the 1600s, John Locke, an English philosopher, formulated natural rights by incorporating the principles of equality and freedom, such as the right to life and property rights.[39] Blackstone introduced "natural rights" of humans to the realm of common law.[40] Kant described human beings as possessing intrinsic universal value, which is absent in inanimate objects.[41] Goodhart perceived the common law as "a method of administering justice" which requires the recognition and enforcement of human rights.[42] Some of the laws and legal instruments that recognised human rights are the Magna Carta (1215), the Petition

---

36 Peter Leyland, *The Constitution of the United Kingdom: A Contextual Analysis (Constitutional Systems of the World)* (2nd ed.) (Oxford: Hart Publishing, 2012), 50; Muhamad Hassan Ahmad, Ashgar Ali Ali Mohamed, and Chithra Latha Ramalingam, "Constitutional Supremacy and the Rule of Law: The Emergence of Constitutional Oath Doctrine," *MLJ*, no. 3 (2021): lvi.

37 [2020] MLJU 694.

38 This practice is generally known as the "parliamentary supremacy." *See* also *Kerajaan Malaysia v Syarikat Ismail Ibrahim Sdn Bhd & Ors* [2020] MLJU 52; Muhamad Hassan Ahmad, Ashgar Ali Ali Mohamed, and Chithra Latha Ramalingam, "Constitutional Supremacy and the Rule of Law: The Emergence of Constitutional Oath Doctrine," *MLJ*, no. 3 (2021): lvii.

39 Pauline Maier, "The Declaration of Independence and Natural Rights," Constitutional Rights Foundation, accessed April 4, 2022, https://www.crf-usa.org/foundations-of-our-constitution/natural-rights.html; Syed Hamid Albar, "Human Rights: High Time to Enforce Seriously," *MLJ*, ccclxx.

40 James Spigelman, *Statutory Interpretation and Human Rights* (Brisbane: University of Queensland Press, 2008), 23.

41 Luigi Caranti, "Kant's Theory of Human Rights," in *Handbook of Human Rights*, ed. Thomas Cushman (London: Routledge, 2012), accessed April 4, 2022, https://www.routledgehandbooks.com/doi/10.4324/9780203887035.ch3; Syed Hamid Albar, "Human Rights: High Time to Enforce Seriously,"*MLJ*, ccclxx.

42 Goodhart AL, "What Is the Common Law," *Law Quarterly Review* 76, (1960): 46.

of Rights (1628), the Habeas Corpus Act (1679), and the English Bill of Rights (1688), to name but a few.[43]

Some of the human rights recognised under common law are the freedom of speech; the freedom of movement; the right of access to the courts; the right to access legal counsel in a criminal case; the right to procedural fairness; the right not to deprive property without compensation; the privilege against self-incrimination; among others.[44] The common law has long covered some of the fundamental rights and freedoms mentioned in contemporary international human rights conventions and legal instruments. For example, the freedom from slavery under the common law corresponds with article 8 of the ICCPR, and the concept of personal liberty under the common law corresponds with article 9 of the ICCPR.[45]

According to Bailey, the "freedom" in common law is a general principle established on a case-by-case basis.[46] Lumb described the common law method well by saying that it is "based on a step by step approach, with the recognition and development of rights reflecting a casuistic approach to the interpretation of a 'rights' issue in the light of relevant remedies and legislative restrictions."[47] In interpreting human rights statutes, O'Connor J suggested in the case of *Potter v Minahan*[48] that judges should interpret the statute law relating to fundamental rights and freedoms in consistent with the common law to the extent the statute permits.[49]

Even in the setting of parliamentary supremacy as practiced in the UK, the Parliament cannot just simply override the fundamental rights and freedoms of its subjects.[50] For example, freedom of speech has long been recognised as one of the fundamental human rights under the common law. Blackstone described this freedom as "essential

---

43 *See* Youth for Human Rights International, "The Background of Human Rights," 2002–2021, https://www.youthforhumanrights.org/course/lesson/background-of-human-rights/the-background-of-human-rights.html; Syed Hamid Albar, "Human Rights: High Time to Enforce Seriously," *MLJ*, ccclxxi.

44 Corrin J, "Australia: Country Report on Human Rights," *Victoria University of Wellington Law Review* 37, (2009): 41–42.

45 *See* also Australian Human Rights Commission, "Common Law Rights, Human Rights Scrutiny and the Rule of Law," accessed April 4, 2022, https://humanrights.gov.au/our-work/rights-and-freedoms/common-law-rights-human-rights-scrutiny-and-rule-law#:~:text=Common%20law%20recognition%20of%20rights,from%20acting%20inconsistently%20with%20rights.

46 Bailey P, *The Human Rights Enterprise in Australia and Internationally* (Chatswood: LexisNexis, 2009), 1–11.

47 Lumb RD, *Australian Constitutionalism* (Sydney: Butterworths, 1983), p. 102.

48 [1908] 7 CLR 277, 304.

49 RS French CJ, "The Common Law and the Protection of Human Rights," Anglo Australasian Lawyers Society, September 4, 2009, 5–7, https://www.hcourt.gov.au/assets/publications/speeches/current-justices/frenchcj/frenchcj4sep09.pdf.

50 *R v Secretary of State for the Home Department; Ex parte Simms* [2000] 2 AC 115, 131.

to the nature of a free State"[51] while Lord Coleridge characterised it as "one which it is for the public interest that individuals should possess, and, indeed, that they should exercise without impediment, so long as no wrongful act is done."[52] Thus, the Parliament cannot override or impair the freedom of speech recognised under the common law. According to this presumption, the courts have to interpret and apply the Parliament's legislation without limiting or impairing the freedom of expression well recognised under the common law.

This notion was again recognised in the case of *Derbyshire County Council v Times Newspapers Ltd.*[53] Balcombe and Butler-Sloss LJJ opined that: "where the law is uncertain, the courts should approach it in such a way as to ensure that it does not involve a breach of the statutory provision."[54] Again, in the case of *Metric Martyrs,*[55] Laws LJ characterised it as "protecting rights of a constitutional character recognised by the common law." According to him, this approach provides "the benefits of a written constitution where fundamental rights are accorded with special respect while preserving the sovereignty of the legislature and the flexibility of the uncodified British Constitution."[56] It can be observed from the above that the common law gives a high value to fundamental rights and freedoms despite the fact that they could be subjected to statutory limitations.[57]

Julius Stone criticised this approach as the presumptions made by judges upon legislation would not be well suited in the setting of parliamentary supremacy.[58] Roscoe Pound preferred statute law over common law in order not to interfere with the status quo in the democratic environment, as he regarded the legislation as "the more truly democratic form of law-making."[59] At any rate, it is undeniable that the common law still has a significant role to play, especially in protecting human rights while operating in line with the practices of parliamentary supremacy.[60]

---

51 William Blackstone, *Commentaries on the Laws of England* (Vol 4) (Oxford: Clarendon Press, 1769), 151–152.

52 *Bonnard v Perryman* [1891] 2 Ch 269, at 284; *R v Police of the Metropolis; Ex parte Blackburn (No 2)* [1968] 2 QB 150, at 155; *Wheeler v Leicester City Council* [1995] AC 105, at 106; *Attorney-General v Guardian Newspapers Ltd (No 2)* [1990] 1 AC 109, at 220.

53 *Derbyshire County Council v Times Newspapers Ltd* [1992] QB 770, 813.

54 RS French CJ, "The Common Law and the Protection of Human Rights," Anglo Australasian Lawyers Society, 04 September 2009, pp. 8–14., available at: <https://www.hcourt.gov.au/assets/publications/speeches/current-justices/frenchcj/frenchcj4sep09.pdf> (accessed on 04 April 2022).

55 *Thoburn v Sunderland City Council* [2003] QB 151.

56 *Thoburn v Sunderland City Council* [2003] QB, at 187.

57 RS French CJ, "The Common Law and the Protection of Human Rights," 8.

58 Julius Stone, *The Province and Function of Law: Law Logic, Justice and Social Control: A Study in Jurisprudence* (Sydney: Associated General Publications Pty Ltd, 1946), 199.

59 Roscoe Pound, "Common Law and Legislation," *Harvard Law Review* 21, no. 6 (April 1908): 387–407.

60 RS French CJ, "The Common Law and the Protection of Human Rights," 16.

Presently, in the UK, human rights are protected under the Human Rights Act 1998, which gives legal effect to the European Convention on Human Rights. Some of the human rights and freedoms covered by this convention are the right to life, prohibition of torture, prohibition of slavery and forced labour, right to liberty and security, right to a fair trial, no punishment without law, right to respect for private and family life, freedom of thought, conscience and religion, freedom of expression, freedom of assembly and association, right to marry, prohibition of discrimination, and so forth.[61]

If there is a violation of any right or freedom mentioned in the convention, the victim can take action under the Human Rights Act before the courts in the UK. In the case of *Derbyshire County Council v Times Newspapers Ltd*,[62] the Court of Appeal referred to article 10 of the European Convention on Human Rights, which relates to freedom of expression. On the other hand, if the victim finds that the domestic remedy granted by the UK court is not satisfactory and when all local remedies have been exhausted, the victim can also take the case to the European Court of Human Rights[63] in accordance with the "generally recognised rules of international law and within a period of four months from the date on which the final decision was taken."[64] In such a case, the European Court of Human Rights may receive applications from "any person, nongovernmental organisation or group of individuals" who claim to be the victim of a violation by one of the parties to the convention. The contracting parties are obliged not to hinder the effective exercise of this right in any way.[65]

In the past few years, there have been calls to repeal the Human Rights Act 1998. This move may pave the way for the resurgence of the wide-ranging application of common law in the future in the protection of human rights without the need to refer to the said statute and thereby the European Convention on Human Rights.[66] Some senior judges, namely, Lord Reed and Lord Mance, promote the common law as "a primary source of fundamental rights and values." They described it as "the origin and promoter of individual rights"[67] and "the guarantor of

61 The Human Rights Act 1998, s 1(1)(a); The European Convention on Human Rights, arts 2–12 and 14.

62 *Derbyshire County Council v Times Newspapers Ltd* [1992] QB 770, 813.

63 The European Court of Human Rights is the court of the Council of Europe based in Strasbourg, France. The court ensures the countries of the Council of Europe respect the European Convention on Human Rights. *See* Citizens Advice, "What Are Human Rights?," accessed April 4, 2022, https://www.citizensadvice.org.uk/law-and-courts/civil-rights/human-rights/what-are-human-rights/#:~:text=In%20the%20UK%2C%20human%20rights,Act%20in%20the%20UK%20courts.

64 The European Convention on Human Rights, art 35.

65 The European Convention on Human Rights, art 34.

66 *See Osborn v The Parole Board* [2013] UKSC 61 and *Kennedy v The Charity Commission* [2014] UKSC 20.

67 Lord Neuberger, "*The Role of Judges in Human Rights Jurisprudence: A Comparison of the Australian and UK Experience*," Address to the Supreme Court of Victoria, August, 2014.

human rights."[68] The Supreme Court urged the claimants to use the common law at the initial stage of any dispute relating to the violation of human rights and then resort to the European Convention on Human Rights through the Human Rights Act 1998 only when the common law is lacking. This recent approach taken by the courts can be counterproductive as the protection of human rights available under the common law is not codified and thus lack clarity as to which rights are protected compared to the European Convention on Human Rights.[69] Besides, the victim will not have access to a more reliable and impartial court of law when the domestic remedy granted by the local court is not satisfactory.[70]

12.6 Human Rights from Shari'ah Perspective

Islam strongly upholds the honour and dignity of another person irrespective of his or her religious faith. Further, the religion thus requires its followers to maintain and practice all the noble qualities of ethical values such as honesty, sincerity, and benevolence. Further, man must exhort and commend each other to do good and forbid all that is wrong, which should be in harmony with what Allah (*SWT*) loves and hates.[71] Allah (*SWT*) has imbued a conscience and the cognition of good and evil into human nature.[72] Besides, Islam also strongly upholds the honour and dignity of another person irrespective of their religious faith. As Allah's vicegerent on earth, man has been created in a position of honour above the brute creation. The Qur'an provides that: "We have honoured the sons of Adam."[73] As Allah (*SWT*) has honoured mankind, surely mankind is also under "a duty to observe the same

68 *Commissioner of Police of the Metropolis v DSD and NBV* [2015] EWCA Civ 646, [27], per Laws LJ.
69 Lady Hale, "*UK Constitutionalism on the March*," Keynote Address delivered at the Constitutional and Administrative Law Bar Conference, July, 2014.
70 Hodge Jones & Allen, "Common Law: A Poor Substitute for the Protections Afforded by the Human Rights Act," October 30, 2015, https://www.hja.net/expert-comments/opinion/civil-liberties-human-rights/common-law-a-poor-substitute-for-the-protections-afforded-by-the-human-rights-act/.
71 *See Surah Ali 'Imran* (3): Verse 110, "Ye are the best of peoples, evolved for mankind, enjoining what is right, forbidding what is wrong, and believing in Allah." Again in *Surah Al-Tawbah* (9): Verse 71, "The believers, men and women, are protectors, one of another: they enjoin what is just, and forbid what is evil. They observe regular prayers, practice regular charity, and obey Allah and His Messenger." *See* also *Surah Al Hajj* (22): Verse 41.
72 *See Surah As-Sham* (91): Verse 8.
73 *Surah Al Isra* (17): Verse 70. This verse emphasises among others, fairness, just in treatment of workers, protection of their honour and dignity. An employer must therefore refrain from defaming or damaging employee's reputation, honour and dignity.

among them, to preserve its integrity and avoid its violation."[74] Further, there are many verses in the Qur'an affirming Allah's love and compassion for mankind, and this sets a basic framework for the relationship between mankind.[75]

Love for other members and respect for their rights, concern for their welfare and reputation are the commandments of Allah (*SWT*). As Allah (*SWT*) proclaims: "Avoid aggression, for Allah loves not aggressors."[76] The use of abusive language or strong words of condemnation is equally prohibited. It is provided that: "Allah loveth not that evil should be noised abroad in public speech, except where injustice hath been done; for Allah is He who heareth and knoweth all things."[77] The Prophet Mohammad (peace be upon him) said: "It is not for a believer to indulge in insults, sarcasm or cursing."[78] He further stated: "Whoever saved the honour of his brother, God will save his countenance against the blaze of fire in the day of judgment."[79] He further stated that: "Do not annoy the Muslims, nor defame them, and do not expose their nakedness, for one who exposes the nakedness of his Muslim brother, Allah will expose his own nakedness."[80] Hence, the honour and dignity of each individual have been regarded as sacred. In fact, Islam enjoins the believers to uphold justice and kindness, which call for just standards of behaviour to all, irrespective of whether they belong to the fold of Islam.

In Islam, human life is sacred, and therefore it must be protected and preserved at all costs regardless of one's religious, ethnic, cultural, and linguistic backgrounds. Allah (*SWT*) reveals in the Qur'an that: "If anyone killed a person – unless it is a legal retaliation for murder or for spreading mischief in the land – it would be as if he killed all mankind; and if anyone saved a life, it would be as if he saved the life of all mankind."[81] It is an inherent duty for all Muslims to defend and save all mankind without any discrimination.

Further, the Qur'an reminds mankind in the following verse which states: "O mankind! We created you from a single (pair) of a male and a female, and made you into

74 Mohammad Hashim Kamali, *The Dignity of Man: The Islamic Perspective* (Cambridge: The Islamic Foundation UK and Iimiah Publishers, 1999), 30.

75 For example, in the Quran, *Surah Al-Tawbah* (9): Verses 4 and 7 state, "Allah truly loves those who are conscious of Him"; *Surah Al-Baqarah* (2): Verse 195, "Allah loves those who are good to others"; *Surah Ali 'Imran* (3): Verse 159, "Allah (SWT) loves those who place their trust on Him"; *Surah Al-A'rfah* (7): Verse 156, "My mercy engulfs everything and extent beyond everything"; and *Surah Al-Zumar* (39): Verse 53, "O my servants who transgressed against their souls! Do not despair of the mercy of God. For God forgives all sins. He is most forgiving, most merciful."

76 *See Surah Al-Baqarah* (2): 190.

77 *Surah An-Nisa* (4): Verse 148.

78 Al Tabrizi, *Mishkat* Vol. 1, Hadith No: 4847.

79 Cited in Mohammed Hashim Kamali, *Freedom of Expression in Islam* (Cambridge: Iimiah Publishers, 1994), 119.

80 Tirmidhi, *Sunna al Tirmidhi* Vol. III, Hadith No: 84.

81 *Surah Al-Ma'idah* (5): Verse 32.

nations and tribes, that ye may know each other (not that ye may despise each other)."[82] This verse offers the reason for the creation of mankind into different tribes, races, colour and creed is for us to be able to recognise each other and also learn to live together and love each other but not to draw the division along the line of these differences and fight one another. In corresponding to the above Qur'anic verse, the Prophet Mohammad (peace be upon him) further emphasised this point in his final sermon in the Uranah valley of Mount Arafat in Mecca in the following words: "All mankind is from Adam and Eve, an Arab has no superiority over a non-Arab nor a non-Arab has any superiority over an Arab; also a White has no superiority over a Black nor a Black has any superiority over a White except by piety and good action . . . "[83] Therefore, in Islam, all humans are considered equal in dignity and rights.

Apart from that, Muslims are ordained to deal justly in a dignified manner with other fellow human beings regardless of whether the other is a Muslim or not. This can be observed from the following Qur'anic verse, which states: "O ye who believe! Stand out firmly for justice, as witnesses to Allah, even as against yourselves, or your parents, or your kin, and whether it be (against) rich or poor: for Allah can best protect both. Follow not the lusts (of your hearts), lest ye swerve, and if ye distort (justice) or decline to do justice, verily Allah is well-acquainted with all that ye do."[84] Again, the Prophet Mohammad (peace be upon him) reminded Muslims in his final sermon to act justly in all of their dealings with others in life by saying that: "O People! . . . Return the goods entrusted to you to their rightful owners. Hurt no one so that no one may hurt you . . . You will neither inflict nor suffer any inequality . . . It is true that you have certain rights with regard to your women but they also have rights over you . . . Do not therefore do injustice. Remember one day you will meet Allah and answer your deeds. So beware, do not astray from the path of righteousness after I am gone."[85]

As from the above, it is prudent to assume that all kinds of human rights are generally recognised as long as a particular principle of rights does not go against the principles of Shari'ah. Thus, it would be a daunting task to list down all the human rights that can be protected under the Shari'ah, which is again subjected to various interpretations and analogies made by countless Islamic scholars belonging to numerous schools of thought. In fact, in Islam, human dignity and human rights are accepted to be equal (except where it explicitly mentions in the Qur'an and Sunnah not to be treated equally but fairly depending on the physical and mental capacity of

82 Surah Al-Hujurat (49): Verse 13.

83 IIUM, "The Last Sermon of Prophet Muhammad (p.b.u.h.)," accessed April 4, 2022, https://www.iium.edu.my/deed/articles/thelastsermon.html.

84 Surah An-Nisa (4): Verse 135.

85 IIUM, "The Last Sermon of Prophet Muhammad (p.b.u.h.)" and Syed Hamid Albar, "Human Rights: High Time to Enforce Seriously," *MLJ*, ccclxix-ccclxx.

human in general – especially in terms of gender), universal and inalienable to all humans. It can be observed from the mentioned Qur'anic verses and sayings or customs (*Ahadith*) of the Prophet Mohammad (peace be upon him) that human rights are intertwined with the "principle of justice" itself.[86]

Every single person claiming to be a Muslim should ask themselves the following three questions.

(1) Whether he/she loves justice for himself/herself where all other humans should treat him/her in a manner consistent with what justice would require?
(2) Whether he/she loves justice for other humans where he/she should treat all other humans in a manner consistent with what justice would require?
(3) Whether he/she would still love justice even when the justice would go against himself/herself, his/her parents, or next of kin and their interests?

Islam and the Shari'ah require every Muslim to answer all the above three questions in the affirmative. It can therefore be observed that the recognition and protection of human dignity and human rights is an intrinsic and integral part of the Islamic justice system regardless of whether Muslims around the world are really up to the benchmark in their actual practices.

12.7 The Cairo Declaration on Human Rights in Islam (CDHRI)

Muslim nations view that some of the principles of human rights mentioned in the UDHR are not in line with the Shari'ah, which Muslims are bound to follow as the religious law. There was a dilemma among the Muslim nations as they could not follow the contemporary principles of human rights which are against the principles of Shari'ah. The compromise was to draft a similar human rights declaration that adopts the contemporary principles of human rights which are in line with the principles of Shari'ah and restricts which are not.

Accordingly, on 05 August 1990, "the Cairo Declaration on Human Rights in Islam" (CDHRI) was adopted by the state members of the Organisation of Islamic Cooperation (OIC) in Cairo, Egypt. On 28 November 2020, its revised version entitled: "the Cairo Declaration of the Organisation of Islamic Cooperation on Human Rights" was further adopted at the 47th Session of the Council of Foreign Ministers of the Organisation of Islamic Cooperation (United Against Terrorism for Peace and Development) held in Niamey, Republic of Niger. Generally, both versions of the CDHRI provide principles of human rights and freedoms which are in line with the

86 Syed Hamid Albar, "Human Rights: High Time to Enforce Seriously," *MLJ*, ccclxx.

Shari'ah while conforming to the contemporary notion of human rights. The interpretation of CDHRI Version 1990 is specifically subjected to Shari'ah[87] as it is the "only source of reference for the explanation or clarification of any of the Articles of this Declaration."[88] On the other hand, the CDHRI Version 2020 does not directly invoke Shari'ah, but it states that "the right to exercise and enjoy the rights and freedoms set out in the present declaration, without prejudice to the principles of Islam."[89] The following discourse will only focus on the CDHRI Version 2020.

In the Preamble of the CDHRI Version 2020, the state members of the OIC acknowledge "the principles of brotherhood and equality among all human beings which are firmly established by all Divine religions." At the same time, they strongly believe that mankind – as the vicegerent of Allah (*SWT*) on Earth in Islam – has to commit to ensuring and protecting human dignity and human rights, which have already been safeguarded by the teachings of Islam, and those rights which do not prejudice the principles of Islam. In this regard, they recall the earliest human rights pact in Islam, i.e., the "Charter of Medina"; the final sermon of the Prophet Mohamed (peace be upon him); the "values of justice, equality and peace of Islamic civilisation which should underpin the conception of human rights; the Charter of the United Nations, the International Bill of Human Rights; the Vienna Declaration and Program of Action, Durban Declaration and Programme of Action, and the Outcome Document of the Durban Review Conference 2009, and other relevant international human rights conventions and instruments."[90]

The CDHRI Version 2020 regards all human beings as one family. Hence, it recognises that all humans are equal in dignity, rights, and obligations "without any discrimination on the grounds of race, colour, language, sex, religion, sect, political opinion, national or social origin, fortune, age, disability or other status."[91] It prohibits gross and systematic violation of human rights in all forms and under any circumstances.[92]

The CDHRI Version 2020 outlines the following principles of human rights, namely, right to life; entitlement to inviolability; right to liberty and safety and not to be subjected to torture; protection of the family and marriage; rights of women; rights of the child; right to recognition before the law; right to education; right to self-determination; freedom of movement; rights of migrants and refugees; nationality rights; right to work; right to legitimate economic and financial gains; right to own property; intellectual property rights; right to the enjoyment of the highest attainable standard of physical and mental health; protection of privacy; right to

87 The Cairo Declaration on Human Rights in Islam, art 24.
88 The Cairo Declaration on Human Rights in Islam, art 25.
89 The Cairo Declaration on Human Rights in Islam, art 25(a).
90 The Cairo Declaration of the Organization of Islamic Cooperation on Human Rights, Preamble.
91 The Cairo Declaration of the Organization of Islamic Cooperation on Human Rights, art 1(a).
92 The Cairo Declaration of the Organization of Islamic Cooperation on Human Rights, art 1(b).

freedom of thought, conscience and religion; right to freedom of opinion and expression; right to access to justice and fair trial; right to participate in the conduct of public affairs and freedom of peaceful assembly and association; and fair treatment during situations of war and armed conflict.[93]

It can be observed that the human rights and freedoms recognised in the CDHRI Version 2020 are more detailed than those mentioned in the UDHR. Nevertheless, the enjoyment of these rights and freedoms shall not be prejudiced against the principles of Islam and national legislation. The CDHRI Version 2020 shares the same fate with the UDHR as both are merely declarations that do not have binding legal effects on the state members. Looking at the bright sight, the CDHRI Version 2020 could pave the way – at least among Muslim nations – to adopt human rights treaties that are not prejudiced against the principles of Islam.

12.8 Conclusion

The UDHR was created to achieve common standards of achievements for all people and all nations, to the end that every individual and every organ of society should strive by teaching and education to promote respect for these rights and freedoms and by progressive measures, national and international, to secure their universal and effective recognition and observance, both among the peoples of the member states themselves and among the peoples of territories under their jurisdiction. Meanwhile, the CDHRI was created as a reminder to man of the ideal code of human rights that was revealed more than 1400 years ago. As Allah (*SWT*) says: "This is a declaration for mankind, a guidance, and instruction to those who fear God."[94] Human rights in Islam are firmly rooted in the belief that Allah (*SWT*), and Allah (*SWT*) alone, is the Law Giver and the Source of all human rights. Due to this divine origin, no ruler, government, assembly, or authority is expected to curtail or violate in any way the human rights conferred by the creator of the universe. The above is reiterated in the foreword to the CDHRI: "Islam gave to mankind an ideal code of human rights fourteen centuries ago. These rights aim at conferring honour and dignity on mankind and eliminating exploitation, oppression, and injustice."

93 The Cairo Declaration of the Organization of Islamic Cooperation on Human Rights, arts 2–24.
94 *Surah Ali 'Imran* (3): Verse 138.

Ashgar Ali Ali Mohamed and Muhamad Hassan Ahmad

13 Alternative Dispute Resolution: The Conventional and Shari'ah Perspective

13.1 Introduction

Disputes and conflicts are common to any organisation and may arise between and among staff, customers, and suppliers, between and across organisational units, departments, and even between countries. In an organisation, any unresolved conflict may have a significant negative impact on the commitment to the organisation and/or productivity, among others. Likewise, international disputes, if not addressed immediately, may escalate into war with severe loss of lives and damage to properties, as the world is currently witnessing in Ukraine. Early recognition of conflict and an effective resolution process can lead to unity by addressing concerns or issues rather than suppressing them, getting people to talk to solve the problem, and above all, enabling people to be part of a team that cares. It promotes, *inter alia*, compromise or collaboration as people learn how to work harmoniously, develop creative solutions to problems, and reach outcomes that mutually benefit those involved. Unfortunately, however, human conflicts or disputes are commonly referred to and adjudication in the courts. The undue delay in settlement of disputes in courts which is common in many common law countries, including Malaysia, has seen an increase in the backlog of cases. As efforts to eliminate the backlog of cases are not showing positive results, the Malaysian judiciary has time and again proposed Alternative Dispute Resolution (ADR) as a mode of dispute settlement of civil and criminal matters, making court appearances as the last resort.

It is worthwhile noting that in Malaysia, the ordinary courts of law administer justice according to common law precedents and statutes based on the fundamental principles derived from English law. The process of litigation is based on the adversarial process, which was inherited from the common law and the English legal procedure. In this system, the parties, through their advocate, generally control the course of the trial, where they are given the freedom to present their case and set forth their points of view. In fact, before the case may be set down for trial, the parties are required to comply with the stringent civil and criminal procedural rules of the court; for example, in a civil dispute, the requirement of filing pleadings and other originating documents, service of documents, "discovery," "interrogation," and pre-trial case management, among other. During the hearing of the case, which is normally held in open court, the parties may raise preliminary objections. Upon determination of the preliminary objection, the case may proceed for a full hearing with the parties adducing evidence and the examination of witnesses. Thereafter, the parties would be required to make a submission of their case.

https://doi.org/10.1515/9783110766707-013

The presiding judge merely adjudicates the pleadings and evidence produced by the parties. In order to ascertain the truth, the judge would thoroughly elucidate the facts and issue of the case at hand and thereafter, make a decision that attains a reasonable degree of certainty. The judge acts as an impartial referee and may only ask questions to witnesses when it is necessary to clear up any point that has been overlooked or left obscure; to *see* that the advocates behave themselves seemly and keep the rules laid down by the law; to exclude irrelevancies and discourage repetition; to make sure that by wise intervention he follows the points that the advocates are making and to assess their worth, and at the end to make up his mind where the truth lies.[1]

While admitting that the enforcement of the above processes will ensure, *inter alia*, that the decision arrived at is fair and based on justifiable reasons, what needs to be emphasised herein is that such a process would certainly consume substantial time and costs. Many of the problems associated with the process of litigation in Malaysia are common to the adversarial process. Litigation in the courts is costly, time-consuming with unpredictable outcomes, and above all, it has the potential to damage irreparably the relationships between the parties. The presiding judge will then deliver his written grounds of judgment. An aggrieved party may appeal against the decision of the trial court to the superior courts.

It must be added that the disposal of cases vides the traditional litigation approach would not help in reducing the backlog of cases, even if there is an increase in the number of judges and courtrooms. This is because of the ever-increasing volume of cases filed in the courts annually. In fact, there are many disputes that could be resolved outside the framework of conventional litigation using the ADR mechanisms such as mediation and conciliation. Hence, this chapter discusses the conventional as well as Islamic ADR mechanisms in practice and further identifies the similarities as well as differences of ADR mechanisms between the two systems.

13.2 ADR from the Conventional Perspective

Unlike the traditional litigation in the ordinary courts of law, which is adversarial, costly, unpredictable, rigid, slow, damaging to relationships, and limited to narrow rights-based remedies compared to creative problem solving, the ADR process is flexible, adaptable, neutral, and confidential. As the phrase suggests, ADR is an alternative to the traditional legal system, and the processes therein consist of negotiation, mediation, conciliation, early neutral evaluation, expert determination, mini-trial, arbitration, and Med-Arb. From the above lists, mediation/conciliation and arbitration are proving to be popular and effective means of settling disputes. The choice of a

1 Per Lord Denning in *Jones v National Coal Board* [1957] 2 QB 55, 64.

suitable ADR mechanism would depend on the type of dispute, circumstances of the parties, the urgency of resolving the dispute, and financial circumstances of the parties. Specific ADR processes can be devised to suit complex disputes in commercial and non-commercial sectors.

Community dispute would, in most circumstances, require an amicable resolution with the hope of promoting harmony in the neighbourhood and creating a safer environment for the community. Hence, it is prudent to settle the dispute out-of-court by application of conciliation or mediation. Likewise, in family disputes, the conciliation process is absolutely relevant as the conciliator would have the requisite skill and knowledge in terms of understanding the parties' desires, collecting information, facilitating communication, facilitating agreement, and ability to manage cases and documents, among others. His ability to be creative, to be able to deal with strong emotion, sensitivity, reasoning, emotional stability, analytical skills, interviewing techniques, and a sense of commitment to the whole exercise of conciliation would certainly have an impact on the resolution of the dispute. Again, in a commercial dispute where such disputes would involve substantial monetary interests, early settlement of the dispute is warranted to ensure minimum interruption of business, and thus arbitration may be a good option, even if it is expensive.

Mediation or conciliation is also suitable to resolve international conflicts, for example, the Russian and Ukraine conflict. The world is currently witnessing the Western world supporting Ukraine with weapons and with Russia threatening the use of nuclear weapons if any foreign powers intervene to support Ukraine. The threat is undoubtedly real, and it thus calls for an immediate solution to prevent the nuclear-armed countries from going into war. A harmonious world will be a distant dream if states resort to using force or violent means to resolve their disputes. The world had formerly witnessed that war brings nothing but destruction to lives and properties. The human and the environmental atrocity will be to unimaginable amount if the war is launched between the great nuclear powers. No country should provoke another into war more so involving the big nuclear powers, as no peace lovers would want to recall the distractions arising from the First and the Second World Wars.

The tension involving the big powers over Ukraine could be resolved by peaceful means. In fact, the peaceful settlement of international disputes is a cardinal principle of the law of the United Nations (UN). Article 33(1) of the UN Charter broadly categorises dispute settlement mechanisms into three categories, i.e., the diplomatic means; legal, judicial, or adjudicative means; and political means. It provides that the parties to any disputes shall, first of all, seek a solution by negotiation, inquiry, mediation, conciliation, arbitration, judicial settlement, resort to regional agencies or arrangements, or other peaceful means of their own choice. Negotiation helps to prevent a dispute from becoming a major source of conflict. The UN Charter obliges the member states to refrain from threatening or using force against the territorial integrity or political independence of any state in their international relations.

13.3 Mediation or Conciliation

It would certainly be helpful to briefly discuss the process in conciliation or mediation. The conciliator/mediator as a neutral third party would assist the parties in reaching a settlement. He would listen to the arguments forwarded by the parties and may, where necessary, intervene to ask questions to help the disputants understand the issues. Further, he would guide the parties through the process to develop a mutually acceptable solution. He would also maintain a safe and respectful atmosphere. Besides, he would explore the strength of the parties' case with a view to reconciling the parties' positions to the extent possible and assisting them in reaching a consensus on the resolution of the dispute. The mediator may offer suggestions, recommendations, and alternatives for consideration by the parties to resolve the dispute. If desired, he would assist the parties in preparing a written agreement that could benefit both the disputants and everyone involved. The mediator, however, has no power to compel or even recommend a resolution or settlement.

In international disputes, where the disputing parties are in most circumstances unwilling to negotiate or fail to negotiate effectively, the assistance of a third party may be necessary to help in procuring a settlement. This assistance may be requested by one or both of the parties, or it may be voluntarily offered by a third party. The mediators may be individuals, neutral third states, or institutions and organisations. Whoever is the mediator, what is important is that they must be impartial and must enjoy the confidence of both sides of the dispute. The conflict between Iran and the United States (US) over hostages was mediated by Algeria, a move that averted a potential war; the Falkland Islands dispute was mediated by the US followed by UN Secretary-General; and the dispute relating to the breakup of Yugoslavia was mediated by European Union (EU) and the UN.

Unlike a lawsuit where there would be a winner and a loser, a settlement *vide* mediation or conciliation, while it cannot guarantee specific results, the mediator can help the disputants to find a mutually acceptable solution. In fact, mediation, in most circumstances, is able to improve the relationship between the parties rather than straining it further. Through this process, resolutions are based on the voluntary choice of the parties, where the decision to settle the dispute is solely up to the choice of the parties. The mediator does not impose the terms of the resolutions or force the parties to agree. It is for the parties to arrive at an amicable resolution of their differences. If termination of a relationship is the option, mediation can make the termination more amicable. The success of mediation depends on the willingness of the parties to work together in good faith and the ability of the mediator to properly manage the mediation process.

It must be added that mediation is not and should never be assumed to be a substitute for the judicial system. It is only an alternative mode of dispute resolution, and where mediation fails to bring about an amicable resolution, the dispute will be referred to and adjudicated in court. For mediation to procure maximum results, the disputants must embrace mediation and appreciate its true value, such as its ability to save costs and the potential for repairing relationships. It is reiterated that the mediation process is principally aimed at exploring options for an amicable settlement of a dispute and facilitating negotiations between the parties. It is conducted in private settings by a neutral third party who is a skilled or trained mediator. The disputing parties are able to speak for themselves and work together to find a lasting solution to their conflict under the guidance of the mediator. The process works because the parties are given the power and obligation to seek solutions that meet their own needs and interests. The mediator has no authority to decide on the issues in dispute but to assist the parties in voluntarily reaching a mutually acceptable settlement with the mediator controlling the proceedings and the flow of communication between the parties.

At this juncture, it is also worthwhile mentioning the UN Convention on International Settlement Agreements resulting from Mediation or also known as the Singapore Mediation Convention. This convention was adopted by the UN General Assembly on 20 December 2018 to deal with the promotion of mediation as an alternative and effective method of resolving commercial disputes. It excludes consumer transactions for personal, family, or household purposes, inheritance, and employment law. This convention is similar to the New York Convention on the Recognition and Enforcement of Foreign Arbitral Awards, which is also known as the New York Arbitration Convention, adopted on 10 June 1958 to provide the framework for the recognition and enforcement of foreign arbitral awards and the referral by a court to arbitration. The Singapore Mediation Convention imposed an obligation on the parties with respect to both enforcement of a settlement agreement and the right of a disputing party to invoke a settlement agreement covered by the convention. Pursuant to this convention, the settlement agreement has cross-border enforcement where the agreement arrived thereto can be enforced in another convention Ssate, if it involves foreign parties.

13.4 Arbitration

In relation to arbitration, it is a system of private justice to settle disputes privately outside the jurisdiction of state courts through persons chosen by the parties to adjudicate the dispute. The law on arbitration is based upon the principle of withdrawing the dispute from the ordinary court and enabling the parties to resolve the dispute through the setting up of a private tribunal. An arbitrator could be a professional lawyer, an economist, or a distinguished businessman, among others. For the business community, arbitration is highly preferred because of their often highly specialised and complicated disputes with the resulting effect of saving costs, delay, and, more importantly, preserving commercial goodwill. Arbitration is used in a variety of subject matters, ranging from specialised adjudications such as building contracts, insurance, patents, employment, and breach of contract to more general disciplines of law, for example, sale and purchase of goods, loan transactions, and so on. The reference of disputes to arbitration is of two principal types, namely, the conventional, where the parties agree to refer their present or future disputes to an arbitrator of their own choice; and statutory, where such reference is imposed on them by the terms of a particular statute.

In Malaysia, the arbitration proceedings are regulated by the Arbitration Act 2005,[2] which came into force on 15 March 2006.[3] The 2005 Act vested choice of jurisdictional preference of arbitration proceedings on the parties to the arbitration agreement. They may choose the appropriate law in the jurisdiction of their choice as the governing law should any dispute arises. An arbitrator must decide the dispute in accordance with the choice of law of the parties.[4] In relation to this, section 30(1) of the Act provides that in respect of a domestic arbitration where the seat of arbitration is in Malaysia, the arbitral tribunal shall decide the dispute in accordance with the substantive law of Malaysia. In respect of international arbitration, section 30(2) provides that the arbitral tribunal shall decide the dispute in accordance with the law as agreed upon by the parties as applicable to the substance of the dispute. Further, the parties are free to agree on the language to be used in the arbitral proceedings. Where the parties fail to agree on the language, the arbitral tribunal shall determine the language to be used in the arbitral proceedings. The arbitral tribunal may order that any documentary evidence shall be accompanied by a translation into the language agreed upon by the parties or determined by the arbitral tribunal.[5]

Upon hearing of the dispute, the arbitrator will make a decision known as an "award." The term "award" is defined in the 2005 Act as "a decision of the arbitral tribunal on the substance of the dispute and includes any final, interim, or partial award and any award on costs or interest but does not include interlocutory orders."[6] The award of an arbitrator shall be deemed final and conclusive between the parties on all matters referred to by the submission. Pursuant to section 36(1) of the 2005 Act, an award made by an arbitral tribunal pursuant to an arbitration agreement shall be final and binding on the parties and may be relied upon by any party by way of defence, set-off, or otherwise in any proceedings in any court. A valid award is like the judgment of a competent court of judicature, conclusive evidence as between the parties to it, regarding all matters included therein.[7] The

2 Act 646.

3 PU (B) 65/2006.

4 *See Lembaga Pelabuhan Kelang v Kuala Dimensi Sdn Bhd & Another Appeal* [2010] 9 CLJ 532; *R Kathiravelu Ramasamy v American Home Assurance Company Malaysia* [2009] 1 CLJ 708 CA.

5 The Arbitration Act 2005, s 24.

6 The Arbitration Act 2005, s 2.

7 *See Cairns Energy India Pty Limited & Anor v The Government of India* [2009] 1 LNS 1128.

award, if not performed, the successful party may, by leave of the High Court, pursuant to section 38 of the 2005 Act, enforce the award in the same manner as a judgment or order to the same effect, and where leave is so given, judgment may be entered in terms of the award. In short, the award could be adopted by the High Court and enforced as if it were a judgment of the High Court.

It is worth mentioning that in relation to the international arbitral award, the New York Convention 1958 and the UNCITRAL Model Law on International Commercial Arbitration 1985 obligate the contracting parties to recognise and enforce international arbitration award made in its own state and/or foreign state provided that it is in compliance with terms set out in articles I to V of the 1958 Convention. In fact, the recognition and enforcement of arbitral awards as contained in articles 35 and 36 of the UNCITRAL Model Law are reproduced in sections 38 and 39 of the 2005 Act.

Section 38 of the 2005 Act states that on an application in writing to the High Court, an award made in respect of a domestic arbitration or an award from a foreign state shall, subject to this section and sections 39, be recognised as binding and be enforced by entry as a judgment in terms of the award or by action. The applicant shall produce the duly authenticated original award or a duly certified copy of the award and the original arbitration agreement or a duly certified copy of the agreement. Where the award or arbitration agreement is in a language other than the national language or the English language, the applicant shall supply a duly certified translation of the award or agreement in the English language. Section 39 (1) of the 2005 Act provides, *inter alia*, that recognition or enforcement of an award, irrespective of the state in which it was made, may be refused only at the request of the party against whom it was invoked where that party provides to the High Court proof that the award has not become binding on the parties or if the High Court finds that the award is in conflict with the public policy of Malaysia.

13.5 ADR from the Shari'ah Perspective

In Islam, the alternative modes of dispute settlements include *sulh* (negotiation, mediation/conciliation and compromise of action); *tahkim* (arbitration); Med-Arb; *muhtasib* (ombudsman) *wali al-mazalim* (Special Tribunal/Chancery); and *fatawa* of *muftis* (expert determination). In fact, the settlement of dispute vides conciliation (*sulh*) and arbitration (*hakam*) has been commended in the Qur'an.

The adoption of *sulh* in settlement of disputes is propounded through several Qur'anic verses and *Sunnah*. In the Qur'an, Allah (SWT) proclaims: "If two parties among the believers fall into a quarrel, make ye peace between them: but if one of them transgresses beyond the bounds against another, then fight ye (all) against the one that transgresses until it complies with the command of Allah; but if it complies, then make peace (*sulh*) between them with justice, and be fair: For Allah loves those who are fair (and just). The believers are but a single brotherhood: so make peace and reconciliation (*sulh*) between your two (contending) brothers; and fear Allah, that ye may receive mercy."[8] From the above verse, the Qur'an stresses the concept of Muslim brotherhood and, therefore, disputes or quarrels between the parties or groups of believers should be settled peacefully in accordance with perfect justice and fairness.

Moreover, the settlement of disputes amicably connotes *iman* (faith); hence it ought to be implemented, as Allah (SWT) proclaims: "But no, by the Lord, they can have no (real) faith, until they make thee judge in all disputes between them, and find in their souls no resistance against thy decisions, but accept them with the fullest conviction."[9] According to the commentary of the above verse, Abdullah Yusuf Ali noted that: "the test of true faith is not mere lip profession, but bringing all our doubts and disputes to the one in whom we profess faith. Further, when a decision is given, we are not only to accept it, but find in our inmost souls no difficulty and no resistance, but on the contrary, a joyful acceptance springing from conviction of our own faith."[10]

Again, Allah (SWT) proclaims: "In most of their secret talks there is no good; but if one exhorts to a deed of charity or justice or conciliation (*sulh*) between men (secrecy is permissible): to him who does this, seeking the good pleasure of Allah, We shall soon give a reward of the highest (value)."[11] What is apparent from the above verses of the Qur'an is that Islam recognises the amicable settlement of disputes vide *sulh* which aims at ensuring the cordial relationship is not disrupted, and brotherhood is maintained provided it is made on just, equitable and fair terms.

Apart from the above verses of the Qur'an, there are many traditions of the Prophet Mohammad (peace be upon him) on *sulh*. It was narrated by Sahl bin Sa'd that once there was a dispute among the people from the tribe of Bani Amr bin Auf where the Prophet Mohammad (peace be upon him) himself went to the group along with some of his companions in order to make peace between the people in the group.[12] In another tradition, it was narrated by Umm Kalthum Bint Uqba that she heard the Prophet Mohammad (peace be upon him) saying: "He who makes peace (*sulh*) between the people by inventing good information or saying good things, is not a liar."[13]

8 *Surah Al-Huju'rat* (49): Verses 9 and 10.
9 *Surah Al Nisa* (4): Verse 65.
10 Abdullah Yusuf Ali, *The Meaning of the Holy Qur'an* (Amana Corporation, 1991), p. 205.
11 *Surah Al Nisa* (4): Verse 114.
12 *Sahih al-Bukhari* (Vol. 3), English Translation by Dr. Muhammad Muhsin Khan (1986), 534, para 858.
13 *Sahih al-Bukhari* (Vol. 3), English Translation, p. 533.

Again, it was narrated by Abu Hurairah that the Prophet Mohammad (peace be upon him) had once said: "There is a *sadaqa* (charity) to be given for every joint of the human body, and for every day on which the sun rises, there is a reward of a *sadaqa* for the one who established *sulh* and justice among people."[14] Also, Abu Hurairah reported that the Prophet Mohammad (peace be upon him) said: "conciliation between Muslims is permissible."[15] In another *hadith*, it was reported from Shurayh al-Qadi that the Prophet Mohammad (peace be upon him) said to the disputing parties: "make peace between you."[16] The above authorities from the *Sunnah* likewise signify the importance of *sulh* as a peaceful mode of dispute settlements.

The implementation of *sulh* by the Prophet Mohammad (peace be upon him) could be observed in the case of making the Treaty of *Hudaibiyah*, where it was narrated by Al-Bara Bin Azid that: "when the Prophet Mohammad (peace be upon him) made the peace treaty with the people of *Hudaibiyah*, Ali Bin Abi Talib wrote on the document and stated in it: '*Muhammad, Allah*'s Apostle'. The pagans asked not to write '*Muhammad, Allah*'s Apostle', for if he is an apostle, they could not fight with him. The Prophet Mohammad (peace be upon him) then asked Ali to obliterate the same, but Ali refused to do so, then the Prophet Mohammad (peace be upon him) himself erased and later made peace with them."[17] It is obvious that in the peace treaty of *Hudaybiyyah*, the Prophet Mohammad (peace be upon him) continued with the process of *sulh* to conclusion despite the displeasing remarks made against him. The Madinah Constitution, which was enacted during the time of the Prophet Mohammad (peace be upon him), included provisions on conciliation to settle any disputes emanating from the groups of people in Madinah.

Apart from the above, the practice of *sulh* can further be seen during the tenure of the pious Caliphs. Caliph Umar Al-Khattab wrote a letter addressed to Abu Musa Al-Ash'ari on his appointment as a judge (*qadi*). The said letter contained several instructions on the administration of justice, which also included the implementation of compromise and conciliation (*sulh*), which is permissible among Muslims, except for those making unlawful as lawful and *vice versa*. Based on *ijma* (consensus of opinion), Muslim scholars are unanimous in holding that conciliation is lawful due to its benefits of resolving disputes amicably.[18] Hence, Shari'ah judges are highly encouraged to persuade the litigants to settle their disputes peacefully. This is based on the *hadith* narrated by Abdullah bin Ka'ab to the effect that: "Abdullah bin Abu Hadrad al-Aslami owed Ka'ab bin Malik some money. One day the latter met the former and demanded his right, and their voices grew very loud. The Prophet Mohammad (peace be upon him) passed by them and said: 'O, Ka'ab

14 *Sahih al-Bukhari* (Vol. 3), English Translation, p. 543.
15 *Sunan Abu Dawud* (Vol. 3), English Translation by Ahmad Hassan (1948), ch 1349, para 3587.
16 Abu Bakr Muhammad Ibn Khalaf Ibn Hayyan Al Waki', *Akhbar al-Qudah* (Vol. 2), (1980), 39.
17 *Sahih al-Bukhari* (Vol. 3), English Translation by Dr. Muhammad Muhsin Khan (1986), 536.
18 Muhammad al-Sharbini al-Khatib, *Mughni al-Muhtaj* (Vol 2.), (1933), 177.

(beckoning with his hand as if intending to say), deduct half the debts'. So, Ka'ab took half what the other owed him and remitted the other half."[19]

The process of conciliation in Shari'ah is the same as in the conventional system as outlined earlier. It involves the intervention by a third party who attempts to mediate between the disputing parties. In effect, conciliation means that the two disputing parties would get together to work out a solution to the matter in dispute, and the third party can intervene to assist the parties in settlement of their dispute. The third person or the conciliator acts not in a judicial capacity but a purely administrative one. The conciliator's task is essentially to convene the parties to resolve the issues, find points of common interest and defuse tension. It is understood that the conciliator cannot mediate a dispute in the manner adopted by the courts. The conciliator will not take the side of either party to the dispute and will remain impartial at all times; neither does he make a decision on the merits of the case nor recommend the acceptance of any possible solution. It is entirely up to the parties concerned to reach a settlement and the proposed terms of the settlement.

Where the parties amicably arrive at a settlement, an agreement setting out the terms of the settlement is drawn up and signed by the parties or by their representatives. It is highly recommended that the agreed terms of the settlement are to be in writing, and this is consonant with the provision of the Qur'an, where Allah (SWT) proclaims: "O ye who believe, when ye deal with each other in transaction involving future obligations in a fixed period of time reduce them to writing. Let a scribe write down faithfully as between the parties; let not the scribe refuse to write: as Allah has taught him. So let him write. Let him who incurs the liability dictate but let him fear His Lord and not diminish aught of what he owes. If the party liable is mentally deficient, or weak, or unable himself to dictate, let his guardian dictate faithfully and get two witnesses out of your own men and if there are not two men, then a man and two women such as ye choose for witnesses so that if one of them errs the other can remind her."[20]

The legal effect of the agreed settlement is that it shall bind the parties, and any decision recorded in the agreement becomes part of the contract. Muslims are obliged through the Qur'anic injunction to fulfil all of their obligations. As Allah (SWT) proclaims: "O you who believe, fulfil all obligations."[21] To ensure the agreed settlement is valid and enforceable, the parties to the agreed settlement must be in a state of consciousness and qualified to sign the contract. Anything done by a person who is mature, sane, and *mukallaf* (free), is binding on him, and he is responsible for all his actions.

19 *Sahih al-Bukhari* (Vol. 3), English Translation by Dr. Muhammad Muhsin Khan (1986), para 869.
20 *Surah Al-Baqarah* (2): Verse 282.
21 *Surah Al-Maidah* (5): Verse 1.

It is worth mentioning that, in Malaysia, for civil matters, the applicable conciliation in the Federal Territories Syariah Court is governed by the Syariah Court Civil Procedure (Federal Territories) Act 1998, section 247(1)(c) with the procedure contained in the Syariah Court Civil Procedure (*Sulh*) (Federal Territories) Rules 2004.[22]

13.6 Arbitration in Islam

In relation to marital disputes, they are excluded from being subjected to *sulh* under rule 1(3) of the Syariah Court Civil Procedure (*Sulh*) (Federal Territories) Rules 2004 Rules. The reason for the exclusion is that in a divorce situation, the Qur'an sanctions the institution of *hakam* (arbitration), where arbiters, one from each side, should be appointed to find the settlement of such dispute. Allah (SWT) proclaims: "If you fear a break between them two, appoint (two) arbiters, one from his family and the other from hers; if they wish for peace, Allah will cause them reconciliation: for Allah has full knowledge and is acquainted with all things."[23] This is now reflected in section 47(5) of the Islamic Family Law (Federal Territories) Act 1984. It provides *inter alia*, that in the event that one party does not consent to the divorce a reconciliation effort through a third party, usually an officer from the religious department, should be resorted. The court shall, where possible, give preference to close relatives of the parties having knowledge of the circumstances of the case. The main function of the conciliatory committee is to reconcile matrimonial disputes of the parties with the aim that they may resume cohabitation.

Aside from the above, the practices of *tahkim* by the Prophet Mohammad (peace be upon him) can be seen in relation to the dispute involving the replacement of *hajar al-aswad* (the Black Stone) after the rebuilding of the *Ka'ba*. As per the agreement of the disputing tribe in Mecca then, it was agreed that the first person to enter the premises was entrusted with the above task. Prophet Mohammad (peace be upon him) happened to be the first person to enter the mosque. In resolving the dispute, the Prophet Mohammad (peace be upon him) requested for a cloak to be laid in the middle of the circle of the representatives of the disputing clans, and the Black Stone was placed on it. The Prophet Mohammad (peace be upon him) invited all the disputants to raise the cloak to an appropriate level near the actual place. He then took the Black Stone and laid it in its rightful place. The conduct and

---

22 Similar rules are also enforced in other States such as for Selangor – the Syariah Court Civil Procedure (*Sulh*) (Selangor) Rules 2001; for Melaka – the Syariah Court Civil Procedure (*Sulh*) Rules 2004; for Johor – the Syariah Court Civil Procedure (*Sulh*) Rules 2004; and for Penang – the Syariah Court Civil Procedure (*Sulh*) (State of Penang) Rules 2006, among others.

23 *Surah An- Nisa* (4): Verse 35. The procedure involving arbitration by *hakam* in marital disputes is provided in section 48 of the Islamic Family Law (Federal Territories) Act 1984.

decision of the Prophet Mohammad (peace be upon him) were acceptable to all the disputants as it resulted in a win-win outcome.

Reverting back to matrimonial dispute, the arbitration by *hakam*, which has the authority to dissolve the marriage, is contained in section 48 of the Islamic Family Law (Federal Territories) Act 1984, which provides that:

(1) If satisfied that there are constant quarrels (*shiqaq*) between the parties to a marriage, the Court may appoint in accordance with Hukum Syarak two arbitrators or *Hakam* to act for the husband and wife respectively.
(2) In appointing the *Hakam* under subsection (1), the Court shall, where possible, give preference to close relatives of the parties having knowledge of the circumstances of the case.
(3) The Court may give directions to the *Hakam* as to the conduct of the arbitration and they shall conduct it in accordance with such directions and Hukum Syarak.
(4) If the *Hakam* are unable to agree, or if the Court is not satisfied with their conduct of the arbitration, the Court may remove them and appoint other *Hakam* in their place.
(5) The *Hakam* shall endeavour to obtain from their respective principals full authority, and may, if their authority extends so far, pronounce on *talaq* before the Court if so permitted by the Court, and in that event the Court shall record that pronouncement of one *talaq*, and send a certified copy of the record to the appropriate Registrar and to the Chief Registrar for registration.
(6) If the *Hakam* are of the opinion that the parties should be divorced but are unable for any reason to order a divorce, the Court shall appoint other *Hakam* and shall confer on them authority to order a divorce and shall, if they do so, record the order and send a certified copy of the record to the appropriate Registrar and to the Chief Registrar for registration.
(7) Unless he is a close member of the family of the parties, no person or *Peguam Syarie* shall be allowed to be present or represent any of the parties in the presence of the *Hakam*.

It is worthwhile noting that under the original Shafii law, the *hakam* are arbitrators and may only act as agents for the parties. However under the Maliki School, they can become independent and have the authority to order a divorce, as provided in sub-section (6) above.[24] Further, the *hakam* must immediately address the issues before there is a further breakdown of the relationship. They should encourage the parties to discuss their concerns and consider options for resolving their conflicts.

24 *See Che Pa v Siti Rahmah* [1976] 2 JH 244, [1982] 3 LNS 4, [1982] SYA 24; *Talib bin Salleh v Che Sepiah* [1979] 1 JH (1) 84; *Nerat Musa v Ahmad Kanchil* [1965] 3 JH 101, [1983] 3 LNS 13, [1983] SYA 213; *Abdul Razak v Siti Jarnah* [1988] 7 JH 84.

This often improves relationships and/or keeps the conflict out of the court system, and this is the probable reason why *Peguam Syarie* (Shari'ah lawyer) is not allowed to be present or represent any of the parties in the presence of the *hakam*.

13.7 Conclusion

The adversarial nature of dispute resolution in the court has led to the continuous search for the extra-judicial ways of dispute resolution, which include negotiation, mediation, conciliation, and arbitration. The ADR mechanisms have now become the practice in civil cases where the trial judge may, with the consent of litigants, order mediation. This mechanism allowed the parties, with the assistance and guidance of the court, to suggest and adopt ways and means to justly, expeditiously, and economically dispose of the case.

Similarly, the non-adjudicatory process of dispute settlement is also commended in Islam. In fact, the non-adjudicatory process of resolving disputes is divinely commanded where the Qur'an and *Sunnah* mentioned *sulh* and *tahkim* processes. It was even affirmed by Umar Ibn Khattab, the second Caliph, when he said: "Avoid as much as possible going to court and settle your disputes by way of *Sulh* for compulsory judgment of a court may create enmity among you."[25]

Just like in the convention system, the objective of the ADR in Shari'ah is to ensure that such disputes are resolved quickly and amicably with a view to ensuring that the dispute does not escalate to the destruction of relations, life, and wealth.[26] *Sulh* is now integrated into the Shari'ah Court system and is primarily intended to help the disputants to find mutually acceptable solutions. It is reiterated that litigation of disputes in the ordinary courts of law and the Shari'ah Courts are associated with disadvantages such as high costs, delays, legal acrobatics, endless frustration or mischief, bad publicity, and acrimony.

That is not so in the ADR mechanisms where as noted earlier, the advantages of resolving disputes by the ADR mechanisms include that it is non-adversarial, the disputing parties are involved in the decision-making, the dispute is resolved amicably, there is no application of complexities of procedural laws, cases can be resolved in a flexible manner, for example, a negotiator can talk separately, bring parties to negotiate face-to-face or talk to them on various electronic modes of communication, the decisions are to the satisfaction of parties as disputing parties may mutually explore and choose from various options. In fact, options are never imposed on any of the

25 Quoted in Sabiq, S., *Fiqhus-Sunnah* (Vol. 3), (Beruit: Shar'iyyatul-Sabi'ah Publishers,1980): 375.
26 Haroon, I.A., "The Use of Alternative Dispute Resolution (*Sulh*) in Sharia Cases," Paper Presented at the National Workshop for Area/Sharia/Customary Court Judges/Directors and Inspectors of Area/Sharia/Customary Courts, 3–5 April 2017.

parties, for example, in family mediation where parties are themselves family members. The success rate is better and more sustainable than any other means of dispute resolution.

When consensus fails, arbitration would be the preferred choice. A third party has to come in as an arbitrator on mutual consent basis to resolve the dispute. It is also worthwhile adding that in Islam, the conciliator and arbitrator are always subject to Allah's command to be just and fair in the decision-making process. As the Qur'an proclaims: "Allah doth command you to render back your Trusts to those to whom they are due; And when ye judge between man and man that ye judge with justice; verily how excellent is the teaching which He giveth you! For Allah is He who hearth and seeth all things."[27]

27 *Surah Al Nisa* (4): Verse 58.

Julio C. Colón

14 Muslims in the US and State Involvement in Religion

14.1 Introduction

The early history of Muslims in the United States (US) began long before the signing of the Declaration of Independence. For example, Muslims were among the slaves brought to the US from Africa.[1] Years later, the first mosque in the US was built in 1893 in Chicago, and though it was included as part of World's Columbian Exhibition, other purpose-built mosques would be built in the next several decades in various other US cities.[2] Despite the small influence that early Muslims in the US had, prominent political figures corresponded with Muslims outside of the country. For example, in 1777, Morocco was the first country to recognise the US as a sovereign nation by order of Sultan Mohammed III, and the two nations signed the Peace and Friendship Treaty of 1786.[3] Business transactions with Muslim entities stretch back nearly as long. In fact, Winchester, a US firearms manufacturer, supplied the Ottoman military under Sultan Abdul Hamid II with 50,000 lever-action repeating rifles during the 1877 Russo-Turkish War.[4] Lastly, various prominent US citizens had at least basic knowledge of the religion of Islam. Examples include Thomas Jefferson, who possessed an English translation of the Qur'an in his personal library,[5] and Mohammed Alexander Russell Webb, a prominent 19th century convert to Islam, the US consul to the Philippines, and Honorary Turkish Consul in New York.[6]

While interesting historical notes, none of these interactions implicated the courts. For that to happen, two phenomena had to develop – the growth of Muslim communities within the country and the surge of capital invested in cross-border

1 Michael A. Gomez, "Muslims in Early America," *The Journal of Southern History* 60, no. 4 (1994): 671.

2 Jennifer Williams, "A Brief History of Islam in America," *Vox*, Jan. 29, 2017, https://www.vox.com/2015/12/22/10645956/islam-in-america.

3 "U.S. Relations with Morocco," Nov. 5, 2020, US Dept. of State, https://www.state.gov/u-s-relations-with-morocco/.

4 Richard Trenk, "The Plevna Delay: Winchesters and Peabody-Martinis in the Russo-Turkish War," *Man At Arms* 19, no. 4 (August 1997): 29–36.

5 Denise A. Spellberg, *Thomas Jefferson's Qur'an: Islam and the Founders* (New York: Vintage, 2013).

6 Mohammed Alexander Russell Webb, *Islam in America: A Brief Statement of Mohammedanism and an Outline of the American Islamic Propaganda* (New York: Oriental Publishing Company, 1893).

https://doi.org/10.1515/9783110766707-014

transactions.[7] These two developments are at the inception of nearly every single court opinion and article cited in this chapter. As for the growth of Muslim communities in the US, disputes involving divorce, employee/employer relations, business dealings, and probate began to appear in courts as local Muslim communities developed. Regarding cross-border transactions, Muslim capital in the form of Shari'ah-compliant banks, funds, and partnerships investing in businesses in the US raised other questions, such as those involving matters of civil and contractual terms native to Shari'ah-influenced jurisdictions.[8] Terms such as *riba*, *gharar*, and *musharaka* have all appeared in decisions published by US courts presiding in cases involving cross-border transactions.[9]

Generally, commentators have to date focused on the processes and outcomes of these cases because for practitioners, pragmatic knowledge of Shari'ah-related concepts is required to draft contracts, advise clients, or even mediate disputes. That stated, the boundaries of US law pertaining to the adjudication of such disputes deserve more attention. The courts are bound by the US Constitution ("Constitution"), and with regard to the matters covered in this chapter, the First Amendment of the Constitution ("First Amendment"). The jurisprudence in this field of law is what marks the borders of when and how courts can entertain cases implicating Shari'ah-related legal concepts. So, rather than inquire how did the courts decide a case, the question is, why did the courts decide a case in light of First Amendment law, and how did that influence the result? As a practical matter, it is an important question to understand in order to advise clients seeking Shari'ah-compliant legal instruments in both personal and business matters, as well as during litigation.

This chapter begins with a brief overview of First Amendment law as it relates to religious matters in courtrooms. Then, several types of cases are discussed as they often raise First Amendment issues within the context of disputes involving Muslim litigants. These cases deal with religious institutions, contractual disputes, and personal litigation between two parties sharing the same religious background. Next, various cases are analysed with regard to how the court confronts making judgments in religious matters, what US legal concepts are employed in resolving the underlying dispute, and how this affects the intention of the parties. Lastly, the chapter takes the information presented and draws conclusions on why Shari'ah-

---

7 "Muslim Immigration After 1965," last accessed February 21, 2022, Carleton College, https://religionsmn.carleton.edu/exhibits/show/history-muslims/immigration-after-1965, and Dr. Majid Al-Moneef, "The Contribution of the Oil Sector to Arab Economic Development," *Ofid Pamphlet Series*, no. 34 (May 2006).

8 Term adapted from João Ribeiro and Jin Lee, "Overview of UNCITRAL Texts on International Commercial Arbitration in Islamic Law Influenced Jurisdictions (ILIJ)," *VUWLR* 46 (2015): 139.

9 Some of the earliest US legal scholarship mentioning the Shari'ah was written with regard to doing business internationally. *See* Jeanne Asherman, "Doing Business in Saudi Arabia: The Contemporary Application of Islamic Law," *The International Lawyer* 16, no. 5 (1982): 321.

related issues continue to appear in US courts and the reasons jurisdiction has or has not been limited by First Amendment principles.

14.2 The First Amendment and Religion: Background, Major Inflection Points, and Current State of the Law

The first ten amendments to the Constitution ratified by the US Congress in 1791 are known as the Bill of Rights. The First Amendment of the Bill of Rights states: "Congress shall make no law respecting an establishment of religion, or prohibiting the free exercise thereof; or abridging the freedom of speech, or of the press; or the right of the people peaceably to assemble, and to petition the Government for a redress of grievances."[10] The first two provisions are important to understand for the purposes of this chapter. They are known as the Establishment Clause and the Free Exercise Clause, respectively.[11]

At its inception, the premise of the law was to prevent the government from adopting an official religion or advancing a particular religion on behalf of the nation.[12] This motivation is generally understood as illustrated by the quote attributed to President Thomas Jefferson in his letter to Danbury Baptist Association of Connecticut, "[. . . T]heir legislature should make no law respecting an establishment of religion, or prohibiting the free exercise thereof thus building a wall of separation between Church & State."[13]

Soon enough, the courts would hear cases brought from individuals asserting the First Amendment as a protection for their personal rights. For example, in 1878, in *Reynolds v. United States*, the Supreme Court ("the Court") upheld a federal law that banned polygamy, ruling that the First Amendment forbids the government from regulating belief but not actions such as marriage.[14] Incidental intrusions on individual

---

10 US Constitution Amend. 1.

11 Jesse H. Choper, "The Religion Clauses of the First Amendment: Reconciling the Conflict," *U. Pitt. L. Rev.* 41 (1979): 673, 673–674.

12 For a historical understanding of how colonial American governments treated religion, *see* for example Arlin M. Adams and Charles J. Emmerich, "Heritage of Religious Liberty," *U. Pa. L. Rev. 137* (1988): 1562 ("The famous Lawes Divine, Moral and Martial (1610–11), the first English legal code in the New World, required daily church attendance and imposed harsh penalties for blasphemy, Sabbath-breaking, and speaking maliciously against the Trinity, God's holy word, or Christian doctrine.").

13 Daniel L. Driesbach and John D. Whaley, "What the Wall Separates: A Debate on Thomas Jefferson's Wall of Separation Metaphor," Const. Comment. 16 (1999): 627.

14 Reynolds v. United States, 98 US 145 (1878).

religious liberty continued to stand as lawful in the US. In 1961, the Court in *Braunfeld v. Brown* upheld to Orthodox Jewish business owners the application of a Pennsylvania law requiring the closure of all stores on Sunday.[15] This decision was in spite of the disadvantage they suffered from also having to close their stores on Saturday due to their religious convictions.[16] In making its decision, the Court ruled in favour of the state because the law was not intended to impede the practice of religion.[17]

In 1963 in *Sherbert v. Verner*, the Court examined the constitutionality of the denial of state unemployment benefits to a worker that was required to work on Saturdays, which was against her religious convictions.[18] In that case, Adell Sherbert, a Seventh Day Adventist, refused to work on Saturdays at her job at a textile mill in response to a change in schedule by the employer.[19] The state subsequently denied her unemployment benefits because it found that in quitting her job, Sherbert had denied suitable work when offered.[20] Upon deciding the case, the Court applied a stricter standard which required that a state policy that infringes on the practice of religion be solely in response to a compelling government interest.[21] In doing so, the state would also have to show that no alternative means were available to achieve said interest before it infringed on religious practice.[22]

These cases were foundational interpretations of the limits of the right to free exercise of religion and its protection under the First Amendment. With regard to the Establishment Clause, in 1971, the Court in *Lemon v. Kurtzman* struck down a Pennsylvania law that allowed the state to reimburse Catholic schools for the salaries of their teachers.[23] In doing so, the Court determined that in order for a law to remain consistent with the Establishment Clause 1) the statute must have a secular legislative purpose; 2) the primary effect of the statute must not advance or inhibit religion; and 3) the statute must not result in an "excessive government entanglement" with religion.[24] Known as the Lemon Test, this reasoning has been called into question by the court on various occasions without explicitly being overruled, and it remains the primary mechanism by which lower courts judge Establishment Clause cases.[25]

---

15 Braunfeld v. Brown, 366 US 599 (1961).
16 *Braunfeld*, 366 US 599.
17 *Braunfeld*, 366 US at 607.
18 Sherbert v. Verner, 374 US 398, 399 (1963).
19 *Sherbert*, 374 US at 399–402.
20 *Sherbert*, 374 US at 399–402.
21 *Sherbert*, 374 US at 407–408.
22 *Sherbert*, 374 US at 407–408.
23 Lemon v. Kurtzman, 403 US 602 (1971).
24 *Lemon*, 403 US at 612–613.
25 For one recent criticism of the Lemon Test, *see* Charles Adside III, "The Establishment Clause Forbids Coercion, Not Cooperation, between Church and State: How the Direct Coercion Test Should Replace the Lemon Test," *NDL Rev.* 95 (2020): 533.

In 1990, the Court seemed to take a step back from its decision in *Sherbert v. Verner* concerning the free practice of religion in *Employment Division v. Smith.*[26] Once again, the appellants protested the state's denial of unemployment compensation, this time on the basis of "misconduct," as appellants were terminated from their employment due to ingesting the hallucinogen peyote.[27] However, the use of peyote was part of a ritual conducted by the Native American Church, of which appellants were members.[28] The Court decided that the Free Exercise Clause of the First Amendment was not violated because "an individual's religious beliefs" do not "excuse him from compliance with an otherwise valid law prohibiting conduct the State is free to regulate."[29]

While called into question at times,[30] the Court has not made a new ruling with regard to such cases. For example, in 2021, in *Fulton v. Philadelphia*, the city of Philadelphia ceased to contract with the company Catholic Social Services for the provision of foster care services because it would not certify same-sex couples as foster parents.[31] Because the law forced Catholic Social Services to either stop providing services or violate its religious beliefs by certifying same-sex couples, this was found to be a burden on its religious practice.[32] While this law appeared on its face to apply generally across the population, the Court decided that it was not a situation in which religious practice would have to give way to compliance with an otherwise valid law because the statute gave expansive powers to grant exemptions to the city's Commissioner of the Department of Human Services.[33] As such, it was deemed not to be generally applicable and hence was judged under a stricter standard than in *Employment Division v. Smith.*[34] Therefore, the Court required a finding that the law served a compelling interest and showed itself to be narrowly tailored to achieve that interest.[35]

The above cases all concern either legislative (as in *Braunfeld v. Brown*) or executive action (such as in *Fulton v. Philadelphia*). However, what is a US court's process when confronted regarding its own authority to preside over cases in which its decisions will implicate religious rights protected by the First Amendment? More specifically, how will courts handle situations which involve religious schism or doctrinal issues?

---

26 Employment Division, Department of Human Resources of Oregon v. Smith, 494 US 872 (1990).
27 *Smith*, 494 US at 874.
28 *Smith*, 494 US at 874.
29 *Smith*, 494 US at 879.
30 *See* Gary J. Simson, "The Uncertain Good of Overruling Employment Division v. Smith," *Canopy Forum on the Interactions Between Law and Religion, Emory University Center for the Study of Law and Religion* (October 2020).
31 Fulton v. Philadelphia, 141 S.Ct. 1868, 1874 (2021).
32 *Fulton*, 141 S.Ct. at 1876.
33 *Fulton*, 141 S.Ct. at 1882.
34 *Fulton*, 141 S.Ct. at 1882.
35 *Fulton*, 141 S.Ct. at 1882.

Regarding the judicial resolution of disputes implicating religion, the Court adopted two important principles – government neutrality in religious disputes and application of neutral principles of law. As for government neutrality in religious disputes, this principle was described in *Serbian Eastern Orthodox Diocese v. Milivojevich,* a case in which the Court was called upon to determine the true leadership of a church after a schism occurred which called its rightful governance into question.[36] The appellate court, in that case, determined that the process by which church authorities made a legal determination as to which bishop was legitimate, and hence the trustee who would control various properties located in the state, was invalid according to the very regulations of the church.[37] The Court overruled the decision, holding that the ruling of a hierarchical church authority in a matter of its religion is, in fact, part of the free practice of religion afforded by the First Amendment.[38] This principle has been applied to various civil cases involving transactions between Muslims. For example, in *El-Farra v. Sayyed,* an imam sued an Islamic center for terminating his contract after having been warned by the committee for causing "disunity and 'fitna' among the community," among other things.[39] Upon review, the Supreme Court of Arkansas affirmed the lower court's dismissal of the case due to a lack of subject matter jurisdiction.[40] It applied the principle of neutrality in religious disputes and refused to become involved in what otherwise was a cognisable employment claim.[41] Citing to *Serbian Eastern Orthodox Diocese, the court wrote,* "The United States Supreme Court, applying the First Amendment, has held that civil courts are not a constitutionally permissible forum for a review of ecclesiastical disputes."[42]

Regarding the application of neutral principles of law – the courts view it in the public interest for courts to be available to resolve disputes.[43] In cases in which a hierarchical church has made a dispute regarding matters dealt with by state laws, the Court has ruled that it may apply neutral principles of law in those cases because the religious institution would have had notice regarding the necessary steps to fulfil its intention under the prevailing law.[44] This principle was formed in *Jones v. Wolf,* a case in which the Court affirmed the state of Georgia's use of the neutral principles of law doctrine in order to adjudicate church property disputes. This entailed using state law and hearing evidence to determine whether there was a trust created and then granting the property to the general church if there was indeed a trust.[45] And, if

36 Serbian Eastern Orthodox Diocese v. Milivojevich, 426 US 696 (1976).
37 *Serbian Eastern Orthodox Diocese*, 426 US at 698.
38 *Serbian Eastern Orthodox Diocese*, 426 US at 722.
39 El-Farra v.Sayyed, 226 SW3d 792, 793 (2006).
40 *El-Farra*, 226 SW3d at 793.
41 *El-Farra* 226 SW3d at 794.
42 *El-Farra*, 226 SW3d at 794.
43 Jones v. Wolf, 443 US 595, 602 (1979).
44 *Jones*, 443 US at 602–603.
45 *Jones*, 443 US 595 at 600.

it was found that no such trust existed, then property ownership was determined on the basis of legal title – even though the result was that courts could occasionally rule against the decision of a governing religious body.[46] Reconciling this with *Serbian Eastern Orthodox Diocese*, the Court pointed out that Georgia law provided that if a property was obtained by a trustee, then the deed of that property needed to stipulate how the property would transfer in case of schism.[47] Thus, Georgia law did indeed provide a means by which church disputes could be resolved under the dictates of their religion.[48] Yet, despite these provisions, the deed in question made no such stipulation, hence it was not the state's action that caused any perceived interference in the free practice of religion.[49] A similar application of the principle can be seen in *Seifeddine v. Jaber*, regarding the enforcement of a *mahr*, or dowry gifted to the wife as part of a Muslim marriage.[50] In that case, the husband argued regarding the court's awarding of the mahr that the "trial court erred by enforcing [. . .] because the Legislature has not prescribed a method to resolve religious issues."[51] The court upheld the decision, citing *Jones v. Wolf* that "a civil court may review religious documents if the court applies neutral principles of law" and noting that "the trial court applied Michigan common law regarding contracts and determined that each of the elements for establishing a valid contract was met."[52]

Must courts resort to these principles more often in the way of resolving disputes involving one or more Muslim parties? In principle, of course, the faith background of the participants is a non-issue, though the reality is that such matters can colour the litigation either in its inception or by argumentation on the part of counsel.[53] That stated, when religious issues are raised, the scope of the court's authority to decide on the issue is guided by the aforementioned principles. These will lead the court to either not exercise jurisdiction, judge the matter according to the prevailing law, or judge the matter while delving into religious doctrine. Typically, such cases fall into several broad factual categorisations, which are 1) disputes involving an institution; 2) cases that require the court to apply the law from a Shari'ah-influenced jurisdiction; 3) cases that implicate religious principles due to the

46 *Jones*, 443 US 595 at 600.
47 *Jones*, 443 US 595 at 603–605.
48 *Jones*, 443 US 595 at 606.
49 *Jones*, 443 US 595 at 606.
50 Seifeddine v. Jaber, 934 NW 2d 64, 69 (Mich. Court of Appeals 2019).
51 *Seifeddine*, 934 NW 2d at 69.
52 *Seifeddine*, 934 NW 2d at 67–69.
53 This is essentially what occured in *Shamil Bank v. Beximco*, and it was not lost upon the court, apparently. *See Shamil Bank of Bahrain EC v. Beximco Pharm. Ltd.*, [2004] EWCA (Civ) 19, [1] at para. 10, [2004] 1 W.L.R. 1784 (appeal taken from Eng.) ("Until their defences were filed in this action, the appellants had never given any indication to the bank that they were dissatisfied on religious grounds with the arrangements agreed between the parties or that they sought to challenge them on the grounds that they did not comply with the principles of Sharia.").

identity of the parties themselves; and 4) cases in which the free practice of religion is itself in conflict with the law or policy of the US.

14.3 Religious Inquiry: Four Types of Disputes

14.3.1 Disputes Involving Institutions

As can be gathered from the discussion so far, the courts may be required to give deference to the decisions of hierarchical churches. However, this principle is in practice broader than the literal meaning of the phrase "hierarchical church." After all, various churches in the US are local to their specific congregants and not aligned with a larger institution, as opposed to the organisation of parochial churches such as the Catholic Church or the various orthodox churches. This situation is similar for Muslims in the US, given that there is no sanctioned legal authority regarding religious practice, such as the *mufti* of a country that makes official religious recommendations to the citizens of Muslim-majority countries.[54] Therefore, in the US, few mosques are affiliated with an official religious ministry. In these cases, the court looks at the nature of the transaction to understand whether there is a sufficient connection to the propagation of religion in order to decide whether to defer to the institution's judgment.

Accordingly, issues regarding faith and doctrine are considered part of the governance of religious institutions, even at the level of singular congregations. For this reason, courts will not take jurisdiction over legal disputes that are on the bare facts justiciable according to the neutral principles doctrine if the matter involves the carrying on of the religious mission of the institution. This class of cases will tend towards government neutrality in otherwise justiciable contract disputes involving the employment of individuals for the institution's ministry.[55] Recently, in *Our Lady of Guadalupe Sch. v. Agnes Morrissey-Berru*, the Court tested this principle in a case in which it overruled the appellate court, deciding to apply the "ministerial exception" to teachers at a Catholic school.[56] This exception prevented the teachers from pursuing discrimination claims against their former employer, as the Court noted the key roles they fulfilled in the church's mission.[57]

---

54 "[A] muftī, a Muslim jurist who issues an expert legal opinion in response to a question or writes a legal opinion on a subject that he considers significant." Muhammad Khalid Masud, "Adab al-muftī," in *Encyclopaedia of Islam, THREE*, eds. Kate Fleet, Gudrun Krämer, Denis Matringe, John Nawas, Everett Rowson (Brill, 2008), http://dx.doi.org/10.1163/1573-3912_ei3_COM_26301.

55 Hosanna-Tabor Evangelical Lutheran Church and School v. EEOC, 565 US 171, 186 (2012).

56 Our Lady of Guadalupe Sch. v. Agnes Morrissey-Berru, 140 S. Ct. 2049 (2020).

57 *Our Lady of Guadalupe Sch.*, 140 S. Ct. 2049.

Compare the principle described above with the decision in *National Group for Communications & Computers v. Lucent Technologies*, another case alleging breach of contract but for which the court cited actual primary sources of Shari'ah in making its decision.[58] The case in *Our Lady of Guadalupe Sch. v. Agnes Morrissey-Berru*, did not require analysis of religious texts, and neither party in *National Group for Communications & Computers v. Lucent Technologies* represented a religious institution. However, the employment contract in *Our Lady of Guadalupe Sch. v. Agnes Morrissey-Berru* was between an individual and a religious institution and involved at a basic level the propagation of religion. On the other hand, in *National Group for Communications & Computers v. Lucent Technologies* the reading of Islamic source material was only necessary for the purpose of interpreting the terms of a normal transaction for services.

14.3.2 Governing Law

Many nations incorporate Shari'ah principles into their legal systems to varying extents.[59] As such, occasionally, a matter will arise in US courts that requires the analysis and perhaps even the application of Shari'ah principles. Generally, this may occur in three situations. The first takes place when a contract that is the subject of dispute contains within it a reference to a specific Shari'ah principle. For example, in *In Re East Cameron Partners, L.P.*, a complex oil and gas financing arrangement was structured as a *sukuk*.[60] In that case, a party to the agreement and the original owner of the royalty interests which underlined the *sukuk* argued that the court should treat the *sukuk* as a mere loan.[61] The court ultimately denied this argument and ruled on that issue in favour of the *sukuk*-holders.[62] This decision was possibly based on the sukuk-holders' argument that by asking the court to recharacterise the *sukuk* as a loan, the petitioners failed to state a claim because they did not describe the details of the alleged loan agreement.[63]

The second situation which may require an analysis of Shari'ah principles in US courts is when the parties to an agreement select that the law of a Shari'ah-

58 Nat'l Grp. for Commc'ns & Computers v. Lucent Techs. Int'l, 331 F. Supp. 2d 290, 293–301 (D.N.J 2004).

59 Julio C. Colón, "Choice of Law and Islamic Finance," *Texas International Law Journal* 46, no. 2 (Spring 2011): 412, 418.

60 Julio C. Colón, "Settlement of Islamic Finance Disputes in the United States of America," in *Dispute Resolution in Islamic Finance: Alternatives to Litigation?*, eds. Adnan Trakic, John Benson, and Pervaiz K. Ahmed (New York: Routledge, 2019), 82 (citing to memoranda filed in support of parties' pretrial motions).

61 Colón, "Settlement of Islamic Finance Disputes in the United States of America," 82–85.

62 Colón, "Settlement of Islamic Finance Disputes in the United States of America," 82–85.

63 Colón, "Settlement of Islamic Finance Disputes in the United States of America," 82–85.

influenced jurisdiction should govern the contract. For example, in *National Group for Communications & Computers v. Lucent Technologies*, the trial court determined that the contract to a major telecommunications project was governed by Saudi Arabian law.[64] In doing so, the court made findings that designated the "Qur'an, the Sunnah, and fiqh" as the primary legal sources in Saudi Arabia and Hanbali fiqh as controlling.[65] Then, it determined based on its findings that expectation damages as requested by the plaintiff fell under the legal prohibition of *gharar*.[66]

Lastly, courts may also find themselves analysing Shari'ah principles on the basis of comity, in which courts will generally give deference to the decisions of foreign courts out of mutual respect rather than obligation.[67] For example, in *Elahham v. Al-Jabban*, evidence of the plaintiff's remarriage was at issue.[68] The court understood that there was a strong case that plaintiff was remarried under Shari'ah law in Egypt, and although "Michigan courts recognize marriages solemnized in foreign nations as a matter of comity," expert testimony suggested that further steps needed to be taken in order to solemnise the marriage under Egyptian law.[69]

As can be seen from the previous examples, religious principles can be implicated in a case, even blatantly quoted, and the court will typically exercise jurisdiction and possibly even analyse the religious texts themselves, often in the light of expert testimony. However, what is necessary is that the matter at hand must deal with issues judicable under prevailing laws while not implicating the mission of religious institutions.

14.3.3 Religious Identity of Opposing Parties

Occasionally, cases arise in which there is no religious institution involved, nor does the choice of law implicate Shari'ah or concepts from Islamic jurisprudence, but due to the religious and cultural background of the parties, religious issues arise before the court. These cases typically involve personal controversies, such as divorce and inheritance. Courts generally resolve disputes in such cases by first determining whether there is jurisdiction to hear the case, and settling the dispute according to the procedure and laws in the jurisdiction of the presiding court.

For example, in *Falah v. Falah*, a court in the US state of Ohio had to decide whether a divorce obtained in a Shari'ah court was valid.[70] The couple originally

---

64 *Nat'l Grp. for Commc'ns & Computers*, 331 F. Supp. 2d at 293–301.
65 *Nat'l Grp. for Commc'ns & Computers*, 331 F. Supp. 2d at 293–301.
66 *Nat'l Grp. for Commc'ns & Computers*, 331 F. Supp. 2d at 293–301.
67 *Black's Law Dictionary*, 6th Edition, s.v. "comity."
68 Elahham v. Al-Jabban, 899 NW 2d 768 (Mich. Court of Appeals 2017).
69 *Elahham*, 899 NW 2d at 784–786.
70 Falah v. Falah, 87 NE 3d 763 (Ohio Court of Appeals, 9th Appellate Dist. 2017).

married in Israel and later moved to the US.[71] In 2013, the couple decided to divorce, and while both parties were in Israel, the husband filed for divorce.[72] After initially refusing service, the wife eventually obtained an attorney in Israel, and the couple obtained a divorce in a Shari'ah court, which was binding under Israeli law.[73] However, while the case was pending in Israel, the wife returned to Ohio and filed for divorce there.[74] In response, the husband filed a motion to dismiss the petition for divorce in Ohio for lack of jurisdiction.[75] The trial court denied the motion to dismiss, and although it accepted the existence of the Israeli divorce decree on the basis of comity, it still issued its own decree of divorce while including various other orders regarding property division and spousal support.[76] On appeal, the appellate court decided that the trial court was correct in exercising jurisdiction in the divorce because the wife had never abandoned her Ohio residency.[77] As for the issue of granting "comity" to the decision of the Shari'ah court, the appellate court viewed it as merely "additional evidence that the parties had decided to terminate their marriage and that Husband had already paid Wife a certain sum of money as a result of that decision [. . .]."[78]

Compare that case to *Jabri v. Qaddura*, a divorce case in the US state of Texas involving a Muslim couple.[79] With the advice of their respective counsels, the couple agreed to arbitration through a local arbitration committee according to "Islamic rules of law."[80] Following a disagreement concerning the scope of issues covered by the arbitration, the wife moved the trial court to stay proceedings and compel arbitration, which the court denied.[81] The appellate court reversed the denial of the motion by the trial court because under the prevailing law "arbitration of a particular grievance should not be denied unless it can be said with positive assurance that the arbitration clause is not susceptible of an interpretation that covers the asserted dispute."[82] Noting the language of the arbitration agreement that "[the parties] agree to submit *all claims and disputes among them* to arbitration" and the lack of language limiting the arbitration to certain issues, the appellate court ruled that it was an abuse of discretion to not stay litigation and compel arbitration.[83]

---

71 *Falah*, 87 NE 3d at 766.
72 *Falah*, 87 NE 3d at 766.
73 *Falah*, 87 NE 3d at 766.
74 *Falah*, 87 NE 3d at 766.
75 *Falah*, 87 NE 3d at 766.
76 *Falah*, 87 NE 3d at 766–767.
77 *Falah*, 87 NE 3d at 771–773.
78 *Falah*, 87 NE 3d at 771–773.
79 Jabri v. Qaddura, 108 S.W.3d 404, 407 (Tex. App. – Fort Worth 2003, no pet.).
80 *Jabri*, 108 S.W.3d at 408.
81 *Jabri*, 108 S.W.3d at 408–409.
82 *Jabri*, 108 S.W.3d at 411.
83 *Jabri*, 108 S.W.3d at 412–413.

Falah v. Falah and *Jabri v. Qaddura* both raised similar issues. Firstly, in each case, the parties consented to the jurisdiction of a forum, only to later attempt to move the divorce proceedings to the trial court. Secondly, both proceedings, at some point, were conducted in forums that operated according to the principles of Shari'ah.

Though quiet on the matter of the First Amendment, the decisions were both sound with regard to the First Amendment. Regarding government neutrality in religion, both cases involved single individuals rather than institutions with religious objectives. Though the marriages being dissolved did implicate religious principles at certain times in the proceedings, both disputes were entirely personal between two individuals. As in *Jones v. Wolf*, a notice of the law regarding the issue before the court allowed parties to resolve any matter according or not according to religious principles before availing themselves of the local court. In *Falah v. Falah*, this meant that parties were on notice regarding residency rules and the jurisdiction of the Ohio court. Thus, the court exercised jurisdiction in spite of the wife's original consent.[84] In *Jafari*, the court relied on local jurisprudence favouring arbitration, and the petitioner's original agreement to arbitrate was a deciding factor in that case.[85]

Finally, *Falah v. Falah* and *Jabri v. Qaddura* both are demonstrative of the neutral principles doctrine. In both cases, parties voluntarily placed themselves under the jurisdiction of the courts at some point and, at least in theory, could have utilised laws in place to effectuate their wishes before the actual divorces.

14.3.4 The Equality of All Parties Before the Law

The fourth type of case which will often require the court to consider First Amendment principles are cases in which the free practice of religion is itself in conflict with the law or policy of the US. The conflict behind these cases tends to be between the Free Exercise Clause and the neutral application of the law. Such is the law regarding the First Amendment that it does not always protect the free exercise of religion, and constitutionally permissible state actions have often inhibited religious practices – examples range from polygamy to the use of banned substances.[86]

The seminal case in this field of law is *Employment Division v. Smith*, which while criticised by legal scholars and legislatures, is still standing law.[87] In that case, two members of the Native American Church were fired from their job in the US state of Oregon for ingesting peyote, a hallucinogenic substance used as part of

---

84 *Falah*, 87 NE 3d at 771–773.

85 *Jabri*, 108 S.W.3d at 412–413.

86 *See* for example *Reynolds*, 98 US 145, in which the Court upheld a conviction for bigamy despite appellant's argument that he was required to marry multiple women on religious grounds.

87 *See* Simson, "The Uncertain Good of Overruling Employment Division v. Smith."

the church's religious rites.[88] Because possession of peyote was illegal in Oregon, the employees (the respondents in the case on appeal) were denied benefits by Employment Division as it was determined that they were fired for "misconduct."[89] The Oregon appellate court reversed that decision on the basis of "holding that the denial of benefits violated respondents' free exercise rights under the First Amendment."[90] However, when that decision was eventually reviewed by the Supreme Court, it decided that the First Amendment's Free Exercise Clause does not permit a person to disobey a generally applicable criminal law, even if it would require the violation of that person's religion.[91] The Court further elaborated that in the case of generally applicable law – one that does not itself lend to individual assessments – then the state is not held to the "compelling governmental interest" standard of lawmaking.[92] This would require the government to show that the law is essential to achieving a compelling governmental interest.[93]

Various cases have come before courts that require the court to sort out whether a generally applicable policy can be upheld in the face of religious practice.[94] For example, in *Bey v. Tennessee*, a Muslim prisoner sued the US state of Tennessee for disallowing the purchase of meals containing *halal* meat,[95] claiming an infringement of his free practice of religion.[96] In response, the court noted that previous decisions have already decided that the provision of *halal* meat is not a violation of the First Amendment so long as the Muslim prisoners are provided food that is not *haraam*.[97,98]

Thus, the courts will typically seek to leave government policies that affect everyone in place without granting specific accommodations, so long as the free practice of one's religion is not directly targeted.

---

88 Employment Division, Department of Human Resources of Oregon v. Smith, 494 US 872, 874 (1990).

89 *Smith*, 494 US at 874.

90 *Smith*, 494 US at 874.

91 *Smith*, 494 US at 883–884.

92 Smith, 494 US at 884–889.

93 *Smith*, 494 US at 884–889.

94 Bey v. Tennessee, No. 3:19-cv-00486 (M.D. Tenn. Feb. 12, 2020).

95 *Halal* is an Arabic term used by Muslims to denote something that is legally permissible. "Ḥalāl," in *Encyclopaedia of Islam, First Edition*, eds. M. Th. Houtsma, T.W. Arnold, R. Basset, R. Hartmann (Brill, 1913–1936), http://dx.doi.org/10.1163/2214-871X_ei1_SIM_2637.

96 *Bey*, No.: 2:15-cv-21-JRG-DHI at 5.

97 *Bey*, No.: 2:15-cv-21-JRG-DHI at 17 (citing to Robinson v. Jackson, 615 F. App'x 310, 313–14 (6th Cir. 2015).

98 *Haraam* is a term meaning impermissible, the opposite of *halal*. "Ḥalāl," *Encyclopaedia of Islam, First Edition.*

14.4 Islam in Common Law Courts: Specific Cases

Specifically, regarding cases involving Shari'ah, Islamic principles, or Muslim-specific issues in US courts, the facts regarding the cases are as varied as the experiences of the litigants themselves.

In *Seifeddine v. Jaber*, a First Amendment issue arose due to the religious background of the parties. In that case, the trial court enforced the provisions of a *mahr*[99] agreement upon divorce.[100] The plaintiff appealed, stating that the trial court did not apply "neutral principles of law in determining that the *mahr* provision in the parties' Islamic marriage certificate constituted a contract requiring plaintiff to pay $50,000 to defendant."[101] The appellate court acknowledged the First Amendment issue and cited *Jones v. Wolf*, stating:

> Civil courts may not decide religious doctrinal matters. [. . .] But [. . .] in the context of resolving a church property dispute, a civil court may review religious documents if the court applies neutral principles of law. [. . .] By applying neutral principles of law, civil courts avoid "entanglement in questions of religious doctrine, polity, and practice." [. . .] Therefore, when examining a religious document, "a civil court must take special care to scrutinize the document in purely secular terms, and not to rely on religious precepts [. . .]."[102]

The court proceeded to rule against the appellant, citing that various courts have concluded that "religious marital agreements may be examined when a court applies neutral [. . .] principles of law."[103] The court proceeded to note that "the relief sought by plaintiff in this action is simply to compel defendant to perform a secular obligation to which he contractually bound himself,"[104] and that this principle also applied specifically to *mahr* agreements.[105]

No facts, in this case, compelled the court to decide whether the parties could have a *mahr*. The court emphasised that it was applying neutral principles of law, and in this case, contract law. In fact, one could say that the court's decision is consistent with the Lemon Test in that it has a secular purpose, its principal or primary effect neither advances nor inhibits religion, and it does not result in excessive government entanglement with religion. However, the court noted that the appellant failed to make his argument in various respects.[106] One plausible argument that

99 In Islamic law, a *mahr* is "[a] gift of money or property that must be made by a man to the woman he marries." *Black's Law Dictionary 11th ed.*, ed. Bryan A. Garner (Thompson Reuters, 2019).
100 *Seifeddine*, 934 N.W.2d at 67.
101 *Seifeddine*, 934 N.W.2d at 67.
102 *Seifeddine*, 934 N.W.2d at 67.
103 *Seifeddine*, 934 N.W.2d at 68.
104 *Seifeddine*, 934 N.W.2d at 68–69.
105 *Seifeddine*, 934 N.W.2d at 68–69.
106 *Seifeddine*, 934 N.W.2d at 68. ("Plaintiff does not challenge any particular element establishing the existence of a contract. Nor does plaintiff cite any authority for his contention that a neutral

was not made was to emphasise that the exercise of neutral principles of law should have been outweighed by government neutrality in religious disputes. Because regardless of the ability of the court to neutrally apply state contract law, it was still, in essence, a religious dispute. In other words, because the appellant only set a *mahr* for religious purposes, and the appellee only accepted the *mahr* for religious purposes, the court effectively decided to enforce the dictates of their religion. After all, various contracts could be valid under the letter of the law; however, the court would refuse to exercise jurisdiction on the basis of the ministerial exception. Perhaps the prenuptial requirement of a *mahr* fulfils key roles of advancing religion in a similar way. On the other hand, an argument in favour of exercising jurisdiction is that the dispute is not schismatic, and all parties were on notice concerning Michigan law regarding marriage, divorce, and contracts.

Other US courts have also interpreted *mahr* agreements according to the local laws controlling contracts. In *Ali v. Syed*, the appellant argued that the trial court erred when it enforced a *mahr* upon a divorce on the basis that it constituted a valid simple contract under Michigan law.[107] Among other arguments, the appellant argued that because the *mahr* was made under Shari'ah rather than any state law, it was, therefore, a religious obligation rather than a contract under state law.[108] As such, his argument followed that "under the ecclesiastical abstention doctrine, the courts of the state of Michigan lack jurisdiction to enforce Islamic marriage contracts."[109] The court rejected this argument, essentially weighing in favour of the neutral principles of law doctrine against the government neutrality in religious disputes doctrine, stating "we are not interpreting or applying the contract between the parties under Shariah law, but are applying Michigan law to the review of the parties' contract [. . .]."[110] Once again, this distinction walks a fine line, and it is a dispute that could be decided either way by a trial court within the same framework of law. However, in cases in which both parties are individuals and avail themselves of a court for dispute resolution, there is a tendency for the court to favour neutral application of law, and the doctrine of government neutrality in religious disputes is reserved for the institutions set up to facilitate the practice of religion itself.

In fact, cases before *Our Lady of Guadalupe Sch. v. Agnes Morrissey-Berru* were decided by US state courts according to similar reasoning. For example, the Supreme Court of Arkansas ruled on whether or not the trial court correctly declined to exercise subject matter jurisdiction in the case of *El-Farra v. Sayyed*. In that case, the former imam of the Islamic Center of Little Rock ("the Center"), Monir Y. El-

---

principle of law must be derived from a statute rather than from Michigan common law when examining a religious document.").

107 Ali v. Syed, No. 342196 at 2 (Mich. Ct. App. Jan. 29, 2019).

108 *Ali*, No. 342196 at 4.

109 *Ali*, No. 342196 at 4.

110 *Ali*, No. 342196 at 4.

Farra, sued the Center and its executive committee.[111] El-Farra had previously been under contract to serve as the Center's imam.[112] As part of the agreement, the executive committee was able to end El-Farra's employment by unanimous vote on the grounds of "Islamic Jurisdiction (Shari'a)."[113] Throughout several months, El-Farra was warned by the Center's executive committee regarding the content of his sermons until he was placed on probation due to allegations of conduct that "contradicts the Islamic law."[114] He was eventually terminated and afterwards filed a lawsuit alleging defamation and breach of contract.[115] Lawyers for the defence responded with a motion for summary judgment, claiming that "the First Amendment to the United States Constitution [. . . prohibited] the circuit court from exercising jurisdiction in this case."[116] The trial court granted the motion and dismissed the case.[117] On appeal, plaintiff's lawyers contended that his breach of contract claim did not involve "matters related to Islamic doctrine, but only interpersonal matters concerning his relationship with the Executive Committee."[118] Therefore, his argument followed that in view of the fact that he was seeking damages rather than reinstatement, "his claim is purely secular, does not involve the court in selection of a minister."[119] The appellate court disagreed, however, and cited several US Supreme Court and various appellate court rulings; including the United States Supreme Court ruling in *Serbian Eastern Orthodox Diocese v. Milivojevich*, which applied the First Amendment and "held that civil courts are not a constitutionally permissible forum for a review of ecclesiastical disputes."[120] In arriving at its decision, the Arkansas Supreme Court referred extensively to *Kaufmann v. Sheehan*:

> [. . .] such decisions [as] would require the courts to determine the meaning of religious doctrine and canonical law and to impose a secular court's view of whether in the context of the particular case religious doctrine and canonical law support the decision the church authorities have made [. . . are] precisely the kind of judicial second-guessing of decision-making by religious organizations that the Free Exercise Clause forbids.[121]

Finally, in affirming the decision of the lower court, the court noted that "the First Amendment protects the act of decision rather than the motivation behind it,"[122]

111 *El-Farra*, 226 SW3d at 793.
112 *El-Farra*, 226 SW3d at 793.
113 *El-Farra*, 226 SW3d at 793.
114 *El-Farra*, 226 SW3d at 793.
115 *El-Farra*, 226 SW3d at 793.
116 *El-Farra*, 226 SW3d at 793.
117 *El-Farra*, 226 SW3d at 793.
118 El-Farra, 226 SW3d at 795.
119 *El-Farra*, 226 SW3d at 795.
120 *El-Farra*, 226 SW3d at 794.
121 *El-Farra*, 226 SW3d at 794 (quoting Kaufmann v. Sheehan, 707 F.2d 355, 358 (8th Cir. 1983)).
122 *El-Farra*, 226 SW3d at 796.

and "whether the termination [. . .] was based on secular reasons or Islamic doctrine, this court will not involve itself in ICLR's right to choose ministers without government interference."[123]

Nevertheless, litigants have successfully employed First Amendment arguments in order to protect their ability to engage in affairs otherwise covered by laws which apply to all citizens, yet clearly impede religious practice. For example, in 2013, in *Awad v. Ziriax* a federal court ruled in favour of the plaintiff Muneer Awad's claims that a state law violated the Establishment Clause.[124] In that case, the US state of Oklahoma attempted to amend the state constitution with language that would "[forbid] courts from considering or using Sharia Law."[125] Awad claimed that the possible amendment threatened injury by preventing him from practicing his faith in matters such as probating his will, which contained direct references to Shari'ah.[126] The trial court agreed with his Establishment Clause claim, finding that the defendants had not shown any evidence of a "compelling state interest" and as such the clear reference to Shari'ah violated the Establishment Clause.[127]

Choice of law disputes represent an interesting genre of cases which implicate religion, particularly Shari'ah, because of the combination of US choice of law doctrine and the various Shari'ah-influenced jurisdictions that incorporate religious principles into the legal system. For example, the US bankruptcy court in the case of *In Re Arcapita Bank* has at times required the parties to explain religious law as it relates to Shariah-compliant finance.

In that case, among various issues, the court had to determine the validity of setoffs under the laws of Bahrain.[128,129] The plaintiffs, a group of Arcapita's creditors, were attempting to secure the transfer of funds that Arcapita invested with the companies Bahrain Islamic Bank and Tadhamon Capital B.S.C. ("defendants") before Arcapita filed for bankruptcy.[130] However, the defendants contended that under Bahraini law, those funds were properly offset for debts owed to them by Arcapita.[131] Each party filed motions for summary judgment regarding this issue.[132] As part of their argument, the defendants contended that the claimed setoffs were

123 *El-Farra*, 226 SW3d at 796.
124 Awad v. Ziriax, 966 F. Supp. 2d 1198, 1203 (Dist. Court, WD Oklahoma 2013).
125 *Awad*, 966 F. Supp. 2d at 1201.
126 Awad v. Ziriax, 670 F.3d 1111, 1120 (10th Cir. 2012).
127 *Awad*, 966 F. Supp. 2d at 1204.
128 In Re Arcapita Bank B.S.C., 628 BR 414, 431 (Bankr. S.D. N.Y. 2021).
129 "Setoff is an equitable right of a creditor to deduct a debt it owes to the debtor from a claim it has against the debtor arising out of a separate transaction." Samuel R. Maizel, "Setoff and Recoupment in Bankruptcy," January 26, 1996, US Depart. of Justice, https://www.justice.gov/jm/civil-resource-manual-65-setoff-and-recoupment-bankruptcy.
130 *Arcapita Bank*, 628 BR at 422.
131 *Arcapita Bank*, 628 BR at 422.
132 *Arcapita Bank*, 628 BR at 422.

rightful according to "'law merchant' and 'normal business practice' in Bahrain and within Islamic finance generally."[133] As such, defendants argued, the setoffs are to be considered "contractual rights" according to the safe harbour provisions of the Bankruptcy Code.[134,135] However, the court found that the applicability of "law merchant" to the bankruptcy code's safe harbours provisions was not well supported.[136] It also rejected the argument that setoff constituted a standard part of Shari'ah-compliant business practice based on defendant's argument that the codification of setoff in the law of Bahrain "reflects a long-standing transnational custom of Shari'a compliant financing and, therefore, the Defendants' setoffs fall under the umbrella of law merchant."[137]

According to the court, defendant's arguments were contradictory, as they "assert that they executed the setoffs pursuant to Bahraini statute," but the transactions that they wanted to constitute a setoff "were viewed as improper by Bahrain's own regulatory authority."[138] Of particular importance to the court was what expert testimony revealed to be a fairly new acceptance of setoffs within the Islamic finance industry:

> [. . . T]here are ten "central attributes" of a modernized law merchant, including that it is "transnational in character," expressed "through international commercial codes and conventions," or "endorsed by transnational institutions – legal economic, and political institutions – by nation-states and by stratified communities of transnational merchants alike." [. . .] They do cite to the setoff statutes of Qatar and the United Arab Emirates. [. . .] But these two examples hardly amount to a "transnational body of informal law, created by the industry customs and practices of merchants, which is endorsed and codified in domestic and international law." [. . .] Furthermore, while "Shari'a does allow for set-off of countervailing debts in certain circumstances, it has only been relatively recently that the modern Islamic finance market has applied this broad principle, only in those jurisdictions where set-off is possible, and with particular reference to murabaha contracts." [. . .] This evidence is scarcely the "longstanding" customs upon which law merchant is based, rather appearing to be a phenomenon that has recently been codified in the commercial laws of certain jurisdictions in the twenty-first century.[139]

Thus, the court decided that setoffs could not be considered a normal business practice against an insolvent entity such as Arcapita.[140]

The court was obviously a neutral party in this case, attempting to reconcile the traditions of the industry of the companies involved in the proceedings. Though the business practices of Islamic finance were at times discussed, the case at its core

133 *Arcapita Bank*, 628 BR at 473.
134 *Arcapita Bank*, 628 BR at 473.
135 11 U.S.C. §§ 555, 556, 559, 560.
136 *Arcapita Bank*, 628 BR at 474.
137 *Arcapita Bank*, 628 BR at 475.
138 *Arcapita Bank*, 628 BR at 475.
139 *Arcapita Bank*, 628 BR at 475–476.
140 *Arcapita Bank*, 628 BR at 476.

was a commercial dispute rather than a schism within a religious body. The court's decisions in this matter were for the purpose of determining the rights of creditors, neither advancing nor inhibiting religion, and did not result in government entanglement with religion.

14.5 Final Comments

The case of Shari'ah-based jurisprudence and law derived from nations that require an inquiry into sources from the canon of Islamic law presents a rare example of the scope of First Amendment law. This includes analysis of the doctrines of neither advancing nor inhibiting religion, government non-entanglement in religion, government neutrality in religious disputes, and application of neutral principles of law. Two phenomena account for this situation.

The first is the expansive influence of Shari'ah and the status that it holds among nations and individuals. That is to say, in an era where secular courts and laws have supplanted the religiously-minded avenues of dispute resolution, possibly overtaking the latter in prestige in the psyches of the governed, many people maintain that Shari'ah principles are sufficient as a basis by which to judge matters. Furthermore, various nations incorporate the foundations of Shari'ah into their laws at a constitutional level.[141]

The second reason for the peculiar presence of Islamic jurisprudence in US courts is the nation's choice of law jurisprudence, as well as the courts' preference to exercise jurisdiction rather than passively dismiss cases at the mere mention of a religious subject. The Court has given presumptive validity to choice-of-law clauses, and overcoming that presumption requires showing that it would be unreasonable under the circumstances.[142] Furthermore, courts are not inclined to dismiss cases for want of jurisdiction solely because there may be a religious theme in the background. In fact, one of the policy reasons cited by the Court in *Jones v. Wolf* in arriving at its decision was the state's "obvious and legitimate interest in the peaceful resolution of property disputes."[143]

These characteristics of US law and the respect for Shari'ah among its proponents in the US and abroad created a situation in which unambiguously religious topics would be addressed by the courts. Though, such decisions would normally

141 Colón. "Choice of Law and Islamic Finance, " 418.
142 John Bourdeau, et al., "Definition; general enforceability," in *American Jurisprudence, Second Edition* (Thomson Reuters, 2018), 17A Am. Jur. 2d Contracts § 255 ("Choice-of-law provisions are recognized as valid and will generally be enforced by the courts as long as they are reasonable, and good morals and fundamental policies of law are not violated.").
143 *Jones*, 443 US 595 at 602.

only occur in cases between private individuals and businesses, not between religious institutions such as private schools, religious centres, and organised congregations of worshippers. Thus, the courts are at times presented with facially secular matters regarding contract or civil law, but at times, they cannot avoid examining religious doctrine due to choice of law issues or the necessity of deciphering technical, Shari'ah-related terms.

Interestingly, this has resulted in courts being asked to dismiss cases for lack of jurisdiction based on First Amendment grounds of government neutrality, but more often than not, the courts exercise jurisdiction based on the doctrine of neutral principles of law. These doctrines are what the courts use in order to attempt to maintain both the freedom of the citizens to practice their religions without government involvement and the authority of the government notwithstanding that freedom.

Adnan Trakic

15 Harmonisation of Shari'ah and Common Law: Findings and Recommendations

15.1 Introduction

"Harmonisation of law," a term that refers to an effort to bring two different legal traditions in harmony with one another, has over time developed a rather negative connotation when mentioned in the context of Shari'ah and common law. Harmonisation began to be looked at as an attempt by one legal system to impose its values on another. There seems to be a great deal of hostility and resistance towards even a mention of harmonisation of law, particularly in jurisdictions where both Shari'ah and common law are practiced. One major reason for that is the lack of understanding of the scope to which these two legal traditions are similar.

One of the principal findings of this book is that Shari'ah and common law have many more commonalities than differences. As a result, the need for harmonisation between the two is exaggerated. The similarities do not need to be harmonised. Rather, they need to be acknowledged and appreciated. If the differences between Shari'ah and common law, which undoubtedly exist as evidenced in this monograph, are approached from the position of appreciation for commonalities, the ambiance to reconcile the differences would be more conducive to the harmonisation process, which would, in that case, be reflective of compromise and an amicable solution.

15.2 Findings and Recommendations

It is worthwhile mentioning that the findings and recommendations are produced by scholars with expertise in the area of law discussed in their respective chapters. The summary of the findings and recommendations in this chapter, however, represents the editor's review of the main points discussed by the authors in their respective chapters. As such, the editor was at liberty to provide his own commentary where he felt that was necessary. Also, this summary is limited to the points that, in editor's estimation, are the most applicable in the context of the harmonisation theme identified in the first chapter of this monograph. For the full and accurate representation of what was discussed in the relevant chapters, readers are encouraged to read actual chapters written by the respective authors.

https://doi.org/10.1515/9783110766707-015

15.2.1 Contract Law

In Chapter 2, Aishath Muneeza compares the contract law principles in common law and Shari'ah. Contract law under common law is often discussed on its own or in comparison with the codified statutory provision of some countries. The same can be said for Shari'ah-based contract law. Therefore, research of this sort is rare, particularly in the comparative context.

Aishath's approach to the topic was guided by the notion that not everything that is different in the two legal systems needs to be necessarily harmonised. If the actual or perceived differences do not contradict the fundamentals of the legal systems, they should be able to co-exist. The author cites an example of statements that are traditionally referred to as invitations to treat by the common law courts. The display of goods with a price tag, for example, is not an offer capable of acceptance but only an invitation to others to make an offer that is capable of acceptance. However, the same example is likely to be considered an offer capable of acceptance under Shari'ah provided the seller intended it to be. The intention of the seller/offeror will determine what that statement ought to be regarded as. Despite these differences, there should be flexibility in pursuing the approach that may be more in line with the needs of the community and business practice, especially if the approach does not contravene Shari'ah. Thus, in this example, the common law approach may be given preference if it protects the seller from having to deal with multiple potential buyers when there is only one or a limited number of items displayed with a price tag.

While this example shows the readiness of Shari'ah to accept the common law principles that do not oppose its value system, this readiness should also be reciprocated by the common law. A good example of that was provided by Abdul Hamid Mohamad J (as he then was) in the case of *Nepline Sdn Bhd v Jones Lang Wootton*,[1] where instead of applying the common law "caveat emptor" (let the buyer beware) principle, the learned judge applied the Islamic law concept which imposes the duty on the seller to disclose to the buyer defects related to the item being sold. So, Islamic law shits the burden from the buyer to the seller. This approach is in line with the need to provide greater protection to the consumers. At the time the decision was delivered, the learned judge did not deliberate on the source of law that made him depart from the common law concept. It is only later that he explained in one of his speeches that he, in fact, was inspired by Islamic law in the decision he

1 [1995] 1 CLJ 865.

made.[2] These two examples show us how the two systems of laws should co-exist and supplement each other to produce beneficial results for the country and its civic and business community.

That being said, Aishath mentions areas where the two law systems contradict when it comes to contract law principles. The most notable and irreconcilable differences relate to the elements that are strictly prohibited in Shari'ah, such as interest (*riba*), excessive uncertainty and speculation (*gharar*), gambling (*maysir*), and other things that are not seen as having any value in Islam or are considered as impure like intoxicants including alcohol and drugs. Contracts involving elements not permitted in Islam are invalid under Shari'ah even though they may be viewed as permissible under the common law. There are also significant differences between the two legal systems when it comes to the concepts like unilateral contracts, binding nature of promises, intention to create a legally binding relationship, and damages. At the end of the chapter, Aishath provides a list of areas, in the form of a table, that are different in the two systems of law with the suggestion as to whether the differences can remain or whether they require harmonisation.

15.2.2 Islamic Finance

An interesting example where harmonisation of contract law might be required was discussed in Chapter 3 by Noor Suhaida Kasri. In this chapter, she explores harmonisation efforts in Islamic finance. While Islamic financial contracts such as *murabahah* (markup sale), *bay al 'inah* (sale and repurchase), *tawarruq* (monetisation), and *musharakah* and *mudarabah* (partnerships) have the unique features, they, nonetheless, are subject to the same laws that apply to conventional contracts. As such, they have to comply, among others, with the provisions of the Contracts Act 1950 (in the Malaysian context). Non-compliance with the law would render the contract null and void. Noor Suhaida raises an interesting question in this context: whether the non-compliance with Shari'ah would render an Islamic financial contract null and void? This question was adjudicated recently by the High Court and Court of Appeal in the case of *Maybank Islamic Berhad v Golden Base Construction Sdn Bhd*.[3] The High Court thought that these were triable issues worth exploring further. However, on the appeal, the Court of Appeal categorically held that Shari'ah non-compliance does not affect contract's validity from a conventional contract law point of view. The court cited section 281 of the Islamic Financial Services Act 2013 (IFSA), which upholds the contract's validity despite its Shari'an non-compliance.

---

2 Tun Abdul Hamid Mohamad, "Review of the Civil Law Act 1956 (Act 67): Comments," November 3, 2013, https://tunabdulhamid.me/2013/11/review-of-civil-law-act-1956-act-67-comments/.

3 [2019] 1 LNS 1785. The written grounds by the Court of Appeal were not available at the time of writing this chapter.

This decision by the Court of Appeal presents a real challenge in at least two aspects. First, it places Shari'ah non-compliance and, by necessary extension, the requirement of Shari'ah compliance stipulated by the regulators like the Central Bank and Securities Commission of Malaysia in a subsidiary position compared to the compliance with conventional laws. If non-compliance with conventional laws, including subsidiary legislation like those passed by the regulators, would render the contract null and void under section 24 of the Contracts Act 1950, why then Shari'ah non-compliance with the subsidiary legislation passed by the same regulators does not invalidate the contract under the same section. This dichotomy discriminates Islamic financial contracts against their conventional counterparts. Another aspect worth mentioning is that there are other cases, including the recent Federal Court decision in *JRI Resources Sdn Bhd v Kuwait Finance House (Malaysia) Berhad*,[4] where the court emphasised that "Contracts containing Shariah repugnant elements which had already been executed are liable to be deemed null and void, which would in turn render the profits derived thereof non-halal."[5] As such, the practical utility of section 281 of the IFSA needs to be reconsidered in view of this development.

That being said, there are many examples in the Islamic finance industry where harmonisation efforts were successful. The author specifically commends the role of the Shari'ah Advisory Council of the Central Bank of Malaysia (SAC) in resolving Islamic finance disputes. Since the SAC was designated the final arbiter of Shari'ah issues that may arise in Islamic finance disputes by virtue of sections 56 and 57 of the Central Bank of Malaysia Act 2009 (CBMA), the problem of having the different judicial decisions on Shari'ah compliance of the same Islamic financial contracts ceased. The impugned sections took away the power from judges to make Shari'ah rulings on Islamic finance matters and instead placed it into the hands of the SAC. Moreover, the SAC's rulings were made mandatory on the court and arbitrator deciding the dispute.

Therein, however, lies the problem that Noor Suhaida deals with in this chapter. The problem relates to the constitutionality of sections 56 and 57 of the CBMA. The question is simple: did Parliament, by passing these two sections, usurp the court's judicial power in view of the constitutional doctrine of separation of powers? If the answer to this question is in the affirmative, the SAC's role as prescribed by sections in the resolution of Islamic finance disputes is unconstitutional. Noor Suhaida refers to the landmark Federal Court decision in *JRI Resources*, where the court upheld the constitutionality of sections 56 and 57 by a split majority of five to four. Even though the constitutional dilemma may seem to have been resolved, for now, the fact that almost half of the judges in the panel dissented shows that the solution provided by these two sections is questionable, to say the least. Perhaps this is where greater

4 [2019] 3 MLJ 561.

5 [2019] 3 MLJ 588.

harmonisation efforts may be required so that judges can judge Islamic finance disputes without having to abdicate their judicial power. The SAC's role too is crucial, but how it offers its rulings perhaps needs to be revisited so that they are not made mandatory on the judges. There is indeed a thin line between what SAC does in this respect and the judges' exercising of the judicial power, and the line should not be crossed. Therein lies the challenge of harmonisation.

On the brighter side, Noor Suhaida points out that many aspects of Islamic finance are in line with conventional laws. She adds that the civil courts, which have jurisdiction over Islamic finance disputes, have been forthcoming when harmonisation is required. She cites an example of the Federal Court decision in *Latifah Mat Zin v Rosmawati Sharibun & Anor.*[6] In this case, as mentioned earlier in the chapter, the issue pertained to the jurisdiction of the courts. The Federal Court held that while the civil court had jurisdiction over the probate and letter of administration, the Shari'ah court had jurisdiction to decide the question on *hibah* (gift), i.e., whether it formed part of the estate, thereby being subject to *faraid* (Islamic inheritance laws) or not. This is an example of the two courts working together harmoniously to resolve a dispute that may include elements of both conventional and Islamic law.

15.2.3 Islamic Financing of Energy Projects: The Need for Standardisation

The Islamic finance theme continues in Chapter 4, in which Ridoan Karim calls for the standardisation of Islamic finance contracts in relation to the financing of energy projects. In many countries with a major Muslim population, the need for financing for energy projects, particularly for renewable energy, has increased in recent years. However, there is an obstacle that makes many parties, including multinational corporations involved in the energy sector, hesitant when it comes to Islamic finance. They all want certainty when dealing with Islamic finance institutions. There seems to be fear that Islamic finance contracts typically used by the Islamic finance providers are inundated with unhealthy levels of uncertainty, particularly when it comes to enforcing Shari'ah compliance. They fear that a contract that may be viewed as perfectly compliant under the conventional law (be it common law or civil law) may be non-compliant with Shari'ah. Or, in some cases, it may be viewed as non-compliant according to one school of thought while valid according to another. In the same fashion, a contract that may be in contravention of Shari'ah principles of financing could eventually be enforced as valid under the conventional laws and courts thereby completely disregarding the Shari'ah underlying nature of the contract.

6 [2007] 5 CLJ 253.

All of the above fears are justified. In fact, cases with similar concerns have already been adjudicated by the courts, most prominently in Malaysia,[7] the UK,[8] and UAE.[9] As seen in the earlier chapter, Malaysia seemed to have resolved this issue by reinforcing the role of the Shari'ah Advisory Council of the Bank Negara Malaysia (SAC) and making the necessary amendments in the relevant legislation to ensure that the SAC has the final word in Shari'ah compliance questions. Since this approach has been criticised for overstepping into the protected space of the judiciary, the approach suggested by Ridoan for other countries is worth considering.

Ridoan encourages the parties (including Islamic finance providers) as well as regulators to incorporate Accounting and Auditing Organization for Islamic Financial Institutions (AAOIFI) standards into the contracts concluded by the parties.[10] This could be done by developing standard form contracts or clauses that are reflective of AAOIFI's standards. However, Ridoan warns that this must be done with caution as standard form contracts may bring along many other issues, such as unfairness and inequality of bargaining power. The parties in cross-border contracts need to be careful with the choice of law and court clauses. The jurisdictions that have proven to be indifferent to enforcing Shari'ah compliance of impugned Islamic finance contracts should not be selected. Instead, countries with a proven track record of recognising both the conventional and Islamic aspects of Islamic finance contracts are preferred as a forum for settling disputes.

15.2.4 Insubordination in Employment Law

From Islamic finance, we now move to employment law. In Chapter 5, Ashgar Ali and Mohammad Hassan explore the employer-employee relationship, particularly how employees' insubordination is dealt with under common law and Shari'ah. They try to determine the extent to which an employee's duty to obey the employer's lawful and reasonable orders applies. They make reference to the landmark Malaysian Federal Court decision in *Ngeow Voon Yean v Sungei Wang Plaza Sdn Bhd / Landmarks Holdings Bhd*,[11] where the court laid down the related common law principles that equally apply in Malaysia. The authors also cite several verses from the

7 *Arab-Malaysian Finance Bhd v Taman Ihsan Jaya Sdn Bhd & Ors* [2009] 1 CLJ 419; *Bank Islam Malaysia Berhad v Lim Kok Hoe & Anor (and 8 Other Appeals)* [2009] 6 CLJ 22.

8 *Islamic Investment Company of the Gulf (Bahamas) Ltd v Symphony Gems NV. & Ors* [2002] WL 346969 (QB Com Ct, 13th Feb 2002); *Shamil Bank of Bahrain EC v Beximco Pharmaceuticals Ltd* [2004] EWCA Civ 19.

9 *See* Omair Haroon, Sameen Fatima Meenai and Aun Raza Rizvi, "Dana Gas: The *Sukuk* Dispute," *Asian Journal of Management Cases* 17, no. (IS) (2020): 42S-54S, DOI: 10.1177/0972820119884395.

10 *See* Accounting and Auditing Organization for Islamic Financial Institutions (AAOIFI), accessed May 21, 2022, http://aaoifi.com/?lang=en.

11 [2006] 5 MLJ 113.

Qur'an and sayings of the Prophet (SAW) that demonstrate the importance of obeying the lawful work-related orders of the superior based on trust (*amanah*). A true believer, as they argue, must not betray the employer's trust and must at all-time fulfil the duties entrusted with full competence, dedication, and honesty. So the finding that this duty exists under both common law and Shari'ah, is not a surprise.

What is less clear is how an employee should respond to employer's orders that he/she is in doubt as to whether they are lawful or not? If the employee has doubts, the proper thing to do under common law, the authors argue, is to perform such orders. Later on, if he finds that the orders are illegal or dangerous, he can refer the case to the relevant department in the company to look into it. Alternatively, there is always an option of bringing the case before the court to adjudicate the matter. What does not seem to be an option is not obeying such orders. The reason for that is that the employer would, if found that the orders were indeed lawful and reasonable, have good grounds to ask for the dismissal of the employee on the basis of insubordination. This is a risk that employees, as noted by the Federal Court in *Ngeow Voon Yean*, should not take.

While the common law position regarding the dubious employer's orders is documented in several court cases that the authors have discussed in this chapter, it is less clear as to what extent the position under Shari'ah is aligned with it. Shari'ah recognises the importance of obeying lawful and reasonable orders. It is equally explicit that illegal and dangerous orders must not be obeyed. In this respect, both legal systems share the same views. But, matters that are of dubious nature are contentions. It is a general principle under Islamic law that Muslims should stay away from matters that are dubious. So if an employee has some doubts but thinks that there is a good chance that the order given by the employer is unlawful or dangerous (i.e., manifestly wrong), there seems to be an argument under Islamic law that such an order should not be obeyed. That might not be the case under the common law, as presented earlier. Also, disobeying orders simply because the employee "thinks" that they are unlawful or would place him or others in a state of danger may lead to disharmony in the employment workplace. The authors have given this aspect of the insubordination theme special attention in this chapter. They provide clear answers and also their views as to the areas in which the two legal systems agree and areas where there could be some tensions.

15.2.5 Corporate Governance

While the above chapter clarifies how employees should deal with lawful, unlawful, and dubious employers' orders, Chapter 6 shifts the attention to corporate governance. In this chapter, Elsa Satkunasingam highlights the importance of good corporate governance practices, particularly in institutions that carry the label Islamic or are associated with it. One such institution is Tabung Haji (TH), the Malaysian hajj pilgrimage fund board. TH was established primarily to enable Muslims to save safely and prudently for the hajj pilgrimage to Macca, which is one of the five pillars of the Islamic faith. Before TH, Muslims had no choice but to save their funds in their homes as placing them in conventional interest-bearing banks was not an option due to the prohibition of interest in Islam. Therefore, the objective behind the establishment of TH is truly noble.

Besides providing safekeeping for hajj based on Islamic principles of *wakalah* and *amanah*, TH also provides dividends and bonuses to the depositors, which have been relatively competitive compared to other institutions. Perhaps it is the over-emphasis on the provision of dividends and bonuses that seem to have created many challenges for the TH as its primary role of safekeeping for hajj pilgrimage became somewhat overshadowed by the desire to provide good investment returns to the depositors. However, profits can only be declared if certain conditions are fulfilled, according to section 22 of the Tabung Haji Act 1995. One of the conditions is that TH's liabilities cannot exceed the value of its assets.

Not being able to declare bonuses and dividends if its liabilities are higher than its assets appears to be a genuine issue for TH, Elsa explains. TH's depositors are voters, and the Government of the day, which has direct oversight over the TH's board, may consider it necessary to declare the dividends and bonuses. The higher they are, the better perception by the voters (depositors) of the management of the business by the Government would be. However, there are no guarantees that the business conducted and investments made by TH would always yield good returns. If they do not, it is reasonable to expect that the bonuses and dividends would not be great. This is particularly so when some companies in which TH owed shares had not been performing well.

As a senior corporate governance expert with both industry and academic experience in the field, Elsa examines the corporate governance practices of the TH roughly from 2015 until 2020. Her analysis is based on the publicly available information in the TH annual reports and media reporting on the matter. For the details of the analysis, one would need to refer directly to Chapter 6. However, suffice to say here is that TH was referred to as a case study only. The objective is not to point out TH's weaknesses or strengths, for that matter. Rather, the objective is much broader. It relates to the context of harmonisation of laws, and that is: good corporate governance based on the principles of transparency and accountability is viewed as a cornerstone under both common law and Islamic law. As such harmonisation is not really necessary as both legal systems seem to share the same values in this respect. Given its faith-based approach, one may say that transparency, accountability, and good governance are perhaps accentuated more in Islamic law. Therefore, it is inconceivable that institutions that operate on the basis of Shari'ah-compliant principles are lacking in good corporate governance. In fact, non-compliance with good corporate governance would likely be tantamount to a non-compliance with Shari'ah-based principles.

Elsa concludes that the operational independence, which is embedded in the application of the transparency and accountability principles, is a solution to the challenges that TH and any other companies may face in view of pressures to do things that may not be in the best interest of the company. Having the company's board appointed by the Government Minister is not a problem per se, provided the board members are prepared to genuinely practice Islamic and common law principles of transparency and accountability. This is why, Elsa suggests, the boards need to build a strong relationship with the regulators, civil societies, and media members so that any undue pressure or improprieties would be immediately reported. The board also needs to stay united and make decisions with strong ethical beliefs and convictions.

15.2.6 Defamation

Ethical beliefs and convictions should be guiding principles not only in corporate governance and commercial law matters but should also inform one's right to free speech and expression. While people have the right to speak freely without fear or favour, they must endeavour only to speak the truth. In Chapter 7, Farheen Baig Sardar Baig and Ashgar Ali Ali Mohamed explore limits to the freedom of speech and expression. They begin by stating that both the common law and Shari'ah recognise persons' right to freedom of speech and expression. Shari'ah, in particular, accentuates this freedom by encouraging true believers to speak up freely when that is in the interest of justice. That said, the right to freedom of speech and expression, like all other rights, has limits. Both legal systems recognise that the right to freedom of speech ends when it begins to violate the rights of others, such as the right to honour and reputation.

The right to live an honourable life implies the right not to be defamed by others. Defamation, as the word suggests, infers the act of taking away someone's reputation by making false accusations that have the effect of lowering the defamed person's reputation in the eyes of ordinary people. The defamed person would normally have two legal options depending on the facts. One is to lodge a police report for criminal defamation provided elements of that crime are fulfilled. Both common law and Shari'ah consider certain types of defamation as criminal offences, and both systems provide severe punishments for it. While the authors' discussion is mostly limited to defamation as a civil wrong (civil cause of action), they have dedicated a significant part of the chapter to one particular form of criminal defamation under Islamic law known as *qazaf* (false accusation of unlawful sexual intercourse). From their discussion, it can be seen that besides the punishment of 80 lashes prescribed in the Qur'an for the offence of *qazaf*, there is also an element of faith-based punishment where the defamer should fear the punishment by God in the hereafter.

The faith-based argument is particularly interesting in this context as it has elements of a preventive measure. The authors explicate that a statement made with malice would attract responsibility before God in the hereafter even if it does not rise to the level of an offence sanctionable by law. So, for example, backbiting and gossiping, which may not have elements of criminal or even civil liability, is condemned in Islam and described as a gruesome act comparable to that of "eating the flesh of his brother"[12] in the hope of discouraging believers from making statements that would lead to defaming others.

As for the common law, authors note that their discussion is limited to the tort of defamation. At the same time, they acknowledge the importance of criminal defamation that deserves a detailed analysis in separate research. Defamation tort is a civil wrong that entitles the defamed person to claim damages (monetary compensation) if elements of the tort are fulfilled, namely, the impugned statement must be defamatory, the statement must refer to the defamed person, and there needs to be the publication of the statement. The extent to which the elements would apply may vary, however, depending on the form of defamation, i.e., whether it is a slander (defamatory statement in a transient form) or liable (defamation in written or printed form). In any case, the common law is clear in that the defamed person is entitled to damages if elements of defamation are fulfilled.

The situation does not seem to be as clear in Shari'ah. On the one hand, there is a concept of discretionary punishment (*ta'zir*) where the court may impose punishment as it deems appropriate, including monetary ones but only on matters on which the punishment has not been prescribed in the Qur'an. So while discretionary punishment would not apply to *qazaf*, it may apply, for example, if there is sufficient evidence to show that the defamer made inappropriate remarks that do not necessarily amount to *qazaf*. But perhaps a more important question in this context that the authors attempt to answer is: could there be any damages awarded for defamation other than *qazaf*?

15.2.7 Privacy and Data Protection

In Chapter 8, Ridoan Karim and Normann Witzleb discuss privacy and data protection laws with reference to several jurisdictions. They examine the extent to which national privacy and data protection laws, in both common law and non-common law jurisdictions, align with the Islamic laws on the subject and also how Islamic law can contribute to the development of better privacy and data protection framework.

There is no doubt that Islam values privacy, which is considered both an individual human right and the right accorded to God in the sense that it is reserved for the

12 Qur'an, *Surah Al-Baqarah* (Chapter 2) verse 190.

entire humanity. Breach of privacy carries both criminal and civil liability. As private data (information) is not considered property in Islam, the breach of privacy and personal information theft is not theft of property warrantying *hudud* punishment (i.e., the exact punishment prescribed by the Qur'an and Sunnah). Rather, it is a crime punishable with *tazir* (i.e., the amount and severity of punishment are determined by the court depending on the facts and the circumstances of the case). Breach of privacy resulting in economic loss would also entitle the victim to sue for damages. As such, breach of privacy is considered a civil wrong besides being a crime.

The EU General Data Protection Regulation (GDPR) is said to be the most advanced privacy and security law globally. It provides the highest standards for the protection of privacy and personal data. GDPR is often used as a benchmark model law by countries in developing their privacy and data protection laws. The authors explain that it was this law that most of the Arab countries in the GCC have referred to when developing their domestic laws. There seems to be no reference to Shari'ah principles in the legislation dealing with privacy and data protection. Instead, the desire to create a favourable economic environment for investments and business operations led these countries to adopt the Western privacy and data protection standards into their national laws.

Other Muslim majority countries like Pakistan, Malaysia, and Bangladesh seem to have relied on the common law and equity developments in the area of privacy like the doctrines of confidentiality, which later on developed into a tort of misuse of public information. Some of these countries have complemented the common law developments with specific legislation, like Malaysia, which has introduced Personal Data Protection Act 2010. The act, however, the authors argue, is not as comprehensive as GDPR and legislation of other countries that have implemented it.

While GDPR is a good law and is worth emulating, it may be worthwhile exploring Islamic law aspects of privacy and data protection that are equally forward-looking. The authors have singled out specifically *muhasabah* (self-accountability) and *amanah* (preservation of trust) as Islamic law concepts that could complement the conventional date protection laws. The authors argue that there is a clear nexus between legal responsibility and self-accountability. The former ensures compliance with public law obligations and is enforced by the regulators, while the latter pertains to the data processor's commitment to comply with moral and ethical obligations and is self-enforced. In the case of data processors, for instance, it is recognised that they first must be accountable to themselves and their stakeholders. The importance of self-accountability should not be underestimated, according to the authors. If we were to rely on the regulators to ensure compliance with the law, many breaches of privacy and data protection laws would go unnoticed as the regulators are often under-resourced to ensure complete compliance with the law, the authors argue. Another concept of practical utility mentioned by the authors is *amanah* (trust). Self-accountability presumes a healthy dose of trust in data processors that they will do the right thing. In the context of privacy, that would mean that they are entrusted with ensuring that private and confidential information must be safe and secure. The breach of trust endowed on an individual is considered a sin in Islam.

15.2.8 Environmental Law

The practical utility of Islamic law principles is not limited to privacy and data protection law. One area in which their implementation could generate enormous benefits is environmental law. In Chapter 9, Maizatun Mustafa explains that the world is at the stage where immediate and concrete actions must be taken to protect and preserve the environment, or the damage to the environment will be irreversible. The rapid climate change and various environmental disasters have resulted in serious adverse effects on not only flora and fauna but also on humans.

Malaysia has not been spared from the dreadful effects of environmental pollution and neglect. The most common examples are air pollution in the form of transboundary haze caused by open burning for agricultural purposes and industrial dumping of harmful chemical waste into rivers and seas. Maizatun reports that such instances of pollution have resulted in serious health issues, particularly for the young and elderly. There have been times when the schools in the entire district or even nationwide had to be closed due to environmental pollution.

There is no doubt that rapid economic development and industrialisation are the main contributors to environmental pollution and denigration. Thus, it appears as if economic development and environmental protection are exclusive of each other. However, it does not have to be this way. The two competing interests are not necessarily incompatible. While countries have a legitimate right to pursue economic development to improve people's lives and livelihoods, that right, Maizatun argues, cannot be devoid of environmental protection and preservation. The two seemingly competing objectives are compatible if approached from a sustainability point of view.

The keyword here is "sustainability." Therefore, countries are responsible for introducing laws and policies that will enable sustainable economic activities and development. This is in line, the author expounds, with the United Nation's Rio Declaration on Environment and Development of 1992 and the 17 Sustainable Development Goals (SDGs) of 2015. A closer look at these international instruments reveals that the sustainability concept is not only limited to the protection and preservation of the environment. Rather, the author argues, sustainability includes more complex social and ethical dimensions. Thus, some of the SDGs emphasise the importance of protecting human rights and social justice and highlight the importance of the values like accountability, transparency, access to justice and information, and public participation. All of these, Maizatun suggests, need to be applied more extensively within national policies and laws.

Having comprehensive environmental laws and hefty penalties imposed on those who breach the laws is important. But, prosecution of offenders alone is not enough. Greater emphasis needs to be placed on preventive measures, and this is where the Islamic law approach to the topic can be of great use. Maizatun talks about Islamic concepts that are of interest here. First is the concept of *khalifa*, which means that God has created a human being as His vicegerent on earth. This reinforces that humans are not owners of the earth. Rather, they are entrusted with it to manage its resources in accordance with the wishes of the actual Owner, God Almighty. This now brings us to the concept of *mizan*, which means the management of the earth and its resources needs to be done in a sustainable manner. Central to the topic of sustainability is the concept of *maqasid* Shari'ah, which highlights the need for the protection of religion, life, intellect, family (linage), and property. For example, protection of life implies the need for a healthy environment. Hence, any action that would pollute the air and water, or the environment in general, contravenes *maqasid* Shari'ah. Also, preserving the environment for the future generation is reflected in the need to protect family (linage).

Therefore, sustainable economic development and the use of the environment and its resources is an injunction ordained by God to all human beings. Having environmental protection enunciated as an important pillar in the religion of Islam should help countries, particularly those with a major Muslim population like Malaysia, achieve their SDGs as sustainable development and environmental protection are part and parcel of the religious belief.

15.2.9 Family Law

At first sight, family law and its application in Malaysia appear to be straightforward. Shari'ah, codified in the form of state enactments, applies to Muslims, while non-Muslims' family law matters are regulated under federal legislation known as Law Reform (Marriage and Divorce) Act 1976 (LRA). The courts, too, seem to have a pretty clear jurisdictional demarcation line. Shari'ah courts hear disputes on Muslim marriage, divorce, and related ancillary orders, while the civil courts hear disputes involving non-Muslims. The problem, however, arises when one party to a marriage, which is solemnised under LRA, converts to Islam. In case of a dispute, which law should apply to them, the LRA or relevant Islamic law enactment? Likewise, which court should have jurisdiction to hear the dispute, the Shari'ah or the civil court? Sridevi Thambapillay answers these and similar questions in Chapter 10.

Sridevi explains that there are three main issues that may arise when a spouse to a marriage that is solemnised under the LRA later converts to Islam. The first two issues relate to divorce and child custody. Under the old LRA, conversion to Islam was a ground for a non-Muslim spouse to initiate divorce proceedings. However, the same right was not available to the converted Muslim spouse. In this way, the

LRA discriminated against the Muslim spouse by treating the conversion to Islam almost like a fault entitling the other spouse to divorce. Perhaps even more worrying consequence of that pertained to ancillary matters such as custody over children. The legislature soon realised the need for the amendment of the LRA to resolve these problems, and, in 2017, the LRA was amended, more specifically sections 3(3) and 51. The amended LRA provides the same rights to the converted Muslim spouse in terms of the divorce and ancillary matters as those provided to the non-Muslim spouse. While issues pertaining to divorce and child custody seem to have been resolved by the 2017 amendments to the LRA, the third, perhaps the most complex and warring issue according to Sridevi, remains somewhat unresolved, and that is the ongoing problem of unilateral conversion of children by the converted Muslims spouse.

Article 12(4) of the Federal Constitution provides that the religion of a child (a person under the age of 18) shall be decided by the child's "parent or guardian." Notably, the words "parent or guardian" are singular, suggesting that one parent alone can decide the child's religion. In Malaysia, there have been cases where converted Muslim parents converted their children to Islam without prior consent from the other spouses. This puts a non-Muslim spouse in an unenviable situation as, once converted to Islam, the Muslim spouse and children might wish to resolve their dispute in Shari'ah court applying Islamic law. The non-Muslim spouse, however, cannot appear before the Shari'ah court as it has no jurisdiction over the non-Muslims. The worries of the non-Muslim spouses were somewhat alleviated when in 2018, the Federal Court delivered a decision in the case of *Indira Gandhi Mutho v Pengarah Jabatan Agama Islam Perak & Ors and Other Appeals.*[13] The court clarified that the words "parent or guardian" in article 12(4) must be read in the plural to mean "parents or guardians." This was also supported by section 2 (95) in the Eleventh Schedule of the Federal Constitution that states the following: "words in the singular include the plural, and words in the plural include the singular." As such, the court concluded that the conversion of a child by one parent without the other parent's consent is unlawful, and the state law that allows it is null and void to the extent of inconsistency with the Federal Constitution.

While the Federal Court decision in *Indira Gandhi* has somewhat resolved the problem with unilateral conversions, the fear remains that in the future, the issue could resurface before a different panel of Federal Court judges who may arrive at a different decision. Therefore, Sridevi suggests that this issue should be resolved in one of the following three ways. First, she proposes the establishment of a special tribunal to hear disputes involving a converted Muslim spouse and the non-Muslim spouse. The tribunal should consist of judges who are familiar with both civil law as well as Shari'ah so that they can arrive at a solution that would be acceptable under both legal

13 [2018] 3 CLJ 145.

systems. In the alternative, she suggests that such issues could be resolved through mediation without the need to have the case publicised. Unilateral conversion tends to be a sentimental issue that is best resolved among the spouses amicably. And the last and perhaps most workable solution should come from the legislators. Just as Parliament amended the LRA in 2017, Parliament should amend the laws related to the unilateral convention, Sridevi argues, so that the problem is resolved once and for all.

15.2.10 Criminal Justice System

Another area of law where one would think harmonisation is close to impossible is criminal law. Undoubtedly, crimes and punishments in Shari'ah and common law have major differences. For instance, there are types of acts that are considered crimes under Islamic law, such as adultery and drinking intoxicating drinks. The same acts are not offences under common law. Despite the differences, there is so much more that the two systems of law share in common, and these commonalities are often left unnoticed. In Chapter 11, Hanifah Haydar Ali Tajuddin and Nasimah Hussin call for the harmonisation of Malaysia's criminal justice system.

They begin by bringing into the picture the important historical context. They explain that the Shari'ah, particularly Islamic criminal law elements, have been practiced in this country long before the British imposition of the common law through colonisation. This goes to show that Islamic criminal law is not alien to this land. Despite that, the applicability of Islamic criminal law was gradually replaced with the common law-based system through multiple interventions during the British colonisation. What is left of Islamic criminal law is a very limited application in the offences against the precepts of Islam, and those are only applicable to Muslims as per the Federal Constitution. The authors contend that whenever there is a dual legal system in place, there will always be a tendency for one to dominate the other, especially in a country like Malaysia, where the common law elements of the criminal law system are predominant compared to the Shari'ah counterpart. Nevertheless, one should never give up efforts to come to a compromise when there is a conflict between the two. Harmonisation is the way forward in such instances.

Contrary to the views that depict Islamic criminal law as barbaric and archaic, especially in relation to the *hudud* and *qisas* crimes for which punishments are prescribed in Qur'an and Hadith, the objective behind these crimes and punishments is not punitive in nature. Quite the contrary, the authors argue, the evidentiary requirements for the convictions in *hudud* and *qisas* offences make it almost impossible to have them implemented. So one may wonder what is their practical utility then? The authors explain that the main purpose behind these offences is deterrence. While *hudud* and *qisas* do not apply in Malaysia, other types of offences, known as *ta'zir*, do. These are the offences for which the court can prescribe the appropriate punishment.

Talking about punishments, the authors put forward the concept of restorative justice as an area where the two systems of law could work together to make major improvements in Malaysia's criminal justice system. Restorative justice is not punitive. The emphasis is not only on the prosecution and the offender's punishment. Rather, the concept brings into picture other stakeholders involved in the crimes committed, most notably, the victims of the crime and society. The current criminal justice system, authors maintain, has tendencies to overlook the needs of the victims, who should be involved in the sentencing and rehabilitation of the offenders. Non-custodial sentencing, including community service, compulsory attendance order, and parole, are good examples of restorative justice as they are rehabilitative. Rehabilitative elements can also be seen in the Victim Impact Statement and the plea bargaining process. These are all worth exploring further, and the best thing about it is that restorative justice has strong support in the jurisprudence of both legal systems. So there is plenty of space for both Shari'ah and common law legal systems to collaborate for the betterment of the overall criminal justice system.

15.2.11 Human Rights

In Chapter 12, Muhamad Hassan Ahmad, Muhammad Naqib Ishan Jan, and Ashgar Ali Ali Mohamed, offer a perspective on the topic of human rights with reference to international law, the common law as well as Shari'ah. Everyone would agree that respect for human rights and the rule of law are the cornerstones of our societies. As such, all legal systems, including Shari'ah provide for the protection of these rights. The difference, however, may arise as to the scope or the so-called "universality" of the concept of human rights. What constitutes human rights in one jurisdiction may not be the same in another. The reason for this is the conventional difference in the approach to human rights between Shari'ah and secular legal systems.

Shari'ah views human rights as a constant and unchanging category that has its basis in the wholly Qur'ah and the Sunnah of the Prophet Muhammad (PBUH). Human rights in Islam are intrinsic to the creation of human beings. They existed from the time of the creation of the first humans, Adam and Eve, and remained unchanged until contemporary times. The right of equality, as reflected in the last sermon of Prophet Mohammad (PBUH), was nothing short of revelatory for its time when he said: "All mankind is from Adam and Eve, an Arab has no superiority over a non-Arab nor a non-Arab has any superiority over an Arab; also a White has no superiority over a Black nor a Black has any superiority over a White except by piety and good action."[14] Slavery, racism, and mistreatment of women were still rampant at that time. Hence, Islamic teachings were not necessarily reflective of the societal norms at the time. Quite the contrary, Qur'an and the Prophet were sent by God (SWT), Muslims believe, to correct the societal norms and guide humanity to their success in this world and Hereafter.

On the other hand, the concept of human rights in the secular legal systems reflects the societal norms and values that are prevalent when these rights are introduced. So, for example, before World War II and the creation of the United Nations with all its agencies, many western countries felt it appropriate to colonise African and Asian countries, use their natural resources, and enslave many of their people. At that time, racism and inequality were rampant and acceptable in many western societies. It was only later that the changes began to take place. Thus, the concept of human rights in the West is not constant, and it fluctuates to be in line with the popular views.

The authors conclude that while most of the human rights contained in the UN documents and conventions are in line with the concept of human rights under Islamic law, there are some differences. The point of difference arises when the western concept of human rights is not aligned with Shari'ah. Thus, Shari'ah compliance is a must for a certain right to be recognised as legitimate under Islamic law.

15.2.12 Alternative Dispute Resolution

In Chapter 13, Ashgar Ali Ali Mohamed and Muhamad Hassan Ahmad stressed the importance of the Alternative Dispute Resolution (ADR) mechanisms in the resolution of disputes. It is hard to point out any substantial differences in approach to the ADR between the common law and Shari'ah. Both legal systems maintain that the ADR modes, such as mediation, conciliation, and arbitrations, are more beneficial to the disputing parties than the conventional litigation before the courts. In litigation, one party wins while the other loses. In ADR, the authors argue, the emphasis is on amicable comprise so that both parties can win. The good outcomes of an amicable comprise may have much broader effects. The authors refer to the ongoing Russia and Ukraine conflict as an example. Appointing a third party independent mediator to bring both parties to the negotiating table seems like the only reasonable option. Any other option would result in more bloodshed and suffering.

An out-of-court settlement has many benefits, especially in family and commercial disputes. Islamic state enactments in Malaysia make specific reference to the use of *sulh* (mediation) and *hakam* (arbitration) in resolving marital disputes. Arbitration has proven to be an effective mode of resolution in commercial disputes,

---

14 International Islamic University Malaysia, "The Last Sermon of Prophet Muhammad (p.b.u.h.)," accessed May 9, 2022 https://www.iium.edu.my/deed/articles/thelastsermon.html.

especially when parties are from different jurisdictions. One, often neglected major benefit of mediation and arbitration is the preservation of confidentiality. Unlike litigation in an open court setting (except for cases involving children), the resolution of the disputes through mediation and arbitration remains private. The world does not need to know the details of marital disputes or important information pertaining to the parties' commercial dispute.

The authors also acknowledge that there have been some criticisms of the ADR, such as that the arbitration can be expensive. Those criticisms are noted, and they deserve to be considered so that the ADR is strengthened and not abolished altogether. The weaknesses like that of costliness need to be fixed. Recently, a former Court of Appeal judge, Dr Hamid Sultan Abu Backer, suggested an excellent initiative to address this problem. He called on universities to be involved in providing their expertise and support so as to make arbitration more affordable.

15.2.13 Shari'ah and the US Courts

Chapter 14 is different than the other chapters in that it attempts to explain the US courts' approach to disputes that are related in some way to Shari'ah. This is intriguing because, on the one hand, the US is a secular country with no state religion, and yet here, we are talking about its courts being asked to adjudicate matters that may pertain to religious doctrines. At the start of the chapter, Julio C Colon reiterates that the US courts' approach to Shari'ah and all other religions and their doctrines is guided by the US Constitution's neutrality doctrine. The First Amendment of the Bill of Rights states: "Congress shall make no law respecting an establishment of religion, or prohibiting the free exercise thereof . . . "[15] The words "Congress shall make no law respecting an establishment of religion" is known as the Establishment Clause, which essentially preserves the secular nature of the Federation. In other words, there shall be no state religion. The other is the Free Exercise Clause contained in words "prohibiting the free exercise thereof." These two clauses read together can be referred to as neutrality doctrine. The state and church are to be separated. Religion is a personal matter, and the state should have a neutral approach; that is, it should neither promote nor inhibit it.

Julio explains that adjudication of Shari'ah-related matters before the US courts is inevitable for two reasons. First Muslim community in the US is gradually but steadily growing. Thus, the number of disputes in family, employment, probate, or business dealings is bound to increase. Another reason is the source of capital invested in cross-border transactions. Some of that capital comes from jurisdictions that practice Islamic finance, which must comply with Shari'ah principles. All this

15 U.S. Constitution Amend. 1.

said, the US courts will not readily adjudicate Shari'ah matters in disputes related to Islamic doctrine due to neutrality principle subsumed in the First Amendment. At the same time, Julio cites several cases involving private parties (not religious institutions) where it appears as if the courts abandoned their neutrality principle and enforced the positions that are aligned with the religious doctrines. So how do we reconcile these on the first sight opposing positions?

As a general rule, Julio clarifies, the US courts will only adjudicate Shari'ah-related matters and enforce the same if they are "justiciable under prevailing laws." As such, if a Shari'ah compliance is provided through a contract clause, for example, the court is likely to enforce the compliance with Shari'ah not because Shatri'ah requires it but rather because the prevailing domestic contract law principles require the courts to enforce what the parties have mutually agreed in their contract. This is, of course, contingent on the assumption that the Shari'ah law principles agreed on by the parties in their contract are consistent with the prevailing domestic laws. Julio brings into light many other fascinating examples like those pertaining to *mahr* in family disputes and the choice of clause of a jurisdiction influenced by Shari'ah in cross-border disputes. To have an accurate and complete understanding of the topic, the readers are encouraged to read Chapter 14 in this monograph.

15.3 Conclusion

Harmonisation of Shari'ah and common law is an effort or process that requires good faith from the representatives of both legal traditions. If the harmonisation effort is approached knowing that Shari'ah and common law are not so different as some represent them to be, and certainly not different to the extent that their differences are irreconcilable, the likelihood of achieving a compromise and workable solutions would be higher. That is why we should talk more about the commonalities of the two legal traditions and celebrate them. There are many lessons that one can learn from this monograph but if the editor was pressured to single out one, that would be that Shari'ah and common law share many more commonalities than differences, and the differences can be reconciled through a constructive harmonisation process so that the final solutions are acceptable under both legal systems. This is not wishful thinking or some sort of utopian idea. This is a finding based on the expert discussions of both legal systems. But now, this and many other findings and recommendations from this book need to reach out to the relevant decision-makers and stakeholders. It is our sincere hope that the regulators, legislators, members of the judiciary, and ordinary people will heed these lessons and do their part in making the harmonisation process work for the betterment of everyone because that is ultimately what the laws, including Shari'ah and common law ones, are all about: they are there to ensure justice, peace, and prosperity for everyone.

Notes on Contributors

Muhamad Hassan Ahmad is an Assistant Professor at the Civil Law Department, Ahmad Ibrahim Kulliyyah of Laws (AIKOL), International Islamic University Malaysia (IIUM). He graduated with Bachelor of Law (LLB), Master of Comparative Laws (MCL) and Doctor of Philosophy (PhD). He has special research interest in Public International Law, Private International Law, Alternative Dispute Resolution, Comparative Law, and Jurisprudence. He published a number of research articles in various local as well as international academic journals and presented several research papers at numerous local as well as international conferences.

Dato' Sri Ashgar Ali Ali Mohamed is a Professor at Ahmad Ibrahim Kulliyyah of Laws, International Islamic University Malaysia. He graduated with Bachelor of Law (LLB (Hons)) and Master of Comparative Laws (MCL) from the International Islamic University Malaysia (IIUM); Master of Laws (LLM (Hons)) from the University of Auckland, New Zealand; and Doctor of Philosophy in Business Law (PhD) from the Graduate School of Management, University Putra Malaysia. His area of interest includes Employment Law, Civil Litigation, and Alternative Dispute Resolution.

Julio C. Colón graduated from the University of Texas School of Law, where he was conferred a Juris Doctor. During law school, he was active in the international law society and published an article in the *Texas International Law Journal*, which was well received by scholars internationally. Following law school, Mr Colón began his career as a lawyer working in non-profit and immigration law. He later shifted to practising full time in civil law while serving as an adjunct professor at his alma mater. During this time, he published several articles on Islamic finance and dispute resolution, and presented at various conferences in the United States and Asia. He currently resides in San Juan, Puerto Rico, where he continues to write and develop his practice.

Mohammad Naqib Eishan Jan is a Professor at Ahmad Ibrahim Kulliyyah of Laws, International Islamic University Malaysia (IIUM). He graduated with Bachelor of Laws (LLB (Hons)), Master of Comparative Laws (MCL) and Doctor of Philosophy (PhD) from IIUM. His areas of expertise include Public International Law, International Humanitarian Law, International Human Rights Law, International Dispute Resolution, International Commercial Arbitration, Use of Force in International Relations, Refugee Law, and the Law of the United Nations. He has taught and published extensively in these specialised areas. Further, he has published a number of books and numerous articles in refereed law journals, and presented papers at various conferences.

Hanifah Haydar Ali Tajuddin is a Senior Assistant Director at the Policy and Research Division of the Syariah Judiciary Department of Malaysia and, before that, she served as a Syariah Prosecutor at the Syariah Prosecution Department of the Federal Territories. She is actively involved in the making of policies for the implementation and administration of Shari'ah law in Malaysia. She completed her PhD in 2020 at the International Islamic University Malaysia, focusing on restorative justice in Islamic Criminal Law. She is also an active researcher and has published articles and book chapters in the areas of Islamic law and criminal justice system.

Nassimah Bt Hussin is an Associate Professor at the Department of Islamic Law, Ahmad Ibrahim Kulliyyah of Laws (AIKOL), International Islamic University Malaysia (IIUM). She obtained her Bachelor of Syariah (Hon) from University of Malaya (1991), Master of Comparative Laws (MCL) from IIUM (1992) and PhD from University of Edinburgh (1997) in Islamic Criminal Law. The areas of her research interests are Islamic Law, Criminal Law, Victimology, *Usul Fiqh*, Women and Child Issues, etc. She has published several articles, some of them being: "Sulh as a Method of Alternative

https://doi.org/10.1515/9783110766707-016

Dispute Resolution in Criminal Cases: An Islamic Perspective," "Factors which Influence the Degree of Punishment: The Practice in the Syariah Court of Malaysia" and "Abortion and Causing Miscarriage: Islamic Medical Perspective." In 2012, she was appointed the Head of the Islamic Law Department, AIKOL. She has been serving as a member of the Student Disciplinary Board IIUM since 2003.

Ridoan Karim is a Lecturer at the Department of Business Law and Taxation, School of Business, Monash University Malaysia. He graduated with an LLB (Hons) from Brac University, MCL from IIUM, and a PhD from the UM. Being a passionate researcher and academic, Ridoan has widely published in peer-reviewed journals and presented papers at several national and international conferences in his areas of interest, that is "legal and regulatory aspects of energy", "science, technology and law," "business law," "data privacy and protection" and so on. Ridoan acted as a consultant and fellow in projects funded by the University of Malaya before joining Monash.

Noor Suhaida binti Kasri is a Senior Research Fellow and the Deputy Director of Research Development and Innovations Department at ISRA Research Management Centre, INCEIF University. She received her Doctor of Philosophy in Islamic Banking Finance and Management from the University of Gloucestershire (in collaboration with Markfield Institute of Higher Education), UK, under the sponsorship of ISRA. Her Master in Laws was from King's College London under the funding of the British Chevening Scholarship Award. Her Bachelor of Laws and Diploma in Shariah Legal Practice were from the International Islamic University of Malaysia. Prior to joining ISRA, she had almost twelve years of experience as a Malaysian advocate and solicitor as well as a Syarie lawyer. She sat as one of MUFG Bank (Malaysia) Berhad's Shariah Committee from 2017 to 2020.

Aishath Muneeza is an Associate Professor at INCEIF University, Malaysia. She has served as the first female Deputy Minister of Ministry of Islamic Affairs in Maldives; Deputy Minister of Ministry of Finance and Treasury in Maldives; Head of Islamic Finance of Capital Market Development Authority of Maldives; member of Islamic Fiqh Academy (National Fatawa Council of Maldives); first chairperson of Hajj pilgrimage fund, Maldives Hajj Corporation Limited; and chairperson of Maldives Center for Islamic Finance Limited which was set by Government of Maldives to strategise Maldives as the hub of Islamic finance in South Asia.

Maizatun Mustafa is an Associate Professor with the Legal Practice Department, Ahmad Ibrahim Kulliyyah of Laws at IIUM. Her expert areas are environmental law, climate change, and sustainable development. She is currently the coordinator for Climate Change Policy and Law Centre, IIUM. Dr Maizatun has authored many articles and books, including a book entitled *Environmental Law in Malaysia*. Her book project on climate change litigation with the National University of Singapore and Yale University has been published by Cambridge University Press. At the international level, she is an active member of the International Union for Conservation of Nature (IUCN) Academy of Environmental Law and the IUCN World Commission on Environmental Law.

Farheen Baig Sardar Baig is an Associate Professor at Ahmad Ibrahim Kulliyyah of Laws, International Islamic University Malaysia (IIUM). She has a Diploma in Islamic Studies, Bachelor of Law (LLB (Hons)), Master of Comparative Laws (MCL) and Doctor of Philosophy in Law (PhD), all from the IIUM. She was admitted to the Malaysian Bar as an Advocate and Solicitor by the High Court of Malaya in 1995 and, thereafter, joined the Ahmad Ibrahim Kulliyyah of Laws. Dr Farheen has co-authored several books on Employment Law, including *Retrenchment: The Law and Practice in Malaysia* (Sweet and Maxwell Asia, 2012); *Migrant Workers Law and Practice in Malaysia* (Malaysian Current Law Journal (MCLJ), 2012); *Sexual Harassment at the Workplace in Malaysia*

(Malaysian Current Law Journal (MCLJ), Ampang, 2011); and *Procedure for Unfair Dismissal Claims in Malaysia* (Petaling Jaya: LexisNexis, 2009). In addition, she has written numerous articles published in both local and international journals/reports and has also presented papers at conferences in the areas of Employment Law and Civil Litigation.

Elsa Satkunasingam is a Senior Business Development Adviser, Corporate Governance and Sustainability at the Iclif Executive Education Center at Asia School of Business. She conducts training and research in corporate governance for financial institutions and companies. She was formerly the Deputy General Manager, Corporate Secretariat Division at the Malaysia Deposit Insurance Corporation (PIDM) specialising in research and training on corporate governance and compliance. Prior to that, she was the head of the Corporate Governance Department at Bursa Malaysia and was involved in the development of corporate governance and sustainability programs and publications. She has also published several book chapters and journal articles in the area of corporate governance. She holds a PhD from Monash University and a Master of Laws and Bachelor of Laws from University Malaya.

Sridevi Thambapillay obtained her LLB (Hons) with an Upper Second Class from the University of Malaya in 1995. She was admitted as an Advocate and Solicitor of the High Court of Malaya in 1996. She completed her Masters in Law (LLM) at the University of Malaya in 1997 and thereafter began her career as a Senior Officer at the Loan Documentation Department in the United Overseas Bank (Malaysia) Berhad. Her passion for teaching law resulted in her joining as a lecturer at HELP Institute in 1998. Wanting to enhance her teaching career in a public university, she was indeed fortunate to be offered a tutor's post at the Faculty of Law, University of Malaya, in 2001. She is currently a Senior Lecturer at the same place. Her area of research is in Family Law and Elderly Law, and she has written various articles and edited several books in this area, individually and jointly. She teaches Administrative Law, Legal Method, and Family Law subjects at the Faculty of Law. She was conferred a PhD in Law in 2017 by the University of Malaya.

Adnan Trakic is an Associate Professor and Head of Business Law and Taxation Department at the School of Business, Monash University Malaysia. He graduated with a LLB (Hons)), Master of Comparative Laws (MCL), Doctor of Philosophy (PhD) from the International Islamic University Malaysia (IIUM), and Graduate Certificate in Higher Education (GCHE) from Monash University. He has taught and researched in the fields of conventional and Islamic finance law, business law, and dispute resolution. A co-author of several books, his published work extends to many articles, book chapters, and other contributions.

Normann Witzleb is an Associate Professor at The Chinese University of Hong Kong, Faculty of Law, where he chairs the Obligations Lab Asia in the Centre for Comparative and Transnational Law. He is also an Adjunct Associate Professor at Monash University, Faculty of Law, where he convenes the Privacy and Access to Information Group of the Castan Centre for Human Rights Law. He has published widely on Australian and European private law, in particular the areas of privacy rights, torts and remedies. His recent book publications include *Big Data, Political Campaigning and the Law: Democracy and Privacy in the Age of Micro-Targeting* (Routledge, 2020), with M. Paterson and J. Richardson (eds). Prof Witzleb is admitted to practice in the Australian Capital Territory, a barrister of the High Court of Australia and a fully qualified German lawyer. In 2019 and 2020, he consulted with the Australian Attorney-General's Department and the Office of the Australian Information Commissioner on law reform projects in privacy and information law.

Printed in the USA
CPSIA information can be obtained
at www.ICGtesting.com
CBHW051113050124
3181CB00009B/152

9 783110 766684